Murray's Daily Companion

This book is a chance to eavesdrop on history. A rich collection, drawn from nine centuries of daily writings and with a page for each day of the year, it reveals what was flowing through the lives, minds and pens of some of history's most celebrated figures. At the start of each entry are also featured the anniversaries of a host of curious and arresting events connected with that day – for instance, the day Don Juan lost his virginity, a man-powered plane crossed the Channel, the Battle of Hastings was fought.

The names that dance across these pages capture the very spirit of a succession of ages: we hear Elizabeth I addressing her troops, walk across London with Samuel Pepys, meet the mad George III with Fanny Burney, escape from the *Titanic* with its wireless operator, and see the aftermath of the terror attacks on New York on that most resonant of recent dates, 9/11. A great many of the authors drawn on have been published by one of Britain's oldest publishers – John Murray, established in 1768 – including Jane Austen, Lord Byron, Charles Darwin and Freya Stark.

Utterly absorbing whatever the day and month, handsomely presented and decorated with fine woodcuts, this is a reader's treasure trove that will inspire and delight.

Roger Hudson was educated at Cambridge, worked as an editor at John Murray for many years and has compiled a number of books for the Folio Society.

Murray's DAILY COMPANION

A Literary and Historical Almanac of Readings
and Anniversaries

From Diaries, Letters, Eyewitness Accounts, Some
Speeches and a Few Sermons

Written on Each Day of the Year Over Many Centuries

Edited by Roger Hudson

John Murray

Compilation © The Folio Society Ltd 2002
Compilation and additional material this edition © Roger Hudson 2005

This revised edition is based on *The Folio Book of Days*
first published by the Folio Society Ltd in 2002
and is published by arrangement with the Folio Society

This edition first published in Great Britain in 2005 by John Murray (Publishers)
A division of Hodder Headline

Engravings on pages vi, 1, 35, 67, 101, 133, 167, 199, 233, 267, 299,
333 and 365 © Estate of Eric Ravilious 2005. All rights reserved, DACS.

1

A CIP catalogue record for this title is available from the British Library

ISBN 0 7195 6744 0

Typeset in Century 725 BT by Servis Filmsetting Ltd, Manchester

Printed and bound by Clays Ltd, St Ives plc

Hodder Headline policy is to use papers that are natural, renewable and recyclable products
and made from wood grown in sustainable forests. The logging and manufacturing processes
are expected to conform to the environmental regulations of the country of origin.

John Murray (Publishers)
338 Euston Road
London NW1 3BH

CONTENTS

INTRODUCTION

It is natural to be curious about what people might have been up to, or thinking, or writing to each other on a particular day in a previous century. This book provides one set of answers among the myriad available to satisfy such inquisitiveness. It draws not merely on diaries but on letters, on eyewitness accounts, on a few speeches and a few sermons as well, by more than a hundred people; in fact, on any source that is dated – and for once, the day of the month is more important than the year. Kings and queens, presidents, loiterers in the corridors of power, avid diarists and compulsive letter-writers, profligate lords and sharp-tongued ladies, politicians, poets, painters, literary figures, historians, soldiers, sailers, clergymen, farmers, explorers, reporters – all are to be found here. It also features at the top of each day's entry curious and arresting events whose anniversaries occur on that day – for instance, the day Don Juan lost his virginity, a man-powered plane crossed the Channel, the Battle of Hastings was fought.

Each day of the year has a page devoted to it, and there is often more than one passage for one date. Extracts from one diary or letters from one correspondence are quite likely to appear in the wrong chronological order. As well as simple juxtapositions there are links between a number of passages, links sometimes, but not always, mentioned in the text. Apart from the account of the battle of Waterloo itself, there are Creevey's encounters with the Duke of Wellington before and after it, on 29 May and 19 June, together with his and Georgiana Capel's descriptions of the battlefield on 20 June and 15 July and Lady Granville's account of the French depicting the battle in ballet form on 31 July. Charles I's attempted arrest of the five members in January 1642 finds a strong echo in Oliver Cromwell's eventual dissolution of the Rump of the same Long Parliament in April 1653. General Thomas Harrison, who assisted in this last, is executed in front of Pepys on 13 October 1660. Jack London's picture of San Francisco devastated by the fire that followed the earthquake of April 1906 is qualified by William James's letter in May looking on the bright side. Three different views of the Great Exhibition of 1851 are given by Walter Bagehot, Jane Welsh Carlyle and Charles Dickens on 8 and 11 May and 11 July 1851. Covent Garden Opera House is seen on 8 December 1762 through the eyes of James Boswell, and of Charles Dickens on 26 December 1860; Drury Lane

Theatre is visited by Pepys on 5 October 5 1667, Boswell on 3 February 1763 and Edward FitzGerald on 6 February 1842.

With a few exceptions, the writers' first language is English. The names of the exceptions – for example, Blériot and Columbus – will indicate why they have been allowed in. The earliest piece in the book, perversely falling almost at the end on 29 December, is an eyewitness account of the murder of Archbishop Thomas à Becket in 1170. The most recent description is of a desolated Manhattan on 11 and 12 September, in 2001.

At various points there tends to be a concentration of extracts from one particular source, and there are reasons why. For example, Boswell's tour of Scotland with Dr Johnson took place in August and September 1773. Lord Byron's Ravenna Journal, though he only kept it between 4 January and 27 February 1821, is one of the most remarkable diaries ever written, matched, but in a very different key, by the passages of Dorothy Wordsworth's Grasmere Journal written during the spring months of 1802.

The justification for calling this *Murray's Daily Companion* is not merely that it is published under John Murray's imprint, but also that so much of its content comes from books and authors published by John Murray over the last two hundred years. And, as a look at the sources at the back of the book will show, it is not merely the obvious big names among Murray authors, such as Byron, Jane Austen, Coleridge, Walter Scott, Charles Darwin, Freya Stark and John Betjeman, that will be found here, but a great many lesser-known ones as well. Important dates from the history of this publishing house will be found among the anniversaries at the head of each daily entry – Byron's and Scott's first meeting at Murray's, Darwin's *Origin of Species* sharing its publication day with the great Victorian bestseller, Samuel Smiles's *Self Help*. Among the Byron letters quoted here there are several to his publisher, including one in verse. The final link between book and firm is provided by the compiler, who worked for John Murray's for eighteen years.

There are many pitfalls to avoid when making compilations such as this, but two of the biggest are including overmuch by Sydney Smith, and having too many executions. There may appear to be a generous helping of the former, but what is here is as nothing to what cried out to be included. As to blocks and scaffolds, these have been restricted to four of the great set-pieces – Joan of Arc, Mary, Queen of Scots, Sir Walter Raleigh, John Brown – and Pepys's brief but unforgettable picture of General Harrison meeting his death at Charing Cross. There are also a poem and two letters written from the Tower of London shortly before execution, by Chideock Tichborne, Queen Anne Boleyn and Sir or Saint Thomas More. A brake has also been kept on the number of battles. The aim throughout has been to keep a balance between the eyewitnesses to great events and the more intimate and personal; between the big names like Pepys, Dorothy Wordsworth, Dickens, Keats, Horace Walpole and Robert Louis Stevenson, the less well known such as Emily Eden, William James, Mr Justice Holmes, Barbara Castle and Sylvia Townsend Warner, and the virtually unknown or forgotten like Pamela, Lady Campbell, Conrad Russell, George Beardmore, Keith Vaughan and Henrietta, Countess of Bessborough.

There are passages of high drama, such as Queen Elizabeth's Armada speech, the passing of the Great Reform Bill, the sinking of the *Titanic* as experienced by her wireless operator, Hiroshima's destruction recounted by the pilot who dropped the bomb, Buzz Aldrin on the Moon, or journalists' accounts, such as Elliot Bell's picture of the Wall Street Crash of 1929, Relman Morin at Little Rock in 1957, Max Hastings walking into Port Stanley at the end of the Falklands War in 1982 and John Simpson in Baghdad under attack from Cruise missiles in 1991.

There are moving passages full of humanity and dignity – often in adversity – such as William Wilberforce's speech against slavery, Chief Seattle on the lot of the American Indian, Lincoln's inauguration as US President for a second term seen through the eyes of Walt Whitman, Mahatma Gandhi on trial for sedition.

There are also many other less public entries, and among them various categories are discernible. There are the moments arrested or frozen in time, which seem to come down to us as fresh as when they were recorded. A perfect example is John Keats's letter of 12 March, in which he remarks how 'it would be a great delight . . . to know in what position Shakespeare sat when he began "To be or not to be".' This delight is exactly what we experience when their words allow us to join John Ruskin at Coniston in the Lake District on 25

February, James Boswell sitting up all night on 21–2 March, or Dorothy Wordsworth sitting by the fire with her brother William on 23 March. In the right hands, like those of Francis Kilvert, Gerard Manley Hopkins or Dorothy Wordsworth, there is another approach which speaks to us as powerfully as these 'time capsules'. This relies on a minute and detailed observation of nature, of colour, movement, effects of light and of weather. Dorothy Wordsworth's description of Rydale on 18 March is a splendid example.

The changing seasons are an obvious spur, John Evelyn describing the frozen Thames, for example, or Kilvert on the autumn tints of the beeches at Bowood (the great Whig country house in Wiltshire belonging to Lord Lansdowne, which in fact appears on two other occasions: when Pamela, Lady Campbell endures party games there after Christmas, and when Emily Eden observes Lady Holland's perverse way of playing whist at the end of October). Food, drink and clothes, as might be expected, get a certain amount of attention: Sydney Smith giving his recipe for salad-dressing in verse, Keats praising claret and Lamb pork, Byron and Scott both calculating how much of a man's life is taken up with buttoning and unbuttoning, Lady Mary Wortley Montagu on undress in Italy and Pamela, Lady Campbell on the unsatisfactory nature of 'home-brewed bonnets'. A less obvious recurring theme is railways, starting with Fanny Kemble's trip on the footplate with Robert Stephenson on the new Liverpool to Manchester line on 26 August 1830, before its official opening. Keith Vaughan's prose evocation of a country railway station on 5 June 1962 is almost as moving as Edward Thomas's famous poem 'Adlestrop', to be found on 24 June. A. C. Benson warns of the hazards of travelling with women on 3 July 1911. The other really widespread new means of conveyance in the late Victorian and Edwardian eras was the bicycle, and it was thanks to his that Benson could go on a magical excursion on 15 May 1905 which we can share with him here. We can also enjoy his acid comments on a service at King's College Chapel, Cambridge, on 12 April 1914. In York Minster on 8 September 1904 he is much less critical, but then he is not attending a service. His attitude there is in some respects like that of Thomas Carlyle in Ely Cathedral two days (or sixty-two years) before.

Both the origins and beginnings of the two World Wars have entries: a description of Archduke Franz Ferdinand's assassination in Sarajevo on 28

June 1914 and the scene in the House of Commons before Chamberlain's fateful flight to Munich in September 1938, as well as Henry James deploring the wreck of civilization on 10 August 1914 and Harold Nicolson's diary entry on 3 September 1939. The moment of armistice on 11 November 1918 and the 1919 signature of the Treaty of Versailles are seen through the eyes of Virginia Woolf and Harold Nicolson. The actual fighting and conditions on the Western Front in the First World War are related by those two good friends Raymond Asquith and Conrad Russell as well as by Wilfred Owen. By contrast it is the Home Front, in particular as seen through the eyes of civilians George Beardmore, Chips Channon, James Lees-Milne and James Agate, that stands for the years 1939 to 1945.

As well as categories and themes that recur throughout the book, there are a few individuals who regularly crop up, in particular Queen Victoria and Winston Churchill. Victoria's father, the Duke of Kent, appears on 11 December 1817, talking to Thomas Creevey about the need to abandon his mistress and take a wife in the hope of siring an heir to the throne. Then there is a report of Victoria as a baby, her diary entry on the day of her accession on 20 June 1837, a description of her conduct at her first Privy Council, her touching remark on her honeymoon on 13 February 1840, details of how Prince Albert treated her in the early years, her opening of the Great Exhibition in 1851, the rigours of staying with her at Balmoral, and finally her account of an attempt to assassinate her in 1872. Churchill is first sighted in 1930 at something of a low point in his career, then Stanley Baldwin singles him out in 1935. He is a thorn in the side of Chamberlain during the Munich crisis in 1938, both determined and grim in his speeches in 1940, and finally champion of English usage against creeping political correctness in 1945. The Poet Laureate Alfred, Lord Tennyson and the domineering Whig hostess Lady Holland also feature several times because of their friendships with the diarist William Allingham and Sydney Smith respectively.

While eschewing any real mission, and avoiding like the plague (see 14 September) the sort of homespun philosophy and belabouring of the obvious that is found in the quotations selected for many birthday books, desk calendars and books of days, a number of selections here have to do with the conduct of life and its meaning, death, eternity, and the higher mysteries generally. Sydney Smith's now famous instructions to Lady Morpeth on how to avoid melancholy will be found on 16 February, Keat's 'amulet against the ennui' on 1 May, another Sir Walter Raleigh's brief but telling formula for happiness on 1 October, Thomas Gray's method for raising his own spirits above freezing point on 21 February, Virginia Woolf's horribly clear-eyed view of her depressions on 23 June, and lastly Charles Lamb's precepts for avoiding hypochondria on 22 November.

Readers are free to select from the following for a plausible view of, or at least attitude towards, such matters as God, the meaning of the universe and the life hereafter: Robert Louis Stevenson on 2 January, Mr Justice Holmes on 15 February, David Hume on 7 July, Conrad Russell on 17 September and Tennyson on 1 November. If that is all too much, then Lord Byron's musings on the relationship between body and soul, inspired first by his own indigestion and secondly by the evisceration of the late Lord Guilford, are recommended and will be found on 27 February and 11 April.

The genesis, or near-genesis, of three famous poems is mentioned: Keats's 'To Autumn' and 'To a Nightingale' on 21 September 1819 and 15 January 1820, and Wordsworth's 'Intimations of Immortality' on 27 March 1802. We hear from Edward Gibbon about his first inspiration to write *The Decline and Fall of the Roman Empire* in Rome on 15 October 1764, and the moment he finished it in Lausanne on 27 June 1787. If reassurance is sought for one's own contradictions and inconsistencies, then all that need be done is to turn to Jane Austen's marvellous letter of 18 November 1814 to her niece, or Byron writing on 6 December 1813 about journal-keeping. For encounters with madness read William Cowper on 16 January 1786, Fanny Burney on 2 February 1789 or Charles Lamb on 10 June 1796. Two views of the *vie de château*, at very different times and places, will be found on 22 August and 19 October. On the latter date Lady Granville rather dreads going to stay with her brother, the sixth Duke of Devonshire, at Chatsworth because of all the smartness and dressing up; also on that day, Emily Eden points out the drawbacks to being master of such a place.

Sydney Smith gives brilliant lessons on the accepting and declining of invitations (23 May, 6 November), while Edward Lear declines one in verse on 14 November. Gerard Manley Hopkins and Samuel Taylor Coleridge are both fascinated by how starlings fly when in great numbers (on 8 and 27 November). Finally, there is an early nineteenth-century sailor on 24 March desperate for a chew of pigtail tobacco, the selfsame substance that cures Lady Granville's toothache on 16 December 1811.

No one would expect a book of this kind to be read through in short order, from cover to cover, like a novel. On the other hand, it is hard to imagine anyone being so disciplined as to read only one day's entry at a time. If its fate is to become part of the clutter on the bedside table or one of that select band of books in the smallest room, who would grumble? The aim is to have filled it with old friends and new acquaintances, like the best sort of party, and to have caught them when they were at their wittiest, wisest, most indiscreet or most compelling.

Roger Hudson

JANUARY

1 JANUARY

1904 *The first car registration number, A1, is awarded to Earl Russell.*

1951 *The first episode of* The Archers *is broadcast.*

1961 *The birth control pill is launched in Britain.*

On Monday we had Rossini. The King [George IV] all graciousness to him. He sang, which went to our musical hearts, 'Otello' and 'Figaro', etc. but the courtiers and the rest of the society were indignant at his familiarity. Being fat and lazy, and consequently averse to standing, he took a chair and sat by the King, who, however, gave him the kindest reception, and, less petit than his suite, understood the man, and treated him as his enthusiasm for music disposed him to do. I hope to hear more of him, for it is an unspeakable pleasure. We have had one assembly, all Brighton. Tonight there is a child's ball . . . Nothing ever equalled the King's kindness. You see I am quite touched.

Harriet, Countess Granville to her brother, the Duke of Devonshire,
from the Royal Pavilion, Brighton, 1824.

To Carlyle's [in Cheyne Row, Chelsea]. We walk out. 'This morning', he said, 'after midnight, we heard a chorus of male voices outside the window singing *Auld Lang Syne*. We peeped out, and saw five or six figures on the other side of the street. I was really touched. I put up the window and said "Goodnight!" One of them eagerly replied "Good-night!" and then they all vanished silently away.' . . . He spoke of 'Hogmanay' in the streets of Edinburgh, hot punch and kissing. There used to be gangs of footpads in Edinburgh. C. was once struck on the head by them and had his hat broken. He saw three young men of this kind hanged.

William Allingham, Diary, 1873.

2 JANUARY

1815 *Lord Byron marries Annabella Milbanke, only to separate from her a year later. He commemorates the date in verse in 1821:*

> *This day of all our days has done*
> *The worst for me and you;*
> *'Tis now six years since we were one*
> *And five since we were two.*

A woman in Whitefriars held her maid's head so long in a tub of water that she drowned her. And a player about the town, upon some displeasure to the Lord of Doncaster's barber (that was very dear to him) ran him through and killed him unawares.

John Chamberlain to Dudley Carleton, 1619.

I must take my old way, and write myself into good humour with my task. It is only when I dally with what I am about, look back, and aside, instead of keeping my eyes straight forward, that I feel these cold sinkings of the heart. All men I suppose do, less or more. They are like the sensation of a sailor when the ship is cleared for action, and all are at their places – gloomy enough; but the first broadside puts all to rights.

Sir Walter Scott, Journal, 1826. See also 4 May.

Yes, if I could believe in the immortality business, the world would indeed be too good to be true; but we were put here to do what service we can, for honour and not for hire: the sods cover us, and the worm that never dies, the conscience, sleeps well at last; these are the wages, besides what we receive so lavishly day by day . . . Happinesses are but [a man's] wayside campings; his soul is in the journey; he was born for the struggle, and only tastes his life in effort and on the condition that he is opposed. How, then, is such a creature, so fiery, so pugnacious, so made up of discontent and aspiration, and such noble and uneasy passions – how can he be rewarded but by rest?

Robert Louis Stevenson to Edmund Gosse, 1886.

3 JANUARY

The Feast of Fools, when medieval priests and monks parodied services, eating sausages before the altar, burning old sandals in place of incense, singing, swearing.

1870 *Brooklyn Bridge begun in New York.*

1892 *J.R.R. Tolkien born in South Africa.*

Sir Richard Hoare having invited me to attend the Annual Meeting of the gentlemen engaged with himself in examining the Antiquities of Wiltshire, I . . . found no very great difficulties to Maiden Bradley, but was constrained to move slowly beyond this village as the roads were much less taken care of – I mean by removing the snow, which had fallen so deep as to equal the tops of the hedges. I never remember to have experienced anything like the cold whilst driving from Maiden Bradley to Stourhead, and my nose and ears were so much affected I hesitated once or twice whether I should not dismount and rub them with the snow, according to the Russian recipe; our delays were such, it was nearly six before we arrived at Stourhead. I say 'we' because I had taken my servant with me by desire of Sir Richard, as his party was larger than usual. I found dinner was over; but the worthy owner of the mansion left the company to see proper care taken of me, and after a hearty meal on a smoking hot beef steak I joined the party in the dining-room.

The Revd John Skinner, Journal, 1824.

I have been walking . . . with Lady Cowper and Mr Sneyd. She talked of Lord Melbourne and Prince Albert. She said Lord Melbourne . . . told her he had never seen the Queen angry but once. When talking of the Prince one day when she was not long married, he (Lord M.) said, 'But damn it, Madam, you don't expect that he'll always be faithful to you, do you?' These two people have an immense idea of the Prince. They say he has great knowledge, and great abilities, and great ambition, and will be a power in the state. He has great influence over the Queen gained by degrees; he judiciously gave way at first, never finished a game of chess with her for the first three years.

Chichester Fortescue, Diary, 1852.

4 JANUARY

1885 *The first appendicitis operation performed.*

1985 *The first commercial surrogate mother, Mrs Kim Cotton, gives birth to a baby girl.*

A little after, the king came, with all his guard, and all his pensioners, and two or three hundred soldiers and gentlemen. The king commanded the soldiers to stay in the hall, and sent us word he was at the door. . . . Then the king came upwards, towards the chair, with his hat off, and the Speaker stepped out to meet him. Then the king stepped up to his place, and stood upon the step, but sat not down in the chair. And, after he had looked a great while, he told us, he would not break our privileges, but treason had no privilege; he came for those five gentlemen, for he expected obedience yesterday, and not an answer. Then he called Mr Pym, and Mr Hollis, by name, but no answer was made. Then he asked the Speaker if they were here, or where they were. Upon that the Speaker fell on his knees, and desired his excuse, for he was a servant to the house, and had neither eyes, nor tongue, to see or say anything but what they commanded him. Then the king told him, he thought his own eyes were as good as his, and then said, his birds were flown, but he did expect the house should send them to him, and if they did not he would seek them himself, for their treason was foul, and such an one as they would all thank him to discover. Then he assured us they should have a fair trial, and so went out, putting off his hat till he came to the door.

Sir Ralph Verney, who was there, describes King Charles I's attempt to seize the Five Members of Parliament, in 1642. The three he does not name were John Hampden, Sir Arthur Hazlerigg and William Strode.

5 JANUARY

1896 *Discovery of X-rays announced.*

1919 *The Nazi - National Socialist - Party formed in Munich.*

1964 *The first automatic ticket barrier on the London Underground.*

Rose late – dull and drooping – the weather dripping and dense. Snow on the ground, and sirocco above in the sky, like yesterday. Roads up to the horse's belly, so that riding (at least for pleasure) is not very feasible. Added a postscript to my letter to Murray. Read the conclusion, for the fiftieth time (I have read all W. Scott's novels at least fifty times) of the third series of 'Tales of my Landlord' [*Legend of Montrose*] – grand work – Scotch Fielding, as well as great English poet – wonderful man! I long to get drunk with him.

Dined versus six o' the clock. Forgot that there was a plum-pudding (I have added, lately, eating to my 'family of vices'), and had dined before I knew it. Drank half a bottle of some sort of spirits – probably spirits of wine; for what they call brandy, rum, etc., etc., here is nothing but spirits of wine, coloured accordingly. Did *not* eat two apples, which were placed by way of dessert. Fed the two cats, the hawk, and the tame (but not tamed) crow. Read Mitford's *History of Greece* – Xenophon's *Retreat of the Ten Thousand*. Up to this present moment writing, six minutes before eight o' the clock – French hours, not Italian.

Hear the carriage – order pistols and greatcoat, as usual – necessary articles. Weather cold – carriage open, and inhabitants somewhat savage . . . – rather treacherous and highly inflamed by politics. Fine fellows, though – good materials for a nation. Out of chaos God made a world, and out of high passions comes a people.

Clock strikes – going out to make love. Somewhat perilous, but not disagreeable.

Lord Byron, Ravenna Journal, 1821.

6 JANUARY

Twelfth Night (Boxing Day is the first of the Twelve Days of Christmas).

871 *King Ethelred and his brother Alfred defeat the Danes at the Battle of Ashdown.*

1945 *The Battle of the Bulge ends, and with it, the last German offensive of the war.*

A dreary red-nosed dyspeptic clergyman at one table, at another a young man who smiles brilliantly to himself, at another a gloomy whiskered man, with brows drawn up and corrugated with care, who feeds himself carefully and compassionately and takes salt with his bananas – I like to watch all his little ways and manners; at another an elderly couple, a gross slow-moving old man, and a haughty female who has once been beautiful and now looks unutterably bored. A shifting pageant of human lives, like a big hotel, isn't a very encouraging affair. It doesn't give one the idea that life is very happy or satisfactory. At a place like this the people who come are mostly fortunate people – with more wealth than the run of men; but there seem few happy parties or happy faces – much that is tired and cross and bored and disillusioned. There is a cross man by the window with a waxed moustache, whose wife, a spectacled wretch, spends the end of every meal in shaking up for him a phial of purple medicine. It's no good saying people *ought* to be more cheerful; it requires a good deal of character to be cheerful if you don't feel it. The wonder to me is why more of them are *not* cheerful, why life *should* be disappointing, what it is in experience which drains people of joy and hope, and whether they could help it.

A. C. Benson describes the Riviera Palace Hotel,
Penzance, Cornwall in his Diary, 1912.

8

7 JANUARY

Christmas Day in the Orthodox Church.

1558 *England loses Calais, her last French possession.*

1927 *A Transatlantic telephone service opens, costing £15 for three minutes.*

Many thanks, my darling Emmy, for your delightful letter. Till you are shut up for six months in an old rambling house on the coast of the Isle of Bute in January, you cannot know the value, the intrinsic sterling, of such a letter as yours . . . I think, if God grants us life, we are likely to settle, when we do settle, somewhere near London. It is bad for the mind to live without society, and worse to live with mediocrity; therefore the environs of London will obviate these two evils. But I like the idea . . . I cannot bear Scotland in spite of every natural beauty, the people are so odious . . . Their hospitality takes one in, but that is kept up because it is their pride. Their piety seems to me mere love of argument and prejudice; it is the custom to make a saturnalia of New Year's Eve, and New Year's Day they drown themselves in whisky. Last New Year's Eve being Sunday, they would not break the Sabbath, but sat down after the preaching till twelve o'clock; the moment that witching hour arrived, they thought their duty fulfilled, seized the whisky, and burst out of their houses, and ran about drinking the entire night, and the whole of Monday and Monday night too. This is no exaggeration, you have no idea the state they are in – men lying about the streets, women as drunk as they – in short, I never was more disgusted.

Pamela, Lady Campbell, recently married, to Emily Eden, 1821.

8 JANUARY

1815 *The last battle between Britain and the United States is fought, at New Orleans.*

1886 *The Severn railway tunnel is opened, 4 miles and 624 yards long.*

1940 *Food rationing (initially for butter, sugar and bacon) is introduced.*

Again all day in our bags, suffering considerably physically from cold hands and feet, and from hunger, but more mentally, for we cannot get on south, and we simply lie here shivering. Every now and then one of our party's feet go, and the unfortunate beggar has to take his leg out of the sleeping-bag and have his frozen foot nursed into life again by placing it inside the shirt, against the skin of his almost equally unfortunate neighbour. We must do something more to the south, even though the food is going, and we weaken lying in the cold, for with 72° of frost the wind cuts through our thin tent, and even the drift is finding its way in and on to our bags, which are wet enough as it is . . . We are so short of food, and at this high altitude, 11,600 feet, it is hard to keep any warmth in our bodies between the scanty meals. We have nothing to read now, having depoted our little books to save weight.

> *Ernest Shackleton, attempting to be the first to the South Pole,*
> *at 90° South, Diary, 1909.*

Early in the morning the Thames broke through in several places and flooded river London . . . Fourteen people were drowned in basements, poor souls, and a fish was caught in the kitchen of Battersea police station. The basement of the Tate Gallery was filled, which may help to settle the question of [where to keep] the twenty thousand Turner sketches.

> *Sylvia Townsend Warner, Diary, 1928.*

9 JANUARY

1799 *Pitt the Younger introduces income tax, two shillings in the pound.*

1806 *Nelson is buried in St Paul's Cathedral.*

1969 *The first trial flight of Concorde at Bristol.*

Blessed be God, the King is well amended, and hath been sin Christmas Day; and on Saint John's Day commanded his almoner to ride to Canterbury with his offering, and commanded the secretary to offer at Saint Edward [in Westminster Abbey]. And on the Monday after noon the Queen came to him, and brought my Lord Prince with her. And then he asked what the Prince's name was, and the Queen told him Edward; and then he held up his hands and thanked God thereof. And he said he never knew him till that time, nor wist [knew] not what was said to him, nor wist not where he had be whiles he hath be sick till now. And he asked who was godfathers, and the Queen told him, and he was well apaid [pleased].

> *Edmund Clere to John Paston I, 1455. The king, Henry VI,*
> *had been mad when his son Edward was born.*

At 4 a.m. started south, with the Queen's Union Jack, a brass cylinder containing stamps and documents to place at the furthest south point, camera, glasses, and compass. At 9 a.m. we were in 88° 23' south, half running and half walking over a surface much hardened by the recent blizzard. It was strange for us to go along without the nightmare of a sledge dragging behind us. We hoisted Her Majesty's flag and the other Union Jack afterwards, and took possession of the plateau in the name of His Majesty. While the Union Jack blew out stiffly in the icy gale that cut us to the bone, we looked south with our powerful glasses, but could see nothing but the dead white snow plain. There was no break in the plateau as it extended towards the Pole, and we feel sure that the goal we have failed to reach lies on this plain . . . Homeward bound at last. Whatever regrets may be, we have done our best.

> *Ernest Shackleton, Diary, 1909.*

10 JANUARY

1840 *The penny post is introduced.*

1863 *The first section of the London Underground, between Paddington and Farringdon Street, is opened by Mr Gladstone.*

1929 *Tintin appears for the first time, in a comic strip in a Belgian newspaper.*

The Duchess [of Albemarle] cried mightily out against the having of gentlemen captains with feathers and ribands, and wished the King would send her husband to sea with the old plain sea-captains that he served with formerly, that would make their ships swim with blood, though they could not make legs [make a bow] as captains nowadays can.

Samuel Pepys, Diary, 1666.

If you attend at all to Natural History I send you this P.S. as a memento, that I continue to collect all kinds of facts about 'Varieties and Species', for my some-day work to be so entitled; the smallest contributions thankfully accepted; descriptions of offspring of all crosses between all domestic birds and animals, dogs, cats, etc., etc., very valuable. Don't forget, if your half-bred African cat should die, that I should be very much obliged for its carcase sent up in a little hamper for the skeleton; it, or any cross-bred pigeons, fowl, duck, etc., etc., will be more acceptable than the finest haunch of venison, or the finest turtle.

Charles Darwin to his cousin William Darwin Fox, 1841.

11 JANUARY

1922 *Insulin given to a diabetic for the first time, in Toronto.*

1963 *The first disco opened, the Whisky-a-Go-Go in Los Angeles.*

1974 *First surviving sextuplets born, to Mrs S. Rosenkowitz in Cape Town.*

A very cold day. William promised me he would rise as soon as I had carried him his breakfast, but he lay in bed till between twelve and one. We talked of walking, but the blackness of the cold made us slow to put forward, and we did not walk at all. Mary [Wordsworth's wife] read the Prologue to Chaucer's tales to me in the morning. William was working at his poem to Coleridge [the *Prelude*] . . . Before tea I sat two hours in the parlour. Read part of *The Knight's Tale* with exquisite delight. Since tea Mary has been down stairs copying out Italian poems for Stuart [editor of the *Morning Post*]. William has been working beside me, and here ends this imperfect summary . . . Now I am going to take tapioca for my supper, and Mary an egg, William some cold mutton – his poor chest is tired.

Dorothy Wordsworth, Journal, 1803.

All idea of study is dissipated; the boys took their gun and their skaites immediately after our breakfast and went to the basin at Bengrove, but as the snow had fallen in the night were obliged to employ sweepers. I went to see whether it was hard enough to bear them with safety. They did not arrive at Camerton till nearly dinner time, having spent the morning in shooting. I regret the gun was purchased, as it has been a sad obstacle to reading; indeed it seems now considered that nothing more is to be done in the way of study this vacation. When once the bow is unloosed it is difficult to new string it again.

The Revd John Skinner, Journal, 1826.

12 JANUARY

1895 *The National Trust founded.*

1948 *The first full-size UK supermarket is opened, belonging to the London Co-op, at Manor Park.*

The son of the White Chief says his father sends us greetings of friendship and good will. This is kind of him, for we know he has little need of our friendship in return because his people are many. They are like the grass that covers the vast prairies, while my people are few; they resemble the scattering trees of a storm-swept plain.

The Great and – I presume – good White Chief sends us word that he wants to buy our lands but is willing to allow us to reserve enough to live on comfortably. This indeed appears generous, for the Red Man no longer has rights that he need respect, and the offer may be wise, also, for we are no longer in need of a great country.

There was a time when our people covered the whole land as the waves of a wind-ruffled sea cover its shell-paved floor, but that time has long since passed away with the greatness of tribes now almost forgotten. I will not dwell on nor mourn over our untimely decay, nor reproach my pale-face brothers with hastening it, for we, too, may have been somewhat to blame . . .

It matters little where we pass the remnant of our days. They are not many. The Indian's night promises to be dark. No bright star hovers above his horizon. Sad-voiced winds moan in the distance. Some grim Fate of our race is on the Red Man's trail, and wherever he goes he will still hear the sure approaching footsteps of his fell destroyer and prepare to stolidly meet his doom, as does the wounded doe that hears the approaching footsteps of the hunter.

Chief Seattle responds to the Governor of the State of Washington following the decision to place the Indian tribes on reservations, 1855.

13 JANUARY

1929 *Wyatt Earp dies, frontier Sheriff and victor of the Gunfight at the OK Corral.*

1964 *The Beatles' breakthrough record, 'I Want to Hold Your Hand', reaches No.1 in the US charts.*

I had the gratification of seeing the whole party swamped in crambo [a word game involving rhyming], and water-logged in charades, and a large party writhing in the agonies of English Xmas conviviality, without any young ladies, without any music to break the awful solemnity of the evening, and no Lord Auckland [Emily's brother] to make them gamesome . . .

Sir Guy [her husband] nearly died of crambo, and was very near taking a dictionary with him the next time. But as he is not at all of the go-along tribe he kicked, and would not cramb. The event of the next time was charades, and our enthusiasm knew no bounds when Lord Dudley joined the crew, and appeared with his coat turned inside out, and enacted a chimney-sweeper, and rattled a stick upon a bit of wood. Our rapture was indescribable, and it reminded me of the feelings of those who in ancient times beheld great men doing little things! . . . It was that day too he said when they offered him toasted cheese, 'Ah! yes; today is Toasted-cheese day, and yesterday was Herring day!!'

How we all laughed!!! . . .

We had a ball at Bowood the night before Twelfth Night. It went off very well indeed. I had the pleasure of cramming my small Pam [her daughter, aged five] into a pink body and seeing it dance, and seeing everybody make a fuss with it because it was by many degrees the smallest thing in the room.

Pamela, Lady Campbell to Emily Eden, on aspects of Christmas at Bowood, Lord Lansdowne's house in Wiltshire, 1826.

14 JANUARY

Mallard Day at All Souls College, Oxford. A 'boisterous torch-lit duck hunt' is held through the college buildings and over the roofs, but now only in the first year of each century. It supposedly commemorates a duck found when the college foundations were being dug in 1437.

1896 *The first public screening of a film in the UK, at the Royal Photographic Society in London.*

I have sent you a little purse with some small money in it, all the pence I had, that you may have a penny to give a poor body, and a pair of gloves; not that I think you have not better in Oxford, but that you may sometimes remember her, that seldom has you out of my thoughts.

Brilliana, Lady Harley to her son Edward at Oxford, 1639.

The gentleman [Grenville] tells us America is obstinate; America is in almost open rebellion. I rejoice that America has resisted. Three million of people so dead to all feelings of liberty as voluntarily to submit to be slaves would have been fit instruments to make slaves of the rest. I come not here armed at all points, with law cases and acts of parliament, with the statute book doubled down in dog's ears, to defend the cause of liberty . . . but upon a general principle, upon a constitutional principle . . .

The gentleman asks, when were the colonies emancipated? But I desire to know when they were made slaves . . . I will be bold to affirm that the profit to Great Britain from the trade of the colonies, through all its branches, is two millions a year . . . And shall a miserable financier come with a boast that he can bring a peppercorn into the exchequer, to the loss of two millions to the nation? . . .

In the House of Commons in 1766 William Pitt (the Elder), Prime Minister during the recently concluded Seven Years' War, attacks his brother-in-law George Grenville's proposal to help pay for it by taxing the American colonies.

The nipple should always be a little above the centre. In Rubens and common nature it is below, which gives a flabby, infirm look.

Benjamin Robert Haydon, Diary, 1825.

15 JANUARY

1759 *The British Museum is opened.*

1880 *The first British telephone directory is published, 255 names in London.*

1913 *The first unemployment, sickness and maternity benefits are paid out.*

What I learn comes from newspapers, that collect intelligence from coffee-houses, consequently what I neither believe nor report. At home I see only a few charitable elders, except about four-score nephews and nieces of various ages, who are each brought to me about once a-year, to stare at me as the Methusalem of the family, and they can only speak of their own contemporaries, which interest me no more than if they talked of their dolls, or bats and balls. Must not the result of all this, Madam, make me a very entertaining correspondent? And can such letters be worth showing? or can I have any spirit when so old and reduced to dictate?

Oh! my good Madam, dispense with me from such a task, and think how it must add to it to apprehend such letters being shown. Pray send me no more such laurels, which I desire no more than their leaves when decked with a scrap of tinsel and stuck on twelfth-cakes that lie on the shop-boards of pastry-cooks at Christmas. I shall be quite content with a sprig of rosemary thrown after me, when the parson of the parish commits my dust to dust.

Horace Walpole to the Countess of Ossory, 1797.
He died the following March, aged 79.

George [their brother] is busy this morning in making copies of my verses. He is making now one of an ode to the nightingale, which is like reading an account of the Black Hole at Calcutta on an iceberg.

John Keats to his sister Georgiana, 1820.

16 JANUARY

1809 *Death of General Sir John Moore at Corunna in the early stages of the Peninsular War: 'Not a drum was heard, not a funeral note . . .'*

1920 *Prohibition - the outlawing of the sale of alcohol - introduced in the US.*

It will be thirteen years in little more than a week, since this malady [mental illness] seized me. Methinks I hear you ask – your affection for me will, I know, make you wish to do so – Is it removed? I reply, in great measure, but not quite. Occasionally I am much distressed, but that distress becomes continually less frequent, and I think less violent. I find writing, and especially poetry, my best remedy. Perhaps had I understood music, I had never written verse, but had lived upon fiddle-strings instead. It is better however as it is. A poet may, if he pleases, be of a little use in the world, while a musician, the most skilful, can only divert himself and a few others. I have been emerging gradually from this pit. As soon as I became capable of action, I commenced carpenter, made cupboards, boxes, stools. I grew weary of this in about a twelvemonth, and addressed myself to the making of birdcages. To this employment succeeded that of gardening, which I intermingled with that of drawing, but finding that the latter occupation injured my eyes, I renounced it, and commenced poet. I have given you, my dear, a little history in shorthand.

William Cowper to Lady Hesketh, 1786.

John Pounds was an interesting creature – a man who, lamed for life, took up shoe-mending in a little shop, open to the air in a bye-street of Portsmouth . . . And then, being full of affection for children, he took a wild little boy, and while he cooked taught him to read and spell. He soon had a class of 20 or 30 in his shop, and fed them with potatoes cooked in his little stove, and in this way, during his life, he taught hundreds for love. He was the real founder of the Ragged School movement . . . 'May I die', he said, 'as a bird dies' (he kept a number of them and a cat and rabbits) 'when he drops off his perch.' And so he did . . . He seems to me the nearest of all I have known to the heart of the Kingdom of God.

Stopford Brooke at Portsmouth, Diary, 1899.

17 JANUARY

1874 *The original Siamese twins, Chang and Eng Bunker, die within three hours of each other.*

1929 *The character 'Popeye' appears for the first time, in a cartoon strip.*

1983 *Breakfast TV starts in Britain, with Frank Bough and Selina Scott of the BBC.*

Mrs C——, I have settled, is a publican's daughter, and Mr C—— is running away with her, the till, the time-piece off the bar mantel-shelf, the mother's gold watch from the pocket at the head of the bed; and other miscellaneous property . . . Apropos of rolling, I have forgotten to mention that in playing whist we are obliged to put the tricks in our pockets, to keep them from disappearing altogether; and that five or six times in the course of every rubber we are all flung from our seats, roll out at different doors, and keep on rolling until we are picked up by stewards. This has become such a matter of course, that we go through it with perfect gravity; and when we are bolstered up on our sofas again, resume our conversation or our game at the point where it was interrupted.

Charles Dickens describes fellow-passengers and
conditions, sailing to America in 1842.

Close by [the Al Rasheed Hotel], a two-thousand-pound penetration bomb landed, but contrary to the gossip in the hotel neither my eyeballs nor the fillings in my teeth came out. I switched on the radio I found by the bed and listened to President Bush explaining what was going on. It was 5.45 a.m. and I was soon asleep . . .

Someone shouted that a cruise missile had just passed the window. Following the line of the main road beside the hotel and travelling from south-west to north-east, it flashed across at five hundred miles an hour, making little noise and leaving no exhaust. It was twenty feet long, and was a good hundred yards from our window. It undulated a little as it went, following the contours of the road. It was like the sighting of a UFO.

John Simpson of the BBC describes the first day of the bombing
of Baghdad during the Gulf War, 1991.

18 JANUARY

1778 *Captain Cook discovers and names the Sandwich Islands, now Hawaii.*

1871 *Unified Germany is proclaimed an Empire at Versailles.*

1912 *Scott reaches the South Pole.*

Eamonn [his producer] was having trouble locking the dish on to the satellite . . . The reason seemed to be the jamming waves put out by American Awacs aircraft, which were accompanying an attack by B-52 bombers.

The security people and the minders started to panic, shouting at us to get inside fast. The bombing started, a rumble that shook the ground and rippled the water in the stagnant pool of sewage that had formed twenty yards from where we had set up the phone . . . Annoyed by the nervousness of the minders, I stayed by the satellite phone, finishing off my script. 'Keep calm,' I called out. 'It's perfectly safe.' There was a thick whistling sound beside my head, and a heavy machine-gun bullet, near the end of its flight, flattened itself on the step in front of me. A minder picked it up and waved it in my face. 'You see? You see? And you say it's safe!' . . .

That night Anthony [cameraman] camped out in the hotel grounds. I eluded the security man in the darkness and found him lurking near the swimming pool. I gave him a hip-flask of Laphroaig and helped him settle on a bench from which he could film the night's attacks . . . I made it up to the fifth floor . . . took off my dirty clothes for the first time since the war began, arranged the necessary equipment in case my room took a hit (pain-killers, field dressings, torch) and read a little Evelyn Waugh by candlelight. The crump of a missile made the flame flicker, but I blew it out and fell asleep.

John Simpson, Baghdad, 1991.

19 JANUARY

1348 *Edward III establishes the Order of the Garter.*

1841 *Hong Kong is ceded to Great Britain by China.*

This being the day for the Queen's birthday [Charlotte, consort of George III] to be kept, Bill fired my blunderbuss three times, each charge three caps of powder with a good deal of paper and tow on it. I fired him off in the evening with three caps of powder also.

Parson James Woodforde, Diary, 1778.

With regard to the Poeshie [poetry] – I will have no cutting and slashing . . . Don Juan shall be an entire horse or none . . . I will not give way to all the Cant of Christendom – I have been cloyed with applause and sickened with abuse; at present – I care for little but the Copyright – I have imbibed a great love for money – let me have it – if Murray loses this time – he won't the next . . .

When he [Lord Lauderdale] landed at the [Venice] custom house from Corfu – he called for 'Post horses – directly' – he was told that there were no horses except mine nearer than the Lido – unless he wished for the four bronze coursers of St Mark – which were at his service . . .

P.S. – Whatever brain-money – you get on my account from Murray – pray remit me – I will never consent to pay away what I earn – that is mine – and what I get by my brains – I will spend on my bollocks – as long as I have a tester [sixpence] or a testicle remaining – I shall not live long – and for that reason – I must live while I can – so – let him disburse – and me receive – 'for the Night cometh'.

Lord Byron to John Cam Hobhouse and Charles,
Lord Kinnaird, from Venice, 1819.

20 JANUARY

1265 *The first English Parliament meets in Westminster Hall.*

1961 *Inauguration of J.F. Kennedy as 35th President - but first Roman Catholic President - of the USA.*

I am now the owner of an estate [Vailima] . . . three streams, two waterfalls, a great cliff, an ancient native fort, a view of the sea and lowlands, or (to be more precise) several views of them in various directions, are now mine. It would be affectation to omit a good many head of cattle; above all as it required much diplomacy to have them thrown in, for the gentleman who sold to me was staunch. Besides all this, there is a great deal more forest than I have any need for; or to be plain the whole estate is one impassable jungle, which must be cut down and through at considerable expense. Then the house has to be built; and then (as a climax) we may have to stand a siege in it in the next native war.

I do feel as if I was a coward and a traitor to desert my friends; only, my dear lady, you know what a miserable corrhyzal (is that how it is spelt?) creature I was at home: and here I have some real health, I can walk, I can ride, I can stand some exposure, I am up with the sun, I have a real enjoyment of the world and of myself; it would be hard to go back again to England and to bed; and I think it would be very silly.

Robert Louis Stevenson, from Samoa, to Lady Taylor, 1890.

21 JANUARY

1793 *Louis XVI guillotined in Paris.*

1976 *Concorde enters service on the London-to-Bahrain and Paris-to-Rio de Janeiro routes.*

Rode out, as usual, and fired pistols. Good shooting – broke four common, and rather small, bottles, in four shots, at fourteen paces, with a common pair of pistols and indifferent powder. Almost as good *wafering* or shooting – considering the difference of powder and pistol – as when in 1809, 1811, 1812, 1813, 1814, it was my luck to split walking-sticks, wafers, half-crowns, shillings, and even the *eye* of a walking-stick, at twelve paces, with a single bullet – and all by *eye* and calculation; for my hand is not steady, and apt to change with the very weather. To the prowess which I here note, Joe Manton [famous gunmaker] and others can bear testimony; for the former taught, and the latter has seen me do, these feats.

Tomorrow is my birthday – that is to say, at twelve o' the clock, midnight, i.e. in twelve minutes, I shall have completed thirty and three years of age!!! – and I go my bed with a heaviness of heart at having lived so long, and to so little purpose.

It is three minutes past twelve. ' 'Tis the middle of the night by the castle clock' [the opening line of Coleridge's *Christabel*], and I am now thirty-three! . . . I don't regret them [the years] for what I have done, as for what I *might* have done.

Lord Byron, Ravenna Journal, 1821.

22 JANUARY

1788 *Lord Byron born.*

1901 *Queen Victoria dies.*

1972 *Great Britain joins the Common Market.*

Leaving the Embankment we drove up Constitution Hill, and saw the whole sky lit up by about a dozen search-lights. They made a splendid show, sweeping to and fro in the thin clouds and crossing one another in lanes of fire. Zeppelins were expected. The Abbey and Parliament Houses were without lights, and solemn and sombre they were against the dark sky. Every now and then Jupiter peered through the flying clouds, wondering what folly Earth was at, but with no notion of the boundlessness of the madness of Europe . . . Bryce, who was deputed to bring the OM to Henry James, found him unable to speak, unable save for a minute to understand what the Order was. Why does Government always delay? A year ago he would have received it with keen pleasure. Now it is Dead Sea fruit, and he deserved it then as much as now. I suppose they said he was not then an Englishman – and if they *said* that, what asses they were!

Stopford Brooke, Diary, 1916. The American-born writer Henry James had been awarded the Order of Merit. He had lived in England for several decades before becoming a British subject in 1915. He died in March 1916. See 7 August.

This morning I walked to the foot of St James's Street to witness the proclamation, and found a crowd already gathered before St James's Palace. Soon the carriages of the Herald's Office arrived; very grand, very gold and scarlet and heraldic were the various Heraldic Kings, Norroy, Garter, Clarenceux, etc. In the first carriage sat Bernard [Duke of] Norfolk, Earl Marshal of England. The trumpeters blew a bugle, and proclaimed the accession of King Edward VIII. It was a fleeting brilliant ceremony which I shall surely never see again. Afterwards I saw a large black car (the King's) drive away, with the blinds pulled half down. The crowd bowed, thinking that it contained the Duchess of Kent, but I saw Mrs Simpson . . .

We are all riveted by the position of Mrs S. No man has ever been so in love as the present King; but can she be another Mrs Fitzherbert [to whom George IV was secretly married]?

Sir Henry (Chips) Channon, Diary, 1936.

23 JANUARY

1806 *Death of William Pitt the Younger. His last words: 'Oh my country! How I leave my country.'*

1879 *Eleven VCs are won at the Battle of Rorke's Drift against the Zulus.*

1924 *The first Labour government is formed, under Ramsay MacDonald.*

So to my wife's chamber, and there supped and got her [to] cut my hair and look [at] my shirt, for I have itched mightily these six or seven days; and when all came to all, she finds that I am lousy, having found in my head and body above twenty lice, little and great; which I wonder at, being more than I have had almost these twenty years. I did think I might have got them from the little boy, but they did presently look [at] him, and found none – so how they came, I know not; but presently did shift myself [change my shirt], and so shall be rid of them, and cut my hair close to my head. And so, with much content to bed.

Samuel Pepys, Diary, 1669.

I was to have dined with Gwen [his sister], but was summoned by Lord Beaverbrook and chucked. I arrived at Stornoway House to find him alone writing a cross letter to his son about bills. In a few minutes Winston Churchill slouched in. Very changed from when I had last seen him. A great round white face like a blister. Incredibly aged. Looks like pictures of Lord Holland [Whig grandee, 1773–1840]. An elder statesman. His spirits also have declined and he sighs that he has lost his old fighting power.

Harold Nicolson, Diary, 1930.

24 JANUARY

1848 *Gold discovered in California, at Sutter's Mill.*

1935 *Beer sold in cans for the first time, in the US.*

1965 *Death of Winston Churchill.*

The frost continuing more and more severe, the Thames before London was still planted with booths in formal streets, all sorts of trades and shops furnished and full of commodities, even to a printing press, where the people and ladies took a fancy to have their names printed, and the day and year set down when printed on the Thames; this humour took so universally, that 'twas estimated the printer gained £5 a day, for printing a line only, at sixpence a name, besides what he got by ballads, etc. Coaches plied from Westminster to the Temple, and from several other stairs to and fro, as in the streets, sleds, sliding with skates, a bull-baiting, horse and coach races, puppet plays and interludes, cooks, tippling, and other lewd places, so that it seemed to be a bacchanalian triumph, or carnival on the water, whilst it was a severe judgement on the land, the trees not only splitting as if by lightning struck, but men and cattle perishing in divers places; and the very seas so locked up with ice, that no vessels could stir out or come in. The fowls, fish, and birds, and all our exotic plants and greens universally perishing. Many parks of deer were destroyed, and all sorts of fuel so dear that there were great contributions to preserve the poor alive . . . London, by reason of the excessive coldness of the air hindering the ascent of the smoke, was so filled with the fuliginous steam of the sea-coal, that hardly could one see across the streets, and this filling the lungs with its gross particles, exceedingly obstructed the breast, so as one could scarcely breathe.

John Evelyn, Diary, 1684.

25 JANUARY

———◆◆◆◆◆———

1533 *Henry VIII marries Anne Boleyn as his second wife.*

1947 *Chicago gangster Al Capone dies virtually penniless.*

The generality of the [French] men, and more than the generality, are dull and empty. They have taken up gravity, thinking it was philosophy and English, and so have acquired nothing in the room of their natural levity and cheerfulness. However, as their high opinion of their own country remains, for which they can no longer assign any reason, they are contemptuous and reserved, instead of being ridiculously, consequently pardonably, impertinent.

Horace Walpole to Thomas Gray from Paris, 1766.

My birthday – and let me count up all the things I had. Leonard had sworn he would give me nothing, and like a good wife, I believed him. But he crept into my bed, with a little parcel, which was a beautiful green purse. And he brought up breakfast, with a paper which announced a naval victory (we have sunk a German battleship) and a square brown parcel, with *The Abbot* [by Sir Walter Scott] in it – a lovely first edition. So I had a very merry and pleasing morning – which indeed was only surpassed by the afternoon. I was then taken up to town, free of charge, and given a treat, first at a picture palace, and then at Buszards [Tea Rooms]. I don't think I've had a birthday treat for ten years; and it felt like one too – being a fine frosty day, everything brisk and cheerful, as it should be, but never is. We exactly caught a non-stop train, and I have been very happy reading father [Sir Leslie Stephen] on Pope, which is very witty and bright, without a single dead sentence in it. In fact I don't know when I have enjoyed a birthday so much – not since I was a child anyhow.

Virginia Woolf, Diary, 1915.

26 JANUARY

1788 *The first shipload of convicts arrives in Botany Bay, Australia.*

1871 *The Rugby Football Union is founded.*

1885 *General Gordon is killed at Khartoum in the Sudan by followers of the Mahdi.*

The following is the account nearest the truth that I can learn of the fatal duel:
a club of Nottinghamshire gentlemen had dined at the Star and Garter, and
there had been a dispute between the combatants, whether Lord Byron, who
took no care of his game, or Mr Chaworth, who was active in the association,
had most game on their manor. The company, however, had apprehended no
consequences, and parted at eight o'clock; but Lord Byron stepping into an
empty chamber, and sending the drawer for Mr Chaworth, or calling him thither
himself, took the candle from the waiter, and bidding Mr Chaworth defend himself, drew his sword. Mr. Chaworth, who was an excellent fencer, ran Lord
Byron through the sleeve of his coat, and then received a wound fourteen inches
deep into his body. He was carried to his house in Berkeley Street – made his
will with the greatest composure, and dictated a paper, which, they say, allows
it was a fair duel, and died at nine this morning. Lord Byron is not gone off, but
says he will take his trial, which, if the Coroner brings in a verdict of manslaughter, may, according to precedent, be in the House of Lords, and without the
ceremonial of Westminster Hall.

*Horace Walpole to the Earl of Hertford, 1765. This was the 5th Lord Byron, great-uncle
of the poet. He was tried in Westminster Hall by his fellow peers and found guilty of
manslaughter.*

27 JANUARY

1880 *Patent for an electric lamp granted to Thomas Edison.*

1926 *John Logie Baird gives the first public demonstration of television, in Soho.*

After six fits of a quartan ague [probably malaria] with which it pleased God to visit him, died my dear son Richard, to our inexpressible grief and affliction, five years and three days old only, but at that tender age a prodigy for wit and understanding; for beauty of body a very angel; for endowment of mind of incredible and rare hopes. To give only a little taste of some of them, and thereby glory to God, who out of the mouths of babes and infants does sometimes perfect his praises: at two years and a half old he could perfectly read any of the English, Latin, French, or Gothic letters, pronouncing the three first languages exactly. He had before the fifth year, or in that year, not only skill to read most written hands, but to decline all the nouns, conjugate the verbs regular, and most of the irregular; learned out *puerilis*, got by heart almost the entire vocabulary of Latin and French primitives and words, could make congruous syntax, turn English into Latin, and vice versa, construe and prove what he read, and did the government and use of relatives, verbs, substantives, ellipses, and many figures and tropes, and made a considerable progress in Comenius's *Janua*; began himself to write legibly, and had a strong passion for Greek.

John Evelyn, Diary, 1658.

With characteristic fickleness I have begun a new novel since you left, about ten chapters of it are done. I have dictated it to Belle – part of it, when it was thought better I should not speak, in the deaf and dumb alphabet. I think I ought to charge *extry* for this book! on the principle of the parties who paint pictures with their toes.

Robert Louis Stevenson to his mother, 1893. Belle was Stevenson's step-daughter. The new novel was St Ives.

28 JANUARY

1457 *Henry VII is born.*

1547 *Henry VIII dies. His final words: 'All is lost! Monks, monks, monks!'*

1896 *First British motorist is fined for speeding, doing 8 mph in a 2.5 mph area.*

To pray Greenfield to send me faithfully word by writing how Clement Paston [her son] hath do his devoir [applied himself] in learning. And if he hath not do well, nor will not amend, pray him that he will truly belash him till he will amend; and so did the last master, and the best that ever he had, at Cambridge. And say Greenfield that if he will take upon him to bring him into good rule and learning, that I may verily know he doth his devoir, I will give him ten marks for his labour; for I had liefer he were fair buried than lost for default.

Agnes Paston, Memorandum, 1458.

I tremble for the 'magnificence', which you attribute to the new Childe Harold. I am glad you like it; it is a fine indistinct piece of poetical desolation, and my favourite. I was half mad during the time of its composition, between metaphysics, mountains, lakes, love unextinguishable, thoughts unutterable, and the nightmare of my own delinquencies. I should, many a good day, have blown my brains out, but for the recollection that it would have given pleasure to my mother-in-law; and, even *then*, if I could have been certain to haunt her – but I won't dwell upon these trifling family matters.

Lord Byron to Thomas Moore, 1817.

29 JANUARY

1856 *The Victoria Cross is instituted, the first awards going to combatants in the Crimean War against Russia.*

1916 *The newly invented tank is put on trial for the first time, at Hatfield.*

1942 Desert Island Discs *is broadcast for the first time on BBC radio.*

I want to tell you that I have got my own darling child from London; on Wednesday I received one copy [of *Pride and Prejudice*] . . . Miss Benn dined with us on the very day of the book's coming and in the evening we set fairly at it, and read half the first volume to her, prefacing that, having intelligence from Henry [a brother] that such a work would soon appear, we had desired him to send it whenever it came out, and I believe it passed with her unsuspected. She was amused, poor soul! *That* she could not help, you know, with two such people to lead the way, but she really does seem to admire Elizabeth [Bennet]. I must confess that I think her as delightful a creature as ever appeared in print, and how I shall be able to tolerate those who do not like *her* at least I do not know. There are a few typical errors; and a 'said he', or a 'said she', would sometimes make the dialogue more immediately clear . . . The second volume is shorter than I could wish, but the difference is not so much in reality as in look, there being a larger proportion of narrative in that part. I have lopped and cropped so successfully, however, that I imagine it must be rather shorter than *Sense and Sensibility* altogether. Now I will try to write of something else, and it shall be a complete change of subject – ordination – I am glad to find your enquiries have ended so well. If you could discover whether Northamptonshire is a country of hedgerows I should be glad again.

Jane Austen to her sister Cassandra, 1813. Miss Benn was a Chawton neighbour who did not know Jane Austen was the author of the book. Northamptonshire is the setting for Mansfield Park. *See also 4 February*

30 JANUARY

1606 *Execution of Sir Everard Digby, Gunpowder Plotter, by hanging, drawing and quartering. When the executioner plucked out his heart and said, 'Here is the heart of a traitor', Digby said 'Thou liest', before expiring.*

1649 *Execution of Charles I. He wore two shirts on that cold morning because he did not want to shiver lest his enemies should say it was from fear.*

Wrought hard at *Bon.* [*Life of Napoleon*] all day, though I had settled other-wise. I ought to have been at an article for John Lockhart [his son-in-law, editor of the *Quarterly Review*], and one for poor Gillies [editor of the *Foreign Quarterly*]; but there is something irresistible in contradiction, even when it consists in doing a thing equally laborious, but not the thing you are especially called upon to do. It is a kind of cheating the devil, which a self-willed monster like me is particularly addicted to. Not to make myself worse than I am though, I was full of information about the Russian campaign, which might evaporate unless used, like lime, as soon after it was wrought up as possible . . .

By a letter from Gibson [his solicitor] I see the gross proceeds of *Bonaparte* at

eight volumes are	£12,600
Discount five months	210
Net pounds	£12,390

I question if more was ever made by a single work or by a single author's labours in the same time. But whether it is deserved or not is the question.

[The following morning] Young Murray [John Murray III], son of Mr M. in Albemarle Street, breakfasted with me. English boys have this advantage, that they are well bred and can converse when ours are regular-built cubs – I am not sure if it is an advantage in the long run. It is a temptation to premature display.

Sir Walter Scott, Journal, 1827.

31 JANUARY

1846 *Sir Robert Peel repeals the Corn Laws.*

1858 *The* Great Eastern *steamship is launched sideways into the Thames.*

1953 *The Great Storm that drowned more than 2,000 in Holland and England, where it raged from Lincolnshire down to Canvey Island.*

I heard a carriage drive up, and *men's voices* . . . the men proved to be Alfred Tennyson of all people and his friend Mr Moxon . . . Alfred is dreadfully embarrassed with women alone – for he entertains at one and the same moment a feeling of almost adoration for them and an ineffable contempt! adoration I suppose for what they *might be* – contempt for what they *are*! The only chance of my getting any right good of him was to make him forget my womanness – so I did just as Carlyle would have done, had he been there; got out *pipes* and *tobacco* – and *brandy* and *water* – with a deluge of *tea* over and above. The effect of these accessories was miraculous – he *professed* to be *ashamed* of polluting my room, 'felt', he said, 'as if he were stealing cups and sacred vessels in the Temple' – but he smoked on all the same – for *three* mortal hours! – talking like an angel – only exactly as if he were talking with a clever man – which – being a thing I am not used to – men always *adapting* their conversation to what they *take to be* a woman's taste – strained me to a terrible pitch of intellectuality.

Jane Welsh Carlyle to Helen Welsh, 1845.

Another general came today and he was rather pleased with me. Fortunately he looked at kitchens and not at horses and there was no other squadron leader could touch me on the grease-trap, the stock-pot, the incinerator and the use and abuse of dripping. Would you believe it, I was the only one who had a meat safe and could point out its situation and merits in a clear and soldierlike manner? But dripping is my forte. The ninth man to be killed by that shell died yesterday.

Conrad Russell to Katharine Asquith, from Flanders, 1918. Earlier in January a shell had killed and wounded many of his men.

FEBRUARY

1 FEBRUARY

1884 *The first volume of the* Oxford English Dictionary *is published. The final volume does not appear until 1928.*

1979 *Ayatollah Khomeni returns from exile in France to Iran, having coordinated the revolution there the previous month.*

They [the French] have stated that they would organise every country by a disorganising principle; and afterwards they tell you all this is done by the will of the people. And then comes this plain question, what is the will of the people? It is the power of the French. They have explained what that liberty is which they wish to give to every nation; and if they will not accept of it voluntarily, they compel them. They take every opportunity to destroy every institution that is most sacred and most valuable in every nation where their armies have made their appearance; and under the name of liberty, they have resolved to make every country in substance, if not in form, a province dependent on themselves, through the despotism of Jacobin societies. This has given a more fatal blow to the liberties of mankind, than any they have suffered, even from the boldest attempts of the most aspiring monarch. We see, therefore, that France has trampled under foot all laws, human and divine. She has at last avowed the most insatiable ambition, and greatest contempt for the law of nations, which all independent states have hitherto professed most religiously to observe; and unless she is stopped in her career, all Europe must soon learn their ideas of justice – law of nations – models of government – and principles of liberty from the mouth of the French cannon.

William Pitt the Younger, Prime Minister, in the House of Commons, 1793. France declared war this day, Louis XVI having been executed on 21 January.

2 FEBRUARY

Candlemas: Feast of the Purification of the Virgin Mary, forty days after the Nativity.

1709 *Alexander Selkirk, the model for Robinson Crusoe, is rescued after more than four years marooned on a Pacific island 400 miles off the coast of Chile.*

1880 *The first imported frozen meat is landed in London, from Australia.*

What was my terror to hear myself pursued – to hear the voice of the King himself loudly and hoarsely calling after me, 'Miss Burney, Miss Burney!'. . . I turned round, I saw the two doctors had got the King between them, and three attendants . . . I instantly forced myself forward to meet him . . . I looked up and met all his wonted benignity of countenance, though something still of wildness in his eyes. Think, however, of my surprise to feel him put both his hands round my two shoulders, and then kiss my cheek! . . . the Willises [Dr Willis was assisted by his son], who have never seen him till this fatal illness, not knowing how very extraordinary an action this was from him, simply smiled and looked pleased . . . He now spoke in such terms of his pleasure in seeing me that I soon lost the whole of my terror . . . What a conversation followed! . . . He told me innumerable anecdotes of [Handel] . . . Then he ran over most of his oratorios attempting to sing the subjects of several airs and choruses, but so dreadfully hoarse that the sound was terrible. Dr Willis, quite alarmed at this exertion feared he would do himself harm, and again proposed a separation. 'No, no, no! he exclaimed, 'not yet. I have something I must just mention first.' He pulled out a pocket book and rummaged some time, but to no purpose.

> *Fanny Burney, on a meeting with King George III in Kew Gardens*
> *during his first major fit of insanity, Diary, 1789*

Oh! there is an organ playing in the street – a waltz, too! I must leave off to listen. They are playing a waltz which I have heard ten thousand times at the balls in London, between 1812 and 1815. Music is a strange thing.

> *Lord Byron, Ravenna Journal, 1821*

3 FEBRUARY

1959 *Buddy Holly killed in a plane crash, aged 22.*

1960 *Harold Macmillan makes his 'Wind of Change' speech in Cape Town, heralding the end of British support for South Africa's bar on the advancement of black Africans, and of colonial rule generally.*

This day was the first representation of Mrs Sheridan's comedy, *The Discovery*. As Dempster, Erskine, and I had made a resolution to be present at every first night, I determined to venture abroad . . .

At three I swallowed an apple-tart, then wrapped myself well up in two pair of stockings, two shirts, and a greatcoat; and thus fortified against the weather, I got into a snug [sedan] chair and was carried to Drury Lane. I took up my associates at the Rose Tavern, and we went into the pit at four, where, as they had not dined, they laid down their hats, one on each side of me, and there did I sit to keep their places. I was amused to find myself transported from my room of indisposition [he was suffering from a dose of the clap) to the gay, gilded theatre. I put myself as much as possible into proper humour for seeing the play . . .

I had but a troublesome occupation keeping two seats while my companions were enjoying themselves over a bottle and lolling at their ease, in no hurry to come in. However, I had the satisfaction to see them well punished, for by staying so late they could scarcely squeeze through the crowd, and with the utmost difficulty got to their places. The evening went finely on . . . We had several judicious and lively people round us, and kept up a clever enough chat. I wrought myself up to the imagination that it was the age of Sir Richard Steele [*c.* 1710], and that I was like him sitting in judgment on a new comedy.

James Boswell, Journal, 1763.

4 FEBRUARY

1953 *Sweet-rationing ends in Britain.*

1962 *The* Sunday Times *produces the first colour supplement.*

Our second evening's reading to Miss Benn [from *Pride and Prejudice*, just published] had not pleased me so well, but I believe something must be attributed to my mother's too rapid way of getting on: and though she perfectly understands the characters herself, she cannot speak as they ought. Upon the whole, however, I am quite vain enough and well satisfied enough. The work is rather too light, and bright, and sparkling; it wants shade; it wants to be stretched out here and there with a long chapter of sense, if it could be had; if not, of solemn specious nonsense, about something unconnected with the story, an essay on writing, a critique on Walter Scott, or the history of Buonaparté, or anything that would form a contrast, and bring the reader with increased delight to the playfulness and epigrammatism of the general style.

Jane Austen to her sister Cassandra, 1813.

The harem sees all the events from its rooms: when we hear a noise, a scream, or anything exciting we rush to the window and look out right over the valley . . . I am longing unspeakably for a wash . . . and I have been so uncomfortable, but find that one doesn't get *much* dirtier after the first two days. Anyway I know all about life in the Middle Ages . . . The great amusement of the harem are the children. They can still run in and out, the little girls like thin little butterflies in their yellow hoods and black face veils. The babies are kept to play with, and all suffer from overworked nerves. There is perfect friendly democracy; it is a very nice feeling but makes both cleanliness and privacy impossible: on the other hand it makes saintliness not only possible but frequently almost necessary.

Freya Stark to her mother, 1935, from the Government castle in
Masna'a in the Hadramaut on her first Arabian journey.

5 FEBRUARY

1811 *George, Prince of Wales, becomes Prince Regent as a result of his father George III's final decline into madness.*

1933 *Prohibition is ended in the US.*

I must tell you poor Mr Denison is broken-hearted about his sister Lady Conyngham; and his only relief, he says, is imparting his grief to me. According to his own account, he protested to her from the first against her living under the King's roof; but that the thing, instead of getting better, has become daily worse and worse. Not that even now he can suppose there is anything criminal between persons of their age, but that he never goes into society without hearing allusions too plain to be misunderstood; and he lives in daily fear and expectation of the subject coming before Parliament. In short, such is his feeling that he has called formally upon his sister to leave her fat and fair friend and to go abroad.

Thomas Creevey to his step-daughter Miss Ord, 1828. Lady Conyngham had supplanted Lady Hertford in the affections of George IV in the early 1820s. She was in her fifties, he in his sixties.

My son and my daughter, accompanied by their Uncle Russell and their Cousin Elinor Page, went to the concert at the Rooms [in Bath]. I continued within doors reading Sir Walter Scott's novel of *Rob Roy*. We dined at half-past four, and stayed to drink tea with my Mother; at seven we returned home in a close carriage, as I do not like to expose myself to the open air. The ground was so silppery the horses could not keep their legs descending the hill to Camerton, but absolutely slid down on their haunches. The servants were gone to bed, and I had much ado to awaken them; it was not nine o'clock, and methinks they might have been found watching.

The Revd John Skinner, Journal, 1830.

6 FEBRUARY

1685 *Charles II dies. His last words, according to Lord Macaulay: 'I have been a most unconscionable time in dying; I hope you will excuse it.'*

1918 *The vote is given to women over the age of 30.*

Mr O'Birne, an Irish gamester, had won one hundred thousand pounds of a young Mr Harvey of Chigwell, just started from a midshipman into an estate by his elder brother's death. O'Birne said, 'You can never pay me.' 'I can,' said the youth; 'my estate will sell for the debt.' 'No,' said O.; 'I will win ten thousand – you shall throw for the odd ninety.' They did, and Harvey won.

Horace Walpole to Sir Horace Mann, 1780. Harvey went on to command one of the ships at Trafalgar.

You enter Drury Lane at a quarter to seven: the pit is already nearly full: but you find a seat, and a very pleasant one. Box doors open and shut: ladies take off their shawls and seat themselves: gentlemen twist their side curls: the musicians come up from under the stage one by one: 'tis just upon seven. Macready [the manager] is very punctual: Mr T. Cooke is in his place with his marshal's baton in his hand: he lifts it up: and off they set with Handel's noble overture . . . Do you know the music [to *Acis and Galatea*]? It is of Handel's best: and as classical as any man who wore a full-bottomed wig could write. I think Handel never gets out of his wig: that is, out of his age: his Hallelujah chorus is a chorus not of angels, but of well-fed earthly choristers, ranged tier above tier in a Gothic cathedral, with princes for audience, and their military trumpets flourishing over the full volume of the organ. Handel's gods are like Homer's, and his sublime never reaches beyond the region of the clouds. Therefore I think that his great marches, triumphal pieces, and coronation anthems, are his finest works.

Edward FitzGerald to Frederick Tennyson, elder brother of the poet, 1842.

7 FEBRUARY

1914 *Charlie Chaplin appears on screen in his 'Tramp' costume for the first time.*

1947 *The first of the Dead Sea Scrolls discovered in caves on the west side of the Jordan, the most valuable dating from c. 160 BC to AD 68.*

Seven years, my lord, have now passed, since I waited in your outward rooms, or was repulsed from your door; during which time I have been pushing on my work [the *English Dictionary*] through difficulties, of which it is useless to complain, and have brought it, at last, to the verge of publication, without one act of assistance, one word of encouragement, or one smile of favour. Such treatment I did not expect, for I never had a patron before . . .

Is not a patron, my lord, one who looks with unconcern on a man struggling for life in the water, and when he has reached ground, encumbers him with help? The notice which you have been pleased to take of my labours, had it been early, had been kind; but it has been delayed till I am indifferent, and cannot enjoy it; till I am solitary and cannot impart it; till I am known, and do not want it. I hope it is no very cynical asperity not to confess obligations where no benefit has been received, or to be unwilling that the public should consider me as owing that to a patron, which Providence has enabled me to do for myself.

Having carried on my work thus far with so little obligation to any favourer of learning, I shall not be disappointed though I should conclude it, if less be possible, with less: for I have been long wakened from that dream of hope, in which I once boasted myself with so much exultation, my Lord, your lordship's most humble, most obedient servant, SAM. JOHNSON

Samuel Johnson to the Earl of Chesterfield, 1755.

8 FEBRUARY

1904 *The Russo-Japanese War starts with a surprise attack by the latter on Port Arthur in the Far East.*

1969 *The last issue of* The Saturday Evening Post *appears in the US.*

Then, groping for the block, she laid down her head, putting her chin over the block with both her hands, which, holding there still, had been cut off had they not been espied. . . . Then she, lying very still upon the block, one of the executioners holding her slightly with one of his hands, she endured two strokes of the other executioner with an axe, she making very small noise or none at all, and not stirring any part of her from the place where she lay: and so the executioner cut off her head, saving one little gristle, which being cut asunder, he lifted up her head to the view of all the assembly and bade 'God save the Queen'. Then, her dress of lawn falling from off her head, it appeared as grey as one of threescore and ten years old, polled very short, her face in a moment being so much altered from the form she had when she was alive, as few could remember her by her dead face. Her lips stirred up and down a quarter of an hour after her head was cut off . . .

Then one of the executioners, pulling off her garters, espied her little dog which was crept under her clothes, which could not be gotten forth but by force, yet afterward would not depart from the dead corpse, but came and lay between her head and her shoulders, which being imbrued with her blood was carried away and washed, as all things else were that had any blood was either burned or washed clean, and the executioners sent away with money for their fees, not having any one thing that belonged unto her. And so, every man being commanded out of the hall, except the sheriff and his men, she was carried by them up into a great chamber lying ready for the surgeons to embalm her.

> *Robert Wynkfielde, describing the execution of Mary, Queen of Scots at Fotheringhay Castle, Northamptonshire, 1587.*

9 FEBRUARY

1916 *Military conscription introduced in Britain.*

1933 *The Oxford Union debates the motion that 'This House in no circumstances would fight for King and Country'.*

1969 *The Boeing 747 Jumbo, the largest commercial airliner, makes its first flight.*

Reading a little of *L'Escolle des Filles*, which is a mighty lewd book, but yet not amiss for a sober man once to read over to inform himself in the villainy of the world.

Samuel Pepys, Diary, 1668.

The great excitement of the whole town is that I have hennaed my hands . . . The best beauty specialist in Huraidha was there with a pretty little pointed face and thin fingers sitting crosslegged on the carpets making a green paste of powdered henna leaves and water in a basin . . . and then, being settled with cushions as supports all round me, I handed my hands over beginning with the right one 'for blessing'. The specialist dips her forefinger in the paste which hangs down in a thin drip with which she traces out rings and stars and trees and anything she fancies on your hand. It is no joke. I went at 1 p.m. and came out at five. Meanwhile the ladies came round, pressed glasses of tea in my free hand, looked at the process, and told the gossip. A feeling of leisure hung over the harem: one could not imagine anyone being in a hurry ever. When all was done, I was arranged on cushions full length and told I could sleep while one of the ladies did my feet and the rest had coffee in one corner. I lay with closed eyes, just feeling the little cold drops on my foot: henna is supposed to be very cooling, and they asked if I felt chilled by it. I dozed, and woke to find the work finished, a lovely sun with rays shining on each instep – 'taken', the lady said, 'from a printed book'. My hands had three little branches, and one up the middle finger, besides other small patterns and circles, and the first joint of the palm a solid block of henna: this elaborate affair is only for women who 'have a man', the others can have a simple band or so; but though I pleaded age and spinsterhood I was not to be let so lightly off.

Freya Stark to her mother, from the Hadramaut in Arabia, 1938.

10 FEBRUARY

1840 *Queen Victoria marries Prince Albert of Saxe-Coburg-Gotha.*

1906 *The launch of HMS* Dreadnought, *the first modern battleship.*

1942 *Glenn Miller wins the first gold disc (actually only sprayed gold) for 'Chattanooga Choo-Choo'.*

Went through, for a new day, the task of buttoning, which seems to me somehow to fill up more of my morning than usual – not, certainly, that such is really the case, but that my mind attends to the process, having so little left to hope or fear. The half-hour between waking and rising has all my life proved propitious to any task which was exercising my invention. When I get over any knotty difficulty in a story, or have had in former times to fill up a passage in a poem, it was always when I first opened my eyes that the desired ideas thronged upon me . . . I think the first hour of the morning is also favourable to the bodily strength. Among other feats when I was a young man I was able at times to lift a smith's anvil with one hand by what it called the *horn* or round projecting piece of iron on which things are beaten to turn them round. But I could only do this before breakfast and shortly after rising . . .

Lord Elcho was as is well known engaged in the affair of 1745. He was dissatisfied with the conduct of matters from beginning to end. But after the left wing of the Highlanders was repulsed and broken at Culloden Elcho rode up to the Chevalier [Bonnie Prince Charlie] and told him all was lost and that nothing remained except to charge at the head of two thousand men who were still unbroken and either turn the fate of the day or die sword in hand as became his pretensions. The Chevalier gave him some evasive answer and turning his horse's head rode off the field. Lord Elcho called after him, 'There you go for d—n cowardly b——g Italian', and would never see him again.

Sir Walter Scott, Journal, 1826

11 FEBRUARY

1826 *London University founded to provide education for non-Anglicans excluded from Oxford and Cambridge.*

1975 *Mrs Thatcher becomes the first woman to lead the Conservative Party.*

Nothing would aid more, Natural History, than careful collecting and investigating all the productions of the most isolated islands, especially of the southern hemisphere. . . Urge the use of the dredge in the Tropics; how little or nothing we know of the limit of life downward in the hot seas.

Charles Darwin to Sir Charles Lyell, 1857.

Then to [Westminster] Abbey, so grand in the glimmering light, with a little mist floating in the vault. I sat under the lantern. There was a lovely programme of music – Arcadelt, Bach, Wagner, etc, played by [Sir Frederick] Bridge, with some vocal music – one or two pieces with bells (really metal bars), which he was very keen about, but which I thought hideous – out of tune, and the percussion notes not blending with the wind-notes. But the music stealing or rolling through the aisles, the faint light, the high dim windows, the ghost-like monuments, were as beautiful as anything on earth could be. The best we can do!

A.C. Benson, Diary, 1913.

A new story about Mrs Pat[rick Campbell, the leading actress of the 1890s and 1900s]. Terribly bored by an elderly scientist drooling away about ants – they are wonderful little creatures; they have their own police force and their own army – she leaned forward and said, with an expression of the utmost interest and a voice like damson-coloured velvet, 'No navy, I suppose?'

James Agate, Ego, *1944.*

12 FEBRUARY

1809 *Abraham Lincoln and Charles Darwin born.*

1912 *The Manchu or Qing Dynasty ends and China becomes a republic.*

1956 *The first yellow line in Britain appears, on a road in Slough.*

I agree with you that there is an end for ever of the Whigs coming into power. The country belongs to the Duke of Rutland, Lord Lonsdale, the Duke of Newcastle, and about twenty other holders of boroughs. They are our masters! If any little opportunity presents itself, we will hang them, but most probably there will be no such opportunity; it always is twenty to one against the people. There is nothing (if you will believe the Opposition) so difficult as to bully a whole people; whereas, in fact, there is nothing so easy, as that great artist Lord Castlereagh [leader of the Tory administration in the House of Commons] so well knows.

Let me beg of you to take more care of those beautiful geraniums, and not let the pigs in upon them. Geranium-fed bacon is of a beautiful colour, but it takes so many plants to fatten one pig, that such a system can never answer. I cannot conceive who put it into your head. God bless you.

The Revd Sydney Smith to Mrs Meynell, 1821.

But I am forgetting, after three days, the most important event in my life since marriage – so Clive [Bell] described it. Mr Cizec has bingled [something between a bob and a shingle] me. I am short-haired for life. Having no longer, I think, any claims to beauty, the convenience of this alone makes it desirable. Every morning I go to take up brush and twist that old coil round my finger and fix it with hairpins and then with a start of joy, no I needn't. In front there is no change; behind I'm like the rump of a partridge. This robs dining out of half its terrors.

Virginia Woolf, Diary, 1927.

13 FEBRUARY

1692 *The Massacre of Glencoe, in the Scottish West Highlands, in which members of the Macdonald clan are killed by the Campbells.*

1832 *The first deaths from cholera occur in London.*

My dearest Albert put on my stockings for me. I went and saw him shave; a great delight for me.
Queen Victoria, Journal, the fourth day of her marriage, 1840.

An enormous land deal [is] being made by British Railways over the sites of Liverpool Street and Broad Street Stations. It will mean goodbye to the Great Eastern Hotel with its dome of many-coloured glass, to the Abercorn Rooms and the Masonic Temples; to that glorious elevated walk across from Bishopsgate; through the Miss Hook of Holland part of the station and on to those interlacing Gothic arches of the original Great Eastern. It will mean goodbye to Broad Street echoing and forgotten and to those Lombardic stairs that climb up its southern side to the North London Railway war memorial. Instead the whole area will be covered by offices. We know what they'll look like and under the offices there will be, amid fumes and the tannoy system, some platform for trains to East Anglia. It will be the new Euston only much worse, if that were possible, and much higher of course because the buggers will feel fully justified in being higher than the Stock Exchange or the appalling new Barbican. Much ridicule will be poured on preservation-mad nostalgics such as yours truly, for admiring this 'essentially second-rate' collection of buildings, and for not seeing the glorious smooth-running future the financiers see for their new slabs.
John Betjeman to Auberon Waugh, 1975. Broad Street Station was demolished, while Liverpool Street was part developed and part preserved.

14 FEBRUARY

1779 *Captain Cook killed in the Sandwich Islands (Hawaii).*

1895 *Première of Oscar Wilde's play* The Importance of Being Earnest.

1929 *St Valentine Day's Massacre in Chicago, when seven members of Bugsy Moran's gang are gunned down.*

Right reverend and worshipful and my right wellbeloved Valentine . . . And if it please you to hear of my welfare, I am not in good health of body nor of heart, nor shall he till I hear from you;

> For there wottys [knows] no creature what pain I endure
> And for to be dead, I dare not dysecure [reveal] . . .

But if that ye love me, as I tryste verily that ye do, ye will not leave me therefore; for if that ye had not half the livelode [property] that ye have, for to do the greatest labour that any woman on life might, I would not forsake you.

> And if ye command me to keep me true wherever I go
> I wyse I will do all my might you to love and never no mo.
> And if my friends say that I do amiss, they shall not me let [hinder]
> so for to do.
> My heart me bids ever more to love you
> Truly over all earthly thing.
> And if they be never so wroth, I tyst it shall be better in time coming.

No more to you this time, but the Holy Trinity have you in keeping. And I beseech you that this bill be nor seen of none earthly creature save only yourself.

Margery Brews to John Paston III, 1477.

This morning came up to my wife's bedside, I being up dressing myself, little Will Mercer to be her Valentine; and brought her name writ upon blue paper in gold letters, done by himself, very pretty – and we were both well pleased with it. But I am also this year my wife's Valentine, and it will cost me five pounds – but that I must have laid out if we had not been Valentines.

Samuel Pepys, Diary, 1667.

15 FEBRUARY

1942 *Singapore surrenders to the Japanese.*

1945 *British troops reach the Rhine.*

1971 *Decimal currency introduced to Britain.*

I do not pin my dreams for the future to my country or even to my race. I think it probable that civilization somehow will last as long as I care to look ahead – perhaps with smaller numbers, but perhaps also bred to greatness and splendor by science. I think it not improbable that man, like the grub that prepares a chamber for the winged thing it never has seen but is to be – that man may have cosmic destinies that he does not understand. And so beyond the vision of battling races and an impoverished earth I catch a dreaming glimpse of peace.

The other day my dream was pictured to my mind. I was walking homeward on Pennsylvania Avenue near the Treasury, and as I looked beyond Sherman's statue to the west the sky was aflame with scarlet and crimson from the setting sun. But, like the note of downfall in Wagner's opera, below the skyline there came from little globes the pallid discord of the electric lights. And I thought to myself the *Götterdämmerung* will end, and from those globes clustered like evil eggs will come the new masters of the sky. It is like the time in which we live. But then I remembered the faith that I partly have expressed, faith in a universe not measured by our fears, a universe that has thought and more than thought inside of it, and as I gazed, after the sunset and above the electric lights, there shone the stars.

Mr Justice Holmes's speech at the Harvard Law School dinner, New York, 1913.

16 FEBRUARY

1824 *The Athenaeum Club founded in London largely by those published by John Murray and in the firm's* Quarterly Review, *because Mrs Murray was tired of her drawing room being used as their meeting place.*

1906 *The Kellogg Cornflake Company founded.*

1937 *Nylon patented in the US.*

Nobody has suffered more from low spirits than I have done – so I feel for you. 1st. Live as well as you dare. 2nd. Go into the shower-bath with a small quantity of water at a temperature low enough to give you a slight sensation of cold, 75° or 80°. 3rd. Amusing books. 4th. Short views of human life – not further than dinner or tea. 5th. Be as busy as you can. 6th. See as much as you can of those friends who respect and like you. 7th. And of those acquaintances who amuse you. 8th. Make no secret of low spirits to your friends, but talk of them freely – they are always worse for dignified concealment. 9th. Attend to the effects tea and coffee produce upon you. 10th. Compare your lot with that of other people. 11th. Don't expect too much from human life – a sorry business at the best. 12th. Avoid poetry, dramatic representations (except comedy), music, serious novels, melancholy sentimental people, and everything likely to excite feeling or emotion not ending in active benevolence. 13th. *Do good*, and endeavour to please everybody of every degree. 14th. Be as much as you can in the open air without fatigue. I5th. Make the room where you commonly sit, gay and pleasant. 16th. Struggle by little and little against idleness. 17th. Don't be too severe upon yourself, or underrate yourself, but do yourself justice. 18th. Keep good blazing fires. 19th. Be firm and constant in the exercise of rational religion. 20th. Believe me, dear Lady Georgiana, Very truly yours.

The Revd Sydney Smith to Lady Morpeth, 1820.

17 FEBRUARY

——●●●●●◉◎◉◎●●●●●——

1923 *Lord Carnarvon opens the inner tomb of Tutankhamun, sealed since 1337 BC.*

1979 *War breaks out between Communist China and Communist Vietnam.*

I call your good letter reassuring simply on the general ground of its making you credible for an hour. You are otherwise wholly of the stuff that dreams are made of. I think this is why I don't keep writing to you, don't talk to you, as it were, in my sleep . . . I think I envy you too much – your climate, your thrill of life, your magnificent facility. You judge well that I have far too little of this last – though you *can't* judge how much more and more difficult I find it every day to write . . . Most refreshing, even while not wholly convincing, was the cool trade-wind (is the trade-wind cool?) of your criticism of some of *ces messieurs*. I grant you Hardy with all my heart . . . I am meek and ashamed where the public clatter is deafening – so I bowed my head and let *Tess of the d'Urbervilles* pass. But oh yes, dear Louis, she is vile. The pretence of 'sexuality' is only equalled by the absence of it, and the abomination of the language by the author's reputation for style. There are indeed some pretty smells and sights and sounds. But you have better ones in Polynesia . . .

I know what you all magnificently eat, and what dear Mrs Louis splendidly (but not somewhat transparently – no?) wears. Please assure that intensely-remembered lady of my dumb fidelity. I am told your mother nears our shores and I promise myself joy on seeing her and pumping her. I don't know, however, alas, how long this ceremony may be delayed, as I go to Italy, for all the blessed spring, next week. I have been in London without an hour's absence since the middle of Aug. last. I hear you utter some island objurgation, and go splashing, to banish the stuffy image, into the sapphire sea.

Henry James to Robert Louis Stevenson in Samoa, South Pacific, 1893.

18 FEBRUARY

1478 *The 'false, fleeting, perjur'd' Duke of Clarence put to death, possibly by drowning in a butt of Malmsey wine, by his brother, Edward IV.*

1678 The Pilgrim's Progress *by John Bunyan published.*

1979 *The first edition of* The Antiques Roadshow *is televised.*

You are quite right about happiness. I would always lay a wager in favour of its being found among persons who spend their time dully rather than in gaiety. Gaiety – English gaiety – is seldom come at lawfully; friendship, or propriety, or principle, are sacrificed to obtain it; we cannot produce it without more effort than it is worth; our destination is to look vacant, and to sit silent . . .

I see every day in the world a thousand acts of oppression which I should like to resent, but I cannot afford to play the Quixote. Why are the English to be the sole vindicators of the human race? Ask Mr Meynell how many persons there are within fifteen miles of him who deserve to be horse-whipped, and who would be very much improved by such a process. But every man knows he must keep down his feelings, and endure the spectacle of triumphant folly and tyranny.

The Revd Sydney Smith to Mrs Meynell, 1823.

I finally fell in with the friendly J.R. Tanner [constitutional historian], and mooned about talking of architecture and lecturing. He is a fine, able, solid, sympathetic creature. He said he was fifty-two – how the cataract *rushes* into the abyss – middle-aged men swimming along, grey-headed men on the edge, senile locks in the foam!

A. C. Benson, Diary, 1912.

19 FEBRUARY

1789 *George III recovers from his first attack of madness.*

1897 *The first Women's Institute is founded, not in England but in Canada.*

1985 *The first episode of* EastEnders *is televised.*

The Bishop of Beauvais . . . explained to them that a woman named Jeanne called the Pucelle, who was accused of invoking devils and other crimes, had been delivered and handed over to him from the Very Illustrious Prince the King of France and England [Henry VI].

From the verbatim report of the trial of Joan of Arc, 1431.

Now I like Claret – whenever I can have Claret I must drink it . . . It fills the mouth with a gushing freshness – then goes down cool and feverless – then you do not feel it quarrelling with your liver – no it is rather a peace maker and lies as quiet as it did in the grape. Then it is as fragrant as the queen bee; and the more ethereal part of it mounts into the brain, not assaulting the cerebral apartments like a bully in a bad house looking for his trull [whore] and hurrying from door to door bouncing against the waist-coat [wainscot]; but rather walks like Aladdin about his own enchanted palace so gently that you do not feel his step.

John Keats to the George Keatses, 1819.

Came home solus – very high wind – lightning – moonshine – solitary stragglers muffled in cloaks – women in mask – white houses – clouds hurrying over the sky, like spilt milk blown out of the pail – altogether very poetical.

Lord Byron, Ravenna Journal, 1821.

20 FEBRUARY

1872 *The Metropolitan Museum of Art is opened in New York.*

1962 *John Glenn makes the first orbital flight by a US astronaut, catching up with the Russians in the Space Race.*

This morning I was getting my first experience as Information Officer, having requisitioned the front room of a shattered nursing home which I had turned into an office. (Here I must explain that following raids earlier in the war the Home Office had learned that nothing reassures the bombed more than the simple word 'Information' printed on a card and stuck as near as possible to the site of the disaster. What had been a private catastrophe was turned by this word into a matter of public concern . . .) A stream of the slightly injured, the bereaved, the indignant, the homeless, the bewildered passed through the office. Let's hope to God I was able to satisfy if not comfort them. Bitter cold, alleviated by tea from a mobile canteen opposite, with the clink-clink of tilers employed by the Surveyor's Department and shouts of rescue squads coming through the open windows. The Surveyor's men are the first on the job, after the rescue squads, the fire-brigade, and the police, restoring what houses they could and giving first aid to others by throwing large tarpaulins over broken roofs. The speed with which the operation proceeds is astonishing, I suppose in the first place because the 1940 raids, relatively slight though they were in our district, have perfected method. Ultimately, I imagine that the workmen feel as I do, although many are Irish: as men not in the armed forces they can at last do something to help defeat the enemy. Note: thick-soled shoes are essential for this job (a) because of broken glass, and (b) because they keep the cold out.

George Beardmore, Journal, 1944.

21 FEBRUARY

1916 *The Battle of Verdun begins. By December 1916, when it is over, about 160,000 French are dead and 216,000 wounded, while the Germans have lost 143,000 dead and 187,000 wouned.*

1952 *Identity cards are abolished in Britian.*

Would you know, what I am doing? I doubt, you have been told already, and hold my employment cheap enough: but everyone must judge of his own capabilities, and cut his amusements according to his disposition. The drift of my present studies is to know, wherever I am, what lies within reach, that may be worth seeing. Whether it be building, ruin, park, garden, prospect, picture, or monument; to whom it does, or has belonged, and what has been the characteristic, and taste of different ages. You will say, this is the object of all antiquaries, but pray, what antiquary ever saw these objects in the same light, or desired to know them for a like reason? In short say what you please, I am persuaded, whenever my list is finished, you will approve it, and think it of no small use. My spirits are very near the freezing point, and for some hours of the day this exercise by its warmth and gentle motion serves to raise them a few degrees higher.

Thomas Gray to Thomas Wharton, 1758.

Fletcher, Lord Byron's servant . . . told me, what was very stiking, that even in dying Lord B. shrunk away when those about him put their hands near his foot, as if fearing that they should uncover it. Said, however, that there was nothing wrong in the shape of the foot, except being smaller than the other, and the leg and thigh on that side a little emaciated. Always wore trowsers (nankeen) in bathing. Latterly led a very quiet life in Italy, but while at Venice was as profligate as need be. Great placability in his temper, and used always to make amends for any momentary burst of passion by his kindness afterwards.

Tom Moore, Diary, 1828. Byron had a club foot.

1797 *The last invasion of Britain, when French troops land at Fishguard in Pembrokeshire. They quickly surrender.*

1879 *The first Woolworth store opens in Utica, New York State.*

The mother of the dumb girl . . . was present . . . and I enquired as to the report of her daughter's being with child by the dumb man. She said it was very true . . . but she feared it would cost them much to be separated, they were so attached to each other. Now the fact is they wished to be married two or three years ago, but I dissuaded the mother – who indeed was herself very averse from the match – from giving her consent. They continued the attachment, and the consequence is now become very visible. As they are now both of age, and the young man is able to procure his livelihood, on her removal to Kilmersdon, and *swearing* (if this can be done) to him as the father, I suppose the marriage will be concluded; but *how*, is to me a mystery. I am very glad I shall not have to officiate in the business.

The Revd John Skinner, Journal, 1825.

I once saw a man threshing with a flail and it was near you. At Shophouse [near Guildford]. Have you ever thought how odd it would have been to have lived in 800 or 1200? There was then no idea of change or improvement in any form. You lived in your village and when you died everything was exactly the same as when you were born. Since about 1480 the world has been in a state of constant change and turmoil. And the last sixty years have been the worst.

Conrad Russell to his sister Flora, 1943.

23 FEBRUARY

1827 *Sir Walter Scott confesses to what is by now an open secret, that he is the author of the Waverley novels.*

1863 *The African explorers Speke and Grant announce Lake Victoria to be the source of the White Nile*

1874 *The game of lawn tennis, but called 'Sphairistike', is patented in the UK.*

The siren goes about 2 a.m. or at almost any time. It always wakes me. I rouse Jean, we leap into our outdoor things, and while Jean grabs a bagful of valuables and papers, I come down with Victoria in my arms, as often as not fast asleep, and we hurry out to the reinforced shelter so conveniently placed near the front gate. This has already been opened by the Fire Guard – normally it's kept locked against lovers, and small boys taken short – our paraffin stove is lighted, and we settle down with our neighbours in the three-tier bunks. Other Fire Guards drift in – one night while somnolent we were all roused by the most appalling crash which turned out to have been a visiting Fire Guard's steel helmet dropping onto the concrete floor – while outside the night becomes noisy with bangs, crackles, and rumbles rolling round the heavens. The clouds light up with gun flashes, flares, and path-finding cascades of light globules nicknamed candelabras. Sometimes a green or dusky red ball comes floating through the clouds. Fires are started on the horizon while behind it the clouds glow a dusky red. A plane zooms overhead. Shrapnel cracks on the rooftops. And gradually the noise dies down and the lights go out . . .

The counter this morning is crowded with applicants for Morrison shelters. These are iron-plated cages with lattice sides, about nine feet by five by four, that one erects inside one's home, preferably in the recess provided by the chimney-breast . . . Also the wretched blitzed from London inner boroughs come to implore us for help in finding a roof for them.

George Beardmore, Journal, 1944.

24 FEBRUARY

1920 *American-born MP Nancy Astor becomes the first woman to speak in the House of Commons.*

1938 *The first product to be made from nylon: toothbrush bristles, in New Jersey.*

1981 *The engagement of Prince Charles and Lady Diana Spencer is announced.*

I am going this evening to eat toasted cheese with that celebrated poet Bernard Barton. And I must soon stir, and look about for my greatcoat, brush myself etc. It blows a harrico, as Theodore Hook [novelist and wit] used to say, and will rain before I get to Woodbridge. Those poor mistaken lilac buds there out of the window! And an old robin, ruffled up to his thickest, sitting mournfully under them, quite disheartened. For you must know the mild winter is just giving way to a remarkably severe spring.

Edward FitzGerald to Frederick Tennyson, 1844.

To live in England is, inevitably, to feel the 'imperial' question in a different way and take it at a different angle from what one might, with the same mind even, do in America. Expansion has so made the English what they are – for good or for ill, but on the whole for good – that one doesn't quite feel one's way to say for one's country 'No – I'll have *none* of it!' It has educated the English. Will it only demoralize *us*? I suppose the answer to that is that we can get at home a bigger education than they – in short as big a one as we require. Thank God, however, I've no *opinions* . . . I'm more and more only aware of things as a more or less mad panorama, phantasmagoria and dime museum.

Henry James to his nephew Henry James, Jnr, 1899. As a result of war with Spain, the US had recently acquired the Philippines.

25 FEBRUARY

1774 *The rules of cricket are drawn up at the Star and Garter tavern in Pall Mall.*

1956 *Nikita Khrushchev, ruler of the USSR, denounces Stalin (d. 1953) in a secret speech at the Communist Party Congress.*

It is a bitter black frost, the ground deep in snow, and more falling. I am writing confortable in a perfectly warm room; some of my servants were up in the cold at half-past five to get it ready for me; others, a few days ago, were digging my coals near Durham, at the risk of their lives; an old woman brought me my watercresses through the snow for breakfast yesterday; another old woman is going two miles through it today to fetch me my letters at ten o'clock. Half a dozen men are building a wall for me to keep the sheep out of my garden, and a railroad stoker is holding his own against the north wind, to fetch me some Brobdingnag raspberry plants to put in it. Somebody in the east end of London is making boots for me, for I can't wear those I have much longer; a washerwoman is in suds, somewhere, to get me a clean shirt for tomorrow; a fisherman is in dangerous weather somewhere, catching me some fish for Lent; and my cook will soon be making me pancakes, for it is Shrove Tuesday.

John Ruskin, Fors Clavigera, *written in the Lake District, 1873.*

I was playing cricket on the sands, and presently a huge man with an immense black beard offered to bowl to me. He did not seem much good at bowling on the soft pitch with a tennis ball, and I hit him all over the place. Being a well-brought-up little boy, I presently asked whether the gentleman would not like an innings, for which purpose I handed him my tiny bat. I bowled, the ball hit on a flat pebble, and instead of bouncing slithered between the two walking-sticks which were the wickets.

James Agate, Ego, *1943. The huge man was W.G. Grace.*

26 FEBRUARY

1723 *Sir Christopher Wren dies. He is buried in his greatest work, St Paul's Cathedral, above the North Door of which is carved his epitaph:* Si monumentum requiris, circumspice - *if you want a monument to him, look about you.*

1797 *£1 notes issued by the Bank of England for the first time.*

So took coach and to Windsor, to the Garter [Inn], and thither sent for Dr Childe [the organist], who came to us and carried us to St George's Chapel, and there placed us among the Knights' stalls (and pretty the observation, that no man, but a woman, may sit in a Knight's place, where any brass plates are set). And hither come cushions to us, and a young singing-boy to bring us a copy of the anthem to be sung. And here, for our sakes, had this anthem and the great service sung extraordinary, only to entertain us. It is a noble place indeed, and a good choir of voices. Great bowing by all the people, the poor Knights particularly, to the altar. After prayers, we to see the plate of the chapel and the robes of Knights, and a man to show us the banners of the several Knights in being, which hang up over the stalls. And so to other discourse very pretty, about the Order. Was shown where the late King is buried, and King Henry VIII, and my Lady Seymour [Jane Seymour, Henry's third wife]. This being done, to the King's house, and to observe the neatness and contrivance of the house and gates: it is the most romantic castle that is in the world . . . and so took coach and away to Eton . . . The school good, and the custom pretty of boys cutting their names in the shut[ter]s of the window when they go to Cambridge, by which many a one hath lived to see himself Provost and Fellow, that hath his name in the window standing . . . did drink of the College beer, which is very good; and went into the back fields to see the scholars play.

Samuel Pepys, Diary, 1666.

27 FEBRUARY

1900 *The British Labour Party is founded.*

1933 *The Reichstag (Parliament) building is burnt in Berlin, providing Hitler with an excuse to rush through a law conferring totalitarian power on himself as Chancellor.*

Last night I suffered horribly – from an indigestion I believe. I *never* sup – that is, never at home. But, last night, I was prevailed upon by the Countess Gamba's persuasion, and the strenuous example of her brother, to swallow, at supper, a quantity of boiled cockles, and to dilute them, *not* reluctantly, with some Imola wine. When I came home, apprehensive of the consequences, I swallowed three or four glasses of spirits, which men (the venders) call brandy, rum, or Hollands [gin], but which Gods would entitle spirits of wine, coloured or sugared. All was pretty well till I got to bed, when I became somewhat swollen, and considerably vertiginous. I got out, and mixing some soda-powders, drank them off. This brought on temporary relief. I returned to bed; but grew sick and sorry once and again. Took more soda-water. At last I fell into a dreary sleep. Woke, and was ill all day, till I had galloped a few miles. Query – was it the cockles, or what I took to correct them, that caused the commotion? I think both. I remarked in my illness the complete inertion, inaction, and destruction of my chief mental faculties. I tried to rouse them, and yet could not – and this is the *Soul*!!! I should believe that it was married to the body, if they did not sympathise so much with each other. If the one rose, when the other fell, it would be a sign that they longed for the natural state of divorce. But as it is, they seem to draw together like post-horses.

Let us hope the best – it is the grand possession.

Lord Byron, Ravenna Journal, last entry, 1821.

28 FEBRUARY

1948 *Last British troops leave India.*

1975 *Moorgate Tube crash, in which 43 are killed. It remains a mystery why the driver did not stop.*

1991 *Ceasefire called in the first Gulf War.*

In times like the present, it is impossible to allow private feelings to take place of a public sense of duty. I think your conduct as dangerous in Parliament as it is in your own county. Were you my own brother, therefore, I could not give you my support.
THOMAS LIDDELL

In answer to your letter, I beg to say that I feel gratitude for your frankness, compassion for your fears, little dread of your opposition, and no want of your support.
J.G. LAMBTON

An exchange between John George Lambton, the radical MP for Durham, and a voter, 1820. See 20 December.

Since I saw you something has happened. Bosie's father has left a card at my club with hideous words on it. I don't see anything now but a criminal prosecution. My whole life seems ruined by this man. The tower of ivory is assailed by the foul thing. On the sand is my life spilt. I don't know what to do. If you could come here at 11.30 please do so tonight. I mar your life by trespassing ever on your love and kindness. I have asked Bosie to come tomorrow.

Oscar Wilde to Robert Ross, 1895. Bosie's - Lord Alfred Douglas's - father was the Marquess of Queensberry. His card read, 'For Oscar Wilde posing as a Somdomite'. See 5 April.

29 FEBRUARY

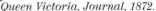

A woman may propose to a man today, but only if wearing petticoats.

2004 Lord of the Rings: Return of the Kings *wins 11 Oscars, equalling* Ben Hur *in 1959 and* Titanic *in 1997.*

At half-past four drove in open landau . . . returning by Constitution Hill, and when at the garden entrance a dreadful thing happened . . . How it all happened I knew nothing of. The equerries had dismounted, Brown had got down to let down the steps and Jane C. was just getting out, when suddenly someone appeared at my side, whom I at first imagined was a footman, going to lift off the wrapper. Then I perceived that it was someone unknown, peering above the carriage door, with an uplifted hand and a strange voice . . . Involuntarily, in a terrible fright, I threw myself over Jane Churchill, calling out, 'Save me', and heard a scuffle and voices! I soon recovered myself sufficiently to stand up and turn round, when I saw Brown holding a young man tightly, who was struggling. They laid the man on the ground and Brown kept hold of him till several of the police came in. All turned and asked if I was hurt, and I said, 'Not at all.' . . . They thought the man had dropped something. We looked, but could find nothing, when Cannon, the postilion, called out, 'There it is,' and looking down I then did see shining on the ground a small pistol! This filled us with horror. All were as white as sheets, Jane C. almost crying, and Leopold [one of the Queen's sons] looked as if he were going to faint. It is to good Brown and to his wonderful presence of mind that I greatly owe my safety.

Queen Victoria, Journal, 1872.

MARCH

1 MARCH

St David's Day

1711 *The* Spectator *magazine, the most famous of the eighteenth century, first published.*

1809 *The* Quarterly Review, *a famous nineteenth-century magazine, first published by John Murray, as a Tory rival to the Whig* Edinburgh Review.

I have all my life been on my guard against the information conveyed by the sense of hearing – it being one of my earliest observations, the universal inclination of humankind is to be led by the ears, and I am sometimes apt to imagine that they are given to men as they are to pitchers, purposely that they may be carried about by them.

Lady Mary Wortley Montagu to her daughter the Countess of Bute, 1752.

Turn where we may, within, around, the voice of great events is proclaiming to us: reform, that you may preserve . . . Pronounce in a manner worthy of the expectation with which this great debate has been anticipated, and of the long remembrance which it will leave behind. Renew the youth of the state. Save property, divided against itself. Save the multitude, endangered by its own ungovernable passions. Save the aristocracy, endangered by its own unpopular power. Save the greatest, and fairest, and most highly civilised community that ever existed, from calamities which may in a few days sweep away all the rich heritage of so many ages of wisdom and glory. The danger is terrible. The time is short. If this bill should be rejected, I pray to God that none of those who concur in rejecting it may ever remember their votes with unavailing remorse, amid the wreck of laws, the confusion of ranks, the spoliation of property, and the dissolution of social order.

Lord Macaulay's speech at the introduction of the Great Reform Bill to the House of Commons, 1831.

2 MARCH

1812 *On this morning Byron 'awoke to find himself famous', the day after the publication of the first two cantos of his poem* Childe Harold's Pilgrimage *by John Murray.*

1969 *Maiden flight of Concorde at Toulouse.*

Home, and there I find my company come . . . I had a noble dinner for them, as almost I ever had, and mighty merry, and particularly myself pleased with looking on Betty Turner, who is mighty pretty. After dinner we fell one to one talk, and another to another, and looking over my house, and closet, and things . . . And thus till night, that our musick come, and the Office ready and candles . . . We fell to dancing, and continued, only with intermission for a good supper, till two in the morning, the music being [by Thomas] Greeting, and another most excellent violin and theorbo, the best in town; and so with mighty mirth and pleased with their dancing of jigs afterwards, several of them, and among others Betty Turner, who did it mighty prettily; and, lastly, W. Batelier's blackamoor and blackamoor maid; and then to a country dance again, and so broke up with extraordinary pleasure, as being one of the days and nights of my life spent with the greatest content; and that which I can but hope to repeat again a few times in my whole life. This done, we parted, the strangers home, and I did lodge my cousin Pepys and his wife in our blue chamber – my cousin Turner, her sister, and The. in our best chamber – Bab., Betty, and Betty Turner in our own chamber; and myself and my wife in the maid's bed, which is very good – our maids in the coachman's bed; the coachman with the boy in his settle-bed, and Tom where he uses to lie. And so I did, to my great content, lodge at once in my house, with the greatest ease, fifteen, and eight of them strangers of quality. My wife this day put on first her French gown, called a sac, which becomes her very well.

Samuel Pepys, Diary, 1669.

3 MARCH

1861 *Serfdom abolished in Russia.*

1875 *First performance of* Carmen, *the world's most popular opera.*

1985 *The year-long miners' strike is called off.*

I drove to Mells to attend a clerical meeting, and arrived a little after two. We sat down fourteen to dinner, which was an uncomfortable one owing to there being only one waiter. After some rather desultory conversation one of the party, of the name of Bumstead, asked me what was the etymon of his name. I did not perceive it at the time, but have every reason to believe, on account of what afterwards occurred, that it was done purposely to put me on the subject of Etymology for the amusement of the company.

The Revd John Skinner, Journal, 1828.

I make remonstrance – for I do remonstrate – bear upon the bad service you have done your cause by riding so hard again that accurst autobiographic form which puts a premium on the loose, the improvised, the cheap and the easy. Save in the fantastic and the romantic (*Copperfield, Jane Eyre*, that charming thing of Stevenson's with the bad title – *Kidnapped*?) it has no authority, no persuasive or convincing force – its grasp of reality and truth isn't strong and disinterested. *R. Crusoe*, e.g., isn't a novel at all. There is, to my vision, no authentic, and no really interesting and no *beautiful*, report of things on the novelist's, the painter's part unless a particular detachment has operated, unless the great stewpot or crucible of the imagination, of the observant and recording and interpreting mind in short, has intervened and played its part – and this detachment, this chemical transmutation for the aesthetic, the representational, end is terribly wanting in autobiography brought, as the horrible phrase is, up to date.

Henry James to H.G. Wells, 1911, about the latter's
use of the first person singular.

4 MARCH

1789 *The US Constitution comes into force and George Washington begins his term of office as President.*

1890 *The Forth Bridge is opened in Scotland.*

Since he [Wordsworth, away for a few days] has left me at half-past eleven (it is now two) I have been putting the drawers into order, laid by his clothes which we had thrown here and there and everywhere, filed two months' newspapers and got my dinner, two boiled eggs and two apple tarts. I have set Molly on to clear the garden a little, and I myself have helped. I transplanted some snow-drops – the bees are busy. William has a nice bright day. It was hard frost in the night. The robins are singing sweetly. Now for my walk. I *will* be busy. I *will* look well, and be well when he comes back to me. O the Darling! Here is one of his bitten apples. I can hardly find in my heart to throw it into the fire.

Dorothy Wordsworth, Journal, 1802.

The President very quietly rode down to the Capitol in his own carriage, by himself, on a sharp trot, about noon, either because he wished to be on hand to sign bills, or to get rid of marching in line with the absurd procession, the muslin temple of liberty, and pasteboard monitor [warship]. I saw him on his return, at three o'clock, after the performance was over. He was in his plain two-horse barouche, and looked very much worn and tired; the lines, indeed, of vast responsibilities, intricate questions, and demands of life and death, cut deeper than ever upon his dark brown face; yet all the old goodness, tender-ness, sadness, and canny shrewdness, underneath the furrows.

Walt Whitman on President Lincoln's second inauguration, 1865.

5 MARCH

1936 *Maiden flight of the Spitfire.*

1946 *Churchill makes 'Iron Curtain' speech in Fulton, Missouri.*

Barclay of the Borough, by far the greatest brewer of ale and beer in England, in the last three, four, or six months of 1826 (I forget the precise number of months) sold 160,000 barrels of beer and ale, and in exactly the corresponding months of 1827 he sold only 90,000, being a falling off of 70,000 out of 160,000, or nearly half. This is entirely owing to . . . taking off the duty upon gin, which is now so cheap that a whole family may and do get drunk with it for a shilling.

Thomas Creevey to Miss Ord, 1828.

The lead-up to this event was more than trying, as the press for some mysterious reason had got it into their heads that I was going either in drag as Madame Tussaud or as Dr Crippen [the murderer]. In the end I plumped for 'Sea-Green' Robespierre and decked myself in 1790s green satin with black frogging hired from Bermans [theatrical costumiers]. I resisted painting a thin red line around my neck as perhaps going a bit far, but it did cross my mind . . .

Great but wholly unnoticed energy had gone into the menu, which worked its way through *Filets de sole Nelson, Noisettes d'agneau Victoria* with *Bombe Gladstone* as a finale. Too much drink flowed and I vaguely remember clambering into the tableau of Madame Tussaud modelling the severed head of Marie Antoinette, grabbing the head and being photographed nursing it by *Time*, something I later regretted. As an evening, however, it all fell curiously flat.

Roy Strong, describing the ball for the bicentenary
of Madame Tussaud's waxwork museum in London, Diary, 1970.

6 MARCH

1899 *Aspirin patented in Berlin.*

1930 *Clarence Birdseye puts frozen foods on sale for the first time, in the US.*

Warm. Sit in Carlyle's room while he is punctuating the *Saga* translation. We walk to Hyde Park, dodging the carriages sometimes, at risk. (He may catch his death thus, for he usually insists on crossing when he has made up his mind to it, carrying his stick so as to poke it into a horse's nose at need.)

> *William Allingham, Diary, 1872. The* 'Saga *translation'*
> *was* The Early Kings of Norway, *Carlyle's final work.*

Henry James had one resemblance to Browning: he was always observing and taking notes of the folk he met at dinners and evening parties, but frequently, while he observed with those large eyes of his, he would, unlike Browning, pass into a questioning and dream and forget where he was and to whom he was talking, as if the conversation had pushed him into analysing some human problem . . . When he could not get the very word or adjective he wanted, it was most amusing to see him with one hand in the air, till he found it, when he flashed his hand down into the palm of the other and brought with a triumphant look the word he wanted, the exact word. Meanwhile when the word delayed, he piled up sentence after sentence and parenthetic side issues – till at last all was obscurity, an obscurity he thought was cleared when he discovered the elusive word he wanted. This was what his style became in his books.

> *Stopford Brooke, Diary, 1916.*

7 MARCH

1876 *The first telephone patented by Alexander Graham Bell.*

1917 *The first jazz record goes on sale - 'The Dixie Jazz Band One-Step'.*

1969 *The Victoria Line on the London Underground opens.*

Worsdale the painter, the pimp [to her husband], the – what you will – once told Mr Thrale as a fact – that he was sitting in the kitchen of a brothel with the mistress of the house.

My Dear Jemmy! exclaims she after a pause – who would do an ill thing? my wicked neighbours here are breaking and bankruptcing every day – but my conscience is clear heaven be praised of wronging any one – and see now how I prosper! Make me thankful! even whilst I am speaking – All my beds are full!

Mrs Hester Thale, Thraliana, 1778. She was Dr Johnson's friend, and looked after him during his attacks of depression. Her husband was a wealthy brewer.

If I had time, or rather, if I took any great interest in two such people as the great thief and the great thief-taker, I would compose a parallel, inch by inch, of these two men. One of them frightened all the good, the other all the bad – one betrayed all his employers, the other all his accomplices – one sacrificed the hopeful to ambition, the other the desperate to justice.

I doubt whether in seven years I could form the corollary more completely than I have done in the seventh of a minute, but it will require a century to make men honest and wise enough to bear the question 'which is best?'

Walter Savage Landor, 1839. The thief is Napoleon and the thief-taker the pioneering French detective - and former criminal - François Eugène Vidocq (1775-1857). Landor was an irascible poet, also famous in his day for his Imaginary Conversations *between historical figures.*

A sudden and blessed change in the weather, a south-west wind, pouring warm rain, and the birds in the garden and orchard singing like mad creatures, the whole air in a charm and tumult of joy and delight.

The Revd Francis Kilvert, Diary, 1875.

8 MARCH

1702 *William III dies after falling from his horse when it stumbles on a molehill. His Jacobite enemies drink the health of 'the little fellow in velvet' - the mole.*

1930 *Gandhi starts his campaign of civil disobedience which eventually leads to Indian Independence in 1947.*

I am really a great admirer of tangible religion; and am breeding one of my daughters a Catholic, that she may have her hands full. It is by far the most elegant worship, hardly excepting the Greek mythology. What with incense, pictures, statues, altars, shrines, relics, and the real presence, confession, absolution – there is something sensible to grasp at. Besides, it leaves no possibility of doubt; for those who swallow their Deity, really and truly, in transubstantiation, can hardly find anything else otherwise than easy of digestion.

I am afraid that this sounds flippant, but I don't mean it to be so; only my turn of mind is so given to taking things in the absurd point of view, that it breaks out in spite of me every now and then. Still, I do assure you that I am a very good Christian.

*Lord Byron to Thomas Moore, 1822. Byron's daughter Allegra, whose mother was
Claire Clairmont, died, aged five, in a convent school near Ravenna a few weeks after
this letter.*

Lunched with Charles Laughton, who . . . won't play Falstaff, whom he hates. 'I had to throw too many of his kind out of our hotel when I was sixteen.' Is making a Henry VIII picture and intends to show him not as a phallus with a crown but as the morbid, introspective fellow he actually was.

*James Agate, Ego, 1933. Charles Laughton's family
ran the largest hotel in Scarborough, Yorkshire.*

9 MARCH

1831 *The French Foreign Legion is founded, to help conquer Algeria.*

1974 *The three-day working week, begun in Britain in December 1973 because of the oil shortage after the Arab-Israeli War, ends.*

t gives me great satisfaction to hear that the pig turned out so well – they are interesting creatures at a certain age – what a pity such buds should blow out into the maturity of rank bacon! You had all some of the crackling – and brain sauce – did you remember to rub it with butter, and gently dredge it a little, just before the crisis? Did the eyes come away kindly with no Oedipean avulsion? Was the crackling the colour of the ripe pomegranate? Had you no complement of boiled neck of mutton before it, to blunt the edge of delicate desire? Did you flesh maiden teeth in it? Not that *I* sent the pig . . . To confess an honest truth, a pig is one of those things which I could never think of sending away. Teal, widgeon, snipes, barn-door fowls, ducks, geese, Welsh mutton, collars of brawn, sturgeon, fresh or pickled, your potted char, Swiss cheeses, French pies, early grapes, muscadines, I impart as freely unto my friends as to myself . . . but pigs are pigs, and I myself therein am nearest to myself.

Charles Lamb to Samuel Taylor Coleridge, 1822.

Right up to 1914 it was *utterly impossible* for two young people to dine at a restaurant together. When Raymond [Asquith] and Katharine were engaged they used to have *breakfast* together at an ABC shop. Except both going to the same ball there was no other way of meeting – at least there would have been the risk of being seen. That's twenty-five years ago. Times have changed.

Conrad Russell to his sister Diana, 1932.

10 MARCH

1801 *The first census of the population of Great Britain and Ireland begins. The total comes to 15,846,000.*

1906 *The Bakerloo Line on the London Underground opens.*

'The wicket was extremely difficult – very hot sunshine pouring down on a pitch which had previously been saturated by rain – and the bowlers one had to face were Barnes, from the Pavilion end, and Tarrant, from the Nursery end I remember saying to Barnes at the fall of a wicket, "You know, Barney, it's an intellectual treat trying to play you on this wicket," and he smiled and said "How long are you going to stay in?" and I replied, "That depends on you." I have a distinct recollection of almost every ball. Barnes was getting so much spin that he literally tore pieces out of the turf. In the end I was caught at the wicket off him – a most magnificent catch by E.J. ("Tiger") Smith, of Warwickshire. The ball off which Smith made this great catch was a leg-break of perfect length, which jumped very quickly and just touched the thumb of my right-hand glove. "Tiger", standing at his full height, caught the ball in front of his right eye, and I remember saying to him afterwards, "I think I was a bit unlucky because most wicket-keepers would have ducked, and I should have scored a four." In his description of the match the *Times* correspondent was kind enough to make some very complimentary remarks about this innings of twenty-four of mine, and finished by saying, "Had Mr Warner not been playing so extremely well he would not have touched that beautiful leg-break from Barnes, off which Smith made his great catch."'

James Agate, Ego, 1943. Sir Pelham Warner describes one of his best innings, in 1913 for the Gentlemen v. the Players at Lord's.

11 MARCH

1682 *The Royal Hospital at Chelsea founded, for army veterans.*

1985 *Mikhail Gorbachev becomes leader of the USSR.*

Lady Augusta called me gently to 'Come and speak with Her Majesty.' I obeyed, first asking, as an old and infirmish man, Majesty's permission to *sit*, which was graciously conceded. Nothing of the least significance was said, nor *needed*; however, my bit of dialogue went very well. 'What part of Scotland I came from?' 'Dumfries-shire (where Majesty might as well go some time); Carlisle, *i.e. Caer-Lewal*, a place about the antiquity of King Solomon (according to Milton, whereat Majesty smiled); Border Ballads . . . Glasgow . . . ending in mere *psalms*, and streets *vacant* at half-past nine p.m. – hard sound and genuine Presbyterian *root* of what has now shot up to be such a monstrous ugly cabbage-tree and hemlock-tree!' all which Her Majesty seemed to take rather well.

Thomas Carlyle on meeting Queen Victoria, to Mrs Aitken, 1869.

Clive [Bell] gave me dinner at the Café Royal, which did not much interest me as a show, rather to his disappointment. However towards the end of dinner a woman of doubtful character dining alone with a man threw her glass on the floor, made a great rattle of knives and plates, upset the mustard pot and marched out like an indignant turkey cock. Was this moment, with the eyes of the diners upon her, what repaid her? Was it for this that she protested? Anyhow she left her man very crestfallen, trying to appear nonchalant; and I daresay that was what she wanted. I couldn't help thinking of the dreary scene in the flat next morning – the tears, the recriminations, the reconciliation – and next Sunday they'll dine, I suppose, at another restaurant.

Virginia Woolf, Diary, 1919.

12 MARCH

1932 *First radio programme from the new BBC Broadcasting House.*

1935 *A 30-mph speed limit introduced in towns.*

1988 *The £1 note no longer legal tender.*

The candles are burnt down and I am using the wax taper, which has a long snuff on it. The fire is at its last click – I am sitting with my back to it with one foot rather askew upon the rug and the other with the heel a little elevated from the carpet. I am writing this on *The Maid's Tragedy* which I have read since tea with great pleasure. Besides this volume of Beaumont and Fletcher, there are on the table two volumes of Chaucer and a new work of Tom Moore's called 'Tom Cribb's Memorial to Congress' – nothing in it. These are trifles, but I require nothing so much of you as that you will give me a like description of yourselves, however it may be, when you are writing to me. Could I see the same thing done of any great man long since dead it would be a great delight: as to know in what position Shakespeare sat when he began 'To be or not be'. Such things become interesting from distance of time or place.

John Keats to the George Keatses, 1819.

Towards eleven o'clock he was so much worse that it was found necessary to muffle the stable-knocker. At half-past, or thereabouts, he was heard talking to himself about the horse and Topping's family, and to add some incoherent expressions which are supposed to have been either a foreboding of his approaching dissolution, or some wishes relative to the disposal of his little property: consisting chiefly of half-pence which he had buried in different parts of the garden. On the clock striking twelve he appeared slightly agitated, but he soon recovered, walked twice or thrice along the coach-house, stopped to bark, staggered, exclaimed *Halloa old girl!* (his favourite expression), and died.

Charles Dickens describes the death of his pet raven
to the painter Daniel Maclise, 1841.

13 MARCH

1954 *The Battle of Dien Bien Phu begins in Indochina. After 57 days the French are defeated by the Vietminh and soon leave Vietnam, Cambodia and Laos.*

1996 *Massacre at a school in Dunblane by a crazed gunman leaves 16 dead.*

Business comes in and being chiefly in the Face way, I'm afraid to put people off when they are in the mind to sit. You please me much by saying that no other fault is found in your picture than the roughness of the surface, for that part being of use in giving force to the effect at a proper distance, and what a judge of painting knows an original from a copy by; in short being the touch of the pencil [brush], which is harder to preserve than smoothness, I am much better pleased that they should spy out things of that kind, than to see an eye half an inch out of its place, or a nose out of drawing when viewed at a proper distance. I don't think it would be more ridiculous for a person to put his nose close to the canvas and say the colours smell offensive, than to say how rough the paint lies; for one is just as material as the other with regard to hurting the effect and drawing of a picture. Sir Godfrey Kneller used to tell them that pictures were not made to smell of: and what made his pictures more valuable than others with the connoisseurs was his pencil or touch.

Thomas Gainsborough to Robert Edgar, 1758.

An art is a fine fortune, a palace in a park, a band of music, health and physical beauty: all but love – to any worthy practiser. I sleep upon my art for a pillow; I waken in my art: I am unready for death, because I hate to leave it. I love my wife, I do not know how much, nor can, nor shall, unless I lost her; but while I can conceive my being widowed, I refuse the offering of life without my art. I *am* not but in my art: it is me; I am the body of it merely.

Robert Louis Stevenson to W.E. Henley, 1884.

14 MARCH

———➤◆◈❋◈◆◄———

1757 *Admiral Byng shot on his own quarter-deck for failing to save Minorca from the French, and 'to encourage the others', in Voltaire's words.*

1885 *First night of* The Mikado, *the most popular of Gilbert and Sullivan's Savoy operas.*

What a detestable feeling this fluttering of the heart is! I know it is nothing organick and that it is entirely nervous but the sickening effects of it are dispiriting to a degree. Is it the body brings it on the mind or the mind inflicts it upon the body? I cannot tell – but it is a severe price to pay for the *Fata Morgana* with which Fancy sometimes amuses men of warm imaginations. As to body and mind I fancy I might as well enquire whether the fiddle or fiddle-stick makes the tune. In youth this complaint used to throw [me] into involuntary passions of causeless tears. But I will drive it away in the country by exercise. I wish I had been a mechanic – a turning-lathe or a chest of tools would have been a Godsend – for thought makes the access of melancholy rather worse than better. I have it seldom thank God and I believe lightly in comparaison of others . . .

Also read again, and for the third time at least, Miss Austen's very finely written novel of *Pride and Prejudice*. That young lady had a talent for describing the involvements and feelings and characters of ordinary life, which is to me the most wonderful I ever met with. The Big Bow-wow strain I can do myself like any now going; but the exquisite touch, which renders ordinary commonplace things and characters interesting, from the truth of the description and the sentiment, is denied to me. What a pity such a gifted creature died so early!

Sir Walter Scott, Journal, 1826.

15 MARCH

44 BC *Julius Caesar is murdered in Rome on the 'Ides of March'.*

1876 *The first eleven-a-side cricket test match is held in Sydney, Australia.*

1917 *Tsar Nicholas II of Russia abdicates.*

I got upon the coach-box today from Stevenage to Hatfield. I was afraid I should fall; and I accustomed myself to overcome fear. The coachman was a stately fellow, as well dressed as a country squire, and quite a bishop in his line of life; for instead of driving one stage out and in, by which at an average two shillings a day may be got, he drove three, so that he got six shillings a day besides wages. There were two outside passengers, who sang and roared and swore as he did. My nerves were hurt at first; but considering it to have no offensive meaning whatever, and to be just the vocal expression of the beings, I was not fretted. They sang, 'And A-Hunting We Will Go', and I joined the chorus. I then sang 'Hearts of Oak', 'Gee Ho, Dobbin', 'The Roast Beef of Old England', and they chorused. We made a prodigious jovial noise going through Welwyn and other villages . . .

The coach had been robbed by footpads in the morning near London; and last night at six another coach had been robbed. It was past six when we were at Highgate. The fear which I felt till we got upon the stones was uneasy. The coachman bid us keep a look-out. Some fellows wanted him to stop under pretence of wanting to be up on the outside; but he drove quickly on, and some of us looked out on each side.

James Boswell, Journal, 1776.

16 MARCH

1872 *The first FA Cup Final: Wanderers beat the Royal Engineers 1-0.*

1935 *Hitler renounces the Treaty of Versailles and reintroduces compulsory military service.*

I have often smiled to myself in viewing our assemblies (which they call conversations) at Lovere [in Italy], the gentlemen being all in light night-caps, night-gowns (under which I am informed they wear no breeches) and slippers, and the ladies in their stays, and smock sleeves tied with ribands, and a single lutestring [glossy silk] petticoat. There is not a hat or a hoop to be seen. It is true this dress is called *vestimenta di confidenza*, and they do not appear in it in town but in their own chambers, and then only during the summer months.

Lady Mary Wortley Montagu to her daughter the Countess of Bute, 1752.

I am not altogether the idle, dreaming being [my first letter] would seem to denote. My father is a clergyman of limited though competent income, and I am the eldest of his children. He expended quite as much in my education as he could afford in justice to the rest. I thought it therefore my duty, when I left school, to become a governess. In that capacity I find enough to occupy my thoughts all day long, and my head and hands too, without having a moment's time for one dream of the imagination . . . I have endeavoured not only attentively to observe all the duties a woman ought to fulfil, but to feel deeply interested in them. I don't always succeed, for sometimes when I'm teaching or sewing I would rather be reading or writing; but I try to deny myself . . . I trust I shall never more feel ambitious to see my name in print; if the wish should rise, I'll look at Southey's letter, and suppress it.

Charlotte Brontë, aged twenty-one, to the Poet Laureate Robert Southey, 1837. She had sent him some of her poems, and he had replied.

17 MARCH

St Patrick's Day

1816 *First steam-powered crossing of the English Channel by the Elise, 38 tons, from Newhaven to Le Havre, taking 17 hours because of stormy conditions.*

1845 *The rubber band is patented in London.*

Tragedy all along the line. At lunch, the day before yesterday, poor Titus Oates said he couldn't go on; he proposed we should leave him in his sleeping-bag. That we could not do, and induced him to come on, on the afternoon march. In spite of its awful nature for him he struggled on and we made a few miles. At night he was worse and we knew the end had come.

Should this be found I want these facts recorded. Oates's last thoughts were of his mother, but immediately before he took pride in thinking that his regiment would be pleased with the bold way in which he met his death. We can testify to his bravery. He has borne intense suffering for weeks without complaint, and to the very last was able and willing to discuss outside subjects. He did not – would not – give up hope to the very end. He was a brave soul. This was the end. He slept through the night before last, hoping not to wake; but he woke in the morning – yesterday. It was blowing a blizzard. He said, 'I am just going outside and may be some time.' He went out into the blizzard and we have not seen him since . . .

We knew that poor Oates was walking to his death, but though we tried to dissuade him, we knew it was the act of a brave man and an English gentleman. We all hope to meet the end with a similar spirit, and assuredly the end is not far.

Captain Robert Falcon Scott, Diary, the Antarctic, 1912.

18 MARCH

1834 *The six Tolpuddle Martyrs, Dorset farm labourers, sentenced to be transported to Australia for forming a trade union.*

1891 *A telephone service between London and Paris begins.*

I felt myself weak and William charged me not to go to Mrs Lloyd's. I seemed indeed to myself unfit for it, but when he was gone I thought I would get the visit over if I could, so I ate a beefsteak thinking it would strengthen me; so it did, and I went off. I had a very pleasant walk – Rydale was full of life and motion. The wind blew briskly, and the lake was covered all over with bright silver waves, that were there each the twinkling of an eye, then others rose up and took their places as fast as they went away. The rocks glittered in the sunshine, the crows and the ravens were busy, and the thrushes and little birds sang. I went through the fields, and sat half an hour afraid to pass a cow. The cow looked at me, and I looked at the cow, and whenever I stirred the cow gave over eating. I was not very much tired when I reached Lloyd's.

. . . When I parted from the Lloyds . . . night was come on . . . There was a vivid sparkling streak of light at this end of Rydale water, but the rest was very dark . . . Once there was no moonlight to be seen but upon the island house and the promontory of the island where it stands. I had many very exquisite feelings, and when I saw this lowly building in the waters, among the dark and lofty hills, with that bright, soft light upon it, it made me more than half a poet. I was tired when I reached home, and could not sit down to reading, and tried to write verses, but alas! I gave up expecting William and went soon to bed.

Dorothy Wordsworth, Journal, 1802. Charles Lloyd and his family
lived at Old Brathay at the head of Lake Windermere.

19 MARCH

1900 *Sir Arthur Evans begins excavating Knossos in Crete.*

1932 *Sydney Harbour Bridge opened.*

1994 *Largest omelette in the world made in Japan, with 100,000 eggs.*

We have every week almost a new proclamation for somewhat or other, as for buildings (forward and backward), for weights and measures, for inns and alehouses, for horse meat, and I know not what else, all for the good of the subject, and yet they either believe it not or will not acknowledge the good pretended.

The Queen's funeral is put off till the 29th of the next month, to the great hindrance of our players, which are forbidden to play so long as her body is above ground. One special man among them, Burbage, is lately dead, and hath left they say better than £300 land.

John Chamberlain to Dudley Carleton, 1619. The Queen was Anne of Denmark, consort of James I; Richard Burbage was the first performer of many of Shakespeare's greatest roles.

The other afternoon I trudged over to Worcester – through a region so thick-sown with good old English 'effects' – with elm-scattered meadows and sheep-cropped commons and the ivy-smothered dwellings of small gentility, and high-gabled, heavy-timbered, broken-plastered farm-houses, and stiles leading to delicious meadow footpaths and lodge-gates leading to far-off manors – with all things suggestive of the opening chapters of half-remembered novels, devoured in infancy – that I felt as if I were pressing all England to my soul. As I neared the good old town I saw the great Cathedral tower, high and square, rise far into the cloud-dappled blue. And as I came nearer still I stopped on the bridge and viewed the great ecclesiastical pile cast downward into the yellow Severn. And going further yet I entered the town and lounged about the close and gazed my fill at that most soul-sustaining sight – the waning afternoon, far aloft on the broad perpendicular field of the Cathedral spire – tasted too, as deeply, of the peculiar stillness and repose of the close.

Henry James to his father, 1870, about the first impact on him of England.

20 MARCH

1819 *The Burlington Arcade of shops opens, off Piccadilly.*

1933 *The Nazis open their first concentration camp at Dachau, outside Munich.*

1974 *Attempt by armed man to kidnap Princess Anne in The Mall.*

If you knew what the address at the head of this sheet meant [Asquith had recently qualified as a barrister] it would give a double zest to your pleasures. It means hundreds of dull men sitting in hundreds of dull rooms with hundreds of dull books – men who bear the same relation to real men as a pianola does to a piano, rooms which bear the same relation to real rooms as a bus does to the Parthenon, books which bear the same relation to real books as beetles bear to butterflies. I take one out of the shelf and the binding crumbles in my hand like a mummy, musty odours of decay exhale from the leaves and clouds of noxious and ancient dust choke my eyes. The window panes are covered with the dung of London pigeons, and from the room above I can sometimes hear the clerks spitting onto the pavement. Once a month or so I have something to do; but the rest of the time I stare with sightless eyes and unregarding brain at books which ought to be burned for dullness by the common hangman. It is the best way ever found out of rotting one's brain. I really believe it would save time and trouble to do it by drink instead. But I have given up drink – as an experiment – for about a fortnight now. The only result is that I sometimes feel faint . . .

I won't write anything about politics – except that . . . I have an idea for you when you go in: go in as a Labour candidate – don't you see the theatrical capability of that? the young aristocrat with ideals and sympathies which carry him passionately out of his class – a tribune of the people – Gracchus, Rienzi, Tolstoi – anyone you like. It would explain your clothes too.

Raymond Asquith to Aubrey Herbert, son of the Earl of Carnarvon,
from 1 Paper Buildings, The Temple, London, 1906.

21 MARCH

Traditionally the Spring Equinox, the first day of Spring, and the first day of more daylight than darkness.

1918 *The last German offensive on the Western Front is launched, leading to the highest one-day loss in the war: 78,000 killed, wounded or captured on both sides.*

My periwig is arrived, and is the very perfection of all periwigs, having only one fault; which is, that my head will only go into the first half of it, the other half, or the upper part of it, continuing still unoccupied. My artist in this way at Olney has however undertaken to make the whole of it tenantable, and then I shall be twenty years younger than you have ever seen me.

William Cowper to Mrs Throckmorton, 1790.

Everybody imagined the Duke would treat what he said with contempt. He thought otherwise, however, and without saying a word to any of his colleagues, or to anyone but Hardinge, his second, he wrote and demanded an apology . . . Lord Winchilsea declined making any apology, and they met [at Battersea] . . . They stood at a distance of fifteen paces. ['Now then, Hardinge,' said the Duke, 'look sharp and step out the ground. I have no time to waste. Damn it! Don't stick him up so near the ditch. If I hit him he will tumble in.'] The Duke fired, and missed; then Winchilsea fired in the air. He immediately pulled out of his pocket a paper . . . in which the word 'apology' was omitted. The Duke read it and said it would not do. Lord Falmouth [Winchilsea's second] said he was not come there to quibble about words . . . and the word was inserted on the ground. The Duke then touched his hat, said 'Good morning, my Lords,' mounted his horse, and rode off . . . At twelve o'clock the Duke went to Windsor to tell the King what had happened. [George IV claimed, rather improbably, he would have acted in the same way.]

Charles Greville, Memoirs (except for matter in square brackets), 1829. Lord Winchilsea had accused the Duke of Wellington, then Prime Minister, of planning to introduce popery into every department of state.

22 MARCH

The earliest date on which Easter can fall.

1312 *The Order of the Knights Templar abolished by the Pope.*

1824 *The National Gallery founded in London.*

About two o'clock in the morning I inadvertently snuffed out my candle, and as my fire was long before that black and cold, I was in a great dilemma how to proceed. Downstairs did I softly and silently step to the kitchen. But, alas, there was as little fire there as upon the icy mountains of Greenland. With a tinder-box is a light struck every morning to kindle the fire, which is put out at night. But this tinder-box I could not see, nor knew where to find. I was now filled with gloomy ideas of the terrors of the night. I was also apprehensive that my landlord, who always keeps a pair of loaded pistols him, might fire at me as a thief. I went up to my room, sat quietly till I heard the watchman calling, 'Past three o'clock'. I then called to him to knock at the door of the house where I lodged. He did so, and I opened it to him and got my candle relumed without danger.

James Boswell, Journal, 1763.

The crowd overflowed the House in every part. When the strangers were cleared out and the doors locked we had 608 members present, more by fifty than ever were at a division before. The Ayes and the Noes were like two volleys of cannon from opposite sides of a field of battle. When the opposition went out into the lobby . . . we spread ourselves over the benches on both sides of the House . . . As the tellers passed along the lowest row . . . the interest was insupportable . . . At 300 there was a short cry of joy, at 302 another, suppressed however in a moment . . . Charles Wood who stood near the door jumped on a bench and cried out, 'They are only 301.' We sent up a shout that you might have heard at Charing Cross.

Lord Macaulay describes the passing of the Great Reform Bill, 1831.

23 MARCH

1861 *The first trams, horse-drawn, run in London, at Bayswater.*

1983 *President Reagan launches the Strategic Defence 'Star Wars' Initiative to counter a nuclear attack in space.*

William is now reading Ben Jonson. I am going to read German. It is about ten o'clock, a quiet night. The fire flutters, and the watch ticks. I hear nothing else save the breathing of my Beloved, and he now and then pushes his book forward, and turns over a leaf.

Dorothy Wordsworth, Journal, 1802.

Non-violence is the first article of my faith. It is the last article of my faith. But I had to make my choice. I had either to submit to a system which I considered has done an irreparable harm to my country or incur the risk of the mad fury of my people bursting forth when they understood the truth from my lips. I know that my people have sometimes gone mad. I am deeply sorry for it; and I am therefore, here, to submit not to a light penalty but to the highest penalty. I do not ask for mercy. I do not plead any extenuating act. I am here, therefore, to invite and submit to the highest penalty that can be inflicted upon me for what in law is a deliberate crime and what appears to me to be the highest duty of a citizen.

Mahatma Gandhi, at his trial on a charge of sedition, 1922.

24 MARCH

1877 *The only dead-heat finish in the Oxford and Cambridge boat race.*

1946 *Alistair Cook broadcasts his first weekly* Letter from America *on BBC radio.*

1956 *Devon Loch, the Queen Mother's horse, ridden by Dick Francis, inexplicably stumbles when seeming an easy winner of the Grand National.*

This cums hopein to find you in good helth as it leaves me safe ankord here yesterday at 4 p.m., arter a plesent vyage tolerable short and few squalls. Dear Tom, hopes to find poor old father stout. Am quite out of pigtail [chewing tobacco]. Sights of pigtail at Gravesend but unfortinly not fit for a dogtochor. Dear Tom, Captains boy will bring you this and put pigtail in his pocket when bort. Best in London at the black boy 7 diles where go, ax for best pigtail, pound a pigtail will do. And am short of shirts. Dear Tom, as for shirts onley took 2, whereof 1 is quite wore out and tother most, but don't forget the pigtail as I arnt had here a quid to chor never sins Thursday. Dear Tom as for the shirts your size will do only longer. I liks um long, got one at present, best at Tower hill and cheap, but be pertickler to go to 7 diles for the pigtail, at the black boy and dear Tom ax for a pound of best pigtail and let it be good. Captains boy will put the pigtail in his pocket, *he likes pigtail so tie it up.* Dear Tom shall be up about Monday or thereabouts. Not so pertickler for the shirts as the present can be washed, but dont forget the pigtail without fail, so am your lovein brother, JACK

    P.S. – Dont forget the pigtail.

A sailor on the Warren Hastings, *East Indiaman, off Gravesend, to his brother, early nineteenth eentury.*

25 MARCH

The Tichborne Dole is distributed in this Hampshire village. A char-itable gift established in the thirteenth century, it was originally 1400 loaves, but now takes the form of flour made from locally grown wheat.

1807 *Britain abolishes the slave trade.*

I have been, during the last three months, undergoing a process of intellectual *exsiccation*. In my long illness I had compelled into hours of delight many a sleepless, painful hour of darkness by chasing down metaphysical game – and since then I have continued the hunt, till I found myself unaware at the root of pure mathematics – and up that tall smooth tree, whose few poor branches are all at its very summit, am I climbing by pure adhesive strength of arms and thighs, still slipping down, still renewing my ascent. You would not know me! All sounds of similitude keep at such a distance from each other in my mind, that I have *forgotten* how to make a rhyme – I look at the mountains (that visible God Almighty that looks in at all my windows) – I look at the mountains only for the curves of their outlines; the stars, as I behold them, form themselves into trian-gles – and my hands are scarred with scratches from a cat, whose back I was rubbing in the dark in order to see whether the sparks from it were refrangible by a prism. The Poet is dead in me – my imagination (or rather the somewhat that had been imaginative) lies, like a cold snuff on the circular rim of a brass candlestick, without even a stink of tallow to remind you that it was once clothed and mitred with flame. That is passed by! I was once a volume of gold leaf, rising and riding on every breath of fancy – but I have beaten myself back into weight and density, and now I sink in quicksilver, yea, remain squat and square on the earth amid the hurricane, that makes oaks and straws join in one dance, fifty yards high in the element.

Samuel Taylor Coleridge to William Godwin, from Keswick, 1801.

26 MARCH

1886 *The first cremation in England, at Woking.*

1923 *The BBC broadcasts its first weather forecast.*

1934 *Driving tests are introduced.*

To make this condiment your poet begs,
The pounded yellow of two hard-boil'd eggs;
Two boiled potatoes, passed through kitchen sieve,
Smoothness and softness to the salad give.
Let onion atoms lurk within the bowl,
And, half-suspected, animate the whole.
Of mordant mustard add a single spoon,
Distrust the condiment that bites so soon;
But deem it not, thou man of herbs, a fault
To add a double quantity of salt;
Four times the spoon with oil of Lucca crown,
And twice with vinegar procur'd from town;
And lastly o'er the flavour'd compound toss
A magic soupçon of anchovy sauce.
Oh, green and glorious! Oh, herbaceous treat!
T'would tempt the dying anchorite to eat;
Back to the world he'd turn his fleeting soul,
And plunge his fingers in the salad-bowl!
Serenely full, the epicure would say,
'Fate cannot harm me, I have dined today.'

The Revd Sydney Smith sends his recipe for salad-dressing to Lady Hardy, wife of the captain of Nelson's Victory, *1839.*

1790 *The shoelace invented.*

1871 *The first rugby international, Scotland v. England, is played in Edinburgh.*

1977 *The world's worst air disaster, when two planes collide on the runway at Tenerife and 582 are killed.*

A divine morning. At breakfast William wrote part of an ode. Mr Oliff sent the dung and William went to work in the garden. We sat all day in the orchard.

Dorothy Wordsworth, Journal, 1802. The ode referred to became 'Intimations of Immortality', of which Gerard Manley Hopkins said: 'For my part I should think St George and St Thomas of Canterbury wore roses in heaven for England's sake on the day that ode, not without their intercession, was penned.'

My present work is to view all facts that I can muster in Natural History to see how far they favour or are opposed to the notion that wild species are mutable or immutable.

Charles Darwin to W.D. Fox, 1855.

Heard a characteristic story of Shelley. Harriet [his first wife] was far too foolish and thought herself too fine to nurse her child. This horrified S. who thought that nature was violated by her refusal and abhorred a hired nurse. The nurse's soul would enter the child. All day he tried to persuade Harriet to do her duty, walking up and down the room, crooning old songs to the child in his arms. At last, in his despair, and thinking that the passion in him would make a miracle, he pulled his shirt away and tried himself to suckle the child. This is [Thomas Love] Peacock's tale, and it is Shelley all over. I believe it. It stamps the man.

Stopford Brooke, Diary, 1899.

1854 *The Crimean War begins. Britain and France take the side of Turkey against Russia.*

1941 *Virginia Woolf drowns herself.*

1964 *Pirate radio ship* Caroline *starts broadcasting off the English coast.*

Sir, we are not weak, if we make a proper use of the means which the God of nature hath placed in our power. Three millions of people, armed in the holy cause of liberty, and in such a country as that which we possess, are invincible by any force which our enemy can send against us. Besides, sir, we shall not fight our battles alone. There is a just God who presides over the destinies of nations; and who will raise up friends to fight our battles for us. The battle, sir, is not to the strong alone; it is to the vigilant, the active, the brave. Besides, sir, we have no election. If we were base enough to desire it, it is now too late to retire from the contest. There is no retreat, but in submission and slavery! Our chains are forged! Their clanking may be heard on the plains of Boston! The war is inevitable – and let it come! I repeat it, sir, let it come!

It is in vain, sir, to extenuate the matter. Gentlemen may cry peace, peace – but there is no peace. The war is actually begun! The next gale that sweeps from the north will bring to our ears the clash of resounding arms! Our brethren are already in the field! Why stand we here idle? What is it that gentlemen wish? What would they have? Is life so dear, or peace so sweet, as to be purchased at the price of chains and slavery? Forbid it, Almighty God! I know not what course others may take; but as for me, give me liberty, or give me death!

Patrick Henry's speech before the Virginia Convention of Delegates at the start of the American War of Independence, 1775.

29 MARCH

1461 *The battle of Towton in North Yorkshire is fought in a snow-storm. It is a defeat for Henry VI in the Wars of the Roses, and the 28,000 slain make it the bloodiest on British soil.*

1871 *Queen Victoria opens the Albert Hall.*

1981 *The first London Marathon is run; 6,700 take part, compared to 30,000 in 2005.*

Now the black trees in the Regent's Park opposite are beginning to show green buds; and men come by with great baskets of flowers; primroses, hepaticas, cro-cuses, great daisies etc., calling as they go, 'Growing, growing, growing! All the glory going!'

Edward FitzGerald to E.B. and Elizabeth Cowell, 1857.

I dined with Lord Houghton – with Gladstone, Tennyson, Dr Schliemann (the excavator of old Mycenae, etc.) and half a dozen other men of 'high culture'. I sat next but one to the Bard and heard most of his talk, which was all about port wine and tobacco: he seems to know much about them, and can drink a whole bottle of port at a sitting with no incommodity. He is very swarthy and scraggy, and strikes one at first as much less handsome than his photos: but gradually you see that it's a face of genius. He had I know not what simplicity, speaks with a strange rustic accent and seemed altogether like a creature of some primordial English stock, a thousand miles away from American manu-facture. Behold me after dinner conversing affably with Mr Gladstone – not by my own seeking, but by the almost importunate affection of Lord H. But I was glad of a chance to feel the 'personality' of a great political leader . . . That of Gladstone is very fascinating – his urbanity extreme – his eye that of a man of genius – and his apparent self-surrender to what he is talking of, without a flaw.

Henry James to his brother William, 1877.

30 MARCH

—————+·|❂|❀|❂|+—————

1856 *The Crimean War ends*

1857 *Russia sells Alaska to the United States for $7.2 million - two cents an acre.*

By looking over my left shoulder I see gorse yellow against the Atlantic blue. And we've been lying on the Gurnard's Head, on beds of samphire among grey rocks with buttons of yellow lichen on them. You look down onto the semi-transparent water – the waves all scrambled into white round the rocks – gulls swaying on bits of seaweed – rocks now dry now drenched with white waterfalls pouring down crevices. We took a rabbit path round the cliff, and I find myself a little shakier than I used to be. Still however maintaining without force to my conscience that this is the loveliest place in the world.

Virginia Woolf, Diary, Zennor, Cornwall, 1921.

Another rocket [a V2], and worst of the lot, landed at the top of Uppingham Avenue [Harrow]. I remember some time ago cycling down Weston Drive into Uppingham and thinking that if a rocket landed there it would make a right mess. And it had, if only because the damned thing had landed plumb on all three mains – water, gas, electricity . . . at 3.40 in the morning, killing nine people among whom was a nine-year-old boy who had been flung out of bed, through the rafters, and into a back garden ten houses away – at first, nobody had been able to find him.

As I watched the mass funeral . . . tears came to my eyes, not with the grief and distress caused to survivors but with the incalculable trouble to which they will be put, months and years of it, before they can resume any sort of normal life and the incident becomes only a tale to tell to the grandchildren. Even obtaining an everyday thing like soap has its problems, let alone the replacement of identity cards, ration books, personal papers, with which I can give some help.

George Beardmore, Journal, 1945.

31 MARCH

1836 *The first instalment of* Pickwick Papers *published, Charles Dickens's first great success.*

1889 *The Eiffel Tower completed.*

1990 *Poll Tax riot in Trafalgar Square.*

It is plain I never knew for how many trades I was formed, when at this time of day I can begin electioneering, and succeed in my new vocation. Think of me, the subject of a mob, who was scarce ever before in a mob, addressing them in the town hall, riding at the head of two thousand people through such a town as [King's] Lynn, dining with above two hundred of them, amid bumpers, huzzas, songs, and tobacco, and finishing with country dancing at a ball and sixpenny whisk [whist]! I have borne it all cheerfully; nay, have sat hours in *conversation*, the thing upon earth that I hate; have been to hear misses play on the harpsichord, and to see an alderman's copies of Reubens and Carlo Marat [Maratta]. Yet to do the folks justice, they are sensible, and reasonable, and civilised; their very language is polished since I lived among them. I attribute this to their more frequent intercourse with the world and the capital, by the help of good roads and post-chaises, which, if they have abridged the King's dominions, have at least tamed his subjects. Well, how comfortable it will be tomorrow, to see my parakeet, to play at loo, and not be obliged to talk seriously!

My ancient aunt said to me, 'Child, you have done a thing today, that your father never did in all his life; you sat as they carried you – he always stood the whole time.' 'Madam,' said I, 'when I cannot imitate my father in great things, I am not at all ambitious of mimicking him in little ones.'

Horace Walpole to George Montagu, 1761. Walpole was MP for King's Lynn from 1757 to 1767. His father had been the first prime minister.

APRIL

1 APRIL

1902 *Treadmills abolished in British prisons.*

1947 *School-leaving age raised to 15.*

1973 *VAT introduced.*

This whisperer wounds thee, and with a stiletto of gold. He strangles thee with scarves of silk, he smothers thee with the down of phoenixes, he stifles thee with a perfume of amber, he destroys thee by praising thee, overthrows thee by exalting thee, and undoes thee by trusting thee – by trusting thee with those secrets that bring thee into a desperate perplexity, either to betray another that pretends to have trusted thee, or to perish thyself for the saving of another that plotted to betray thee. And therefore, if you can hear a good organ at church and have the music of a domestic peace at home, peace in thy walls, peace in thy bosom, never harken after the music of spheres, never hunt after the knowledge of higher secrets than appertain to thee. But since Christ hath made you kings and priests in your proportion, take heed what you hear in derogation of either the State or the Church.

John Donne, a sermon preached before Charles I, in Whitehall, 1627.

Made Bessy turn her cap awry in honour of the day.

Tom Moore, Diary, 1819.

Poor little Goold, the girl I have been so much pleased with as to her constant attendance at Church and desire to improve herself, is laid up with the smallpox. She has been vaccinated by Mr Crang, but it could not have taken properly, as she is fuller with pustules than any person I ever saw, but so very patient. I promised to send her some children's books for her amusement, which I did on my return home.

The Revd John Skinner, Journal, 1825. Vaccination had been
introduced by Edward Jenner in 1798.

2 APRIL

1801 *Nelson wins the Battle of Copenhagen.*

1892 *Death of John Murray III, who initiated Murray's Guides, the first-ever series of guidebooks, and published Darwin.*

1982 *Argentina invades the Falkland Islands.*

My drake (he has four ducks as wives) is absolutely dithering for love of a large speckledy hen – pursues her ceaselessly, covering her with kisses, which she simply hates. He goes to all lengths and never once looks at the thirty other hens.

Conrad Russell to Lady Diana Cooper, 1943.

A bit of ancient masonry stands against the sea, and a castle above patched by all sorts of rough garrisons, and now has a rather pathetic Turkish notice saying 'Danger: don't come near: dynamite'. We did however get in round a wall regardless and saw a toothless old heap of walls and a little hut with cement roof where presumably the dynamite is kept – and there, below the immense sweep of bay, the narrow dark green strip with cracks of gorges spitting out their torrents, the etched line – clean as a cameo – of Cilicia and the hills that fringe the plain. . . .

Alexander descended from this slope at dawn and led his troops along the coast in column till the plain spread out and then he opened out his phalanx and went across what is now olive groves, corn and orange gardens, but was then probably all cistus and asphodel and patches of rushes by the sea. The mountains grow gentler and down one of their passes the armies of Darius had descended. And we reached the bridge on the river which is said to be the right one, and it was rushing down with curls of yellow foam, all the poplars and plane trees out on its banks with tiny leaves and shining white stems, and the river bed itself a light grey, with gravelly banks steep here and there but not high, and loose – so that the horse could manage and the stakes of the Persians on the bank could be pushed about.

Freya Stark to her publisher Jock Murray, 1954, describing the battlefield of Issus on the edge of the Aegean where Alexander defeated the Persians in 333 BC.

3 APRIL

1721 *Sir Robert Walpole becomes the first Prime Minister, and holds the post until 1742.*

1948 *The Marshall Plan for US aid to speed European recovery is signed by President Truman.*

1987 *The sale of the late Duchess of Windsor's jewellery raises £31 million.*

In the morning, I found [Johnson] very busy putting his books in order, and, as they were generally very old ones, clouds of dust were flying around him. He had on a pair of large gloves, such as hedgers use. His present appearance put me in mind of my uncle Dr Boswell's description of him, 'A robust genius, born to grapple with whole libraries'. . . .

I told him that while I was with [Captain Cook the day before] I caught the enthusiasm of curiosity and adventure, and felt a strong inclination to go with him on his next voyage. JOHNSON. 'Why, Sir, a man *does* feel so, till he considers how very little he can learn from such voyages.' BOSWELL. 'But one is carried away with the general, grand, and indistinct notion of A VOYAGE ROUND THE WORLD.' JOHNSON. 'Yes, Sir, but a man is to guard himself against taking a thing in general.'

James Boswell, Life of Johnson, *1776.*

The Tame Celebrity . . . crow's-footed, beginning to be grizzled, general appearance of a blasted boy – or blighted youth – or to borrow Carlyle on De Quincey, 'Child that has been in hell'. Past eccentric – obscure and O no we never mention it – present, industrious respectable and fatuously contented. Used to be very fond of talking about Art, don't talk about it any more . . . Friendly grocer in Sydney: 'It has been a most agreeable surprise to meet you Mr Stevenson. I would never have guessed you were a literary man.' Cigarettes without intermission except when coughing or kissing. Hopelessly entangled in apron strings. Drinks plenty. Curses some.

Robert Louis Stevenson describes himself to J.M. Barrie, 1893.

4 APRIL

1774 *Death of Oliver Goldsmith. Asked 'Is your mind at ease?' he answered, 'No, it is not,' and expired.*

1934 *The first cat's-eyes installed, at a crossroads near Bradford.*

1968 *Martin Luther King assassinated in Memphis.*

There stood before me a little, pale, rather don-like man, quite bald, with a huge head and dome-like forehead, a ragged red beard in odd whisks, a small aquiline red nose. He looked supremely shy, but received me with a distinguished courtesy, drumming on the ground with his foot, and uttering strange little whistling noises. He seemed very deaf. The room was crammed with books: bookcases all about – a great sofa entirely filled with stacked books – books on the table. He bowed me to a chair – 'Will you sit?' On the fender was a pair of brown socks. Watts-Dunton said to me, 'He has just come in from one of his long walks' – and took up the socks and put them behind the coal scuttle. 'Stay!' said Swinburne, and took them out carefully, holding them in his hand: 'They are drying.' Watts-Dunton murmured something about his fearing they would get scorched, and we sat down. Swinburne sat down, concealing his feet behind a chair, and proceeded with strange motions to put the socks on out of sight. 'He seems to be changing them,' said Watts-Dunton. Swinburne said nothing, but continued to whistle and drum. Then he rose and bowed me down to lunch, throwing the window open.

A.C. Benson, Diary, 1903. In 1879 Watts-Dunton, a mediocre novelist of private means, had decided to save the poet Swinburne from drinking himself to death. They lived together thereafter at No. 2, The Pines, on Putney Hill.

5 APRIL

1895 *Oscar Wilde arrested at the Cadogan Hotel on a charge of gross indecency, having lost his libel case against the Marquess of Queensberry.*

1955 *Churchill resigns as Prime Minister.*

She very properly, in consequence of my saying to her it was the right mode of proceeding, attempted to kneel to him. He raised her (gracefully enough), and embraced her, said barely one word, turned round, retired to a distant part of the apartment, and calling me to him, said, 'Harris, I am not well; pray get me a glass of brandy.' I said, 'Sir, had you not better have a glass of water?' – upon which he, much out of humour, said, with an oath, *'No*; I will go directly to the Queen,' and away he went. The Princess, left during this short moment alone, was in a state of astonishment; and, on my joining her, said, *'Mon Dieu! est-ce que le Prince est toujours comme cela? Je le trouve très gros, et nullement aussi beau que son portrait* [My God! Is the Prince always like that? I find him very fat, and nothing like as handsome as his portrait].' I said His Royal Highness was naturally a good deal affected and flurried at this first interview, but she certainly would find him different at dinner.

James Harris, first Earl of Malmesbury, describes the meeting of the future King George IV with his intended bride, Princess Caroline of Brunswick, 1795.

If you have the patience to read all Chapter 1, I honestly think you will have a fair notion of the interest of the whole book . . . I must repeat my request that you will freely reject my work.

Charles Darwin to John Murray III, 1859. Murray had said he would publish the Origin of Species *unseen. In fact he read the first three chapters, the second of which Darwin called dull and abstruse, and stood by his offer.*

6 APRIL

1896 *first modern Olympic Games held in Athens.*

1909 *Robert Peary, his black servant Matthew Henson and four eskimos are the first men to reach the North Pole.*

1917 *The US declares war on Germany.*

I came home FOR EVER on Tuesday in last week. The incomprehensibleness of my condition overwhelmed me. It was like passing from life into eternity. Every year to be as long as three, i.e. to have three times as much real time, time that is my own, in it! I wandered about thinking I was happy, but feeling I was not. But that tumultuousness is passing off, and I begin to understand the nature of the gift. Holydays, even the annual month, were always uneasy joys: their conscious fugitiveness – the craving after making the most of them. Now, when all is holyday, there are no holydays. I can sit at home, in rain or shine, without a restless impulse for walkings. I am daily steadying, and shall soon find it as natural to me to be my own master, as it has been irksome to have had a master. Mary [his sister, now almost continuously insane] wakes every morning with an obsure feeling that some good has happened to us.

. . . I eat, drink, sleep as sound as ever. I lay no anxious scheme for going hither and thither, but take things as they occur. Yesterday I excursioned twenty miles, today I write a few letters. Pleasuring was for fugitive play-days, mine are fugitive only in the sense that life is fugitive. Freedom and life coexistent.

Charles Lamb to William Wordsworth, on his retirement 'after thirty-three years' slavery' in the offices of the East India Company in the City of London, 1825.

7 APRIL

1739 *Dick Turpin the highwayman hanged at York.*

1853 *Queen Victoria given chloroform during the birth of her eighth child. She records the effects as 'soothing, quieting and delightful beyond measure'.*

So far as I can remember, [Byron] appeared to me rather a short man, with a handsome countenance, remarkable for the fine blue veins which ran over his pale, marble temples. He wore many rings on his fingers, and a brooch in his shirt-front, which was embroidered. When he called, he used to be dressed in a black dress-coat (as we should now call it), with grey, and sometimes nankeen trousers, his shirt open at the neck. Lord Byron's deformity in his foot was very evident, especially as he walked downstairs. He carried a stick. After Scott and he had ended their conversation in the drawing-room, it was a curious sight to see the two greatest poets of the age – both lame – stumping downstairs side by side. They continued to meet in Albemarle Street nearly every day, and remained together for two or three hours at a time. Lord Byron dined several times at Albemarle Street. . . . Sometimes, though not often, Lord Byron read passages from his poems to my father. His voice and manner were very impressive. His voice, in the deeper tones, bore some resemblance to that of Mrs Siddons.

John Murray III recalls the first meeting of Lord Byron and
Sir Walter Scott at 50 Albemarle Street, on 7 April 1815.

After all one's thought and search and effort to make some sort of image which would embody the life of our time, it turns out that all that was really significant were toffee wrappers, liquorice allsorts and ton-up motor bikes. So one could have saved oneself the trouble. I understand how the stranded dinosaurs felt when the hard terrain, which for centuries had demanded from them greater weight and effort, suddenly started to get swampy beneath their feet.

Keith Vaughan on the New Generation exhibition at the Whitechapel Gallery which launched the Pop Art movement, Journal, 1964.

8 APRIL

c. **563** BC *The Buddha's birthday.*

1838 *The* Great Western *steamship sets out on her maiden voyage, so signalling the start of a regular Transatlantic steam passenger service.*

1904 *The* Entente Cordiale *alliance signed by France and Great Britain.*

I ought to be writing *Jacob's Room* – I can't and instead I shall write down the reason why I can't – this diary being a kindly blank-faced old confidante. Well, you see, I'm a failure as a writer. I'm out of fashion; old; shan't do any better . . . my book [*Monday or Tuesday*] out (prematurely) and nipped, a damp firework . . . Well, this question of praise and fame must be faced. (I forgot to say that Doran has refused the book in America.) How much difference does popularity make? (I see pretty clearly, I may add . . . that I'm writing a good deal of nonsense) . . . I have still, of course, to gather in all the private criticism, which is the real test. When I have weighed all this I shall be able to say whether I am 'interesting' or obsolete . . . I think the only prescription for me is to have a thousand interests – if one is damaged to be able instantly to let my energy flow into Russian, or Greek, or the [Hogarth] press, or the garden, or people, or some activity disconnected with my own writing . . .

We went to the Bedford Music Hall last night, and saw Miss Marie Lloyd, a mass of corruption – long front teeth – a crapulous way of saying 'desire', and yet a born artist – scarcely able to walk, waddling, aged, unblushing. A roar of laughter went up when she talked of her marriage. She is beaten nightly by her husband. I felt that the audience was much closer to drink and beating and prison than any of us. The coal strike is on.

Virginia Woolf, Diary, 1921.

9 APRIL

—◦|◦|◦|◦——◦◦|◦|◦——

1770 *Botany Bay on the east coast of Australia is discovered by Captain Cook.*

1865 *The Confederate commander, General Robert E. Lee, surrenders to Federal General Ulysses S. Grant at the Appomattox Courthouse, so ending the American Civil War.*

All London is making preparations to encounter a Chartist row tomorrow: so much that it is either very sublime or very ridiculous. All the clerks and others in the different offices are ordered to be sworn in special constables, and to constitute themselves into garrisons. I went to the police office with all my clerks, messengers, etc., and we were all sworn. We are to pass the whole day at the office tomorrow, and I am to send down all my guns; in short, we are to take a warlike attitude. Colonel Harness, of the Railway Department, is our commander-in-chief; every gentleman in London is become a constable, and there is an organisation of some sort in every district.

> *Charles Greville, Memoirs, 1848. The Chartists, twenty thousand in number, were to assemble on Kennington Common.*

The rain roars like the sea; in the sound of it there is a strange and ominous suggestion of an approaching tramp; something nameless and measureless seems to draw near, and strikes me cold, and yet is welcome. I lie quiet in bed today, and think of the universe with a good deal of equanimity. I have, at this moment, but the one objection to it; the *fracas* with which it proceeds. I do not love noise; I am like my grandfather in that; and so many years in these still islands has ingrained the sentiment perhaps. Here are no trains, only men pacing barefoot. No carts or carriages; at worst the rattle of a horse's shoes among the rocks. Beautiful silence; and so soon as this robustious rain takes off, I am to drink of it again by oceanfuls.

> *Robert Louis Stevenson to Sidney Colvin, 1894.*

10 APRIL

1633 *Bananas first on sale in London.*

1849 *The safety pin patented in the US.*

I do not know that I am happiest when alone; but this I am sure of, that I never am long in the society even of *her* I love (God knows too well, and the Devil probably too) without a yearning for the company of my lamp and my utterly confused and tumbled-over library. Even in the day, I send away my carriage oftener than I use or abuse it. *Per esempio* – I have not stirred out of these rooms [in Albany, Piccadilly] for these four days past: but I have sparred for exercise (windows open) with Jackson an hour daily, to attenuate and keep up the ethereal part of me. The more violent the fatigue, the better my spirits for the rest of the day; and then, my evenings have that calm nothingness of languor, which I most delight in. Today I have boxed one hour – written an ode to Napoleon Buonaparte – copied it – eaten six biscuits – drunk four bottles of soda water – read away the rest of my time – besides giving poor —— a world of advice about this mistress of his, who is plaguing him into a phthisic [wasting] and intolerable tediousness. I am a pretty fellow truly to lecture about 'the sect' [the female sex]. No matter, my counsels are all thrown away.

> Lord Byron, Journal, 1814. 'Her *I love*' is his half-sister Augusta Leigh.
> 'Gentleman' Jackson was a famous prize-fighter.

The Chartist movement was contemptible; but everybody rejoices that the defensive demonstration was made, for it has given a great and memorable lesson which will not be thrown away, either on the disaffected and mischievous, or the loyal and peaceful . . . In the morning (a very fine day) everybody was on the alert; the parks were closed; our office was fortified, a barricade of Council Registers was erected in the accessible room on the ground floor; and all our guns were taken down to be used in defence of the building. However, at about twelve o'clock crowds came streaming along Whitehall, going northwards, and it was announced that all was over. The intended tragedy was rapidly changed into a ludicrous farce.

Charles Greville, Memoirs, 1848. Hector Berlioz, in London at the time, said to his hosts, 'My poor friends, you know as much about starting a riot as the Italians know about writing a symphony.'

11 APRIL

1814 *Napoleon abdicates.*

1855 *London's first Royal Mail pillar boxes are installed, painted green.*

1951 *General Douglas MacArthur is sacked as UN/US commander in Korea by President Truman for making political statements and because of fear he might escalate war to nuclear level.*

Lord Guilford died of an inflammation of the bowels: so they took them out, and sent them (on account of their discrepancies), separately from the carcass, to England. Conceive a man going one way, and his intestines another, and his immortal soul a third! – was there ever such a distribution? One certainly has a soul; but how it came to allow itself to be enclosed in a body is more than I can imagine. I only know if once mine gets out, I'll have a bit of a tussle before I let it get in again to that or any other.

Lord Byron to Thomas Moore, 1817.

A cloud comes over Charlotte Street and seems as if it were sailing softly on the April wind to fall in a blessed shower upon the lilac buds and thirsty anemones somewhere in Essex; or, who knows? perhaps at Boulge [his Suffolk cottage]. Out will run Mrs Faiers [his housekeeper], and with red arms and face of woe haul in the struggling windows of the cottage, and make all tight. Beauty Bob [his parrot] will cast a bird's eye out at the shower, and bless the useful wet. Mr Loder [the Woodbridge stationer] will observe to the farmer for whom he is doing up a dozen of Queen's Heads [the new penny-post stamps], that it will be of great use: and the farmer will agree that his young barleys wanted it much. The German Ocean will dimple with innumerable pinpoints, and porpoises rolling near the surface sneeze with unusual pellets of fresh water.

Edward FitzGerald in London to Bernard Barton, 1844.

12 APRIL

1861 *The American Civil War begins.*

1930 *Wilfred Rhodes, aged 52, becomes the oldest man to play in a Test Match, in Kingston, Jamaica.*

1954 *'Rock Around the Clock' recorded by Bill Haley.*

I decided to go to King's [College Chapel, Cambridge] – sat in the antechapel . . . A few imbecile, wild, officious people in the nave; one woman eyed a small book in her hand hungrily and intently, and sang wolfishly; a foolish elderly man handed about books; a young man talked and giggled to a young woman. The music was very characteristic – hymns with tubas, like streams of strawberry jam, and gliding intermediate chords, gross, like German cookery. As for the service, there was no mystery about it, or holiness – it was no more holy than a Union Jack – it was loud and confident . . . Altogether it wouldn't quite do; it was very beautiful both to see and hear, but had no wisdom or depth about it. I had no impulse at all to pray or weep . . .

I felt this morning that though I am happy enough my life is very unsatisfactory. I seem to be floating about experiencing most comforts and prosperities, and yet always on the surface of everything. Love, religion, art, ambition – I have an inkling of all, yet have never dived to any depth or been carried away. I have never been in love; I have abandoned myself to luxurious sentiment, but never ' hungered sore'; I have never really had a personal mystic apprehension of God, never understood art, always at the last moment despised ambition; and the other side of that medal is that I have always been really preoccupied with myself. But how is one to get out of such preoccupation? If any one will tell the human race that, he shall be made a saint.

A.C. Benson, Diary, Easter Sunday, 1914.

13 APRIL

1742 *The first performance of Handel's* Messiah *given, in Dublin.*

1912 *The Royal Flying Corps, from which the RAF developed, is established.*

1975 *The Lebanese Civil War begins.*

I should have mentioned last night that I met with a monstrous big whore in the Strand, whom I had a great curiosity to lubricate, as the saying is. I went into a tavern with her, where she displayed to me all the parts of her enormous carcass; but I found that her avarice was as large as her a[rse], for she would by no means take what I offered her. I therefore with all coolness pulled the bell and discharged the reckoning, to her no small surprise and mortification, who would fain have provoked me to talk harshly to her and so make a disturbance. But I walked off with the gravity of a Barcelonian bishop. I had an opportunity tonight of observing the rascality of the waiters in these infamous sort of taverns. They connive with the whores, and do what they can to fleece the gentlemen. I was on my guard, and got off pretty well. I was so much in the lewd humour that I felt myself restless, and took a little girl into a court; but wanted vigour. So I went home, resolved against low street debauchery.

James Boswell, London Journal, 1763.

Today . . . Count d'Orsay walked in . . . Well! that man understood his trade; if it be but that of dandy, nobody can deny that he is a perfect master of it . . . He had the fine sense to perceive how much better his dress of today sets off his slightly enlarged figure and slightly worn complexion, than the humming-bird colours of five years back would have done.

Jane Welsh Carlyle, Notebook, 1845.

14 APRIL

1865 *President Lincoln is shot at Ford's Theatre in Washington and dies the next day.*

1931 *The Highway Code is first issued.*

On getting into the heat of the fight I found the warfare an unpleasant one, as not a soul could be seen. Now and then a voice in the hedge would say *'Français ou Anglais?'* and a thrust through the bush was an answer. Our Brigade Major, Dreschel, lost his life that way. The same question was put to him and instead of jumping into it, he proudly answered, 'A German,' when a ball in his groin convinced him how much the snake in the bush respected his nativity . . .

By the flashes of light I saw something wrapped in a boat-cloak on the other side of the hedge. Impelled by curiosity as well as humanity, I broke through and on turning it up I washed away the blood and gore from the features with the skirt of the wrapper and discovered the countenance of Lieutenant Köhler of my regiment. My promotion instantly suggested itself, and thoughts of my own danger. I walked up to Captain Bacmeister and, bowing, said in the midst of the shot, 'Allow me to introduce Lieutenant E. Wheatley to your notice.' And I actually received his congratulation. Can there be any thirst for glory when actions like these take place on the field of havoc?

Ensign Edmund Wheatley of the King's German Legion, Diary, 1814. The KGL had been formed after Hanover succumbed to Napoleon in 1803; most of the officers were German, but the other ranks came from every European country except France, Spain and Italy. Here, at the end of the Peninsular War, the French have launched a night attack outside Bayonne.

15 APRIL

1755 *Samuel Johnson's* English Dictionary *published after eight years' work.*

1797 *Mutiny by crews of Royal Navy ships at Spithead.*

1955 *McDonald's hamburger restaurant chain founded by Roy Kroc in De Plaines, Chicago.*

Brewed a vessel of strong beer today. My two large pigs, by drinking some beer grounds taking out of three barrels today, got so amazingly drunk by it, that they were not able to stand and appeared like dead things almost . . . I never saw pigs so drunk in my life – I slit their ears for them without feeling.

Parson James Woodforde, Diary, 1778.

There were men all around me – hundreds of them. The sea was dotted with them, all depending on their lifebelts. I felt I simply had to get away from the ship. She was a beautiful sight then. Smoke and sparks were rushing out of her funnel. There must have been an explosion, but we heard none. We only saw the big stream of sparks. The ship was turning gradually on her nose – just like a duck that goes for a dive. I had only one thing on my mind – to get away from the suction. The band was still playing. I guess all of them went down. They were playing 'Autumn' then. I swam with all my might. I suppose I was 150 feet away when the *Titanic*, on her nose, with her after-quarter sticking straight up in the air, began to settle – slowly.

When at last the waves washed over her rudder there wasn't the least bit of suction I could feel. She must have kept going just so slowly as she had been . . . I felt after a little while like sinking. I was very cold. I saw a boat of some kind near me, and put all my strength into an effort to swim to it. It was hard work. I was all done when a hand reached out from the boat and pulled me aboard.

Harold Bride, wireless operator on the Titanic, *1912.*

16 APRIL

1746 *The Jacobite clans under Bonnie Prince Charlie are defeated at the Battle of Culloden.*

1953 *The Royal Yacht* Britannia *launched by the Queen.*

There was the gentle flowing of the stream, the glittering, lively lake, green fields without a living creature to be seen on them, behind us, a flat pasture with forty-two cattle feeding; to our left, the road leading to the hamlet. No smoke there, the sun shone on the bare roofs. The people were at work ploughing, harrowing, and sowing; lasses spreading dung, a dog's barking now and then, cocks crowing, birds twittering, the snow in patches at the top of the highest hills, yellow palms, purple and green twigs on the birches, ashes with their glittering spikes quite bare.

> *Dorothy Wordsworth at the southern end of Ullswater, Journal, 1802.*

He was wonderful as he was carried past me on his throne, not of flesh and blood, but a white soul robed in white, and an artist as well as a saint – the only instance in history, if the newspapers are to be believed.

I have seen nothing like the extraordinary grace of his gesture, as he rose, from moment to moment, to bless – possibly the pilgrims, but certainly me. Tree [the actor-manager] should see him. It is his only chance. I was deeply impressed; and my walking-stick showed signs of budding . . .

How did I get the ticket? By a miracle, of course . . . Suddenly, as I was eating buttered toast, a man, or what seemed to be one, dressed like a hotel porter, entered and asked me would I like to see the Pope on Easter Day. I bowed my head humbly and said *'Non sum dignus'* [I am not worthy], or words to that effect. He at once produced a ticket!

When I tell you that his countenance was of supernatural ugliness, and that the price of the ticket was thirty pieces of silver, I need say no more.

> *Oscar Wilde to Robert Ross, from Rome, 1900;*
> *he had seen Pope Leo XIII the day before.*

17 APRIL

1521 *Martin Luther is excommunicated at the Diet of Worms.*

1975 *Phnom Penh, capital of Cambodia, falls to the Khmer Rouge.*

On Wednesday morning at a quarter-past five came the earthquake. A minute later the flames were leaping upward . . . And the great water mains had burst. All the shrewd contrivances and safeguards of man had been thrown out of gear by thirty seconds' twitching of the earth crust.

By Wednesday afternoon, inside of twelve hours, half the heart of the city was gone. At that time I watched the vast conflagration from out on the bay. It was dead calm. Not a flicker of wind stirred. Yet from every side wind was pouring in upon the city. East, west, north, and south, strong winds were blowing upon the doomed city. The heated air rising made an enormous suck. Thus did the fire of itself build its own colossal chimney through the atmosphere . . . Wednesday night saw the destruction of the very heart of the city. Dynamite was lavishly used, and many of San Francisco's proudest structures were crumbled by man himself into ruins, but there was no withstanding the onrush of the flames . . .

It was at Union Square that I saw a man offering a thousand dollars for a team of horses. He was in charge of a truck piled high with trunks from some hotel. It had been hauled here into what was considered safety, and the horses had been taken out. The flames were on three sides of the square, and there were no horses . . . An hour later, from a distance, I saw the truckload of trunks burning merrily in the middle of the street.

Jack London witnesses the San Francisco earthquake and fire, 1906.

18 APRIL

1934 *The first launderette - called a washeteria - opens, in Fort Worth, Texas.*

1955 *Albert Einstein dies. His Special Theory of Relativity was published in 1905 and he won the Nobel Prize in 1922.*

Her fair maids were ranged below the sofa . . . Four of them immediately began to play some soft airs on instruments between a lute and a guitar, which they accompanied with their voices, while the others danced by turns. This dance was very different from what I had seen before. Nothing could be more artful, or more proper to raise certain ideas. The tunes so soft! – the motions so languishing! – accompanied with pauses and dying eyes! half-falling back, and then recovering themselves in so artful a manner, that I am very positive the coldest and most rigid prude upon earth could not have looked upon them without thinking of something not to be spoken of. I suppose you may have read that the Turks have no music but what is shocking to the ears; but this account is from those who never heard any but what is played in the streets, and is just as reasonable as if a foreigner should take his ideas of the English music from the bladder and string, and marrow-bones and cleavers . . . When the dance was over, four fair slaves came into the room with silver censers in their hands, and perfumed the air with amber, aloes-wood, and other rich scents. After this they served me coffee upon their knees in the finest japan china, with *soucoupes* of silver, gilt.

Lady Mary Wortley Montagu to the Countess of Mar, 1717, about a visit to the wife of the Grand Vizier's deputy, in Adrianople.

19 APRIL

—————

1775 *The American War of Independence begins.*

1824 *Lord Byron dies at Missolonghi in Greece.*

1928 *The final volume of the* Oxford English Dictionary *is published, the first having appeared in 1884.*

There was a wireless in the restaurant and we listened to a very good blues. I thought how close the analogy is between jazz and plainsong: both so anonymous, so curiously restricted and conventionalised, so perfectly adapted to their *métiers*, both flowing with a kind of devout anonymity.

Sylvia Townsend Warner, Diary, 1928.

Marvellous dry luminous landscape . . . Flocks of black, brown and white goats. Shepherd boys in bluish white djellabas. When we stopped for a moment by the side of the road to smoke a cigarette one left his herd and came running towards us. One's instinct was to think he must want something; but we were wrong. We had stopped on his territory and he came to greet us. He shook us gravely by the hand and stood smiling. He did not understand French and so it was impossible to communicate. We stood silently smiling at each other in the white stillness while storks flew overhead. He indicated his flock and the landscape and his gestures seemed to imply that everything was at our service. When we got up to go he touched his head and his heart and then kissed us gently on the back of the hand and stood quietly to watch our departure. The incident was absurdly moving, hardly believable today. It was like living in the Old Testament.

Keith Vaughan in Morocco, Journal, 1965.

20 APRIL

—◦◦◦◦◦◦~◦~◦◦◦◦◦—

753 BC *Rome founded by Romulus and Remus.*

1902 *Pierre and Marie Curie isolate the radioactive element radium.*

He said: 'It is time for me to put an end to your sitting in this place, which you have dishonoured by your contempt of all virtue and defiled by your practice of every vice. Ye are a factious crew, and enemies to all good government. Ye are a pack of mercenary wretches and would like Esau sell your country for a mess of pottage.' He pointed to individuals, and called them 'whoremasters, drunkards, corrupt and unjust men' adding 'Ye have no more religion than my horse. Ye are grown intolerably odious to the whole nation . . . Perhaps ye think this is not parliamentary language. I confess it is not, neither are you to expect any such from me . . . It is not fit that ye should sit as a parliament any longer. Ye have sat long enough unless you had done more good.' . . . He shouted to Thomas Harrison, 'Call them in,' and the musketeers entered. He pointed to the Speaker: 'Fetch him down.' Harrison hesitated: 'The work is very great and dangerous,' then obeyed. Sir Henry Vane protested: 'This is not honest, yea it is against morality and common honesty.' Cromwell: 'O Sir Henry Vane, Sir Henry Vane, the Lord deliver me from Sir Henry Vane.' Then, turning to the mace: 'What shall we do with this bauble? Here, take it away.' Then, to the Members: 'I command ye therefore, upon the peril of your lives, to depart immediately out of this place. Go, get ye out! Make haste! Ye venal slaves be gone! Take away that shining bauble and lock up the doors.' By 11.40 the House was cleared and locked. Someone put up a poster: 'This House is to be Lett; now unfurnished.'

Oliver Cromwell comes down to the House of Commons in 1653 to dissolve the remainder, the Rump, of the Long Parliament originally elected in 1640, as recounted by S. R. Gardiner in his History of the Commonwealth and Protectorate.

2 1 APRIL

1918 *Manfred von Richthofen, the Red Baron, German air ace, killed.*

1952 *First scheduled jet airline service, by Comet from London to Rome.*

1964 *BBC 2 television channel begins transmissions.*

I went into my garden at half-past six [in] the morning . . . The air was perfectly calm, the sunlight pure, and falling on the grass through thickets of the standard peach (which had bloomed that year perfectly), and of plum and pear trees, in their first showers of fresh silver, looking more like much-broken and far-tossed spray of fountains than trees; and just at the end of my hawthorn walk, one happy nightingale was singing as much as he could in every moment. Meantime, in the still air, the roar of the railroads from Clapham Junction, New Cross, and the Crystal Palace (I am between the three) sounded constantly and heavily, like the surf of a strong sea three or four miles distant; and the whistles of the trains passing nearer mixed with the nightingale's notes. That I could hear her at all, or see the blossoms, or the grass, in the best time of spring, depended on my having been long able to spend a large sum annually in self-indulgence, and in keeping my fellow-creatures out of my way. Of those who were causing all that murmur, like the sea, round me, and of the myriads imprisoned by the English Minotaur of lust for wealth, and condemned to live, if it is to be called life, in the labyrinth of black walls, and loathsome passages between them, which now fills the valley of the Thames, and is called London, not one could hear, that day, any happy bird sing, or look upon any quiet space of the pure grass that is good for seed.

John Ruskin, from Notes on Educational Series, *1870.*

22 APRIL

1662 *The Royal Society founded.*

1838 *The* Sirius *is the first ship to cross the Atlantic using steam power alone.*

1915 *Poison gas used for the first time, by the Germans on the Western Front.*

Now, *Erimus sicut Angeli*, says Christ, *There we shall be as the Angels . . .* There [in Heaven] our curiosity shall have this noble satisfaction, we shall know how the Angels know, by knowing as they know. We shall not pass from author, to author, as in a grammar school, nor from art to art, as in a university; but, as that general which knighted his whole army, God shall create us all doctors in a minute. That great library, those infinite volumes of the books of creatures, shall be taken away, quite away, no more Nature; those reverend manuscripts, written with God's own hand, the Scriptures themselves, shall be taken away, quite away; no more preaching, no more reading of the Scriptures, and that great school-mistress, Experience, and Observation shall be removed, no new thing to be done, and in an instant, I shall know more, than they all could reveal unto me. I shall know, not only as I know already, that a beehive, that an anthill is the same book in *decimo sexto*, as a kingdom is in *folio*, that a flower that lives but a day, is an abridgement of that king, that lives out his threescore and ten years; but I shall know too, that all these ants, and bees, and flowers, and kings, and kingdoms, howsoever they may be examples, and comparisons to one another, yet they are all as nothing, altogether nothing, less than nothing, infinitely less than nothing, to that which shall then be the subject of my knowledge, for, *it is the knowledge of the glory of God.*

John Donne, preaching in 1622 at the open-air pulpit in the churchyard of St Mary Spital (a monastic hospital dissolved in 1538) to the Lord Mayor and Aldermen of London.

23 APRIL

1349 *The Order of the Garter founded by Edward III, on St George's Day.*

1564, 1616 *Shakespeare's birthday - possibly - and date of death.*

1915 *The poet Rupert Brooke dies, on the island of Skyros.*

In these same beds, and close to a gold-mine, I found a clump of petrified trees, standing upright, with layers of fine sandstone deposited round them, bearing the impression of their bark. These trees are covered by other sandstones and streams of lava to the thickness of several thousand feet. These rocks have been deposited beneath water; yet it is clear the spot where the trees grew must once have been above the level of the sea, so that it is certain the land must have been depressed by at least as many thousand feet as the superincumbent subaqueous deposits are thick.

Charles Darwin to his sister, describing one of his geological findings on a trip over the Andes, 1835.

I do not consider that names that have been familiar for generations in England should be altered to study the whims of foreigners living in those parts. Where the name has no particular significance, the local custom should be followed. However, Constantinople should never be abandoned, though for stupid people Istanbul may be written in brackets after it. As for Angora, long familiar to us through the Angora cats, I will resist to the utmost of my power its degradation to Ankara . . . If we do not make a stand we shall in a few weeks be asked to call Leghorn Livorno, and the BBC will be pronouncing Paris Paree. Foreign names were made for Englishmen, not Englishmen for foreign names. I date this minute from St George's Day.

Winston Churchill to the Foreign Office, 1945.

24 APRIL

1900 *The* Daily Express *is launched.*

1916 *The Easter Rising begins in Dublin.*

No one was in the house but Fletcher, of which I was glad. As if he knew my wishes, he led me up a narrow stair into a small room, with nothing in it but a coffin standing on trestles. No word was spoken by either of us; he withdrew the black pall and the white shroud, and there lay the embalmed body of the Pilgrim [Byron] – more beautiful in death than in life. The contraction of the muscles and skin had effaced every line that time or passion had ever traced on it; few marble busts could have matched its stainless white, the harmony of its proportions, and perfect finish; yet he had been dissatisfied with that body, and longed to cast its slough. How often had I heard him curse it! He was jealous of the genius of Shakespeare – that might well be – but where had he seen the face or form worthy to excite his envy?

Edward John Trelawny, 1824.

I worked all day at my chambers, and had a late dinner at a club. I ordered a teal and they brought me a quail: a stone for an egg would have been a trifling disappointment in comparison. Then I went in late to the Palace [Theatre] and saw the Russians [Ballets Russes] who have sadly fallen off. [Mikhail] Mordkin has become a second-rate coquette and Pavlova smothers her genius in technique. She does nothing but dither on the tips of her toes and pretend to be the antennae of a butterfly. This deceives nobody. She and Mordkin will not dance together or even look at one another.

Raymond Asquith to his wife Katharine, 1911.

25 APRIL

The last date upon which Easter can fall.

1915 *The first British troops land at Gallipoli.*

1953 *James Watson and Francis Crick describe the structure of DNA in an article in* Nature.

But, Sir, let it be remembered that the times in which we live are not ordinary times. When we are called to encounter extraordinary and unprecedented dangers, we must lay our account to submitting to extraordinary and unprecedented difficulties. If we are called on to undergo great sacrifices, we must bear in mind the interesting objects which these sacrifices may enable us to defend and to secure. I need not remind the House that we are come to a new era in the history of nations; we are called to struggle for the destiny, not of this country alone but of the civilised world. We must remember that it is not only for ourselves that we submit to unexampled privations. We have for ourselves the great duty of self-preservation to perform; but the duty of the people of England now is of a nobler and higher order. We are in the first place to provide for our security against an enemy whose malignity to this country knows no bounds: but this is not to close the views or the efforts of our exertion in so sacred a cause. Amid the wreck and the misery of nations it is our just exultation that we have continued superior to all that ambition or that despotism could effect; and our still higher exultation ought to be that we provide not only for our own safety but hold out a prospect for nations now bending under the iron yoke of tyranny of what the exertions of a free people can effect, and that, at least in this corner of the world, the name of liberty is still revered, cherished, and sanctified.

William Pitt the Younger, in the House of Commons, 1804. The threat of a French invasion was at its height; Russia, Prussia and Austria were still at peace with France; and Napoleon was about to declare himself Emperor of the French.

26 APRIL

1937 *The Basque town of Guernica bombed by German planes fighting for Franco in the Spanish Civil War.*

1986 *A nuclear power station at Chernobyl in the Ukraine goes out of control.*

Coleridge is printing *Christabel*, by Lord Byron's recommendation to Murray, with what he calls a vision, *Kubla Khan*, which said vision he repeats so enchantingly that it irradiates and brings heaven and elysian bowers into my parlour while he sings or says it; but there is an observation, 'Never tell thy dreams', and I am almost afraid that *Kubla Khan* is an owl that won't bear daylight. I fear lest it should be discovered by the lantern of typography and clear redacting to letters no better than nonsense or no sense. When I was young I used to chant with ecstasy 'MILD ARCADIANS EVER BLOOMING', till somebody told me it was meant to be nonsense . . . Coleridge is, at present, under the medical care of a Mr Gillman (Killman?) a Highgate apothecary, where he plays at leaving off laud—m. I think his essentials not touched: he is very bad; but then he wonderfully picks up another day, and his face, when he repeats his verses, hath its ancient glory; an archangel a little damaged . . . He is absent but four miles, and the neighbourhood of such a man is as exciting as the presence of fifty ordinary persons. 'Tis enough to be within the whiff and wind of his genius for us not to possess our souls in quiet. If I lived with him or the Author of the *Excursion* [Wordsworth], I should, in a very little time, lose my own identity, and be dragged along in the current of other people's thoughts, hampered in a net. How cool I sit in this office, with no possible interruption further than what I may term *material*! . . .

N.B. – Nothing said above to the contrary, but that I hold the personal presence of the two mentioned potent spirits at a rate as high as any; but I pay dearer. What amuses others robs me of myself: my mind is positively discharged into their greater currents, but flows with a willing violence.

Charles Lamb to William Wordsworth, 1816. Coleridge was to spend the rest of his life in Highgate with the Gillmans.

27 APRIL

1828 *London Zoo opened in Regent's Park.*

1945 *American and Russian forces link up at the river Elbe.*

The Duke [of Wellington] was in force, and very frank and amusing. He said all troops ran away – that he never minded; all he cared about was whether they would come back again, and he added that he always had a succession of lines for the purpose of rallying fugitives.

John Wilson Croker, The Croker Papers, 1828. He was an arch-Tory politician, Secretary to the Admiralty and contributor to Murray's Quarterly Review.

I sent you poor old Omar ... I hardly know why I print any of these things, which nobody buys; and I scarce now see the few I give them to. But when one has done one's best, and is sure that that best is better than so many will take pains to do, though far from the best that *might be done*, one likes to make an end of the matter by print. I suppose very few people have ever taken such pains in translation as I have: though certainly not to be literal. But at all cost, a thing must *live*: with a transfusion of one's own worse life is one can't retain the original's better. Better a live sparrow than a stuffed eagle.

Edward FitzGerald to E. B. Cowell, 1859. Cowell, an oriental scholar, had introduced him to the original of The Rubáiyát of Omar Khayyám.

D—— had jokingly proposed to E—— W—— to bring back the Mahdi's toenails from the coming campaign. Kitchener, on this hint, seems to have fancied having the Mahdi's head for himself to make an inkstand of, and gave Gordon [a nephew] the order to dig the body up and keep the head for him. This accordingly was done, and at the same time finger-nails were taken by some of the young officers, but they got talking about it at Cairo and hence the trouble.

Wilfrid Scawen Blunt, Diary, 1899. General Gordon had been killed by the Mahdi's followers in 1885. Kitchener's victory at Omdurman in 1898 was seen as revenge, and after the battle the Mahdi's tomb nearby was desecrated.

28 APRIL

1945 *Mussolini and his mistress shot by partisans while trying to flee from Italy.*

1969 *De Gaulle resigns as President of France after a referendum defeat.*

Just before sun-rising . . . while I was yet asleep, Mr Christian, officer of the watch, Charles Churchill, ship's corporal, John Mills, gunner's mate, and Thomas Burkitt, seaman, came into my cabin, and seizing me, tied my hands with a cord behind my back, threatening me with instant death if I spoke or made the least noise. I called, however, as loud as I could in hopes of assistance; but they had already secured the officers who were not of their party, by placing sentinels at their doors . . .

Particular persons were called on to go into the boat and were hurried over the side; whence I concluded that with these people I was to be set adrift . . . The officers and men being in the boat, they only waited for me, of which the master-at-arms informed Christian; who then said – 'Come, Captain Bligh, your officers and men are now in the boat, and you must go with them; if you attempt to make the least resistance, you will instantly be put to death'; and without further ceremony, with a tribe of armed ruffians about me, I was forced over the side, when they untied my hands. Being in the boat, we were veered astern by a rope, a few pieces of pork were thrown to us, and some clothes, also the cutlasses I have already mentioned; and it was then that the armourer and carpenters called out to me to remember that they had no hand in the transaction. After having undergone a great deal of ridicule, and been kept for some time to make sport for these unfeeling wretches, we were at length cast adrift in the open ocean.

Captain Bligh describes the mutiny on the Bounty, *1789, in his Journal, quoted by John Barrow, Second Secretary of the Admiralty.*

29 APRIL

1914 *The zip fastener as we know it patented by Swedish engineer Gideon Sundback in New Jersey.*

1916 *The Easter Rising in Dublin collapses.*

We then went to John's Grove, sat a while at first. Afterwards William lay, and I lay, in the trench under the fence – he with his eyes shut, and listening to the waterfalls and the birds. There was not one waterfall above another – it was a sound of waters in the air – the voice of the air. William heard me breathing and rustling now and then, but we both lay still, and unseen by one another; he thought that it would be as sweet thus to lie so in the grave, to hear the *peaceful* sounds of the earth, and just to know that our dear friends were near. The lake was still; there was a boat out. Silver How reflected with delicate purple and yellowish hues, as I have seen spar; lambs on the island, and running races together by the half-dozen, in the round field near us. The copses greenish, hawthorns green. Came home to dinner, then went to Mr Simpson – we rested a long time under a wall, sheep and lambs were in the field – cottages smoking. As I lay down on the grass, I observed the glittering silver line on the ridge of the backs of the sheep, owing to their situation respecting the sun, which made them look beautiful, but with something of strangeness, like animals of another kind, as if belonging to a more splendid world.

Dorothy Wordsworth, Journal, 1802.

This is really dreadful news, my dear Louis, odious news to one who had neatly arranged this his coming August should be spent gobbling down your yarns, as the Neapolitan lazzarone puts away the lubricating filaments of the vermicelli.

Henry James to Robert Louis Stephenson, 1889,
on hearing that he is remaining abroad.

30 APRIL

Walpurgisnacht, *when German witches fly out.*

1803 *The US concludes the Louisiana Purchase, buying from Napoleon for $15 million lands to the west of the Mississippi. France had bought them secretly from Spain in 1800.*

1945 *Hitler commits suicide in his Berlin bunker.*

1975 *The Vietnam war ends with the Vietcong capture of Saigon.*

The uproar is begun at Paris, and everybody that can is leaving it . . . The French might have had a good government, if the National Assembly had had sense, experience, moderation, and integrity; but wanting all, they have given a lasting wound to liberty. They have acted, as that nation has always done, from the fashion of the hour, and with their innate qualities, cruelty and insolence.

Horace Walpole to the Countess of Ossory, 1791.

I had an obliquity the other day, an awful longing to be in London for a *leetle*, a very *leetle* while. I tried and tried what you call to reason myself out of it, and I partly succeeded, but the getting out of that folly cost me a great deal, and made me rather rough and uncomfortable. Brushing up one's reason is just as disagreeable as having one's teeth cleaned, it sets one on edge for the while . . .

I am sure you will be obliged to me for telling you, that in a shower in London, a man was running along with an umbrella, and ran against another man, this latter offended man snatched the offending umbrella, out of the umbrel*lee*'s hands, and throwing it away said, 'Where are you running to like a mad mushroom?'

If Aunt gets better soon, I will go up in a week or two, and have a look at you, and get a hat. Your Leghorn [fine-plaited-straw hat] sounds well, but I never yet found home-brewed bonnets answer, they are always ill-disposed, full of bad habits, and get awkward crics about them.

Pamela, Lady Campbell to Emily Eden, 1820.

MAY

1 MAY

1707 *Scotland and England joined by the Act of Union.*

1851 *Opening by Queen Victoria of the Great Exhibition in the Crystal Palace.*

1941 *Première of Orson Welles's film* Citizen Kane, *regularly voted the best-ever.*

I am glad you got on so well with Monsieur le Curé. Is he a nice clergyman? A great deal depends upon a cocked hat and powder – not gunpowder, lord love us, but lady-meal, violet-smooth, dainty-scented, lilywhite, feather-soft, wigsby-dressing, coat-collar-spoiling, whisker-reaching, pig-tail loving, swansdown-puffing, parson-sweetening powder . . .

O there is nothing like fine weather, and health, and books, and a fine country, and a contented mind, and diligent habit of reading and thinking, as an amulet against the ennui – and, please heaven, a little claret-wine cool out of a cellar a mile deep, with a few or a good many ratafia [almond] cakes, a rocky basin to bathe in, a strawberry bed to say your prayers to Flora in, a pad nag to go you ten miles or so, two or three sensible people to chat with, two or three spiteful folks to spar with, two or three odd fishes to laugh at and two or three numbskulls to argue with – instead of using dumb-bells on a rainy day.

Goodbye, I've an appointment – can't stop 'pon my word – goodbye – now don't get up – open the door myself – go-o-o-dbye – see ye Monday.

John Keats to Fanny Keats, from Hampstead, 1819.

It must be very nearly half-past nine I am sure: ring the bell for the tea-things to be removed – pray turn the lamp – at ten the married people go to bed: I sit up till twelve, sometimes diverging into the kitchen, where I smoke amid the fumes of cold mutton that has formed (I suppose) the maids' supper. But the pleasant thing is to wake early, throw open the window, and lie reading in bed. . . . The wheat begins to look yellow; the clover layers are beginning to blossom, before they have grown to any height; and the grass won't grow: stock, therefore, will be very cheap, because of the great want of keep. That is poetry.

Edward FitzGerald to W.F. Pollock, from Geldestone Hall, Beccles, 1840.

2 MAY

1611 *The Authorized (King James) Bible published.*

1982 *The Argentinian cruiser* General Belgrano *is sunk by the submarine HMS* Conqueror *with the loss of 368 lives.*

After inspecting our [the National Trust's] mill at Burnham Staithe I walked to Burnham Market [in north Norfolk]. No food at the Hoste Arms, but at the Nelson I got beer, sausage rolls and hot meat rolls. There were evacuees toping at the bar and recounting their bomb experiences in London. 'The wife said to me, she said, did you ever? Me and my kiddies,' etc. Slightly drunk on a pint of bitter, after my walk, I joined in the conversation and found myself recounting my experiences (they were non-existent) of the Germans and their atrocities. 'Would you believe it,' I said, 'they cut out the heart and began . . . ?' 'Well, I never,' they said in a chorus of delight. Cockneys are good-hearted people. These particularly deplored warfare against women and children. Yes, I said, and put in a plea against the deliberate bombing of our cathedrals and churches, to test their reaction. Reaction: 'One in a hundred may care for such old-fashioned places. They are all right to see now and then. It's flesh and blood what matters. For myself, the whole lot can go. Hear! Hear!' All most good-natured and honestly meant. Philistines!

The old cottages in this part of the world are faced with smooth flints, or large pebbles picked from the shore, and washed smooth by the sea. They give a cream to the strawberry brick walls. Sometimes they look like Easter eggs stacked in a pile by children. All along the coast to Cromer there is a great structure of iron barricading, covered with barbed wire in defence against the invaders, if they should come this way.

James Lees-Milne, Diary, Ancestral Voices, 1942.

3 MAY

---—⊛—---

326 *Discovery of the True Cross by St Helena, mother of the Emperor Constantine, in Jerusalem.*

1951 *The Festival of Britain is opened in London.*

Now we are in the Dardanelles waiting for a wind to proceed to Constantinople. This morning I *swam* from Sestos to Abydos, the immediate distance is not a above a mile but the current renders it hazardous, so much so, that I doubt whether Leander's conjugal powers must not have been exhausted in his passage to Paradise. I attempted it a week ago and failed owing to the north wind and the wonderful rapidity of the tide, though I have been from my childhood a strong swimmer, but this morning being calmer I succeeded and crossed the 'broad Hellespont' in an hour and ten minutes . . .

I see not much difference between ourselves and the Turks, save that we have foreskins and they none, that they have long dresses and we short, and that we talk much and they little. In England the vices in fashion are whoring and drinking, in Turkey, sodomy and smoking; we prefer a girl and a bottle, they a pipe and pathic [catamite] . . . I like the Greeks, who are plausible rascals, with all the Turkish vices without their courage. However some are brave and all are beautiful, very much resembling the busts of Alcibiades, the women not quite so handsome . . .

At Malta I fell in love with a married woman and challenged an aide-de-camp of General Oakes (a rude fellow who grinned at something, I never rightly knew what), but he explained and apologised, and the lady embarked for Cadiz, and so I escaped murder and adultery.

Lord Byron to Henry Drury, on board the frigate Salsette, *1810. In the legend to which he refers, Leander swam the Hellespont every night to be with the priestess Hero; one night he drowned, whereupon Hero threw herself into the sea.*

4 MAY

1780 *The first Derby horse-race is run at Epsom.*

1926 *The General Strike begins.*

1979 *Margaret Thatcher becomes Prime Minister.*

I smoked a pipe and drank a flask of wine on the top of the Antonine Column. Here we found two or three boys amusing themselves with angling for swallows, which they were very dextrous at. They baited their hooks with feathers.

Thomas Jones, Diary, Rome, 1778.

I thought a great deal about beginning my work, but thinking was all I did. I have a positive hatred of the pen. By and by it will die away, and when I begin I shall go on, but to begin is the trial. Folk make light of these sufferings of mine. They are really profound. There is the paper, there the books and there the pen. I look at them, abhor them. They are personal enemies. To touch them is like taking a powder when I was a boy. Then I am afraid of them. Some evil will happen if I lift them: some deadly disease will seize me. Then duty calls, and where duty puts in her oar I run away. And then I take a paint brush. All the pain is overwhelmed with joy. I sweep away books, pen and paper and do my own will and my own pleasure. It is a sorrowful record of iniquity.

Stopford Book, Diary, 1899.

5 MAY

———⊛———

1646 *Charles I surrenders to the Scottish army at Newark at the end of the Civil War.*

1760 *The Earl Ferrers becomes the last nobleman to be hanged after trial by his peers. The 'drop' device is used for the first time, as well as a silk-covered rope, the latter a privilege reserved for the nobility.*

1821 *Death of Napoleon on the island of St Helena.*

My dearest people, I have had a great piece of news. There has been offered for *Treasure Island* – how much do you suppose? I believe it would be an excellent jest to keep the answer till my next letter. For two cents I would do so. Shall I? Anyway I'll turn the page first. No – well – A hundred pounds, all alive, oh! A hundred jingling, tingling, golden, minted quid. Is not this wonderful? Add that I have now finished, in draft, the fifteenth chapter of my novel, and have only five before me; and you will see what cause of gratitude I have.

Robert Louis Stevenson to his parents, 1883. The £100 covered the first 4000 printed. He got £20 per 1000 thereafter. The 'novel' was Prince Otto.

An exact diary of the [General] Strike would be interesting. For instance, it is now a quarter to two; there is a brown fog; nobody is building; it is drizzling. The first thing in the morning we stand at the window and watch the traffic in Southampton Row. This is incessant. Everyone is bicycling; motor cars are huddled up with extra people. There are no buses. No placards. No newspapers. Water, gas and electricity are allowed; but at eleven the light was turned off . . . It is all tedious and depressing, rather like waiting in a train outside a station. One does not know what to do . . . A voice, rather commonplace and official, wishes us good morning at ten. This is the Voice of Britain, to which we can make no reply. The voice is very trivial, and only tells us that the Prince of Wales is coming back, that the London streets present an unprecedented spectacle.

Virginia Woolf, Diary, 1926.

6 MAY

1626 *Manhattan bought by the Dutch for 24 dollars-worth of trade goods.*

1954 *Roger Bannister runs the first four-minute mile.*

1994 *The Channel Tunnel is officially opened.*

Your grace's displeasure and my imprisonment are things so strange unto me, that what to write, or what to excuse, I am altogether ignorant. Let not your grace ever imagine that your poor wife will ever be brought to acknowledge a fault, where not so much as thought thereof proceeded. And to speak truth, never prince had wife more loyal in all duty, and in all true affection, than you have found in Anne Bulen – with which name and place I could willingly have contented myself, if God and your grace's pleasure had so been pleased.

Try me, good king, but let me have a lawful trial, and let not my sworn enemies sit as my accusers and as my judges; yea, let me receive an open trial, for my truth shall fear no open shame . . .

But if you have already determined of me, and that not only my death, but an infamous slander must bring you the joying of your desired happiness, then I desire of God that he will pardon your great sin herein . . .

My last and only request shall be, that myself may only bear the burden of your grace's displeasure, and that it may not touch the innocent souls of those poor gentlemen, who, as I understand, are likewise in strait imprisonment for my sake.

Anne Boleyn to her husband Henry VIII, from her 'doleful prison' in the Tower of London, 1536. She was beheaded at the Tower on 19 May.

7 MAY

1765 *HMS* Victory *is launched at Chatham.*

1915 *The liner* Lusitania *is sunk by a German submarine and among the 1,153 dead are 128 Americans. This does much to turn public opinion in the US against Germany.*

1954 *Fall of Dien Bien Phu to the Vietminh marks end of French rule in Indochina.*

The middle-aged, motherly receptionist said, with a telephone to her ear, 'Sakes alive, Mr Agate, my daughter has just called me to say she's heard on the radio that there's been an explosion in the *Hindenburg* [the German airship] with everybody killed.'

Within a minute people were saying 'Sabotage'. Somebody in the lounge who appeared to know about these things said that normally the ship would have avoided the storm and delayed making her moorings, but that she couldn't afford to do this as she had to return to England last night with a full complement of passengers for the Coronation, and to pick up films. The special editions of the newspapers struck me as being slow in coming out, but the electric news-signs got busy at once and Times Square was almost impassable . . . New York is deeply moved by the tragedy, and nobody can understand why hydrogen was used. It is thought that if not lightning, then some electric friction in the air – supposing there is such a thing – was the cause. If it wasn't, then the disaster happening at the same time as the storm is an extravagant coincidence.

James Agate, Ego, New York, 1937. A new explanation for the fire puts the blame not on the hydrogen inside but on the highly inflammable paint coating the outside, ignited by static electricity.

8 MAY

The Furry, or Floral, Dance is performed through the streets of Helston in Cornwall.

1886 *Coca-Cola goes on sale for the first time, in Atlanta, Georgia.*

1945 *VE (Victory in Europe) Day.*

It went off very well though her Majesty looked matronly and aged and the ladies in attendance on her were an affecting spectacle. The only accurate idea that I can give you of the Exhibition is that it is a great fair under a cucumber frame . . . The Queen sat in the centre with the crowd around and behind her, and I was lucky enough to get a place in the front row of one of the galleries immediately overlooking the chair of state, and almost exactly over the head of your aged and infirm friend the Duke of Wellington. The proceedings were in the nature of pantomime as I could not hear a single syllable either of the address or the answer to it . . . There is an immense amount of wealth, industry and ingenuity and all that sort of thing: and I suppose the best of all things that can be manufactured is there: but no one thing can make much impression in such a mass: the point of the scene is their number and the good effect of the whole . . . The foreign departments are much behindhand: the United States especially: indeed at present nothing satisfactory can be collected except that in that country they are extremely well off for soap. They have an immense compartment all to themselves at the end of the nave and nothing hardly in it except busts in soap of the Queen and other people. It must be amusing to wash yourself with yourself.

The economist and journalist Walter Bagehot to his mother, describing the opening of the Great Exhibition at the Crystal Palace in Hyde Park, 1851.

9 MAY

1785 *The beer pump is patented by Joseph Bramah, who also invented machine tools, a lock, an hydraulic press, a water-closet, and an 'ever-pointed' pencil.*

1936 *The birthday of the actors Glenda Jackson and Albert Finney.*

All the anguish was yours; and in general this experience only rubs in what I have always known, that in battles, sieges and other great calamities, the pathos and agony is in general solely felt by those at a distance; and although physical pain is suffered most by its immediate victims, those at the scene of action have no sentimental suffering whatever. Everyone at San Francisco seemed in a good hearty frame of mind; there was work for every moment of the day and a kind of uplift in the sense of a 'common lot' that took away the sense of loneliness that (I imagine) gives the sharpest edge to the more usual kind of misfortune that may befall a man. But it was a queer sight, on our journey through the city on the 26th (eight days after the disaster), to see the inmates of the houses of the quarter left standing, all cooking their dinners at little brick camp-fires in the middle of the street, the chimneys being condemned. If such a disaster had to happen, somehow it couldn't have chosen a better place than San Francisco (where everyone knew about camping, and was familiar with the creation of civilizations out of the bare ground), and at five-thirty in the morning, when few fires were lighted and everyone, after a good sleep, was in bed. Later, there would have been great loss of life in the streets, and the more numerous foci of conflagration would have burned the city in one day instead of four, and made things vastly worse.

The psychologist and philosopher William James to his son, William James, Junior, and brother, the writer Henry James, after the San Francisco earthquake and fire of 1906. The recipients were in England.

143

10 MAY

1857 *The Indian Mutiny begins.*

1869 *The US transcontinental railroad completed when the Central Pacific meets the Union Pacific in Utah.*

1940 *Churchill becomes Prime Minister.*

Lady Hamilton did attitudes in a shawl of Lady Essex's, who looked inspired and will I hope shortly take to doing them herself . . . Lord Byron is still on a pedestal and Caroline William [Lady Caroline Lamb, Lady Granville's cousin] doing homage. I have made acquaintance with him. He is agreeable and I feel no wish for any further intimacy. His countenance is fine when it is in repose, but the moment it is in play, suspicious, malignant, and consequently repulsive. His manner is either remarkably gracious and conciliatory, with a tinge of affectation, or irritable and impetuous, and then I am afraid perfectly natural.

Lady Granville to her brother, the Duke of Devonshire, 1812. Emma Hamilton first performed her 'attitudes' - tableaux vivants or improvised dramatic poses - in Naples in the 1780s, when she was the British Envoy Sir William Hamilton's mistress, before she met Nelson.

London had its biggest blitz to date. From my attic window the view was one of beauty and awe. Against the glow of the distant fires the Odeon Cinema and other daytime-ugly buildings at Swiss Cottage stood out like the battlements of Elsinore. I could smell my neighbour's thorn and cherry trees, now in full flower, drenched by the full moon. Presently I heard drops of what in that empty sky could not be water. It was shrapnel, and I wondered what Debussy would have made of this garden under that rain.

James Agate, Ego, 1941. The death toll ran to 1,436 and among the buildings hit were the House of Commons, the British Museum and the Inns of Court.

11 MAY

1812 *The Prime Minister, Spencer Perceval, is assassinated.*

1922 *Britain's first radio station, 2LO, goes on air.*

1981 *Première, in London, of the musical* Cats, *based on verses by T. S. Eliot.*

We don't allow it to be a victory on the French side: but that is, just as a woman is not called *Mrs* till she is married, though she may have had half-a-dozen natural children. In short, we remained upon the field of battle three hours; I fear, too many of us remain there still! without palliating, it is certainly a heavy stroke. We never lost near so many officers . . . The whole *hors de combat* is above seven thousand three hundred. The French own the loss of three thousand; I don't believe many more, for it was a most rash and desperate perseverance on our side.

Horace Walpole to Sir Horace Mann, 1745. The British lost
the Battle of Fontenoy against the French.

We went [to the Great Exhibition] and O how – tired I was! Not that it was not really a very beautiful sight – especially at the entrance; the three large trees, built in, because the people objected to their being cut down, a crystal fountain, and a large blue canopy give one a momentary impression of a bazaar in the *Arabian Nights Entertainments;* and such a lot of things of different kinds and of well dressed people – for the tickets were still five shillings – was rather imposing for a few minutes; but when you come to look at the wares in detail there was nothing really worth looking at – at least that one could not have seen samples of in the shops. The big diamond indeed – worth a million! *that* one could not have seen at any jeweller's; but O Babbie what a disappointment! for the big diamond – unset – looked precisely like a bit of crystal the size and shape of the first joint of your thumb!

Jane Welsh Carlyle to Jeannie Welsh, 1851.

12 MAY

Traditionally, the day on which cows are put out to pasture.

1949 *The Berlin blockade, mounted by the Russians, is lifted. It began on 1 April 1948 and some 277,264 flights by the western allies - the Berlin Airlift - have kept the city supplied, even with coal.*

Let us then make such amends as we can for the mischiefs we have done to the unhappy continent [Africa]; let us recollect what Europe itself was no longer ago than three or four centuries. What if I should be able to show this House that in a civilised part of Europe, in the time of our Henry VII, there were people who actually sold their own children? What if I should tell them that England itself was that country? What if I should point out to them that the very place where this inhuman traffic was carried on was the city of Bristol? Ireland at that time used to drive a considerable trade in slaves with these neighbouring barbarians; but a great plague having infested the country, the Irish were struck with a panic, suspected (I am sure very properly) that the plague was a punishment sent from heaven for the sin of the slave trade, and therefore abolished it. All I ask, therefore, of the people of Bristol is, that they would become as civilised now as Irishmen were four hundred years ago. Let us put an end at once to this inhuman traffic – let us stop this effusion of human blood.

William Wilberforce, speaking in the House of Commons, 1789.

The [General] Strike was settled about 1.15 . . . I saw this morning five or six armoured cars slowly going along Oxford Street; on each two soldiers sat in tin helmets, and one stood with his hand at the gun which was pointed straight ahead ready to fire. But I also noticed on one a policeman smoking a cigarette. Such sights I dare say I shall never see again; and don't in the least wish to.

Virginia Woolf, Diary, 1926.

13 MAY

1958 *The Fourth French Republic ends because of the crisis caused by the Algerian civil war.*

1981 *The attempted assassination of Pope John Paul II in St Peter's Square.*

I say to the House as I said to Ministers who have joined this government, I have nothing to offer but blood, toil, tears and sweat. We have before us an ordeal of the most grievous kind. We have before us many, many months of struggle and suffering.

You ask, what is our policy? I say it is to wage war by land, sea and air. War with all our might and with all the strength God has given us, and to wage war against a monstrous tyranny never surpassed in the dark and lamentable catalogue of human crime. That is our policy.

You ask, what is our aim? I can answer in one word. It is victory. Victory at all costs – victory in spite of all terrors – victory, however long and hard the road may be, for without victory there is no survival.

Let that be realised. No survival for the British Empire, no survival for all that the British Empire has stood for, no survival for the urge, the impulse of the ages, that mankind shall move forward toward his goal.

I take up my task in buoyancy and hope. I feel sure that our cause will not be suffered to fail among men.

I feel entitled at this juncture, at this time, to claim the aid of all and to say, 'Come then, let us go forward together with our united strength.'

Winston Churchill's first speech to the House of Commons after becoming Prime Minister, 1940.

14 MAY

1796 *Edward Jenner uses smallpox vaccination for the first time.*

1804 *The Lewis and Clark expedition, the first to reach the Pacific Coast of America, sets out from St Louis.*

1948 *Declaration of Independence by Israel.*

The ladies [John Singer Sargent] paints, according to Meynell, generally bore him so much that he is obliged to retire every now and then behind a screen and refresh himself by putting out his tongue at them.

Wilfrid Scawen Blunt, Diary, 1907.

But I'm not sorry for people who are killed. It must be better to be dead than alive in a world like the present one. I am sure of it but I don't go about saying so. And I don't mind either my own body rotting above ground. But I'm sorry for those who have to live for days in its immediate company.

There's no doubt that there is deep resentment among the troops at the attitude of the press and the old men. Lloyd George brought back the message from the Army 'We are all right. Don't worry.' What does he know after motoring to Abbéville and back and seeing Sir Douglas Haig? Men are naturally reticent and wish to spare others . . . Many of those who have killed a German have it on their minds and it haunts them. But even clever men like Mr Balfour and Lord Curzon have no imagination, it seems. The next time they kill a pig at Whittinghame [Arthur Balfour's house in Scotland] let Mr Balfour take it on single-handed with a bayonet. Then he may get a glimmer of what the 'joy of battle' means.

Conrad Russell to his sister Flora, 1918.

15 MAY

1940 *Nylon stockings launched, in the US.*

1941 *The first flight of Sir Frank Whittle's jet aircraft. The first-ever jet was Ernst Heinkel's He 178, which flew in Germany in August 1939.*

I had one of the most curiously beautiful [bicycle] rides of my life. I got to Milton: saw the church, in its green shade, with its elaborately written monuments, its glorious little window of Jacob, with hands like parsnips: then crossed the line, among the green pastures, so full of great thorn-thickets: and then along the towpath, riding slowly down the Cam. Such a sweet clear, fresh day. I wound slowly along past Baitsbite and the Waterbeach bridge, into the heart of the fen. The space below the towpath full of masses of cow-parsley: the river sapphire blue between the green banks – the huge fields running for miles to the right, with the long lines of dyke and lode; far away the blue tower of Ely, the brown roofs of Reach, and the low wolds of Newmarket. It was simply *enchanting*! . . . So I wound on and on, full of peace and content; I declare that the *absolutely* flat country, golden with buttercups, and the blue tree-clumps far away backed by hills, and over all the vast sky-perspective, is the most beautiful thing *of all* . . . Then Monty [M.R. James] came in to tea, very solemn and well-dressed, blue suit and black tie; the *Provost*! [just elected, of King's College, Cambridge] . . . He told me how he was sent for after the first scrutiny and asked if he would accept. There was a green table set out by the choir door inside, and fellows in nearly all the stalls [of the chapel]. He accepted, and they filed out shaking hands. He told me too how the choir-boys asked to see him, and did him a simple homage in their vestry. Very nice!

A. C. Benson, Diary, 1905.

16 MAY

---•✦•---

1943 *The Dambuster Raid on the Ruhr Valley by 617 Squadron, RAF.*

1983 *The first wheel clamps are used in London.*

When I was sitting in Mr Davies's back parlour, after having drunk tea with him and Mrs Davies, Johnson unexpectedly came into the shop . . . Mr Davies mentioned my name, and respectfully introduced me to him. I was much agitated; and recollecting his prejudice against the Scotch, of which I had heard much, I said to Davies, 'Don't tell where I come from.' – 'From Scotland,' cried Davies, roguishly. 'Mr Johnson,' said I, 'I do indeed come from Scotland, but I cannot help it.' I am willing to flatter myself that I meant this as light pleasantry to soothe and conciliate him, and not a humiliating abasement at the expense of my country . . . He retorted, 'That, Sir, I find, is what a very great many of your countrymen cannot help.' This stroke stunned me a good deal; and when we had sat down, I felt myself not a little embarrassed, and apprehensive of what might come next. He then addressed himself to Davies: 'What do you think of Garrick? He has refused me an order [free ticket] for the play for Miss Williams, because he knows the house will be full, and that an order would be worth three shillings.' Eager to take any opening to get into conversation with him, I ventured to say, 'O Sir, I cannot think Mr Garrick would grudge such a trifle to you.' 'Sir,' said he, with a stern look, 'I have known David Garrick longer than you have done: and I know no right you have to talk to me on the subject.'

James Boswell, Life of Johnson. *The meeting took place in 1763. Mr Davies was an actor and bookseller who lived in Russell Street, Covent Garden.*

17 MAY

1824 *Meeting at 50 Albemarle Street of John Murray II, John Murray III (only 16 years old), Thomas Moore, John Cam Hobhouse and representatives of Lady Byron and Byron's half-sister Augusta Leigh. They decide there and then to burn the only copy of Byron's memoirs, which they do in the drawing room grate.*

1900 *Mafeking relieved in the Boer War.*

A panel slides back discreetly and we find ourselves in Radio City Music Hall [in New York], which is exactly like the interior of an airship hangar. What light there is filters through hundreds of slats. There are six thousand two hundred seats. The screen measures seventy feet by forty. The drop-curtain weighs three tons. A news-budget is in progress with the house in darkness. This over, the lights go up and we become aware of a symphony orchestra; I reflect that here is the concert hall of which Berlioz dreamt. The orchestra plays an overture with Beechamesque punctilio, while changes of lighting bathe the audience in a glow of tender dawn warming to wanton sunset. The band returns hydraulically to the place whence it came, having done great execution. A lady clad entirely in diamonds now goes through the motions of the *haute école* with the assistance of a dazzlingly white horse. This concluded, we arrive at the Rockettes. There are thirty-six of them. They are as good as the Tiller Girls. Then comes the new Fred Astaire–Ginger Rogers picture *Shall We Dance?* Which I permit myself to refrain from seeing.

James Agate, Ego, *1937.*

18 MAY

1803 *War with France recommences after the Peace of Amiens.*

1804 *Napoleon proclaimed Emperor.*

1944 *German stronghold at Monte Cassino captured.*

I write to you in haste and at past two in the morning – having besides had an accident. In going, about an hour and a half ago, to a rendezvous with a Venetian girl (unmarried and the daughter of one of their nobles), I tumbled into the Grand Canal, and not choosing to miss my appointment by the delays of changing, I have been perched in a balcony with my wet clothes on ever since – till this minute that on my return I have slipped into my dressing-gown. My foot slipped in getting into my gondola to set out (owing to the cursed slippery steps of their palaces) and in I flounced like a carp – and went dripping like a triton to my sea-nymph – and had to scramble up to a grated window . . . The fair one is eighteen – her name Angelina – the family name of course I don't tell you. She proposed to me to divorce my mathematical wife – and I told her that in England we can't divorce except for *female* infidelity – 'and pray, (said she), how do you know what she may have been doing these last three years?' – I answered *that* I could not tell – but that the status of Cuckoldom was not quite so flourishing in Great Britain as with us here. – But – She said – 'can't you get rid of her?' – 'not more than is done already' (I answered) – 'you would not have me *poison her*?' – would you believe it? She made me *no answer* – is not that a true and odd national trait? – it spoke more than a thousand words – and yet this is a little – pretty – sweet-tempered – quiet, feminine being as ever you saw – but the Passions of a Sunny Soil are paramount to all other considerations.

Lord Byron to John Murray, 1819.

19 MAY

1588 *The Spanish Armada sets sail from Lisbon.*

1936 *Margaret Mitchell's novel about the American Civil War,* Gone With the Wind, *is published.*

The chamber destined for the Sultan, when he visits his daughter, is wainscoted with mother of pearl fastened with emeralds like nails. There are others of mother of pearl and olive wood inlaid, and several of Japan china. The galleries, which are numerous and very large, are adorned with jars of flowers, and porcelain dishes of fruit of all sorts, so well done in plaster, and coloured in so lively a manner, that it has an enchanting effect. The garden is suitable to the house, where arbours, fountains, and walks, are thrown together in an agreeable confusion. There is no ornament wanting, except that of statues . . . I am almost of opinion they have a right notion of life; while they consume it in music, gardens, wine, and delicate eating, while we are tormenting our brains with some scheme of politics, or studying some science to which we can never attain.

> *Lady Mary Wortley Montagu to the Abbé Conti, 1718, about a house in*
> *Constantinople belonging to a daughter of the Sultan.*

Sauntered a good deal in the garden, bound carpets, mended old clothes. Read *Timon of Athens*. Dried linen. Molly weeded the turnips, John stuck the peas . . . sauntered a long time among the rocks above the church . . . The quietness and still seclusion of the valley affected me even to producing the deepest melancholy. I forced myself from it.

> *Dorothy Wordsworth, Journal, 1800.*

20 MAY

1913 *The Royal Horticultural Society Flower Show is held at Chelsea for the first time.*

1927, 1932 *Charles Lindbergh and Amelia Earhart set off on their solo flights across the Atlantic.*

1941 *Crete is invaded by German airborne troops.*

And as for Hellesdon, my Lord of Suffolk was there on Wednesday in Whitsun week, and there dined, and drew a stew [netted a pond], and took great plenty of fish. Yet hath he left you a pike or two again ye come, the which would be great comfort to all your friends and discomfort to your enemies; for at his being there that day there was never no man that played Herod in Corpus Christi play better and more agreeable to his pageant than he did. But ye shall understand that it was after noon, and the weather hot, and he so feeble for sickness that his legs would not bear him, but there was two men had great pain to keep him on his feet. And there ye were judged. Some said, 'Slay'; some said, 'Put him in prison.' And forth came my lord, and he would meet you with a spear, and have none other mends for that trouble at ye have put him to but your heart blood, and that will he get with his own hands; for an ye have Hellesdon and Drayton ye shall have his life with it.

J. Whetley to John Paston II, 1478. The properties of Hellesdon and Drayton were claimed by John de la Pole, second Duke of Suffolk, and also by the Paston family. The duke held a manorial court to condemn John Paston.

I have at length finished *The Master* [*of Ballantrae*]; it has been a sore cross to me; but now he is buried, his body's under hatches – his soul, if there is any hell to go to, gone to hell; and I forgive him . . .

I love the Polynesian: this civilisation of ours is a dingy, ungentlemanly business; it drops out too much of man, and too much of that the very beauty of the poor beast.

Robert Louis Stevenson, in Honolulu, to W.H. Low, 1889.

21 MAY

1471 *Probable murder of Henry VI in the Tower of London. Eton and King's College, Cambridge, his two foundations, annually provide lilies and roses for the memorial service in Wakefield's Tower oratory there.*

1927, 1932 *Charles Lindbergh and Amelia Earhart complete the first solo Altantic flights - hers the first by a woman.*

Sailed at two, Saturday; landed at passage within the Cove of Cork last night at six. All sick, but the children so good and patient. I was quite proud of my brood, even the baby showed an *esprit de conduite* that edified me. Six boats came out and fought for our bodies under the ship till I thought we should be torn to pieces in the scrimmage. They, however, landed us whole, when another battle was *livrée* for us among the jingle-boys who were to whisk us to Cork. We were stowed in three of these said carrioles called jingles, driven by half-naked barefoot boys who began *whirrrring, harrrrowing*, cutting jokes, talking Irish, and galloping in these skeleton cars till the children caught the infection, laughed and roared and kicked with delight. A violent shower came on. Who cares? thinks I, they must have Irish blood in their veins, for this is very like English misery, but they naturally think it *Fun*. We arrived in tearing spirits, very wet, and were cheated of a considerable sum in shillings. We are in an excellent hotel and set off early for Limerick. Nobody dare travel late in this poor country. Oh, Emily, it is melancholy to see the misery and cunning and degradation of these poor people. I could cry, and I sit looking about, having heard so much of them all, that it appears to me I am recollecting all I see! . . . Such beggars! they show me such legs! and one was driven up in a barrow, legless!

Pamela, Lady Campbell to Emily Eden, 1827.

22 MAY

1455 *The Battle of St Albans, the start of the Wars of the Roses in England.*

1611 *The title of baronet instituted by James I, largely to raise money.*

1915 *Britain's worst train crash, near Gretna Green, 227 killed.*

Passing through Leicester Square, meet Alan Skinner, and walk with him in the flower avenue of Covent Garden . . . Then we dine at Bertolini's pleasantly. I show him the local curiosity, old Mr Seymour, now eighty-two, who has dined here every day for the last forty-three years: he comes at five, stays till eight, sits always in the box on the left-hand of the fireplace as you go up the room, which is kept for him at this time of day; has the joint, college pudding, a gill of Marsala; puts his feet up and sleeps or snoozes for about twenty minutes, then reads the *Daily News*, fidgeting a good deal with the paper, for his hands tremble. Finally he puts on hat, buttons coat up to the throat, straightens his spine and walks down the middle of the room very stiff and wooden, driving off, the waiter says, to his house somewhere near the Regent's Park. I should mention that when he comes in every evening the waiter who receives him invariably says, 'Good evening, Mr Seymour: you are looking very well this evening, Mr Seymour.' Looks like a solitary old bachelor, lawyer or attorney, dried up, penurious; the daily tavern dinner a sort of loophole glimpse of the outside world. Save a word or two to the waiters he never speaks to anyone at Bert's. Skinner departed and I went into the Alhambra and see some good dancing, but the opera-glass is a terrible disenchanter. Next me a bald civil quiet gentleman with his wife and daughters.

William Allingham, Diary, 1868.

23 MAY

1618 *The Defenestration of Prague, when the Emperor's representatives are thrown out of a window, starts the Thirty Years' War.*

1934 *Armed robbers and murderers Bonnie Parker and Clyde Barrow are killed at a police roadblock in Louisiana.*

How very odd, dear Lady Holland, to ask me to dine with you on Sunday, the 9th, when I am coming to stay with you from the 5th to the 12th! It is like giving a gentleman an assignation for Wednesday, when you are going to marry him on the preceding Sunday – an attempt to combine the stimulus of gallantry with the security of connubial relations. I do not propose to be guilty of the slightest infidelity to you while I am at Holland House, except you dine in town; and then it will not be infidelity, but spirited recrimination.

The Revd Sydney Smith to Lady Holland, 1811.

Found Scott sitting to Chantrey, with Rogers, Coke of Norfolk . . . When Sir W. went away Chantrey begged of R. and me to stay and keep Coke in talk during his sitting to him. Got him upon old times; told a strange story (which I find Rogers more inclined to swallow than I am) of a dinner given by Lord Petre to Fox and Burke after their great quarrel, and of a contrivance prepared by Lord Petre to introduce the subject of their difference, and afford an opportunity of making it up. This was no less than a piece of confectionery in the middle of the table representing the Bastille! 'Come, Burke,' said Lord Petre, at the dessert, 'attack that Bastille.' Burke declined. 'Well, Fox,' continued his Lordship, 'Do *you* do it.' 'That I will, by G—,' said Fox, and instantly dashed at it.

Tom Moore, Diary, 1828. Francis Chantrey's bust of Sir Walter Scott was one of the most famous sculptures of the day. Fox favoured the French Revolution; Burke condemned it.

24 MAY

1819 *Queen Victoria born.*

1883 *Brooklyn Bridge opened.*

1972 *Spaghetti Junction of the M5 and M6 opened north of Birmingham.*

There is a distressing taste for sapphism in my herd. They submit to and even provoke the very warmest embraces from their own sex and then when William comes (the bull) they reject his advances. And as soon as he has gone they carry on again among one another. It's very disgusting and such depravity is surprising among creatures that look so gentle and innocent. But one finds vice where it is least expected.

Conrad Russell to Katharine Asquith, 1921.

Ta muchly, ole man, for your very generous present of this superb edition of *Love Among the Ruins*. It could not have come at a more appropriate moment, for only last Sunday I visited Stevenage New Town in the rainy afternoon. It was exactly like your book. Three miles of Lionel Brett-style prefabs interrupted by Hugh Casson blocks of flats and two shopping arcades and concrete roads and lampposts throughout and no trees, only muddy Hertfordshire inclines. I saw through the vast, unprivate ground floor window of a house, grey-faced woman washing up. My goodness, it was terrifying. And kiddies' scooters lying out in the rain on the streets and a big vita-glass school on stilts. The inhabitants have been driven out of Tottenham to live in it.

John Betjeman to Evelyn Waugh, 1953. Lionel Brett and
Hugh Casson were contemporary architects.

25 MAY

1768 *Captain Cook sets sail on his first voyage to the Pacific.*

1977 *The first* Star Wars *film is released.*

By the morning we were come close to the land, and every body made ready to get on shore. The King and the two Dukes did eat their breakfast before they went; and there being set some ship's diet before them, only to show them the manner of the ship's diet, they ate of nothing else but pease and pork, and boiled beef . . . I went, and Mr Mansell, and one of the King's footmen, and a dog that the King loved (which shit in the boat, which made us laugh and me think that a king and all that belong to him are but just as others are) in a boat by ourselves, and so got on shore when the King did, who was received by General Monck with all imaginable love and respect at his entrance upon the land at Dover. Infinite the crowd of people and the gallantry of the horsemen, citizens, and noblemen of all sorts. The Mayor of the town came and gave him his white staff, the badge of his place, which the King did give him again. The Mayor also presented him from the town a very rich Bible, which he took and said it was the thing that he loved above all things in the world. A canopy was provided for him to stand under; which he did; and talked awhile with General Monck and others; and so into a stately coach there set for him; and so away straight through the town towards Canterbury without making any stay at Dover. The shouting and joy expressed by all is past imagination.

Samuel Pepys, Diary 1660. King Charles II and his brothers the dukes of
York and Gloucester return to England at the Restoration.

26 MAY

1868 *Last public execution outside Newgate Prison in London, of an Irish Fenian bomber.*

1908 *First commercial discovery of oil, in Iran.*

1950 *Petrol rationing in Britain ends.*

Rose at three o'clock – Rang the great bell, and roused the girls to milking – went up to the farm, roused the horse-keeper – fed the horses while he was getting up – called the boy to suckle the calves, and clean out the cow-house – lighted the pipe, walked round the gardens to see what was wanting there – went up the paddock to see if the weanling calves were well – went down to the ferry, to see whether the boy had scooped and cleaned the boats – returned to the farm – examined the shoulders, heels, traces, chaff, and corn of eight horses going to plough – mended the acre staff – cut some thongs, whipcorded the boys' plough whips – pumped the troughs full – saw the hogs fed – examined the swill tubs, and then the cellar – ordered a quarter of malt, for the hogs want grains, and the men want beer – filled the pipe again, returned to the river, and bought a lighter of turf for dairy fires, and another of sedge for ovens – hunted up the wheelbarrows and set them a trundling – returned to the farm, called the men to breakfast, and cut the boys' bread and cheese, and saw the wooden bottles filled – sent one plough to the three-roods, another to the three half-acres, and so on – shut the gates, and the clock struck five – breakfasted – set two men to ditch the five roods – two more to chop sads [heavy sods], and spread about the land – two more to throw up muck in the yard – and three men and six women to weed wheat – set on the carpenter to repair cow-cribs, and set them up till winter – the wheeler to mend up the old carts, cart-ladders, rakes, etc., preparatory to hay-time and harvest – walked to the six-acres, found hogs in the grass – went back and sent a man to hedge and thorn – sold the butcher a fat calf, and the suckler a lean one – the clock strikes nine – and walked into barley-field – barleys fine, picked off a few tiles and stones, and cut a few thistles – the peas fine, but foul; the charlock must be topped – the tares doubtful; the fly seems to have taken them – prayed for rain, but could not see a cloud . . .

The Revd Robert Robinson, Baptist pastor and farmer, to an unknown friend, 1784. Robinson's account of his day continues for another 26 lines.

27 MAY

1679 *The Habeas Corpus Act is passed.*

1905 *After it has sailed halfway round the world the Russian Baltic fleet is defeated by Admiral Togo at the Battle of Tsushima off southwest Japan. This leads to Japan's victory in the Russo-Japanese War.*

1941 *The German battleship* Bismarck *is sunk.*

We shall, it is hardly doubted, have a row here, for our Orangemen are frantic, and *will* walk and *will* play their horrid tunes. We had a man killed in a fray a week ago about a drum.

Pamela, Lady Campbell to Emily Eden, from
Armagh in northern Ireland, 1828.

I am exceedingly better in health, I thank the 'powers' – and even presume to figure it out that I shall next slip between the soft swing-doors of Athene [the Athenaeum Club in London] in the character of a confirmed improver, struggler upward, or even bay-crowned victor over ills . . . I am . . . staying with some amiable cousins, of the more amiable sex – supposedly at least (my supposition is not about the cousins, but about sex) – in the deep warm heart of 'New England at its best'. This large Connecticut scenery of mountain and broad vale, recurrent great lake and splendid river (the great Connecticut itself, the Housatonic, the Farmington), all embowered with truly prodigious elms and maples, is very noble and charming and sympathetic, and made – on its great scale of extent – to be dealt with by the blest motor-car, the consolation of my declining years. This luxury I am charitably much treated to, and it does me a world of good. The enormous, the unique ubiquity of the 'auto' here suggests many reflections – but I can't go into these now, or into any branch of the prodigious economic or 'sociological' side of this unspeakable and amazing country; I must keep such matters to regale you withal in poor dear little Lamb House garden; for one brick of the old battered purple wall of which I would give at this instant (homesick *quand même*) the whole bristling state of Connecticut.

Henry James to T. Bailey Saunders, 1911. Lamb House
was his home in Rye, Sussex.

28 MAY

1951 *The first* Goon Show *is broadcast on BBC radio.*

1987 *Mathias Rust manages to land his small aeroplane in Red Square in Moscow after evading Russia's air defence radar: a portent of the coming collapse of the USSR.*

If true [it was], the official news of the surrender [of the Belgian army] would be catastrophic for in that case the BEF [British Expeditionary Force] would be left out on a limb. At 10 a.m. the paper-shop had sold out but I got these details from the man behind the counter (this is the kiosk at Oxford Circus) after hearing rumours from old Charlie Hunt at Broadcasting House. But already the liftman knew, the roadmenders, and the women at their street doors . . .

As a collector of rumours I have heard that (1) Germany has requested a twenty-four-hour armistice in which to bury the dead in front of the Maginot Line (2) Lord Haw-Haw – since identified as William Joyce, an Irishman – has promised from Hamburg that when the bombings begin Harrow School (because Churchill went there) and HM Stationery Office (where the leaflets dropped in the early raids were printed, also situated in Harrow) will be among the first targets (3) an old newspaper-woman living at Bushey noticed a blind man reading a paper which led to the discovery that a local blind school was a nest of spies. 'More tomorrow', as the comics say.

By the way, 'Haw-Haw' isn't a good or accurate nickname. A peer who speaks condescendingly through his nose might be called 'Haw-haw'. Joyce has a heavy voice like that of an old-fashioned schoolmaster, loaded with sarcasm.

George Beardmore, Journal, 1940.

29 MAY

━━━◦❈◦━━━

Oak Apple Day, traditionally to celebrate Charles II's escape from the Roundheads by hiding in an oak tree, but actually the anniversary of his Restoration in 1660.

1453 *Constantinople falls to the Ottoman Turks and the Byzantine Empire ends.*

1953 *Sir Edmund Hillary and Sherpa Tensing are the first to climb Mount Everest.*

I have bespoken a mummy, which I hope will come safe to my hands, notwithstanding the misfortune that befel a very fine one designed for the King of Sweden. He gave a great price for it, and the Turks took it into their heads that he must certainly have some considerable project depending upon it. They fancied it the body of God knows who; and that the fate of their empire mystically depended on the conservation of it. Some old prophecies were remembered upon this occasion, and the mummy committed prisoner to the Seven Towers, where it has remained under close confinement ever since.

> *Lady Mary Wortley Montagu to the Abbé Conti, 1717, from Constantinople.*
> *Egypt was part of the Ottoman Empire.*

'Now then, will you let me ask you, Duke, what you think you will make of it?' He stopped and said in the most natural manner: 'By God! I think Blücher [Prussian commander] and myself can do the thing.' – 'Do you calculate', I asked, 'upon any desertion in Bonaparte's army?' – 'Not upon a man,' he said, 'from the colonel to the private in a regiment – both inclusive. We may pick up a marshal or two, perhaps; but not worth a damn.' – 'Do you reckon', I asked, 'upon any support from the French King's troops at Alost?' – 'Oh!' said he, 'don't mention such fellows! No: I think Blücher and I can do the business.' – Then, seeing a private soldier of one of our infantry regiments enter the park, gaping about at the statues and images: 'There,' he said, pointing at the soldier, 'it all depends upon that article whether we do the business or not. Give me enough of it, and I am sure.'

> *Thomas Creevey reports his conversation with the Duke of Wellington in the park at Brussels, 1815.*

30 MAY

1656 *The Grenadier Guards are formed from Royalists in exile with Charles II.*

1778 *Voltaire dies. When asked on his deathbed to abjure the Devil he replies, 'Is this a time to make enemies?'*

After the sentence was read, the bishop, the Inquisitor, and many of the judges went away, leaving Jeanne upon the scaffold.

Then the Bailli of Rouen, an Englishman, who was there, without any legal formality and without reading any sentence against her, ordered that she should be taken to the place where she was to be burned.

When Jeanne heard this order given, she began to weep and lament in such a way that all the people present were themselves moved to tears.

The said Bailli immediately ordered that the fire should be lighted, which was done.

And she was there burned and martyred tragically, an act of unparalleled cruelty.

And many, both noble and peasant, murmured greatly against the English.

The execution of Joan of Arc, from the official contemporary account, 1431.

A pleasant day, with quick tropical showers that made the hawthorn which now powders the hedges and roads smell most delightfully: after searching the world for shrubs and perfumes, pray what exceeds this plant in its various beauties? . . .

A short road back brought me, at two o'clock, to the George Inn, Silsoe [Bedfordshire] . . . I was too late for their eggs and bacon, so was obliged to have a bad fried beefsteak; but I brought good sauce with me.

The cottagers, everywhere, look wretchedly, like their cows; and slowly recovering from their wintry distress: deserted by the gentry, they lack assistance, protection, and amusement; however my landlord says that in May, there are Mayers (alias Morris dancers) who go about with a fool, a man in woman's clothes (the Maid Marian), and music.

John Byng, Viscount Torrington, Diary, 1789.

31 MAY

1669 *Samuel Pepys gives up keeping his diary, fearing that he is losing his sight.*

1859 *The clock wrongly known as Big Ben (which is the name of the bell that strikes the hours) is wound for the first time.*

1911 *The* Titanic *is launched in Belfast.*

Have you remembered to collect pieces for the patchwork? We are now at a standstill. I got up here to look for the old map, and can now tell you that it shall be sent tomorrow; it was among the great parcel in the dining-room. As to my debt of 3*s*. 6*d*. to Edward [their brother], I must trouble you to pay it when you settle with him for your boots.

We began our China tea three days ago, and I find it very good. My companions know nothing of the matter. As to Fanny and her twelve pounds in a twelve-month, she may talk till she is as black in the face as her own tea, but I cannot believe her – more likely twelve pounds to a quarter . . .

I am very sorry for Mary, but I have some comfort in there being two curates now lodging in Bookham, besides their own Mr Waineford, from Dorking, so that I think she must fall in love with one or the other . . .

I return to my letter-writing from calling on Miss Harriot Webb, who is short and not quite straight, and cannot pronounce an R any better than her sisters; but she has dark hair, a complexion to suit, and, I think, has the pleasantest countenance and manner of the three – the most natural.

Jane Austen to her sister Cassandra, 1811.

There seems to be something wrong with our bloody ships today. Turn two points to port [i.e., steer closer to the German fleet: a battleship, HMS *Queen Elizabeth*, and HMS *Indefatigable*, one of the new lightly armoured battle-cruisers, had blown up].

Admiral Beatty at the Battle of Jutland, 1916.

JUNE

1 JUNE

1915 *First air-raid on Britain, by Zeppelin airships.*

1935 *Driving tests are introduced and L-plates made compulsory.*

1967 *The Beatles' record 'Sergeant Pepper's Lonely Hearts Club Band' goes on sale.*

I was the last to consent to the separation; but the separation having been made and having become inevitable, I have always said, as I say now, that I would be the first to meet the friendship of the United States as an independent power.

George III to John Adams, the first Ambassador to the Court of St James's
from the United States of America, 1785.

I was in my hammock till we arrived at the Canaries, and I shall never forget the sublime impression the first view of Teneriffe made on my mind. The first arriving into warm weather was most luxuriously pleasant; the clear blue sky of the Tropics was no common change after those accursed south-west gales at Plymouth. About the Line it became weltering hot. We spent one day at St Paul's, a little group of rocks about a quarter of a mile in circumference, peeping up in the midst of the Atlantic. There was such a scene here. Wickham (1st Lieutenant) and I were the only two who landed with guns and geological hammers, etc. The birds by myriads were too close to shoot; we then tried stones, but at last, *proh pudor!* [Oh, for shame!] my geological hammer was the instrument of death. We soon loaded the boat with birds and eggs. Whilst we were so engaged, the men in the boat were fairly fighting with the sharks for such magnificent fish as you could not see in the London market.

Charles Darwin to J.M. Herbert about his early experiences
during the voyage of the Beagle, *1832.*

2 JUNE

1780 *The Gordon (anti-Catholic) riots begin in London, led by Lord George Gordon.*

1941 *Clothes rationing begins in Britain: 66 coupons a year, with a suit taking 26.*

Had no difficulty getting to Brooks's [Club] . . . It was bitterly cold with the windows all out and steps up to balconies erected against the façade . . . Watched the Abbey ceremony on the television . . . Certain scenes specially memorable . . . when she walked to the four sides of the Abbey to ask the people if they would accept her as their queen they replying in the affirmative, and she giving a slow half-curtsey of acknowledgement. . . Indeed all day I was choking with emotion and unable to speak or cheer. Am neither proud nor ashamed of this.

The weather was damnable. It rained all day. The moment the procession started it positively poured, and the troops were soaked. Yet the procession was magnificent. The colour and pageantry cannot be described. Uniforms superb and resplendent. The most popular figure Queen Salote of Tonga, a vast, brown, smiling bundle with a tall red knitting needle in her hat: knitting needle having begun as a plume of feathers. Despite the rain she refused to have the hood of her open carriage drawn, and the people were delighted. They roared applause. Extraordinary how the public will take someone to its bosom, especially someone not very exalted who is putting up a good show. All along the route they adored her. Beside her squatted a little man in black and a top hat – her husband. Noël Coward, when asked who he was, said, 'Her dinner.'

James Lees-Milne, Diary, A Mingled Measure, describes the coronation of Queen Elizabeth II, 1953.

3 JUNE

1937 *The Duke of Windsor marries Mrs Simpson in France.*

1940 *The end of the Dunkirk evacuation of British and French troops.*

On Sunday, June 3, we all went to Southill church. Being in a frame of mind which I hope, for the felicity of human nature, many experience – in fine weather – at the country-house of a friend – consoled and elevated by pious exercises – I expressed myself with an unrestrained fervour to my 'Guide, Philosopher, and Friend' [Dr Johnson]. 'My dear Sir, I would fain be a good man; and I am very good now. I fear God, and honour the king; I wish to do no ill, and to be benevolent to all mankind.' He looked at me with a benignant indulgence; but took occasion to give me wise and salutary caution. 'Do not, Sir, accustom yourself to trust to *impressions*. Favourable impressions at particular moments, as to the state of our souls, may be deceitful and dangerous.'

Although upon most occasions I never heard a more strenuous advocate for the advantages of wealth than Dr Johnson, he this day, I know not from what caprice, took the other side. 'I have not observed', said he, 'that men of very large fortunes, enjoy anything extraordinary that makes happiness. What has the Duke of Bedford? What has the Duke of Devonshire? The only great instance that I have ever known of the enjoyment of wealth was that of Jamaica Dawkins, who going to visit Palmyra, and hearing that the way was infested by robbers, hired a troop of Turkish horse to guard him.'

James Boswell, Life of Johnson, *1781. James Dawkins was an archaeologist and Jacobite whose wealth derived from West Indian plantations, hence his particular nomenclature.*

4 JUNE

1944 *Rome is liberated.*

1989 *Massacre of students in Tiananmen Square, Peking, by Chinese army.*

I'm sick of portraits and wish very much to take my viol da gamba and walk off to some sweet village when I can paint landskips and enjoy the fag end of life in quietness and ease. But these fine ladies [his two daughters] and their tea drinkings, dancings, *husband-huntings* and such will fob me out of the last ten years, and I fear miss getting husbands too – But we can say nothing to these things you know Jackson, we must jog on and be content with the jingling of the bells, only damn it I hate a dust, the kicking up of a dust, and being confined *in harness* to follow the track, whilst others ride in the wagon, under cover, stretching their legs in the straw at ease, and gazing at green trees and blue skies without half my *taste*, that's damned hard.

> *Thomas Gainsborough to William Jackson, composer and*
> *Master of Choristers at Exeter Cathedral, late 1760s.*

How the trees must love the wind! They cannot move from their place, they are bound to their neighbours for their lives; they are like monks in a convent, inevitably fixed and hampered. But the wind is the free Bohemian of the Universe, who goes over all the earth, and . . . brings to the trees all the news of all the continents and isles of ocean, and of all the life of men and beasts. Every wood is educated by it, and half the music of the trees is made up of gratitude and of joy for all they hear.

> *Stopford Brooke, Diary, 1899.*

5 JUNE

1916 *Lord Kitchener drowned when the cruiser* Hampshire *carrying him to Russia hits a mine.*

1967 *Six-Day War between Israel and Arab states begins.*

1968 *Robert Kennedy shot. Dies the next day.*

What a *changement de décoration*; no longer George IV, capricious, luxurious, and misanthropic, liking nothing but the society of listeners and flatterers, with the Conyngham tribe and one or two Tory ministers and foreign ambassadors; but a plain, vulgar, hospitable gentleman, opening his doors to all the world, with a numerous family and suite (with a frightful Queen and a posse of bastards *originally*); a Whig minister, and no foreigners, and no toad-eaters at all. Nothing more different, and looking at him one sees how soon this act will be finished, and the scene be changed for another probably not less dissimilar. Queen, bastards, Whigs, all will disappear, and God knows what replace them.
Charles Greville describes dinner at Windsor Castle with William IV during Ascot Races week, Memoirs, 1831. Lady Conyngham had been George IV's last mistress, and the bastards were William IV's children by the actress Mrs Jordan.

Clarbeston Road – 9 a.m. A boy walks slowly down the length of the platform touching the cardboard boxes warming in the morning sun, flicking the string on a parcel, looking down the wide empty rail and waiting for the train to Fishguard, which is puffing quietly and blowing out steam further down the line and getting ready to come in – rather like an elderly actress once famous who knows her best days are over and that it is only a small country theatre half full but determined all the same to do her best. Ugly and uncomfortable, there is a sense of security about railway stations which the luxury and comfort of an airport lounge can never provide.

Keith Vaughan, Journal, 1962.

6 JUNE

1942 *The Japanese navy is defeated at the Battle of Midway in the Pacific, Admiral Yamamoto losing all four of his aircraft carriers while the Americans lose only the* Yorktown.

1944 *D-Day, the Allies land in Normandy.*

Last night we had a magnificent entertainment at Richmond House, a masquerade and fireworks . . . The whole garden was illuminated, and the apartments. An encampment of barges decked with streamers in the middle of the Thames, kept the people from danger, and formed a stage for the fireworks, which were placed, too, along the rails of the garden. The ground rooms lighted, with suppers spread, the houses covered and filled with people, the bridge, the garden full of masks, Whitehall crowded with spectators to see the dresses pass, and the multitude of heads on the river who came to light by the splendour of the fire-wheels, composed the gayest and richest scene imaginable, not to mention the diamonds and sumptuousness of the habits.

Horace Walpole to Sir Horace Mann, on celebrations marking the successful conclusion of the Seven Years' War against France, 1763.

'Twas on a summer's day – the sixth of June: –
I like to be particular in dates,
Not only of the age, and year, but moon;
They are a sort of post-house, where the Fates
Change horses, making history change its tune . . .

> Don Juan, *Canto I, verse CIII, by Lord Byron. This is the day on which Don Juan loses his virginity.*

7 JUNE

1520 *Henry VIII meets Francis I of France at the Field of Cloth of Gold.*

1963 *First appearance on television of the Rolling Stones, and release of their first single 'Come On'.*

This day, much against my will, I did in Drury Lane see two or three houses marked with a red cross upon the doors, and 'Lord have mercy upon us' writ there – which was a sad sight to me, being the first of that kind that to my remembrance I ever saw. It put me to an ill conception of myself and my smell, so that I was forced to buy some roll-tobacco to smell and chaw – which took away the apprehension.

Samuel Pepys on the outbreak of the plague, Diary, 1665.

Well, say as you will, there is not, and never was, such a country as Old England – never were there such a gentry as the English. They will be the distinguishing mark and glory of England in history, as the arts were of Greece, and war of Rome. I am sure no travel would carry me to any land so beautiful, as the good sense, justice, and liberality of my good countrymen make this. And I cling the closer to it, because I feel that we are going down the hill, and shall perhaps live ourselves to talk of all this independence as a thing that has been. To none of which you assent perhaps. At all events, my paper is done, and it is time to have done with this solemn letter. I can see you sitting at a window that looks out on the Bay of Naples, and Vesuvius with a faint smoke in the distance: a half-naked man under you cutting up watermelons, etc.

Edward FitzGerald to Frederick Tennyson, 1840.

8 JUNE

793 *The first Viking raid in Britain, on Lindisfarne off the Northumbrian coast.*

1379 *The Black Prince, father of Richard II, dies in Spain.*

1869 *The first vacuum cleaner is patented.*

I am suffering from my old complaint, the hay-fever (as it is called). My fear is of perishing by deliquescence. I melt away in nasal and lachrymal profluvia. My remedies are warm pediluvium, cathartics, topical application of a watery solution of opium to eyes, ears, and the interior of the nostrils. The membrane is so irritable, that light, dust, contradiction, an absurd remark, the sight of a dissenter – anything, sets me a-sneezing and if I begin sneezing at twelve I don't leave off till two o'clock – and am heard distinctly in Taunton, when the wind sets that way, at a distance of six miles. Turn your mind to this little curse. If consumption is too powerful for physicians at least they should not suffer themselves to be outwitted by such little upstart disorders as the hay-fever.

I have ordered a brass knocker against you come and we have a case of chronic bronchitis next door – some advanced dyspepsia not far off – and a considerable promise of acute rheumatism at no great distance – a neighbouring squire has water forming on the chest so that I hope things will be comfortable and your visit not unpleasant.

The Revd Sydney Smith to his new son-in-law,
Dr Henry Holland, who was coming to stay, 1835.

9 JUNE

1549 *Cranmer's first Book of Common Prayer is issued to the Church of England.*

1958 *The Queen opens the new Gatwick airport.*

1983 *Mrs Thatcher wins her second term as Prime Minister, by a landslide.*

At past twelve I went up to Lord Hertford's: two of his sons came in from the bridge at Blackfriars, where they had seen the toll-houses plundered and burnt. Instantly arrived their cook, a German Protestant, with a child in his arms, and all we could gather was that the mob was in possession of his house, had burnt his furniture, and had obliged him to abandon his wife and another child . . . it had been only some apprentices who supposed him a papist on his not illuminating [putting candles in the windows of] his house . . .

Yesterday was some slaughter in Fleet Street by the Horse Guards, and more in St George's Fields by the Protestant Association, who fell on the rioters, who appear to have been chiefly apprentices, convicts, and all kinds of desperadoes; for popery is already out of the question, and plunder all the object. They have exacted sums from many houses to avoid being burnt as popish. The ringleader Lord George [Gordon] is fled. The Bank, the destruction of all prisons and of the Inns of Court, were the principal aims . . .

The night passed quietly, and by this evening there will be eighteen thousand men in and round the town. As yet there are more persons killed by drinking than by ball or bayonet. At the great Popish distiller's they swallowed spirits of all kinds, and Kirgate saw men and women lying dead in the streets under barrows as he came home yesterday.

Horace Walpole to the Revd William Mason, describing
the anti-Catholic Gordon Riots in London, 1780.

10 JUNE

1829 *The first Oxford v. Cambridge boat race is rowed, at Henley rather than on the Thames between Putney and Mortlake. Oxford wins, after a re-start.*

1938 *Alcoholics Anonymous is founded in the US.*

1943 *The ball-point pen patented by Laszlo Biro in the US.*

I image to myself the little smoky room at the Salutation and Cat, where we have sat together through the winter nights, beguiling the cares of life with Poesy. When you left London, I felt a dismal void in my heart . . . How blest with ye the path could I have trod of quiet life! In your conversation you had blended so many pleasant fancies, that they cheated me of my grief. But in your absence, the tide of melancholy rushed in again, and did its worst mischief by overwhelming my reason. I have recovered. But feel a stupor that makes me indifferent to the hopes and fears of this life . . . A correspondence, opening with you, has roused me a little from my lethargy, and made me conscious of existence. Indulge me in it. I will not be very troublesome. At some future time I will amuse you with an account as full as my memory will permit of the strange turn my phrensy took. I look back upon it at times with a gloomy kind of envy. For while it lasted I had many many hours of pure happiness. Dream not, Coleridge, of having tasted all the grandeur and wildness of Fancy, till you have gone mad. All now seems to me vapid; comparatively so.

Charles Lamb, recently recovered from a fit of insanity,
to Samuel Taylor Coleridge, 1796.

11 JUNE

1860 *The* Evening Standard, *London's evening paper, is first published.*

1987 *Mrs Thatcher wins her third term as Prime Minister.*

Dr Gardiner was married yesterday to Mrs Percy and her three daughters.

Jane Austen, Letters, 1799.

Understanding that Smallcombe had left the field at six o'clock, although Day continued hauling till ten (consequently all the tithing was done by his people), I went to Smallcombe, and, after upbraiding him with his great ingratitude and insolence, dismissed him. This man I have attended and relieved in sickness, employed him when he could not get employment elsewhere during the dead part of the year, and now because work is plenty he behaves in this manner . . . 'You a parson, a shepherd of the flock, to come here,' Mrs Smallcombe vociferated, 'and insult a poor woman like me [because I called her "beldame"]. You will smart for this I assure you, I assure you.' Tyler's wife, a very rank Methodist, who was in the house, then began to join in the contest and asked whether I was not ashamed of myself to call such names . . . When I explained that it meant a scold, both she and Smallcombe's wife became more tranquil, and said they had supposed it meant something much worse.

The Revd John Skinner, Journal, 1822. Tithes were a tax in kind and in labour services owed to the parson.

I was telling someone in the Club today Esmé Percy's story of how Sarah Bernhardt played Lady Macbeth dressed entirely in leopard skins. Howard Young looked up from his paper and said, 'Tell us, James. How did she deal with the line "Out, damned spot"?'

James Agate, Ego, 1944.

12 JUNE

1837 *The Electric Telegraph patented in the UK.*

1979 *The* Gossamer Albatross *becomes the first man-powered aircraft to cross the English Channel, piloted and powered by the Californian racing cyclist Bryan Allen.*

Well, whatever's going on over there [in Normandy], my sympathies as usual are with the unknown, the forgotten, the buried alive, the mutilated and disfigured who won't ever appear except as a name in a paper, or perhaps as a photograph on a piano in a town in Indiana or Alberta or Yorkshire, 'Bugles calling for them in sad shires', anonymously.

One thing about a soldier's death is that it doesn't entail the paper-work that follows on that of a civilian. Following the latest spate of bombing we even had a young fellow call in the site-office asking half-humorously how he could replace his matriculation certificate and letter of reference as to character from an employer now in France. Interesting case in itself as he was a soldier on compassionate leave from the Pay Corps who saw his first bit of action when a bomb fell on a house across the road and deafened him.

Other side-effects of bombs are the stripping of leaves from wayside trees, the deaths by blast of sparrows, chaffinches etc., and the awful things that happen to cats and dogs. We had a man complain that thirty of his forty-odd small birds in a backyard aviary had been killed by blast, half a mile or so away from where the bomb had landed.

George Beardmore, Journal, 1944.

13 JUNE

1842 *Queen Victoria travels by train for the first time, from Slough to Paddington Station in London.*

1944 *The first V1 'doodlebug' flying bombs fall on London.*

The King came from Canterbury thither [to Dover] to visit her, and though she were unready, so soon as she heard he was come, she hastened down a pair of stairs to meet him, and offering to kneel down and to kiss his hand, he wrapped her up in his arms and kissed her with many kisses . . . At dinner being carved pheasant and venison by his Majesty (who had dined before) she ate heartily of both, notwithstanding her confessor (who all this while stood by her) had forewarned her that it was the Eve of St John Baptist, and was to be fasted, and that she should take heed how she gave ill example or a scandal at her first arrival. The same night having supped at Canterbury her Majesty went to bed; and, some space of time after, his Majesty followed her; but being entered his bedchamber, the first thing he did, he bolted all the doors round about (being seven) with his own hand, letting in but two of the bedchamber to undress him, which being done, he bolted them out also. The next morning he lay till seven of the clock, and was pleasant with the Lords that he had beguiled them; and hath ever since been very jocund.

In stature her head reached to his shoulder: but she is young enough to grow taller. Those of our nation that know best her dispositions are very hopeful his Majesty will have power to bring her to his own religion. Being asked, not long since, if she could abide a Huguenot? 'Why not?' said she, 'was not my father one?' [He, Henri IV, had later become a Catholic to secure the throne of France.]

Anonymous letter describing the first meeting of King Charles I with his French wife, Henrietta Maria, to whom he had already been married by proxy, 1625.

14 JUNE

1839 *The first Henley Regatta.*

1905 *Mutiny on the Russian battleship* Potemkin *in Odessa harbour on the Black Sea.*

1940 *Paris falls to the Germans.*

I was looking at the road ahead and there seemed to be no movement. I thought, well I'm a civilian so why shouldn't I go and see what's going on because there didn't seem to be much resistance.

So I stripped off all my combat clothes and walked into Stanley in a blue civilian anorak with my hands in the air and my handkerchief in my hand.

The Argentinians made no hostile movement as I went by the apparently undamaged but heavily bunkered Government House.

I sort of grinned at them in the hope that if there were any Argentinian soldiers manning the position they wouldn't shoot at me.

Nobody took any notice so I walked on and after a few minutes I saw a group of people all looking like civilians a hundred yards ahead and I shouted at them.

I shouted: 'Are you British?' and they shouted back: 'Yes, are you?' I said 'Yes'. . .

I walked on and there were hundreds, maybe thousands, of Argentinian troops milling around, marching in columns through the streets, some of them clutching very badly wounded men and looking completely like an army in defeat with blankets wrapped around themselves . . .

Eventually I reached the famous Falklands hotel, the Upland Goose . . . They offered me gin on the assumption that this is the traditional drink of British journalists, but I asked if they could make it whisky instead and I gratefully raised my glass to them all.

Max Hastings reports in the Evening Standard *how he came to be the first man into Port Stanley at the end of the Falklands War, 1982.*

15 JUNE

1215 *King John seals the Magna Carta.*

1855 *Stamp duty on newspapers is abolished, encouraging rapid growth of the Press.*

1919 *Alcock and Brown fly the Atlantic.*

God sent remedy . . . by the hand of the most renowned man, Sir William Walworthe, the then Mayor; who in Smethefelde, in presence of our Lord the King and those standing by him, lords, knights, esquires, and citizens on horseback, on the one side, and the whole of this infuriated rout on the other, most manfully, by himself, rushed upon the captain of the said multitude, 'Walter Tylere' by name, and, as he was altercating with the King and the nobles, first wounded him in the neck with his sword, and then hurled him from his horse, mortally pierced in the breast; and further, by favour of the divine grace, so defended himself from those who had come with him, both on foot and horseback, that he departed from thence unhurt, and rode on with our Lord the King and his people, towards a field near to the spring that is called 'Whitewelle-beche'; in which place, while the whole of the infuriated multitude in warlike manner was making ready against our Lord the King and his people, refusing to treat of peace except on condition that they should first have the head of the said Mayor, the Mayor himself, who had gone into the City at the instance of our Lord the King, in the space of half an hour sent and led forth therefrom so great a force of citizen warriors in aid of our Lord the King, that the whole multitude of madmen was surrounded and hemmed in; and not one of them would have escaped, if our Lord the King had not commended them to be gone.

The end of the Peasants' Revolt, 1381, from the City Letter Book.

16 JUNE

1880 *The Salvation Army adopts distinctive black straw bonnets for women members.*

1903 *Pepsi-Cola registered as a trade mark, and Henry Ford founds his motor company.*

Certainly my affections to you are so unchangeable, that hostility itself cannot violate my friendship to your person, but I must be true to the cause wherein I serve . . . and where my conscience is interested, all other obligations are swallowed up. I should most gladly wait on you according to your desire, but that I look upon you as you are engaged in that party, beyond a possibility of retreat . . . That great God, which is the searcher of my heart, knows with what a sad sense I go upon this service, and with what a perfect hatred I detest this war without an enemy . . . We are both upon the stage and must act those parts that are assigned us in this tragedy; let us do it in a way of honour, and without personal animosities, whatsoever the issue be.

Sir William Waller to Sir Ralph Hopton, 1643. Waller, Parliamentarian commander in the west of England during the Civil War, replies to a request for a personal interview from his Cavalier opponent Hopton. Twenty years before, they had fought together in Germany.

Friday morning, half-past two – The girls just returned from a ball at the Duke of Richmond's. A battle has taken place today [at Charleroi on 15 June] between Bonaparte and the Prussians: to what extent is not known; result is known, however, to be in favour of the French. Our troops are all moving from this place at present. Lord Wellington was at the ball tonight as composed as ever.

Thomas Creevey, Journal, Brussels, 1815.

17 JUNE

1775 *The Battle of Bunker Hill in the American War of Independence.*

1940 *British troop ship* Lancastria *is bombed and sunk off St-Nazaire with the loss of 2500 lives.*

In this bay we anchored . . . The people of the country, having their houses close by the water's side, showed themselves unto us and sent a present to our general. When they came unto us they greatly wondered at the things which we brought. Our general (according to his natural and accustomed humanity) courteously entreated them, and liberally bestowed on them necessary things to cover their nakedness. Whereupon they supposed us to be gods, and would not be persuaded to the contrary. The presents which they sent unto our general were feathers, and cauls of net work.

Their houses are digged round about with earth, and have from the uttermost brims of the circle clefts of wood set upon them, joining close together at the top like a spire steeple, which by reason of that closeness are very warm. Their bed is the ground with rushes strewed on it and lying about the house; they have the fire in the midst. The men go naked; the women take bulrushes and comb them after the manner of hemp, and thereof make their loose garments; which, being knit about their middles, hang down about their hips, having also about their shoulders a skin of deer, with the hair upon it. These women arc very obedient and serviceable to their husbands.

Sir Francis Drake, sailing off the coast of north-western
California, arrives at Nova Albion, 1578.

18 JUNE

1812 *War declared between Britain and the United States, the 'War of 1812'.*

1975 *The first North Sea oil comes ashore in Britain.*

Our division, which had stood upwards of five thousand men at the commencement of the battle, had gradually dwindled down into a solitary line of skirmishers. The 27th Regiment were lying literally dead, in square, a few yards behind us. My horse had received another shot through the leg, and one through the flap of the saddle, which lodged in his body, sending him a step beyond the pension list. The smoke still hung so thick about us that we could see nothing. I walked a little way to each flank to endeavour to get a glimpse of what was going on; but nothing met my eye except the mangled remains of men and horses, and I was obliged to return to my post as wise as I went.

I had never yet heard of a battle in which everybody was killed; but this seemed likely to be an exception, as all were going by turns . . .

Presently a cheer which we knew to be British commenced far to the right, and made everyone prick up his ears; it was Lord Wellington's long-wished-for orders to advance. It gradually approached, growing louder as it grew near. We took it up by instinct, charged through the hedge down upon the old knoll, sending our adversaries flying at the point of the bayonet. Lord Wellington galloped up to us at the instant, and our men began to cheer him; but he called out, 'No cheering, my lads, but forward, and complete our victory!'

Captain J. Kincaid, Rifle Brigade, describes
the end of the Battle of Waterloo, 1815.

19 JUNE

1829 *The Metropolitan Police founded by Sir Robert Peel. Early nick-names: Bobbies or Peelers.*

1978 *Ian Botham the first cricketer to score a century and take eight wickets in one innings of a Test Match, against Pakistan.*

The first thing I did, of course, was to put out my hand and congratulate him upon his victory. He made a variety of observations in his short, natural, blunt way, but with the greatest gravity all the time, and without the least approach to anything like triumph or joy. 'It has been a damned serious business,' he said. 'Blücher and I have lost thirty thousand men. It has been a damned nice thing – the nearest run thing you ever saw in your life. Blücher lost fourteen thousand on Friday night [at Ligny]: and got so damnably licked I could not find him on Saturday morning; so I was obliged to fall back to keep up my communications with him.' Then, as he walked about, he praised greatly those Guards who kept the farm (meaning Hougoumont) against the repeated attacks of the French; and then he praised all our troops, uttering repeated expressions of astonishment at our men's courage. He repeated so often its being *so nice a thing – so nearly run a thing*, that I asked him if the French had fought better than he had ever seen them do before. 'No,' he said, 'they have always fought the same since I first saw them at Vimeiro [in 1808].' Then he said: 'By God! I don't think it would have done if I had not been there' . . .

There was nothing like vanity in the observation in the way he made it. I considered it only as meaning that the battle was so hardly and equally fought that nothing but confidence of our army in himself as their general could have brought them through.

> *Thomas Creevey talks to the Duke of Wellington*
> *the day after Waterloo, 1815.*

20 JUNE

1756 *Of 147 English confined in the Black Hole of Calcutta after the successful siege of the town by Siraj-ud-daula, the ruler of Bengal, only 23 survive the night.*

1793 *Eli Whitney applies for a patent for his cotton gin, which will transform the economics of the cotton industry and greatly increase the demand for slaves.*

I was awoke at six o'clock by Mamma, who told me that the Archbishop of Canterbury and Lord Conyngham were here, and wished to see me. I got out of bed and went into my sitting-room (only in my dressing-gown), and *alone*, and saw them. Lord Conyngham [the Lord Chamberlain] then acquainted me that my poor uncle, the King, was no more, and had expired at twelve minutes past two this morning, and consequently that I am *Queen* . . .

Since it has pleased Providence to place me in this station, I shall do my utmost to fulfil my duty towards my country; I am very young and perhaps in many, though not in all things, inexperienced, but I am sure, that very few have more real good will and more real desire to do what is fit and right than I have.

Queen Victoria, Journal, 1837.

Just close up to within a yard or two of a small ragged hedge which was our own line, the French lay as if they had been mowed down in a row without any interval. It was a distressing sight, no doubt, to see every now and then a man alive amongst them, and calling out to Lord Arthur [Hill] to give them something to drink. It so happened Lord Arthur had some weak brandy and water in his holster, and he dismounted to give some to the wounded soldiers. It was a curious thing to see on each occasion the moderation with which the soldier drank, and his marked good manners . . .

I rode home with Hume the physician at head quarters, who said . . . upon my expressing regret at the wounded people being still out, 'The two nights they have been out is all in their favour, provided they are now got into hospitals. They will have a better chance of escaping fever this hot weather than our own people who have been carried into hospitals the first.'

Thomas Creevey visits the field of Waterloo, 1818.

21 JUNE

1675 *Foundation-stone of the new St Paul's Cathedral laid.*

1948 *First successful long-playing record demonstrated in the US.*

At twelve She [Queen Victoria] held a Council, at which She presided with as much ease as if She had been doing nothing else all her life, and though Lord Lansdowne or Bathurst had contrived between them to make some confusion with the Council papers, She was not put out by it. She looked very well, and though so small in stature, and without any pretension to beauty, the gracefulness of her manner and the good expression of her countenance give her on the whole a very agreeable appearance, and with her youth inspire an excessive interest in all who approach her, and which I can't help feeling myself . . .

No contrast can be greater than that between the personal demeanour of the present and the late [William IV] Sovereigns at their respective accessions. He was a man who, coming to the throne at the mature age of sixty-five, was so excited by the exaltation, that he nearly went mad, and distinguished himself by a thousand extravagances of language and conduct, to the alarm or amusement of all who witnessed his strange freaks; and though he was shortly afterwards sobered down into more becoming habits, he always continued to be something of a blackguard and something more of a buffoon. It is but fair to his memory at the same time to say that he was a good-natured, kind-hearted, and well-meaning man and he always acted an honourable and straightforward, if not always a sound and discreet, part.

Charles Greville, Memoirs, 1837.

22 JUNE

1814 *First cricket match played at the present Lord's ground, home of the MCC.*

1940 *The French sign armistice with Hitler at Compiègne in the same railway carriage in which the 1918 armistice was signed.*

1941 *Hitler invades Russia.*

We were pushed in to relieve the Canadians opposite Hooge. The Canadians had almost all been killed in the recent fighting there (which was unlucky for them) and hardly any of them had been buried (which was unlucky for us). The confusion and mess were indescribable and the stinks hardly to be borne. No one quite knew where the line was and the men were spotted about in little holes in the ground or in the cellars of ruined cottages and the crypts of crumbling churches . . .

I never saw anything like the foulness and desolation of this bit of the Salient. There were two woods near to us in which we roamed about picking up gruesome relics in the dusk – Maple Copse and Sanctuary Wood – not a leaf or a blade of grass in either of them, nothing but twisted and blackened stumps and a mesh of shell holes, dimpling into one another, full of mud and blood, and dead men and over-fed rats which blundered into one in the twilight like fat moths.

To my mind it was a far more impressive sight than the ruins of Ypres, because it was sheer abomination undiluted by a single touch of beauty, grandeur or sentiment . . . Goodbye, my blessed angel. This morning I took my boots off and washed for the first time these 8 days. It was delicious.

Raymond Asquith to his wife Katharine, 1916.

23 JUNE

Midsummer Eve

1757 *Robert Clive gains control of Bengal for the East India Company by his victory at Plassey.*

1951 *Soviet spies Guy Burgess and Donald Maclean flee to Russia.*

I visited him [Dr Johnson] in the morning, after having been present at the shocking sight of fifteen men executed before Newgate. Talking of the religious discipline proper for unhappy convicts, he said, 'Sir, one of our regular clergy will probably not impress their minds sufficiently: they should be attended by a Methodist preacher, or a popish priest.'

James Boswell, Life of Johnson, *1784.*

What a born melancholiac I am! The only way I keep afloat is by working. Directly I stop working I feel that I am sinking down, down. And as usual, I feel that if I sink further I shall reach the truth. That is the only mitigation; a kind of nobility. Solemnity. I shall make myself face the fact that there is nothing – nothing for any of us. Work, reading, writing, are all disguises; and relations with other people. Yes, even having children would be useless.

We went into the beechwood by the Race Course. I like these woods; and the waters of the greenery closing over one; so shallow, with the sun on them; then so deep in the shade. And I like the beech boughs, laced about, very intricate; like many arms; and the trunks, like the stone pillars in a church. But . . . this thought kept coming to me. What though could one do, at the bottom of that weight? with that incubus of injustice on top of one? Annie Thompsett and her baby live on 15 shillings a week. I throw away 13 shillings on cigarettes, choco-lates, and bus fares. She was eating rice pudding by the baby's cradle when I came in.

Virginia Woolf, Diary, 1923. She later employed Annie as cook and domestic.

24 JUNE

1314 *Robert the Bruce and the Scots defeat Edward II at the Battle of Bannockburn.*

1340 *England's first major victory in the Hundred Years' War against the French, at the sea battle of Sluys.*

1812 *Napoleon invades Russia.*

Yes, I remember Adlestrop –
The name, because one afternoon
Of heat the express-train drew up there
Unwontedly. It was late June.

The steam hissed. Someone cleared his throat.
No one left and no one came
On the bare platform. What I saw
Was Adlestrop – only the name

And willows, willow-herb, and grass,
And meadowsweet, and haycocks dry,
No whit less still and lonely fair
Than the high cloudlets in the sky.

And for that minute a blackbird sang
Close by, and round him, mistier,
Farther and farther, all the birds
Of Oxfordshire and Gloucestershire.

On this day in 1914 Edward Thomas and his wife Helen were going by train to Ledbury in Herefordshire. Thomas made some jottings about these suspended moments in his notebook and much later he wrote this, his most famous poem.

25 JUNE

1876 *Custer's last stand, at the Battle of the Little Big Horn, against the Sioux.*

1891 *The first Sherlock Holmes story appears in the* Strand *magazine.*

1950 *The Korean War begins, the first fought in the name of the United Nations.*

I write in a nook that I call my *Boudoir*. It is a summer-house not much bigger than a sedan chair, the door of which opens into the garden, that is now crowded with pinks, roses, and honeysuckles, and the window into my neighbour's orchard. It formerly served an apothecary, now dead, as a smoking-room; and under my feet is a trap-door, which once covered a hole in the ground where he kept his bottles. At present, however, it is dedicated to sublimer uses. Having lined it with garden mats, and furnished it with a table and two chairs, here I write all that I write in summer-time, whether to my friends, or to the public.

William Cowper to Joseph Hill, 1785.

Return to Farringford. Dinner (which is at 6.30 always). Sitting at claret in the drawing-room we see the evening sunlight on the landscape. I go to the top of the house alone; have a strong sense of being in Tennyson's; green summer, ruddy light in the sky. When I came down to drawing-room found A.T. with a book in his hand . . . He accosted me, 'Allingham, would it disgust you if I read "Maud"? Would you expire?'

I gave a satisfactory reply and he accordingly read 'Maud' all through, with some additions recently made. His interpolated comments very amusing.

'This is what was called namby-pamby!' – 'That's wonderfully fine!' – 'That was very hard to read; could you have read it? I don't think so.'

William Allingham visits Alfred Tennyson on the Isle of Wight, Dairy, 1865.

26 JUNE

1284 *Angry at not being paid for ridding the town of rats, the Pied Piper leads 130 children out of Hamelin to the sound of his pipe, and they are never seen again.*

1945 *The United Nations Charter is signed by 30 nations.*

I hope for [peace], nay and expect it, because it is not yet war. Pride and anger do not deliberate to the middle of the campaign; and I believe even the great incendiaries are more intent on making a good bargain than on saving their honour. If they save lives, I care not who is the better politician; and, as I am not to be their judge, I do not inquire what false weights they fling into the scales. Two-thirds of France, who are not so humble as I, seem to think they can entirely new-model the world with metaphysical compasses; and hold that no injustice, no barbarity, need to be counted in making the experiment. Such legislators are sublime empirics, and in their universal benevolence have very little individual sensibility. In short, the result of my reflections on what has passed in Europe for these latter centuries is, that tyrants have no consciences, and reformers no feeling; and the world suffers both by the plague and by the cure. What oceans of blood were Luther and Calvin the authors of being spilt! The late French government was detestable; yet I still doubt whether a civil war will not be the consequence of the revolution, and then what may be the upshot?

Horace Walpole to the Earl of Strafford, 1790, on the prospect of war with Revolutionary France.

27 JUNE

—————✦✦✤✦✦—————

1843 *John Murray II, Byron's publisher, dies.*

1900 *The Central Line on the London Underground opens.*

1967 *The first cashpoint in Britain is opened, at Enfield.*

I determined to reserve my two last bags of ballast till I was certain of being very near the earth, and fixed one of them to the anchor in order to drop it and break the fall of the machine. When I saw the shadow of the balloon increasing very fast, and could plainly distinguish objects, so small as horses in waggons and in the fields, I threw out my sixth bag, but unluckily when I was preparing the seventh upon the anchor, it slipp'd off, and fell without it. Within a very few seconds I came to the ground on the side of a steep hill, in a corn field. The shock was trifling, but the unevenness of the ground overset the car, and rolled me gently out.

Colonel Richard Fitzpatrick to William Windham, 1785,
describing the end of his balloon trip from Oxford.

Between the hours of eleven and twelve . . . I wrote the last lines of the last page [of *The Decline and Fall of the Roman Empire*], in a summer-house in my garden [in Lausanne, Switzerland]. After laying down my pen I took several turns in a *berceau*, or covered walk of acacias, which commands a prospect of the country, the lake, and the mountains. The air was temperate, the sky was serene, the silver orb of the moon was reflected from the waters, and all nature was silent. I will not dissemble the first emotions of joy on recovery of my freedom, and, perhaps, the establishment of my fame. But my pride was soon humbled, and a sober melancholy was spread over my mind, by the idea that I had taken an everlasting leave of an old and agreeable companion, and that, whatsoever might be the future fate of my *History*, the life of the historian must be short and precarious.

Edward Gibbon, Autobiography, 1787.

28 JUNE

1838 *The Coronation of Queen Victoria.*

1939 *Pan American Airways start first transatlantic passenger service.*

1948 *The Berlin Airlift begins, to circumvent the Soviet blockade of West Berlin.*

The road to the manoeuvres was shaped like the letter V, making a sharp turn at the bridge over the river Nilgacka. Franz Ferdinand's car could go fast enough until it reached this spot but here it was forced to slow down for the turn. Here Princip had taken his stand.

As the car came abreast he stepped forward from the curb, drew his automatic pistol from his coat and fired two shots. The first struck the wife of the Archduke, the Archduchess Sofia, in the abdomen. She was an expectant mother. She died instantly.

The second bullet struck the Archduke close to the heart.

He uttered only one word – 'Sofia' – a call to his stricken wife. Then his head fell back and he collapsed. He died almost instantly.

The assassination of the Austrian Archduke Franz Ferdinand in Sarajavo in 1914, the immediate cause of the First World War, described by Borijove Jevtić, one of the Serbian nationalist conspirators.

And then, isolated and pitiable come the two German delegates. Dr Müller, Dr Bell. The silence is terrifying. Their feet upon a strip of parquet between the Savonnerie carpets echo hollow and duplicate. They keep their eyes fixed away from those two thousand staring eyes, fixed upon the ceiling. They are deathly pale . . . They are conducted to their chairs. Clemenceau at once breaks the silence. '*Messieurs*,' he rasps, '*la séance est ouverte.*' He adds a few ill chosen words. 'We are here to sign a Treaty of Peace' . . . Then St Quentin advances towards the Germans and with the utmost dignity leads them to the little table on which the Treaty is expanded. There is general tension. They sign. There is a general relaxation. Conversation hums again in an undertone.

Harold Nicolson describes the signing of the Versailles Peace Treaty, formally ending the First World War, in 1919.

29 JUNE

1613 *Shakespeare's Globe theatre burnt down in Southwark.*

1855 *The* Daily Telegraph *published for the first time.*

Clear, cold night, slight breeze from the east, day beautifully warm and pleasant. Mr Burke suffers greatly from the cold and is getting extremely weak; he and King start tomorrow up the creek to look for the blacks [aborigines]; it is the only chance we have of being saved from starvation. I am weaker than ever, although I have a good appetite and relish the nardoo [a seed cake] much; but it seems to give us no nutriment, and the birds here are so shy as not to be got at. Even if we got a good supply of fish, I doubt whether we could do much work on them and the nardoo alone. Nothing now but the greatest good luck can save any of us; and as for myself I may live four or five days if the weather continues warm. My pulse is at forty-eight, and very weak, and my legs and arms are nearly skin and bone. I can only look out, like Mr Micawber, 'for *something to turn up';* starvation on nardoo is by no means very unpleasant, but for the weakness one feels, and the utter inability to move one's self; for as far as appetite is concerned, it gives the greatest satisfaction.

Robert Burke and William John Wills accomplished the first crossing of Australia from south to north, reaching the Gulf of Carpentaria in February 1861. Both died of starvation at Cooper's Creek on the return journey; John King, another member of the expedition, survived. Wills's last entry in his Journal, 1861.

30 JUNE

1837 *The pillory is abolished as a form of punishment.*

1894 *Tower Bridge is opened.*

1934 *The Night of the Long Knives in Germany, when Hitler orders the SS to shoot Ernst Roehm and much of the leadership of the SA Brownshirts, seen as potential rivals by himself and the German army.*

I was on volunteer patrol against possible sabotage [of BBC Broadcasting House] . . . We had authority to enter any room, demand anyone's pass. At 8.30 p.m. I was watching the sun sink over Harrow and at 3.30 a.m. observing the first streak of grey-green light over the [Thames] Estuary, the barrage balloons floating in the cool dawn air, the twinkling traffic lights far down in Portland Place. We slept this time in a screened end of the drawing-room . . . the other end was occupied by visitors – a clique of French staff officers – and a wireless receiver giving out the news in French . . .

On Saturday morning I took drill again, shot ten rounds and again excelled with nine bull's-eyes out of ten, and spent the next hour being taught how to take a gun away from a sentry. I tricked him by pretending to drop my guard and ask for a match. Also I got a smack on the jaw from a rifle-butt.

Our first air-raid alarm of the present cycle of alarms took place last Monday (I think). I heard Jean's heart beating within the sounding-board of the pantry's wooden walls. The child slept and played and slept again, all within this three feet of space otherwise occupied by shelves loaded with a bread-bin, sugar, margarine, and tins of this and that. I made tea, walked round, poked my head outside, and went back to bed ten minutes before the All Clear sounded.

George Beardmore, Journal, 1940. General de Gaulle
had arrived in England on 17 June to found the Free French.

JULY

1 JULY

1916 *The Battle of the Somme begins.*

1967 *Regular colour TV broadcasts begin in Britain on BBC2.*

1997 *The 'Chinese Takeaway': Hong Kong is given back to China by Britain.*

Last Saturday night my workmen took their leave, made their bow, and left me up to the knees in shavings. In short, the journeymen carpenters, like the cabinet-makers, have entered into an association not to work unless their wages are raised; and how can one complain? The poor fellows, whose all the labour is, see their masters advance their prices every day, and think it reasonable to touch their share. You would be frightened at the dearness of everything; I build out of economy, for unless I do now, in two years I shall not be able to afford it.

Horace Walpole to Sir Horace Mann, 1762.

As your sincere well-wisher I earnestly require you to abstain from all writing except on broad and general subjects, chiefly allusive to your art. If any severe or unjust remarks are made on you or your works *paint* them down. You can. But if you retort in words, action will produce reaction, and your whole remaining life will be one scene of pernicious contention. Your mind, which should be a mansion for all lovely thoughts, will be for ever disturbed by angry and sarcastic movements, and you will never be in a state to sit down to your easel with that composed dignity which your high calling demands.

Sir George Beaumont to Beujamin Robert Haydon, from Haydon's Autobiography, 1815. Beaumont was a great patron of poets and artists, including Coleridge and Constable. Haydon had been engaged in a controversy with the Royal Academy.

2 JULY

1266 *Norway cedes the Western Isles (Hebrides) and the Isle of Man to Scotland.*

1937 *Aviator Amelia Earhart vanishes over the central Pacific while trying to fly round the world along the Equator.*

1974 *President Lyndon Johnson signs the Civil Rights Bill.*

We never charged but we routed the enemy. The Left Wing, which I commanded, being our own horse, saving a few Scots in our rear, beat all . . . Prince [Rupert]'s horse. God made them as stubble to our swords. We charged their regiments of foot with our horse, and routed all we charged . . .

Sir, God hath taken away your eldest son by a cannon-shot. It broke his leg. We were necessitated to have it cut off, whereof he died.

Sir, you know my own trials this way [one of Cromwell's sons had recently been killed]: but the Lord supported me with this, that the Lord took him into the happiness we all pant for and live for. There is your precious child full of glory, never to know sin or sorrow any more. He was a gallant young man, exceedingly gracious. God give you His comfort. Before his death he was so full of comfort that to Frank Russel and myself he could not express it, 'It was so great above his pain'. This he said to us. Indeed it was admirable. A little after, he said, one thing lay upon his spirit. I asked him, what that was? He told me it was, that God had not suffered him to be any more the executioner of His enemies. At his fall, his horse being killed with the bullet, and as I am informed three horses more, I am told he bid them, open to the right and left, that he might see the rogues run.

Oliver Cromwell to his brother-in-law, Colonel Valentine Walton, immediately after the battle of Marston Moor, the turning-point in the Civil War, 1644.

3 JULY

1866 *The Prussians defeat the Austrians at the Battle of Sadowa/Königgratz, making themselves the most powerful German nation.*

1938 *The Mallard of the LNER establishes the world record of 126 mph for a steam train, between Peterborough and Grantham.*

1940 *The Royal Navy sinks much of the French navy at anchor at Oran and Mers-El-Kebir in Algeria to stop it falling into the hands of the Germans.*

A shell screamed over the house, instantly followed by another and another, and in a moment the air was full of the most complete artillery prelude to an infantry battle that was ever exhibited . . . Through the midst of the storm of screaming and exploding shells an ambulance, driven by its frenzied conductor at full speed, presented to all of us the marvellous spectacle of a horse going rapidly on three legs. A hinder one had been shot off at the hock . . . During this fire the houses at twenty and thirty feet distant were receiving their death, and soldiers in Federal blue were torn to pieces in the road and died with the peculiar yells that blend the extorted cry of pain with horror and despair. Not an orderly, not an ambulance, not a straggler was to be seen upon the plain swept by this tempest of orchestral death thirty minutes after it commenced.

The three-day battle of Gettysburg, Pennsylvania was the turning-point of the American Civil War. Samuel Wilkeson writes his despatch beside the body of his eldest son, killed in the first day's fighting, 1863.

Rule 43: Never travel with women. We had an engaged compartment, which was comfortable; but O the fuss about luggage and wraps. A. and C. had on a moderate computation eighteen packages. Then there was a tyre, a box containing china, a kettle in a sack, a box with some cheese in it. These were all piled up in our compartment – some of them handed out at Kendal. It was a pleasant journey though; the train was a huge one, and it seemed to be just abandoned at stations by all concerned – stood idly waiting until it occurred to some official to try if he could start it.

A.C. Benson, Diary, 1911.

4 JULY

Independence Day, USA.

1829 *First regular bus service in Britain, from Paddington to the Bank of England.*

1954 *End of food rationing in Britain.*

Our breakfast [at Oxford] was excellent; plenty of strawberries and cream. I then tried, in vain, to get into the Ashmolean Museum . . . to know if the woman were yet living who used to show (so well) the picture of the famous sailor, Sir Martin Frobisher: viz., 'Sir Martin Furbisher, an antient navigator, sail'd all round the world and shot the Gulph . . . There's the pistol in his hand he shot it with' . . .

We had been so long on horseback and tormented by flies, in a hot sun (even from ten till three o'clock), that we were as fatigued and peevish as any nervous wretches could be. At one gateway, Colonel Bertie's horse went on his knees to endeavour to drink, to the great alarm of his rider, who thought he had slipped into a deep hole; nor was it possible to refrain from laughter at this camel-like operation.

John Byng, Viscount Torrington, Diary, 1785.

If any extraordinary event happens, who but must hear it before it descends through a coffee-house to the runner of a daily paper? They who are always wanting news, are wanting to hear they don't know what. A lower species, indeed, is that of the scribes you mention, who every night compose a journal for the satisfaction of such *illiterati*, and feed them with all the vices and misfortunes of every private family; nay, they now call it a *duty* to publish all those calamities which decency to wretched relations used in compassion to suppress.

Horace Walpole to Miss Hannah More, 1788.

5 JULY

1948 *The National Health Service comes into operation.*

1954 *Elvis Presley records the first Rock 'n' Roll record, 'That's All Right', an old blues number by Arthur 'Big Boy' Crudup, in Sam Phillips's Memphis studio.*

And therefore tomorrow long I to go to God, it were a day very meet and convenient for me [St Thomas's Eve]. I never liked your manner toward me better than when you kissed me last for I love when daughterly love and dear charity hath no leisure to look to worldly courtesy. Farewell my dear child, and pray for me, and I shall for you and all your friends that we may merrily meet in heaven. I thank you for your great cost.

Sir Thomas More to his daughter Margaret Roper, his last letter, 'written with a coal', before his execution the following day, 1535.

I can never get people to understand that poetry is the expression of *excited passion*, and that there is no such thing as a life of passion any more than a continuous earthquake, or an eternal fever. Besides, who would ever *shave* themselves in such a state?

Lord Byron to Thomas Moore, 1821.

Just back . . . from Knole, where indeed I was invited to lunch alone with his Lordship [Lord Sackville]. His Lordship lives in the kernel of a vast nut. You perambulate miles of galleries; skip endless treasures – chairs that Shakespeare might have sat on – tapestries, pictures, floors made of the halves of oaks; and penetrate at length to a round shiny table with a cover laid for one . . . But the extremities and indeed the inward parts are gone dead. Ropes fence off half the rooms; the chairs and the pictures look preserved; life has left them. Not for a hundred years have the retainers sat down to dinner in the great hall. Then there is Mary Stuart's altar, where she prayed before execution. 'An ancestor of ours took her the death warrant,' said Vita [Lord Sackville's daughter].

Virginia Woolf, Diary, 1924.

6 JULY

1952 *The last London tram is withdrawn.*

1957 *John Lennon meets Paul McCartney for the first time, at a church fête.*

Our window looks over house tops and cliffs onto the sea, so that when the ships sail past the cottage chimneys you may take them for weather-cocks. We have hill and dale, forest and mead, and plenty of lobsters. I was on the Portsmouth coach the Sunday before last in that heavy shower – and I may say I went to Portsmouth by water. I got a little cold and as it always flies to my throat I am a little out of sorts that way. There were on the coach with me some common French people, but very well-behaved. There was a woman amongst them to whom the poor men in ragged coats were more gallant than ever I saw gentleman to lady at a ball. When we got down to walk uphill, one of them picked a rose, and on remounting gave it to the woman with, *'Ma'mselle - voilà une belle rose!'*

. . . Bonchurch too is a very delightful Place – as I can see by the cottages all romantic – covered with creepers and honeysickles with roses and eglantines peeping in at the windows. Fit abodes, for the people I guess live in them, romantic old maids fond of novels or soldiers' widows with a pretty jointure – or anybody's widows or aunts or any things given to poetry and a pianoforte – as far as in 'em lies – as people say.

John Keats to Fanny Keats, from Shanklin on the Isle of Wight, 1819.

7 JULY

1814 Waverley, *the first of Sir Walter Scott's novels, is published anonymously.*

1927 *The first progamme based on gramophone records is broadcast by the BBC.*

1985 *Boris Becker wins Wimbledon for the first time.*

I found him alone, in a reclining posture in his drawing-room. He was lean, ghastly, and quite of an earthy appearance. He was dressed in a suit of grey cloth with white metal buttons, and a kind of scratch wig. He was quite different from the plump figure which he used to present . . .

I had a strong curiosity to be satisfied if he persisted in disbelieving a future state even when he had death before his eyes. I was persuaded from what he now said, and from his manner of saying it, that he did persist. I asked him if it was not possible that there might be a future state. He answered it was possible that a piece of coal put upon the fire would not burn: and he added that it was a most unreasonable fancy that we should exist for ever. That immortality, if it were at all, must be general; that a great proportion of the human race has hardly any intellectual qualities; that a great proportion dies in infancy before being possessed of reason; yet all these must be immortal; that a porter who gets drunk by ten o'clock with gin must be immortal; that the trash of every age must be preserved, and that new universes must be created to contain such infinite numbers . . .

I asked him if the thought of annihilation never gave him any uneasiness. He said not the least; no more than the thought that he had not been, as Lucretius observes, 'Well,' said I, 'Mr Hume I hope to triumph over you when I meet you in a future state; and remember you are not to pretend that you were joking with all this infidelity.' 'No, no,' said he. 'But I shall have been so long there before you come that it will be nothing new.'

James Boswell describes in his Journal his conversation with the philosopher David Hume six weeks before the latter's death in 1776.

8 JULY

━━━◈◈◈◈◈◈◈━━━

1630 *First Thanksgiving Day, held by Massachusetts Bay Colony.*

2000 *J. K. Rowling's fourth Harry Potter children's novel,* Harry Potter and the Goblet of Fire, *published in the US and UK with a combined print run of 5.3 million copies. By this date total sales of the first three are 35 million copies, in 31 languages; by the end of 2001 the figures are 60 million in 200 languages.*

The King [George III] bathes, and with great success; a [bathing] machine follows the royal one into the sea, filled with fiddlers, who play 'God Save the King', as His Majesty takes his plunge!

Fanny Burney, Diary, at Weymouth, 1789.

Oh what anxiety dearest Mary [his wife] and I suffered last night! 'It will succeed,' said she, 'or ruin you.' Had it offended him I should really have had great difficulties, but still I would have got through. Well, at dinner-time he called: I let him in with a beating heart. He walked up, liked Alexander [a painting] very much indeed, and after looking some time said: 'Why what have you been about all your life?' 'Painting large pictures in hopes of the sympathy of the public, my Lord.' 'That was imprudent,' said he. 'It was,' I replied (but I thought, 'I wish I could be as imprudent again'). 'Well, I have brought you £100.' 'My Lord, that's salvation.' He smiled and put five twenties on a chair. He then walked about my plaster-room [a collection of antique casts]; as I followed him – 'Take up your money,' said he. I did so . . . Well, God be thanked, I am once more lifted from a pit by a guardian angel.

Alexander evidently pleased him. 'I wish', said I, 'to make him an aspiring youth,' at which he nodded. 'Don't make the queen d——d ugly.' 'No, my Lord, that I won't' ('I flatter myself I like a handsome woman, and know as much of them as your Lordship,' thought I).

Benjamin Robert Haydon, Memoirs, 1826. Broke as usual, Haydon had written to the great artistic patron Lord Egremont, disclosing his circumstances.

9 JULY

1877 *The first Wimbledon Lawn Tennis Championship begins.*

1984 *Fire at York Minster.*

Yesterday I went to the late King [William IV]'s funeral, who was buried with just the same ceremonial as his predecessor this time seven years. It is a wretched mockery after all, and if I was king, the first thing I would do should be to provide for being committed to the earth with more decency and less pomp. A host of persons of all ranks and stations were congregated, who 'loitered through the lofty halls', chattering and laughing, and with nothing of woe about them but the garb. I saw two men in an animated conversation, and one laughing heartily at the very foot of the coffin as it was lying in state. The chamber of death in which the body lay, all hung with black and adorned with scutcheons and every sort of funeral finery, was like a scene in a play, and as we passed through it and looked at the scaffolding and rough work behind, it was just like going behind the scenes of a theatre. A soldier's funeral, which I met in the morning – the plain coffin slowly borne along by his comrades, with the cap and helmet and sword of the dead placed upon it – was more impressive, more decent, more affecting than all this pomp with pasteboard crowns, and heralds scampering about, while idleness and indifference were gazing or gossiping round about the royal remains.

Charles Greville, Memoirs, 1837. It was this performance which persuaded William IV's brother, the Duke of Sussex, to be buried at the new Kensal Green cemetery on the outskirts of London.

10 JULY

1940 *Luftwaffe attacks on convoys off the south-east coast of England signal the start of the Battle of Britain*

1958 *The first UK parking meters appear, in Mayfair, London.*

I agree with you about the utter senselessness of war, but I do not think about it even so often as one day in seven; one of its chief effects being to make one more callous shortsighted and unimaginative than one is by nature. It extends the circle of one's acquaintance, but beyond that I cannot see that it has a single redeeming feature. The suggestion that it elevates the character is hideous. Burglary, assassination, and picking oakum would do as much for anyone.

We are in the front line now and have two more days there . . . One gets terribly tired of one's clothes after sixteen days without a change. One dozes off in the daytime with a pleasant humming in one's ears which makes one dream of woods and hayfields in England and when one wakes one finds that it is a covey of bluebottles quarrelling over a bit of bully beef that some blasé private has flung into the trenches. Yesterday I saw a very handsome fly with a bottle-green bodice and magenta skirt. This is the nearest I can get to a pretty woman.

Raymond Asquith to his wife Katharine, 1916.

11 JULY

‒‒‒◦❀◦❦❀❅❧◦❀◦‒‒‒

1533 *Henry VIII is excommunicated by Pope Clement VII over the question of his divorce from Catherine of Aragon.*

1798 *The US Marine Corps formally re-established by Act of Congress.*

I find I am 'used up' by the [Great] Exhibition. I don't say 'there is nothing in it' – there's too much . . . I have a natural horror of sights, and the fusion of so many sights in one has not decreased it . . . It is a dreadful thing to be obliged to be false, but when anyone says, 'Have you seen ——?' I say 'Yes', because if I don't, I know he'll explain it, and I can't bear that. —— took all the school one day. The school was composed of a hundred 'infants', who got among the horses' legs in crossing to the main entrance from the Kensington Gate, and came reeling out from between the wheels of coaches undisturbed in mind. They were clinging to horses, I am told, all over the park. When they were collected and added up by the frantic monitors, they were all right. They were then regaled with cake, etc., and went tottering and staring all over the place; the greater part wetting their forefingers and drawing a wavy pattern on every accessible object. One infant strayed. He was not missed. Ninety and nine were taken home, supposed to be the whole collection, but this particular infant went to Hammersmith. He was found by the police at night, going round and round the turnpike, which he still supposed to be a part of the Exhibition. He had the same opinion of the police, also of Hammersmith workhouse, where he passed the night. When his mother came for him in the morning, he asked when it would be over? It was a great exhibition, he said, but he thought it long.

Charles Dickens to Mrs Watkins, 1851.

12 JULY

1910 *Charles Rolls of the Rolls-Royce Company is killed in a plane crash at an air show in Bournemouth. He has recently become the first to make a two-way crossing of the Channel.*

1992 *The* Guardian *newspaper's crop circle competition, first prize £5000, largely debunks the phenomenon, as complex designs are completed a few hours after being given out.*

We had a devil of a business last night altogether. We got off from the House [of Commons] to Sherry's a little before eight – about fourteen of us – without him, so I made him give me a written order to his *two* cooks to serve up the turtle [soup] in his absence, which they did, and which we presently devoured. In the midst of the second course, a black, sooty kitchenmaid rushed into the room screaming 'Fire!' At the house door were various other persons hallooing to the same purpose, and it turned out to be the curtains in Mrs Sheridan's dressing-room in a blaze, which Harry Scott had presence of mind to pull down by force, instead of joining in the general clamour for buckets, which was repeated from all the box-keepers, scene-shifters, thief-takers, and sheriff's officers who were performing the character of servants out of livery. So the fire was extinguished, with some injury to Harry's thumb.

Thomas Creevey to Dr Currie, 1806. 'Sherry' - the playwright Richard Brinsley Sheridan - was an MP and Treasurer of the Navy at this time, and also the proprietor of Drury Lane Theatre, and permanently in debt: hence his peculiar assortment of servants. The sheriff's officers were based at Bow Street Magistrates' Court, next to Drury Lane.

A man brought in a head to Mulinuu in great glory; they washed the black paint off, and behold! it was his brother. When I last heard he was sitting in his house, with the head upon his lap, and weeping. Barbarous war is an ugly business; but I believe the civilised is fully uglier; but Lord ! what fun!

Robert Louis Stevenson, from Samoa where a civil war
had broken out, to Sidney Colvin, 1893.

13 JULY

=⇒:◦|◦|◦|◦➤⟨⟨⟨⟨⟨◦|◦|◦|◦⟨=

1793 *The French Revolutionary, Jean-Paul Marat, is stabbed to death in his bath by Charlotte Corday.*

1985 *The 'Live Aid' pop concerts, organized by Bob Geldof at the Wembley and JFK stadiums in London and Philadelphia, raise over £40 million for Africa and are watched by 1.5 billion people.*

I always thought it very possible that I might be forestalled, but I fancied that I had a grand enough soul not to care; but I found myself mistaken and punished; I had, however, quite resigned myself, and had written half a letter to Wallace to give up all priority to him, and should certainly not have changed had it not been for Lyell's and your quite extraordinary kindness. I assure you I feel it, and shall not forget it. I am *more* than satisfied at what took place at the Linnean Society. I will set to work at the abstract, though how on earth I shall make anything of an abstract in thirty pages of the Journal, I know not, but will try my best.

You cannot imagine how pleased I am that the notion of Natural Selection has acted as a purgative on your bowels of immutability. Whenever naturalists can look at species changing as certain, what a magnificent field will be open – on all the laws of variation – on the genealogy of all living beings – on their lines of migration, etc., etc.

Charles Darwin to the distinguished botanist J. D. Hooker, 1858. In June Darwin had received a letter from Alfred Russel Wallace in Malaysia, from where he had been supplying Darwin with bird skins. Wallace, it seemed, had arrived at the same conclusion about evolution as Darwin. He revealed his own theory to his friends Charles Lyell, the distinguished geologist, and Hooker, who decided the only solution was to go public with Wallace's and Darwin's ideas together. This had just taken place at a meeting of the Linnean Society. The happy outcome was that it forced Darwin to start writing the Origin of Species, *the 'abstract' referred to above.*

14 JULY

1789 *The Fall of the Bastille in Paris and the start of the French Revolution.*

1865 *First ascent of the Matterhorn by a group including Edward Whymper, a John Murray author* (Scrambles Amongst the Alps, *1871*) *and supplier of wood engravings to the firm.*

1902 *Collapse of campanile in St Mark's Square, Venice.*

During the evening service the Church was crowded; and the singers, who have been in a state of constant intoxication since yesterday, being offended because I would not suffer them to chaunt the service after the First Lesson, put on their hats and left the Church. That is the most open breach of all religious decorum I have ever witnessed. However, it is too gross even to excite anger: it induces *awe* at the hardened wickedness of those wretches. Though White and West could fill their houses with oaths and execrations when their daughter and wife was dying above stairs, and under the influence of liquor produced in these injurious revels forget their duties as men to their dearest connections, I was not prepared to expect so open a violation of all decency in the house of God.

The Revd John Skinner, Journal, 1822. There had been a wedding in the family from the big house in the village, with free drink for the singers.

The scent and sound of the great lime tree, full of flowers and bees, came softly to us in the still afternoon. How strange it is that the lime tree smells so perilously sweet, and yet that a single blossom has hardly any fragrance – only a vegetable catkin sort of smell.

A.C. Benson, Diary, 1906.

15 JULY

1815 *Napoleon surrenders to Captain Maitland of HMS* Bellerophon *at Rochefort.*

1869 *Margarine patented in Paris.*

1912 *National Insurance begins.*

A great number of bodies have been found in the corn by the reapers within the last day or two, and it is said that the people living near Waterloo have realised fortunes by plunder. There are remaining upon the field thousands of the most moving English and French letters from the friends of the fallen, and caps pierced with balls and all the inside filled with congealed blood under a tree in the middle. A great number of caps are lying just as they were left and the trunk of a tree quite battered by shots. In this tree a boy of the age of fourteen stood during the battle, and with the most perfect security saw the whole; he had previously asked his father's leave to ride to see it, which being refused, he bethought himself of a better expedient. He is the son of a Belgian marquis and Papa heard this anecdote from him.

Georgiana Capel to her grandmother, the dowager Countess of Uxbridge, from Brussels, 1815. She describes the field of Waterloo. Her uncle, Lord Uxbridge, hit in the knee by a cannon-ball at the end of the battle, exclaimed, 'By God! I've lost my leg!', to which Wellington's characteristically laconic response was 'Have you, by God?'

Alfred Tennyson and I out at twelve. Swan Green, [New] Forest path, Halliday's Hill, we *swim* through tall bracken. T. pauses midway, turns to me, and says solemnly, 'I believe *this* place is quite full of vipers!' After going a little further, he stopped again and said, 'I am told that a viper-bite may make a woman silly for life, or deprive a man of his virility.'

William Allingham, Diary, 1866.

16 JULY

1918 *The former Tsar Nicholas II and his family are shot.*

1945 *The first atomic explosion is carried out in New Mexico.*

Every step one takes brings home the fact that we are not only at war, but in a corner. The fear of invasion hangs over every minute of the day. We hear of bombs shattering a house or two, of Hanley dog-race track being blown up, of Southend's nightly raids, but these rumours only serve to exasperate. It is the preparations for meeting an army among the fields around us, at home, that fill us with dread. The meadows beyond the Iron Bridge over the railway . . . are scarred with long trenches and mounds to prevent the landing of any planes and gliders. Also, in lieu of trees, stakes and poles have been planted. These preparations seem to have taken place overnight. Similarly with all the parks and playing-fields. Concrete gun-emplacements ('pill-boxes') have been created, or are being created, in tactical positions – I saw one behind a cricket pavilion. Old Fords full of bricks are left by the wayside ready to be shoved broadside-on into roads. Poor Laurence Kamm, the most scatterbrained of men, while driving home at 11 p.m. without his papers, was taken to the police station by an LDV [Home Guard] with a fixed bayonet. The whole of the east coast as far as the Humber is said to be under military control, as is the length of the south coast. Passage in and out of this zone is forbidden. Cars and motor-cycles must be rendered useless when left parked. The army is buying up all motor-cycles of over 500 cc newer than 1936.

George Beardmore, Journal, 1940.

17 JULY

1917 *The British Royal Family adopt 'Windsor' as their surname.*

1955 *Disneyland opens in California.*

I have enjoyed weather worthy of Africa, and yet without swallowing mouthfuls of mosquitos, nor expecting to hear hyenas howl in the village, nor to find scorpions in my bed. Indeed, all the way I came home, I could but gaze at the felicity of my countrymen. The road was one string of stage-coaches, loaded within and without with noisy jolly folks, and chaises and gigs that had been pleasuring in clouds of dust; every door and every window of every house was open, lights in every shop, every door with women sitting in the street, every inn crowded with jaded horses, and every ale-house full of drunken topers; for you know the English always announce their sense of heat or cold by drinking. Well! it was impossible not to enjoy such a scene of happiness and affluence in every village and amongst the lowest of the people; and who are told by villainous scribblers, that they are oppressed and miserable. New streets, new towns, are rising every day and everywhere; the earth is covered with gardens and crops of grain.

How bitter to turn from this Elysium to the Temple [prison] at Paris! The fiends there have now torn her son from the Queen [Marie Antoinette]! . . . Well, I will go to bed, and try to dream of peace and plenty; and though my lawn is burnt, and my peas and beans, and roses and strawberries parched, I will bear it with patience till the harvest is got in. Saint Swithin can never hold his water for forty days, though he can do the contrary. Good night!

Horace Walpole to the Hon. H.S. Conway, 1793.

18 JULY

1925 *Volume I of Hitler's* Mein Kampf *is published in Germany, written in prison after he was gaoled for the unsuccessful Beerhall Putsch in Munich in 1923.*

1936 *The Spanish Civil War begins.*

My nerves have for these two or three last days been susceptible of an acute excitement from the slightest causes; the beauty of the evening, the sighing of the summer breeze, brings the tears into my eyes not unpleasingly. But I must take exercise, and case-harden myself. There is no use in encouraging these moods of the mind. It is not the law we live on.

Sir Walter Scott, Journal, 1827.

We went to Mr Murray's and were shown by him most of the modern great authors in their pictures round his rooms. Then Murray showed us MSS of Lord Byron's. There was Scott's review of *Tales of my Landlord* in the MS sent to Murray, and his letter denying the authorship of the *Tales*, but just saving the truth. He gave me a page of Lord Byron's writing. We dined with Mr Clive, Kit Musgrave and Colonel Scudamore being also present. The former was full of Astley's [circus] the latter of Hanwell [asylum]; he went there with a party and found the mad people excellent company.

All the clubs except Crockfords are in St James parish and the managers have agreed to give all the broken victuals to the poor of the parish. A cart with tins is sent round every morning and brings quantities of tea and coffee and about 120 lb of bread and the same of meat which is distributed daily at the vestry.

Caroline Clive, Journal, 1844. She was the wife of the Revd Archer Clive, 'Squarson' of Whitfield in Herefordshire. Scott reviewed his own novels in the Quarterly Review.

19 JULY

⟡⟡⟡⟡⟡⟡⟡⟡⟡⟡⟡

1545 *The Tudor warship* Mary Rose *sinks in the Solent. Recovered four centuries later.*

1588 *The Spanish Armada is first sighted, off the Lizard.*

1837, 1843 *Brunel's ships* Great Western *and* Great Britain *are launched.*

The doors opened about four . . . Many of the doorkeepers were tipsy; quarrels took place. The sun began to light up the old Gothic windows, the peers to stroll in, and other company of all descriptions to crowd to their places. Some took seats they had not any right to occupy, and were obliged to leave them after sturdy disputes. Others lost their tickets . . . Every movement, as the time approached for the King's appearance, was pregnant with interest . . . Something rustles, and a being buried in satin, feathers, and diamonds rolls gracefully into his seat. The room rises with a sort of feathered, silken thunder. Plumes wave, eyes sparkle, glasses are out, mouths smile, and one man becomes the prime object of attraction to thousands . . .

The Hall doors opened again, and outside in twilight a man in dark shadowed armour appeared against the shining sky. He then moved, passed into darkness under the arch, and suddenly Wellington, Howard, and the Champion stood in full view, with doors closed behind them. This was certainly the finest sight of the day. The herald read the challenge; the glove was thrown down.

Benjamin Robert Haydon attends the banquet in Westminister Hall which followed the Coronation of King George IV, Journal, 1821. This was the last coronation at which the King's Champion rode into Westminister Hall to challenge, on the Monarch's behalf, anyone inclined to dispute his claim to the throne. He was accompanied by the High Constable (the Duke of Wellington) and Earl Marshal (Lord Howard of Effingham, deputising for the Catholic Duke of Norfolk).

20 JULY

St Uncumber's Day (alias Wilgefortis). She grew a beard because she did not wish to marry, and as a result was crucified by her irate father, the King of Portugal.

1957 *'Most of our people have never had it so good.' Prime Minister Harold Macmillan's speech at Bedford.*

I cannot give you a better idea of Highland life than by describing the place we are in [south of Oban]. The inn or public is by far the best house in the immediate neighbourhood. It has a white front with tolerable windows. The table I am writing on surprises me as being a nice flapped mahogany one; at the same time the place has no water-closet nor anything like it. You may, if you peep, see through the floor chinks into the ground rooms. The old grandmother of the house seems intelligent though not over clean. N.B. No snuff being to be had in the village, she made us some. The guid man is a rough-looking hardy stout man who I think does not speak so much English as the guid wife, who is very obliging and sensible and moreover though stockingless, has a pair of old shoes. Last night some whisky men sat up clattering Gaelic till I am sure one o' clock to our great annoyance. There is a Gaelic Testament on the drawers in the next room. White and blue chinaware has crept all about here. Yesterday there passed a donkey laden with tin pots. Opposite the window there are hills in a mist – a few ash trees and a mountain stream at a little distance. They possess a few head of cattle. If you had gone round to the back of the house just now, you would have seen more hills in a mist, some dozen wretched black cottages scented of peat smoke which finds its way by the door or a hole in the roof, a girl here and there barefoot. There was one little thing driving cows down a slope like a mad thing – there was another standing at the cow-house door rather pretty faced all up to the ankles in dirt.

John Keats to Tom Keats, 1818.

21 JULY

———◦◦◦◦◦◦⋘⋙◦◦◦◦◦◦———

1797 *Nelson's arm is amputated, following his unsuccessful attack on Tenerife.*

1994 *Tony Blair becomes leader of the Labour Party, soon to be 'New Labour'.*

The blue colour of my boot has completely disappeared now into this – still don't know exactly what colour to describe this other than greyish-cocoa colour. It appears to be covering most of the lighter part of my boot . . . very fine particles . . .

[Later] The Moon was a very natural and pleasant environment in which to work. It had many of the advantages of zero gravity, but it was in a sense less *lonesome* than Zero G, where you always have to pay attention to securing attachment points to give you some means of leverage. In one-sixth gravity, on the Moon, you had a distinct feeling of being *somewhere* . . . As we deployed our experiments on the surface we had to jettison things like lanyards, retaining fasteners, etc., and some of these we tossed away. The objects would go away with a slow, lazy motion. If anyone tried to throw a baseball back and forth in that atmosphere he would have difficulty, at first, acclimatizing himself to that slow, lazy trajectory; but I believe he could adapt to it quite readily . . .

Odour is very subjective, but to me there was a distinct smell to the lunar material – pungent, like gunpowder or spent cap-pistol caps. We carted a fair amount of lunar dust back inside the vehicle with us, either on our suits and boots or on the conveyor system we used to get boxes and equipment back inside. We did notice the odour right away.

Edwin E. (Buzz) Aldrin, the second man to set foot
on the Moon in the Apollo 11 mission, 1969.

22 JULY

1844 *The Revd W. A. Spooner is born, famous for transposing the initial sounds of spoken words: 'You have tasted a whole worm' for 'You have wasted a whole term', 'shoving leopard' for 'loving shepherd', etc.*

1933 *A six-foot-long grey animal spotted crossing a road by Loch Ness begins the craze for the Monster.*

But such green – green – green – as flutters in the vineyard down below the windows, *that* I never saw; nor yet such lilac, and such purple as float between me and the distant hills; nor yet – in anything – picture, book, or verbal boredom – such awful, solemn, impenetrable blue, as is that same sea. It has such an absorbing, silent, deep, profound effect, that I can't help thinking it suggested the idea of Styx. It looks as if a draught of it – only so much as you could scoop up on the beach, in the hollow of your hand – would wash out everything else, and make a great blue blank of your intellect.

When the sun sets clearly, then, by Heaven, it is majestic! From any one of eleven windows here, or from a terrace overgrown with grapes, you may behold the broad sea; villas, houses, mountains, forts, strewn with rose leaves – strewn with thorns – stifled in thorns! Dyed through and through and through. For a moment. No more. The sun is impatient and fierce, like everything else in these parts, and goes down headlong. Run to fetch your hat – and it's night. Wink at the right time of black night – and it's morning. Everything is in extremes . . . The summer gets hotter, hotter, hotter, till it bursts. The fruit gets riper, riper, riper, till it tumbles down and rots.

Charles Dickens writes from Italy to the painter Daniel Maclise, 1844. The Styx was one of the rivers of the Underworld. From what Dickens goes on to say, it would seem he actually means another of them, Lethe: if you drank from Lethe, you forgot the past.

23 JULY

1745 *Bonnie Prince Charlie lands on the Isle of Eriskay in the Outer Hebrides, signalling the start of the Second Jacobite Rebellion.*

1888 *Dunlop patents his pneumatic tyre.*

Flying over Wiltshire yesterday, we followed the course of a little river. Hanging over Cobbett's favourite country, with the sharp downs to provide a skyline of *useful* beauty, and the fertile valleys full of comfort and richness between them, it was almost an agony of affection to look down into the clean water. You could see the whole geography of the stream, the bright green cresses, almost the shadowy trout with their under-shadows.

Nothing will beat the dry-fly . . . the highest of the arts. You have got to endure for a salmon, and there is a pleasure in the absolutely straight sizzle of gut culminating in the plop of a lure that will be fishing efficiently through the whole arc, and the ten minutes with the fish on are at the tip of life. But you can't stalk a salmon. You don't caress your cast on to the water with a feathery anxiety.

There is something in our effete old English waters after all . . . And in them stands absorbed the ruminant angler, unconscious of time, deft with his fingers, puzzling his beloved fly-box, breathing his pipe smoke regularly in the bliss of concentration, pitting his quivering wits and tackle against the rosy-spotted tiger-fighters of the drinkable water, sun-struck into another infinite universe like the heron. I suppose the heron must be the happiest of living creatures.

T. H. White, England Have My Bones, *1934.*

24 JULY

1704 *Gibraltar captured from Spain by the British fleet.*

1851 *The tax on the number of windows in one's house is abolished; first levied in 1696.*

Poor human nature, what a contradiction it is! Today it is all rheumatism and morality, and sits with a death's head before it: tomorrow it is dancing! – Oh! my lady, my lady, what will you say, when the next thing you hear of me after my last letter is, that I have danced three country-dances with a whole set, forty years younger than myself! . . . Danced – I do not absolutely say, *danced* – but I swam down three dances very gracefully, with the air that was so much in fashion after the battle of Oudenarde [1708], and that was still taught when I was fifteen, and that I remember General Churchill practising before a glass in a gouty shoe . . .

Last night we went to Lady Hertford at Ditton . . . All the *jeunesse* strolled about the garden. We ancients, with the Earl and Colonel Keene, retired from the dew into the drawing-room. Soon after, the two youths and seven nymphs came in, and shut the door of the hall. In a moment we heard a burst of laughter, and thought we distinguished something like the scraping of a fiddle. My curiosity was raised, I opened the door and found four couples and a half standing up, and a miserable violin from the ale-house. 'Oh,' said I, 'Lady Bel shall not want a partner'; I threw away my stick, and *me voilà dansant comme un charme*!

Horace Walpole to the Countess of Ossory, 1781.

25 JULY

1952 *The European Coal and Steel Community is founded, precursor of the Common Market and the European Union. Britain is not a member.*

1978 *First test-tube baby born, Louise Brown, in Oldham.*

Four thirty-five a.m. *Tout est prêt!* In an instant I am in the air, my engine making 1,200 revolutions – almost its highest speed – in order that I may get quickly over the telegraph wires along the edge of the cliff. As soon as I am over the cliff I reduce my speed. There is now no need to force my engine. I begin my flight, steady and sure, towards the coast of England. I have no apprehensions, no sensations, *pas du tout*. The [destroyer] *Escopette* has seen me. She is driving ahead across the Channel at full speed. She makes perhaps 26 miles per hour. What matters? I am making over 40 mph. Rapidly I overtake her, travelling at a height of 250 feet . . . Ten minutes go. I turn my head to see whether I am proceeding in the right direction. I am amazed. There is nothing to be seen – neither the destroyer, nor France, nor England. I am alone. I am lost.

Then I saw the cliffs of Dover! Away to the west was the spot where I had intended to land. The wind had taken me out of my course. I turned and now I was in difficulties, for the wind here by the cliffs was much stronger, and my speed was reduced as I fought against it. My beautiful aeroplane responded. I saw an opening and I found myself over dry land. I attempted a landing, but the wind caught me and whirled me round two or three times. At once I stopped my motor, and instantly my machine fell straight on the ground. I was safe on your shore. Soldiers in khaki ran up, and also a policeman. Two of my compatriots were on the spot. They kissed my cheeks. I was overwhelmed.

Louis Blériot makes the first crossing of the English Channel by air, 1909.

26 JULY

1956 *President Nasser of Egypt seizes the Suez Canal Company.*

1958 *Débutantes are presented at Court at Buckingham Palace for the last time.*

[Lady Salisbury, wife of the Prime Minister,] had a yellow satin covering over her as she lay on the sofa. Splendid yellow it was, covered all over with delicate Chinese embroidery. And she asked me if I knew what it was, and when I said no, she told me it was the envelope that had come round the Emperor of China's letter to the Queen.

Sir Edward Burne-Jones, the painter, in conversation, 1897.

I rang up the head waiter at one of my favourite restaurants and said, 'Listen to me carefully, Paul. I am quite willing that in future you address me as "comrade" or "fellow-worker", and chuck the food at me in the manner of Socialists to their kind. But that doesn't start until tomorrow morning. Tonight I am bringing two friends with the intention that we may together eat our last meal as gentlemen. There will be a magnum of champagne and the best food your restaurant can provide. You, Paul, will behave with your wonted obsequiousness. The *sommelier*, the table waiter, and the *commis* waiter will smirk and cringe in the usual way. From tomorrow you will get no more tips. Tonight you will all be tipped royally.' The head waiter said, *'Bien, m'sieu.'* That was at a quarter-past six. At a quarter-past nine I arrived and was escorted by bowing menials to my table, where I found the magnum standing in its bucket, and three plates each containing two small slices of spam! Who would have thought a head waiter to have so much wit in him?

James Agate, after hearing the news of Labour's election victory, Ego, 1945.

27 JULY

1694 *The Bank of England is inaugurated.*

1949 *Maiden flight of the Comet, the first jet airliner.*

'Oh, bless those swamps!' thought I, 'here's another,' but no – not this time. Across the bottom of the steep ravine, from one side to another, lay an enormous tree as a bridge, about fifteen feet above a river, which rushed beneath it over a boulder-encumbered bed. I took in the situation at a glance, and then and there I would have changed that bridge for any swamp I have ever seen, yea, even for a certain bush-rope bridge in which I once wound myself up like a buzzing fly in a spider's web. I was fearfully tired, and my legs shivered under me after the falls and emotions of the previous part of the day, and my boots were slippery with water soaking . . .

Pagan [an Ajumba] thought he would try the bridge, and I thought I would watch how the thing worked. He got about three yards along it and then slipped, but caught the tree with his hands as he fell, and hauled himself back to my side again; then he went down the bank and through the water. This was not calculated to improve one's nerve; I knew by now I had got to go by the bridge, for I saw I was not strong enough in my tired state to fight the water. If only the wretched thing had had its bark on it would have been better, but it was bare, bald, and round, and a slip meant death on the rocks below. I rushed it, and reached the other side in safety.

> *The African explorer and ethnologist Mary Kingsley, travelling in the*
> *Congo accompanied by Fan and Ajumba tribesmen, 1895.*

28 JULY

—————◦|◦|◦|◦————◦—◦————◦|◦|◦|◦————

1586 *The potato introduced to Europe from South America.*

1965 *President Lyndon Johnson orders another 50,000 troops to Vietnam, bringing the total there to 125,000. That figure more than doubles in 1966.*

As we walked along the Strand tonight, arm in arm, a woman of the town accosted us, in the usual enticing manner. 'No, no, my girl,' said Johnson, 'it won't do.' He, however, did not treat her with harshness; and we talked of the wretched life of such women, and agreed, that much more misery than happiness, upon the whole, is produced by illicit commerce between the sexes.

James Boswell, Life of Johnson, 1763. Four nights later Boswell picked up a prostitute in the Strand, arguing this time that 'Surely . . . when the woman is already abandoned, the crime must be alleviated.'

I don't know *why* we live – the gift of life comes to us from I don't know what source or for what purpose; but I believe we can go on living for the reason that (always of course up to a certain point) life is the most valuable thing we know anything about, and it is therefore presumptively a great mistake to surrender it while there is any yet left in the cup. In other words consciousness is an illimitable power, and though at times it may seem to be all consciousness of misery, yet in the way it propagates itself from wave to wave, so that we never cease to feel, and though at moments we appear to, try to, pray to, there is something that holds one in one's place, makes it a standpoint in the universe which it is probably good not to forsake . . . Sorrow comes in great waves – no one can know that better than you – but it rolls over us, and though it may almost smother us it leaves us on the spot, and we know that if it is strong we are stronger, inasmuch as it passes and we remain. It wears us, uses us, but we wear it and use it in return; and it is blind, whereas we after a manner see.

Henry James to Grace Norton, 1883. She was suffering from depression.

29 JULY

1907 *Robert Baden-Powell holds the first Boy Scout camp on Brownsea Island in Poole Harbour, Dorset.*

1981 *Prince Charles marries Lady Diana Spencer in St Paul's Cathedral.*

On the top of a particularly lonely moor passed a little pub at which, on a cycling tour five years ago, Harry [his brother] and a friend stopped for a drink. The pub, he told me, had seemed deserted. They knocked on the counter, and, as nobody came, knocked again. Then the landlord appeared and said, 'Sorry to keep you gentlemen waiting. My wife has just died.' I insisted on going in. No customers, and nobody behind the bar. Only a black cat sitting on the counter, and nothing to be heard but the tick of an invisible clock. I rapped, and nobody came. I was about to rap again, when I noticed that Harry had already got back into the car. I followed him.

Harry told me that in connection with a slum-clearance scheme last winter he came across a room which ran over five cottages. None of the tenants below had ever bothered about it, and one said that so far as he knew the room was empty and had been for years, the property having changed hands half a dozen times, and successive landlords losing sight of the garret. On the door being forced it revealed itself as a joiner's workshop. The tools were neatly arranged on the bench. On a peg hung a working jacket. Dust everywhere. The calendar on the wall bore the date August 10, 1914.

James Agate, Ego, *1938, near Wensleydale.*

30 JULY

1935 *The first Penguin paperbacks go on sale.*

1938 *The first issue of the* Beano *comic appears.*

1966 *England beat Germany to win the soccer World Cup.*

The rain and wind blowing fierce November . . . I kicked along, holding down my head, and would you believe it, rode 12 Welsh miles in two hours! At 4 o'clock I arrived, drenched, at Festiniog Inn . . . I jumped off my mare; sent my great coat and stockings to the fire and put on my dry breeches . . . Mrs O [the landlady] now produced some fresh-caught salmon and some fresh-salted, half hot, roasted beef. I had appetite and played away . . . When I surveyed the outhouses . . . the broken windows I stopped with clouts; my dog was fed with an oatmeal mess; my sheets were aired and my night cap scorched, because I sweated through them last night . . . The rain and tempest increased to a fearful degree, and beat against the windows – as almost to force them in: so I hugged myself over a peat fire and was happy I was not at sea . . . I sit, methinks, as in the cabin of a ship in a storm; for the distant hills appear like approaching waves. At nine o'clock, the roasted leveret was brought in, so delicious and nicely roasted that I suffered none of it be taken out.

John Byng, Viscount Torrington. Diary. 1793, in North Wales.

Introducing 'Miss Zelfredo, the world-famous snake-charmer', the ring-master said: 'It is with great regret that I have to announce one of the great tragedies of the Ring. Doreen Zelfredo's python, which had been with her for six years, died on Friday at Knowle. I am sure the audience will join with me in sympathy for Doreen, and in the wish that she may soon find a new pal. If ever woman loved a snake Doreen did. Miss Zelfredo will now enter the ring and perform her act without her snake.'

James Agate, Ego, *1942.*

31 JULY

1917 *The Battle of Passchendaele (3rd Ypres) begins. It lasts until 10 November and the Allies suffer 300,000 casualties amidst mud and the new German mustard gas.*

1998 *Britain bans landmines.*

We have the army of Spain before us, and mind, with the grace of God, to wrestle a pull with him. There was never any thing pleased better, than the seeing the enemy flying with a southerly wind to the northwards.

Sir Francis Drake, having helped to defeat Philip II of Spain's Armada in the Channel, to Sir Francis Walsingham, 1588.

But now for the cream of the story; we went to the opera – the house was full and brilliant beyond measure and my brother [the Duke of Devonshire] in raptures (as I must say he is from morning till night). All nations, all embassies, all English men and scarcely a *reputable* but myself. Boxes for every King and Emperor of the known world. But what do you think they shout at, applaud, *pâmer de rire* [swoon] over, *dance* in short. They dance the battle of Waterloo – in all its details. The Imperial Guard, wounded, form dejected groups, embrace the National Guard etc. whilst a smart English officer makes most brilliant *entrées*. He is *héros de la pièce*, ends the ballet with presenting a French officer whom he had taken prisoner to his mistress who had imagined him dead. The French all kneel to kiss the hem of his garment and dance a finale of all the nations amidst bursts of applause. Metternich sat by me at supper at Lady Castlereagh's and we agreed it was worth coming any distance, taking any trouble, to see this proof of national character and confirmation of what that character is now reduced to.

Lady Granville, from Paris, to her sister Lady Morpeth, 1815.

AUGUST

1 AUGUST

1740 *'Rule, Britannia' performed for the first time, at Cliveden House, Buckinghamshire.*

1759 *The Battle of Minden, at which the Marquis of Granby is the hero of the day, losing his wig in a cavalry charge and so earning his place on many pub signs.*

1939 *'In the Mood' recorded by Glenn Miller.*

My station was in the powder-magazine with the gunner. As we entered the bay we stripped to our trousers, opened our ports, cleared, and every ship we passed gave them a broadside and three cheers. Any information we got was from the boys and women who carried the powder. They behaved as well as the men, and got a present for their bravery from the Grand Signior [Sultan of Turkey, the ruler of Egypt]. When the French Admiral's ship blew up, the *Goliath* got such a shake we thought the after-part of her had blown up until the boys told us what it was. They brought us every now and then the cheering news of another French ship having struck [surrendered], and we answered the cheers on deck with heartfelt joy. In the heat of the action, a shot came right into the magazine, but did no harm, as the carpenters plugged it up, and stopped the water that was rushing in. I was much indebted to the gunner's wife, who gave her husband and me a drink of wine every now and then, which lessened our fatigue much . . . A lad . . . had the match in his hand to fire his gun. In the act of applying it, a shot took off his arm; it hung by a small piece of skin. The match fell to the deck. He looked to his arm, and seeing what had happened, seized the match in his left hand, and fired off the gun before he went to the cockpit to have it dressed.

John Nichol of HMS Goliath at the Battle of the Nile, 1798.

2 AUGUST

1784 *First Royal Mail coach runs, from Bristol to London.*

1788 *Thomas Gainsborough the painter dies. His last words: 'We are all going to heaven and Van Dyck is of the party.'*

1894 *Death Duties introduced.*

The king started back, scarce believing the testimony of his own eyes; and the woman made a second thrust, which just touched his waistcoat before he had time to prevent her – and at that moment one of the attendants, seeing her horrible intent, wrenched the knife from her hand. 'Has she cut my waistcoat? [said the King] Look! For I have no time to examine.' Thank heaven the poor wretch had not gone quite so far. 'Though nothing [added the King] could have been sooner done, for there was nothing for her to go through but a thin linen, and fat.'

Fanny Burney, Diary, 1786, on the attempt by a mad woman
to stab George III outside St James's Palace.

I went . . . to the sale of the late King [George IV]'s wardrobe . . . He hardly ever gave away anything except his linen, which was distributed every year. These clothes are the perquisite of his pages, and will fetch a pretty sum. There are all the coats, etc. he has ever had for fifty years, three hundred whips, canes without number, every sort of uniform, the costumes of all the Orders in Europe, splendid furs, pelisses, etc., hunting-coats and breeches, and among other things a dozen pair of corduroy breeches he had made to hunt in when Don Miguel [of Portugal] was here. His profusion in these articles was unbounded, because he never paid for them, and his memory so accurate that one of his pages told me he recollected every article of dress, no matter how old, and that they were always liable to be called on to produce some particular coat or other part of apparel of years gone by. It is difficult to say whether in great or little things that man was most odious and contemptible.

Charles Greville, Memoirs, 1830.

3 AUGUST

1858 *John Hanning Speke arrives at the shores of Lake Victoria.*

1914 *The first ship sails through the Panama Canal.*

I am heartily glad it is done – it is almost like a fly crawling up a wainscoat – Imagine the task of mounting 10 Saint Pauls without the convenience of staircases . . . The whole immense head of the Mountain is composed of large loose stones – thousands of acres – Before we had got half way up we passed large patches of snow and near the top there is a chasm some hundred feet deep completely glutted with it – Talking of chasms they are the finest wonder of the whole – they appear great rents in the very heart of the mountain though they are not, being at the side of it, but other huge crags arising round it give the appearance to Nevis of a shattered heart or core in itself – These chasms are 1500 feet in depth and are the most tremendous places I have ever seen – they turn one giddy if you choose to give way to it – We tumbled in large stones and set the echoes at work in fine style . . . After a little time the mist cleared away but still there were large clouds about attracted by old Ben to a certain distance so as to form as it appeared large dome curtains which kept sailing about, opening and shutting at intervals here and there and everywhere; so that although we did not see one vast wide extent of prospect all round we saw something perhaps finer – these cloud-veils opening with a dissolving motion and showing us the mountainous region beneath as through a loop hole.

John Keats to Tom Keats, 1818, describing his ascent of Ben Nevis.

4 AUGUST

1914 *Britain declares war on Germany.*

1964 *The bodies of three civil rights workers found in Mississippi, killed by the Ku Klux Klan; the subject of the 1988 film starring Gene Hackman,* Mississippi Burning.

2000 *The Queen Mother celebrates her 100th birthday.*

Every now and then the Germans sent over a trench mortar bomb – to my mind the most alarming things in this war. It is a thing about the size and shape of a very big rum jar, has a range of four hundred yards or so and goes very high and very slow. At night you see it slowly elbowing through the stars with a trail of sparks behind it, and the probability is that the trench is too full for you to get as far away as you would wish. Then it falls and fizzes for a little in the ground and then the most ear-splitting explosion you can ever hope to hear.

This night I was up at the forward end of this trench, rather engrossed in directing the men's work, when suddenly I found myself surrounded by a mob of terrified figures from the battalion which was holding that part of the line (we were only working on it) who gibbered and crouched and held their hands over their eyes and generally conducted themselves as if the end of the world was at hand. It was very alarming; they had seen one of these damned rum jars coming and I hadn't. Sure enough in about five seconds the thing went off – luckily just the other side of our parapet. The sky was black with smoke and dirt, and the people butted into one in the fog screaming, but much more frightened than hurt . . . In the moment immediately preceding [the explosion] I made up my mind I was dead, and in the moment immediately following I said to myself 'I suppose this is shell-shock at last, now I shall get home.' But it wasn't . . . I felt a piece of the thing hit me on the leg, but alas it only made a small blood-blister. I picked another fragment out of the shoulder of my jacket – it had cut through the khaki but not through my shirt, and there was quite a big dent in my steel helmet. A most disappointing result.

Raymond Asquith to Katharine Asquith, 1916.

5 AUGUST

The oyster season opens. 'He was a bold man that first ate an oyster.'

1962 *Marilyn Monroe found dead.*

Polidori has sent me his tragedy! Do me the kindness to send by return of post a *delicate* declension of it, which I engage faithfully to copy.

John Murray II to Lord Byron, 1817. Polidori was Byron's doctor. Byron obliged his publisher by sending a 'civil and delicate declension' a few weeks later, of which the following is about one-third of the whole:

> Dear Doctor – I have read your play
> Which is a good one in its way
> Purges the eyes and moves the bowels
> And drenches handkerchiefs like towels
> With tears that in a flux of grief
> Afford hysterical relief
> To shatter'd nerves and quickened pulses
> Which your catastrophe convulses.
> I like your moral and machinery
> Your plot too has such scope for scenery!
> Your dialogue is apt and smart
> The play's concoction full of art –
> Your hero raves – your heroine cries
> All stab – and every body dies;
> In short your tragedy would be
> The very thing to hear and see –
> And for a piece of publication
> If I decline on this occasion
> It is not that I am not sensible
> To merits in themselves ostensible
> But – and I grieve to speak it – plays
> Are drugs – mere drugs, Sir, nowadays –

6 AUGUST

————————❖————————

1762 *Lord Sandwich, taking part in an all-night card game, calls for a snack at five in the morning: a slice of meat between two pieces of bread.*

1889 *The Savoy Hotel opens in the Strand, built by Richard D'Oyly Carte with the profits from the operas of Gilbert and Sullivan.*

The problem after the release of the bomb is not to proceed forward but to turn away. As soon as the weight had left the aeroplane I immediately went into this steep turn and we tried then to place distance between ourselves and the point of impact. In this particular case that bomb took fifty-three seconds from the time it left the aeroplane until it exploded and this gave us adequate time of course to make the turn. We had just made the turn and rolled out on level flight when it seemed like somebody had grabbed a hold of my aeroplane and gave it a real hard shaking because this was the shock wave that had come up. Now after we had been hit by a second shock wave not quite so strong as the first one I decided we'll turn around and go back and take a look. The day was clear when we dropped that bomb, it was a clear sunshiny day and the visibility was unrestricted. As we came back around again facing the direction of Hiroshima we saw this cloud coming up. The cloud by this time, now two minutes old, was up at our altitude. We were 33,000 feet at this time and the cloud was up there and continuing to go right on up in a boiling fashion, as if it was rolling and boiling. The surface was nothing but a black boiling, like a barrel of tar. Where before there had been a city with distinctive houses, buildings and everything that you could see from our altitude, now you couldn't see anything except a black boiling debris down below.

Colonel Tibbetts, USAAF, drops the first atomic bomb on Hiroshima, 1945.

7 AUGUST

1914 *£1 and ten-shilling notes issued.*

1998 *US embassies in Kenya and Tanzania bombed by al-Qaeda: 219 killed in Nairobi and 11 in Dar-es-Salaam.*

I became some fortnight ago a British subject. You may perhaps not have been aware that I wasn't one – it showed, I believe, so little; but I had in fact to do things, of no great elaboration, to take on the character and testify to my fond passion for the cause for which you are making so very much grander still a demonstration; so that now at any rate civis Britannicus sum, and there's no mistake about it . . .

Our genius is, and ever has been, to insist *urbi et orbi* [to the city and the world] that we live by muddle, and by muddle only – while, all the while, our native character is never *really* abjuring its stoutness or its capacity for action. We have been stout from the most ancient days, and are not a bit less so than ever – only we should do better if we didn't give so much time to writing to the papers that we are impossible and inexcusable. That is, or seems to be, queerly connected with our genius for being *at all* – so that at times I hope I shall never see it foregone: it's the mantle over which the country truly forges its confidence and acts out its faith.

Henry James to Lieutenant Wilfred Sheridan, 1915.
Sheridan was killed the following month.

8 AUGUST

1963 *Britain's Great Train Robbers get away with £2.5 million.*

1974 *President Nixon announces that he will resign because of the Watergate scandal.*

My loving people, we have been persuaded by some that are careful of our safety to take heed how we commit ourselves to armed multitudes, for fear of treachery; but I do assure you, I do not desire to live to distrust my faithful and loving people.

Let tyrants fear. I have always so behaved myself that, under God, I have placed my chiefest strength and safeguard in the loyal hearts and goodwill of my subjects, and therefore I am come amongst you, as you see, at this time, not for my recreation and disport, but being resolved in the midst and heat of the battle to live or die amongst you all, to lay down for my God and for my kingdom, and for my people, my honour and my blood, even in the dust.

I know I have the body of a weak and feeble woman, but I have the heart and stomach of a king, and of a king of England too, and think it foul scorn that Parma or Spain, or any prince of Europe, should dare invade the borders of my realm; to which, rather than any dishonour shall grow by me, I myself will take up arms, I myself will be your general, judge, and rewarder of every one of your virtues.

> *Queen Elizabeth I addresses her troops at Tilbury, at the mouth of the Thames,*
> *during the Armada conflict, 1588.*

Kew Green was quite filled with all the inhabitants of the place – the lame, old, blind, sick and infants, dressed in their Sunday garb to line the sides of the roads through which their majesties passed, attended by a band of musicians, arranged in the front, who began 'God save the King!' the moment they came on the Green, and finished it with loud huzzas. This was a compliment at the expense of the better inhabitants, who paid the musicians themselves, and mixed in with the group . . . The Queen, in speaking of it afterwards, said, 'I shall always love little Kew for this!'

> *Fanny Burney, Diary, 1786, on how George III's escape*
> *from assassination was celebrated.*

9 AUGUST

1890 *Germany given the North Sea island of Heligoland in return for recognising that present-day Kenya and Uganda fall within the British colonial sphere.*

1949 *Atomic bomb dropped on Nagasaki, killing more than 75,000.*

I am going to stand godfather; I don't like the business; I cannot muster up decorum for these occasions; I shall certainly disgrace the font. I was at Hazlitt's marriage, and had like to have been turned out several times during the ceremony. Anything awful makes me laugh. I misbehaved once at a funeral. Yet I can read about these ceremonies with pious and proper feelings. The realities of life only seem the mockeries.

Charles Lamb to Robert Southey, 1815.

In the course of an hour we were on our way to Cheddar. The young people much enjoyed the drive through the cliffs, which appeared to the greatest advantage of light and shade, the sun being in full splendour. Having put up our horses, we entered the cavern under the direction of some of the old women with candles, and we afterwards made a comfortable luncheon in the open air. I shewed the young people the paper mills, each being permitted to make his own sheet by way of memorial of his visit to the spot. It rained nearly the whole of the way to Wells, but held up, fortunately, to enable us to visit the Cathedral and Bishop's Palace, where we arrived about five o'clock. I meant to have made my visit to the crypt incog., but it happened unfortunately that the Bishop had seen us approaching, and Mr Strachey came down to say he wished to see me. I found the gallery filled with company, and his Lordship in pontificalibus, as he was about to perform the ceremony of Baptism on his great grandson, Strachey's infant. Being myself stained with the variation of each soil from Cheddar to Wells, I was not sorry to retreat as speedily as possible.

The Revd John Skinner, Journal, 1832.

10 AUGUST

1911 *MPs vote themselves salaries for the first time: £400 a year.*

2003 *Britain's hottest day since records began in 1875: 38.1 centigrade, 100.6 degrees Fahrenheit, at Gravesend.*

You and I, the ornaments of our generation, should have been spared this wreck of our belief that through the long years we had seen civilization grow and the worst become impossible. The tide that bore us along was then all the while moving to *this* as its grand Niagara – yet what a blessing we didn't know it . . . The country and the season here are of a beauty of peace, and loveliness of light, and summer grace, that make it inconceivable that just across the Channel, blue as *paint* today, the fields of France and Belgium are being, or about to be, given up to unthinkable massacre and misery. One is ashamed to admire, to enjoy, to take any of the normal pleasure, and the huge shining indifference of Nature strikes a chill to the heart and makes me wonder of what abysmal mystery, or villainy indeed, such a cruel smile is the expression.

Henry James to the novelist Rhoda Broughton, 1914,
writing from Rye, Sussex.

I had to lunch with Charles Fry my publisher at the Park Lane Hotel. He was late, having just got up after some orgy *à trois* with whips, etc. He is terribly depraved and related every detail, not questioning whether I wished to listen. In the middle of the narration I simply said, 'Stop! Stop!' At the same table an officer was eating, and imbibing every word. I thought he gave me a crooked look for having spoilt his fun.

My delight in Churchill's defeat, disapproval of the Socialists' victory, detestation of the atom bomb and disgust with the Allies' treatment of Germany are about equal. Muddle.

James Lees-Milne, Diary, Prophesying Peace, *1945.*

11 AUGUST

1934 *Alcatraz Prison, on an island in San Francisco Bay, receives its first inmates.*

1954 *France's seven-year Indo-China War ends, with the independence of Vietnam, Cambodia and Laos recognised and the Communist Vietminh under Ho Chi Minh in control of North Vietnam.*

At Charleston we had tea from bright blue cups under the pink light of the giant hollyhock. We were all a little drugged with the country; a little bucolic I thought. It was lovely enough – made me envious of its country peace; the trees all standing securely – why did my eye catch the trees? The look of things has a great power over me. Even now, I have to watch the rooks beating up against the wind, which is high, and still I say to myself instinctively 'What's the phrase for that?' and try to make more and more vivid the roughness of the air current and the tremor of the rook's wing slicing as if the air were full of ridges and ripples and roughnesses. They rise and sink, up and down, as if the exercise rubbed and braced them like swimmers in rough water. But what a little I can get down into my pen of what is so vivid to my eyes, and not only to my eyes; also to some nervous fibre, or fanlike membrane in my species.

Janie Julian Leonard and I sat in the orchard till the wind got too strong, and I made them come out on the marsh and was sorry the river was low, or they might have praised it . . . I don't think much either way about Orlando. Odd, how I feel myself under orders; always marching on a definite stage with each book, tho' it is one I set myself.

Virginia Woolf, Diary, 1928.

12 AUGUST

1969 *The Royal Ulster Constabulary use tear-gas for the first time, in the Bogside, Londonderry, after the annual Apprentice Boys' March. This results in the 'Battle of the Bogside', which ends with the first direct intervention by British troops.*

1981 *IBM puts the first personal computer - PC - on sale.*

Not knowing whether you are yet returned from your sea-water, I write at random to you. For me, I am come to my resting place, and find it very necessary, after living for a month in a house with three women that laughed from morning to night, and would allow nothing to the sulkiness of my disposition. Company and cards at home, parties by land and water abroad, and (what they call) *doing something*, that is, racketing about from morning to night, are occupations, I find, that wear out my spirits, especially in a situation where one might sit still, and be alone with pleasure; for the place was a hill like Clifden, opening to a very extensive and diversified landscape, with the Thames, which is navigable, running at its foot.

Cambridge is a delight of a place, now there is nobody in it. I do believe you would like it, if you knew what it was without inhabitants. It is they, I assure you, that get it an ill name and spoil all. Our friend Dr Chapman (one of its nuisances) is not expected here again in a hurry. He is gone to his grave with five mackerel (large and full of roe) in his belly. He ate them all at one dinner; but his fate was a turbot on Trinity Sunday, of which he left little for the company besides bones. He had not been hearty all the week; but after this sixth fish he never held up his head more, and a violent looseness carried him off. They say he made a very good end.

Thomas Gray to John Clerke, 1760. Dr Chapman was Master of Magdalene.

13 AUGUST

1876 *First complete performance of Wagner's Ring Cycle of four operas -* Rhinegold, Valkyrie, Siegfried, Twilight of the Gods *- begins at Beyreuth in Germany.*

1961 *The East Germans begin to erect the Berlin Wall, along the boundary between the Eastern and Western sectors of the city.*

O God, if there be a God, save my soul, if I have a soul!

Prayer of a private soldier just before the Battle of Blenheim, 1704.

I have not time to say more than to beg of you to present my humble duty to the Queen, and to let her Majesty know that her army has had a glorious victory. M. Tallard [French commander], and two other generals, are in my coach, and I am following the rest. The bearer, my aide-de-camp, Colonel Parkes, will give her Majesty an account of what has passed. I shall do it, in a day or two, by another more at large.

The Duke of Marlborough to his wife Sarah, giving news of his victory at Blenheim.
He wrote this note, while still in the saddle, on the back of a tavern bill.

I crossed from Folkestone a week ago, and found Townshend on board, fastened up in his carriage, in a feeble wideawake hat. It was rather windy, and the sea broke pretty heavily over the deck. With sick women lying among his wheels in various attitudes of despair, he looked like an ancient Briton of a weak constitution – say Boadicea's father – in his war-chariot on the field of battle. I could not but mount the Royal Car, and I found it to be perforated in every direction with cupboards, containing every description of physic, old brandy, East India sherry, sandwiches, oranges, cordial waters, newspapers, pocket handkerchiefs, shawls, flannels, telescopes, compasses, repeaters (for ascertaining the hour in the dark), and finger rings of great value. He was on his way to Lausanne, and he asked me the extraordinary question 'how Mrs Williams, the American Actress, kept her wig on?' I then perceived that mankind was to be in a conspiracy to believe that he wears his own hair.

Charles Dickens describes his old and dear friend, the Revd Chauncey
Hare Townshend, to Miss Burdett-Coutts, 1856.

14 AUGUST

1880 *Cologne Cathedral in Germany is completed after 632 years of building.*

1882 *Cetewayo, the defeated King of the Zulus, visits Queen Victoria.*

I received a note from Mr Johnson, that he was arrived at Boyd's inn, at the head of the Canongate [Edinburgh]. I went to him directly. He embraced me cordially; and I exulted in the thought that I now had him actually in Caledonia. Mr Scott told me that, before I came in, the Doctor had unluckily had a bad specimen of Scottish cleanliness. He then drank no fermented liquor. He asked to have his lemonade made sweeter; upon which the waiter, with his greasy fingers, lifted a lump of sugar, and put it into it. The Doctor, in indignation, threw it out of the window. Scott said he was afraid he would have knocked the waiter down . . .

He was to do me the honour to lodge under my roof. Mr Johnson and I walked arm-in-arm, up the High Street, to my house in James's Court; it was dusky night: I could not prevent his being assailed by the evening effluvia of Edinburgh . . . The peril is much abated, by the care which the magistrates have taken to enforce the city laws against throwing foul water from the windows; but, from the structure of the houses in the old town, which consist of many storeys, in each of which a different family lives, and there being no covered sewers, the odour still continues. A zealous Scotsman would have wished Mr Johnson to be without one of his five senses upon this occasion. As we marched slowly along, he grumbled in my ear, 'I smell you in the dark!'

James Boswell, Journal of a Tour to the Hebrides, *1773.*

15 AUGUST

1945 *VJ Day, marking Victory over Japan.*

1969 *Three-day Woodstock music festival begins.*

1987 *Corporal punishment in British state schools is abolished.*

Even Byron was silent and thoughtful. We were startled and drawn together by a dull hollow sound that followed the blow of a mattock; the iron had struck a skull, and the body was soon uncovered. Lime had been strewn on it; this, or decomposition, had the effect of staining it of a dark and ghastly indigo colour. Byron asked me to preserve the skull for him; but remembering that he had formerly used one as a drinking-cup, I was determined Shelley's should not be so profaned. The limbs did not separate from the trunk, as in the case of Williams's body, so that the corpse was removed entire into the furnace . . . After the fire was well kindled we repeated the ceremony of the previous day; and more wine was poured over Shelley's dead body than he had consumed during his life. This with the oil and salt made the yellow flames glisten and quiver. The heat from the sun and fire was so intense that the atmosphere was tremulous and wavy. The corpse fell open and the heart was laid bare. The frontal bone of the skull, where it had been struck with the mattock, fell off; and, as the back of the head rested on the red-hot bottom bars of the furnace, the brains literally seethed, bubbled, and boiled as in a cauldron, for a very long time. Byron could not face this scene, he withdrew to the beach and swam off to the *Bolivar* [his yacht].

Edward John Trelawny arranged for the cremation of Shelley's body, after exhuming it from the beach near Viareggio where it had been buried after he drowned while yachting; he had performed the same service for the body of Edward Williams, Shelley's sailing companion, the day before: 1822.

16 AUGUST

1952 *Flash-flood in Lynmouth, north Devon, kills 34.*

1977 *Elvis Presley dies, aged 42. In 2000 his estate is still earning $35 million a year.*

On the cavalry drawing up they were received with a shout of goodwill, as I understood it. They shouted again, waving their sabres over their heads; and then, slackening rein, and striking spur into their steeds, they dashed forward and began cutting the people.

'Stand fast,' I said, 'they are riding upon us; stand fast.' And there was a general cry in our quarter of 'Stand fast.' The cavalry were in confusion: they evidently could not, with all the weight of man and horse, penetrate that compact mass of human beings; and their sabres were plied to hew a way through naked held-up hands and defenceless heads; and then chopped limbs and wound-gaping skulls were seen; and groans and cries were mingled with the din of that horrid confusion. 'Ah! ah!' 'For shame! for shame!' was shouted. Then, 'Break! break! they are killing them in front, and they cannot get away'; and there was a general cry of 'Break! break' . . .

In ten minutes from the commencement of the havoc the field was an open and almost deserted space . . . The yeomanry had dismounted – some were easing their horses' girths, others adjusting their accoutrements, and some were wiping their sabres. Several mounds of human beings still remained where they had fallen, crushed down and smothered. Some of these still groaning, others with staring eyes, were gasping for breath, and others would never breathe more.

Peterloo: the attack on the peaceful meeting at St Peter's Fields, Manchester, in support of parliamentary reform, described by Samuel Bamford, 1819.

17 AUGUST

1453 *French victory over the English at Castillon ends the Hundred Years' War.*

1978 *Three Americans become the first to cross the Atlantic in a hot-air balloon.*

I have a feel of health and spirits that I certainly have not had before since marriage. Early hours, mixed salts in *eau tiède*, roast meat and rice, Bohea tea, six bunches of currants for supper – but all this *au pied de la lettre* – will procure the same for any body and I think I try it hard; in my eighth month with a little Hercules kicking me till I really can at times hardly forbear screaming. When I arrived here a week ago I looked as if I was expecting to lie in every hour, the second day I was very unwell and bilious. I sent for a ministering angel, a doctor, who gave me a good dose of calomel and ordered me the salts; ever since I have looked a Miss. God bless you, my dear, dearest sister. Granville is putting up all his beautiful regular features and saying – 'Now do leave off – it is really too foolish, tiring yourself.' What an angel he is eating buttered roll.

Lady Granville, who is pregnant, to her sister Lady Morpeth, 1810.

The shouts of the populace announced her near approach, and some minutes after, two folding doors within a few feet of me were suddenly thrown open, and in entered her Majesty . . . I had been taught to believe she was as much improved in looks as in dignity of manners; it is therefore with much pain I am obliged to observe that . . . she popped all at once into the House, made a *duck* at the throne, another to the Peers, and a concluding jump into the chair which was placed for her . . . such a back for variety and inequality of ground as you never beheld; with a few straggling ringlets on her neck, which I flatter myself from their appearance were not her Majesty's own property.

Thomas Creevey describes the arrival of George IV's estranged Queen, Caroline of Brunswick, at the House of Lords on the first day of her trial, 1820.

1958 *Vladimir Nabokov's novel* Lolita, *about an older man's obsession with a twelve-year-old 'nymphet', is published in the US. It has already been published in Paris, in 1955.*

1960 *The birth-control pill is launched, in the US.*

We came to Hampstead Heath, and looked past a foreground of fir-trees over a wide undulating prospect tufted with trees, and richly cultivated, a lake shining in the distance under the evening sky. On the other side huge London lying sombre and silent. We were just in time to see the effect of the lighting of the lamps. The dusky mass awoke, and here and there, and soon all over, glowed with multitudinous sparks – 'like', said Patmore, 'the volcanic crust of the earth not yet cooled' . . .

[After returning to his house in Camden Town] Coventry Patmore went on to tell me: 'I have in this room perhaps the greatest literary treasure in England – the manuscript of Tennyson's *next poem*. It is written in a thing like a butcher's account-book. He left it behind him in his lodging when he was up in London and wrote to me to go and look for it. He had no other copy, and he never remembers his verses. I found it by chance, in a drawer; if I had been a little later it would probably have been sold to a butter-shop [as wrapping-paper].' Before I went away Patmore took out this MS book from a cabinet and turned over the leaves before my longing eyes, but Tennyson had told him not to show it to anybody. Mrs Patmore had copied it out for the press, and T. gave her the original. I was not even told the title at this time. It was *In Memoriam*.

William Allingham, Diary, 1849.

19 AUGUST

———◈———

1942 *The Dieppe Raid ends in disaster, though justified as a dress rehearsal for later combined-operations seaborne landings.*

1991 *Mikhail Gorbachev ousted from power in Russia by a hard-liner coup. The plotters in turn are defeated by Boris Yeltsin, who becomes the new Russian leader.*

Our situation has undergone very little change since the affair of the 17th of June [the Battle of Bunker Hill], except the daily loss of men and officers in the hospitals. I suppose the accounts of that transaction did not meet with credit in England, and that it could not be believed that a thousand men and officers of the bravest troops in the world could in so short a time be cut off by irregulars. After two or three such instances, you good people of old England will find out that five or six thousand men are not sufficient to reduce a country of 1,500 miles in extent, fortified by nature, and where every man from fifteen to fifty is either a volunteer, or compelled to carry arms; amongst whom the number of our countrymen is very great, and they are the most dangerous enemies we have to encounter. [The people of England] will find out that some other mode must be adopted than gaining every little hill at the expense of a thousand Englishmen; and if they mean to continue masters of this country, they will lay aside that false humanity towards these wretches which has hitherto been so destructive to us. They must lay aside the notion that hurting America is ruining Great Britain, and they must permit us to restore to them the dominion of the country by laying it waste, and almost extirpating the present rebellious race, and upon no other terms will they ever possess it in peace.

Captain W.G. Evelyn to the Hon. Mrs Leveson Gower, 1775. He was serving with the British forces in New England fighting the American rebels, and died of wounds the following year.

20 AUGUST

1953 *The USSR explodes its first hydrogen bomb, following its first atomic bomb exploded in 1949.*

1989 *The* Marchioness *pleasure boat sinks after collision with a dredger on the Thames and 51 die.*

I am glad our last day at the seaside was fine, though clouded overhead. We went over to Cummings' (at Margate) in the evening, and as it was cold, we stayed in and played games; Gowing, as usual, overstepping the mark. He suggested we should play 'Cutlets', a game we never heard of. He sat on a chair, and asked Carrie to sit on his lap, an invitation which dear Carrie rightly declined.

After some species of wrangling, I sat on Gowing's knees and Carrie sat on the edge of mine. Lupin sat on the edge of Carrie's lap, then Cummings on Lupin's and Mrs Cummings on her husband's. We looked very ridiculous, and laughed a good deal.

Gowing then said: 'Are you a believer in the Great Mogul?' We had to answer all together: 'Yes – oh, yes!' (three times). Gowing said: 'So am I,' and suddenly got up. The result of this stupid joke was that we all fell on the ground, and poor Carrie banged her head against the corner of the fender. Mrs Cummings put some vinegar on; but through this we missed the last train, and had to drive back to Broadstairs, which cost me seven-and-sixpence.

George and Weedon Grossmith, The Diary of a Nobody, *1894.*

21 AUGUST

1911 *Leonardo da Vinci's portrait of the* Mona Lisa *is stolen from the Louvre in Paris, by an Italian who resents it being in France. It is recovered two years later when he tries to sell it in Florence.*

1968 *Russian tanks in Prague end the liberalising régime of Alexander Dubček in Czechoslovakia.*

I hastened to the kitchen, where I saw the redoubtable Thomas Freeman, who told me, that . . . he attempted to cover her with his hat, but she screamed out, and leaped directly over his head. I then desired him to pursue as fast as possible, and added Richard Coleman to the chase, as being nimbler, and carrying less weight than Thomas . . . He came in sight of a most numerous hunt of men, women, children, and dogs; he did his best to keep back the dogs, and presently outstripped the crowd, so that the race was at last disputed between himself and Puss . . . He got the start and turned her; she pushed for the town again, and soon after she entered it, sought shelter in Mr Wagstaff's tanyard . . . There she encountered the tanpits full of water; and while she was struggling out of one pit, and plunging into another, and almost drowned, one of the men drew her out by the ears, and secured her. She was then well washed in a bucket, to get the lime out of her coat, and brought home in a sack at ten o'clock.

> *William Cowper to the Revd John Newton, 1780. Cowper kept*
> *pet hares and one of them, Puss, had escaped.*

At the revival tonight of *Lady Windermere's Fan* I asked Lady Alexander, exquisite as ever and looking like the lids of Juno's eyes, whether in the 'nineties peeresses at private dances wore tiaras. She said, 'They wore them at the tea-table!'

> *James Agate,* Ego, *1945.*

22 AUGUST

1485 *The Battle of Bosworth brings the first Tudor, Henry VII, to the English throne.*

1642 *Charles I raises his standard at Nottingham and the Civil War starts.*

1988 *All-day drinking in pubs, 11 a.m. to 11 p.m., starts in Britain.*

I believe you would like life in Schloss Pellendorf [in Lower Austria]. The priest rings his bell at the first glimmer of day and *all* the women but *none* of the men go to Mass. The men feed the horses, pigs etc. After Mass the women go into the fields and do the heaviest work conceivable without a break till the last glimmer of day has gone. The women are discalceate [shoeless] but the men wear boots and do the lighter farm jobs.

The Graf is charming and just what I like. He has an English huntsman's face and when Leopold the Hungarian butler announces dinner he, the Count, makes as if he was winding a horn and calls out: Worry, Worry, Worry, Lu Lu, Tear him, Tear him. The cooks are a Hungarian man and his wife and real artists. The footman is a Slovak and the chauffeur kisses Maud's hand every time she gets in and out of the motor. In short we are staying with a Hungarian Nobleman . . .

The battlefield of Wagram is conveniently situated close to the house and the hill on which Mustapha decided not to besiege Vienna . . .

The peasants are so nice. I'm sure we ought all to be like that and personally I do my best. Cocks crow, dogs bark and a delicious hot smell of manure fills the room like Beauty does a brimming cup. It is country life.

Now we have had dinner off crayfish, roebuck's back and champagne and I must get to bed and read a little Hume on Human Nature.

Conrad Russell to Katharine Asquith, 1930.

23 AUGUST

1942 *The Battle of Stalingrad begins.*

1962 *First live TV broadcast is relayed between the US and Europe by Telstar satellite.*

The man who drove our jaunting-car yesterday hadn't a piece in his coat as big as a penny roll, and had had his hat on (apparently without brushing it) ever since he was grown up. But he was remarkably intelligent and agreeable, with something to say about everything. For instance, when I asked him what a certain building was, he didn't say 'courts of law' and nothing else, but: 'Av you plase, sir, it's the foor coorts o' looyers, where Misther O' Connell stood his trial wunst, ye'll remimber, sir, afore I tell ye of it.' When we got into the Phoenix Park, he looked round him as if it were his own, and said: 'THAT's a park, sir, av yer plase.' I complimented it, and he said: 'Gintlemen tills me as they'r bin, sir, over Europe, and never see a park aqualling ov it. 'Tis eight mile roond, sir, ten mile and a half long, and in the month of May the hawthorn trees are as beautiful as brides with their white jewels on. Yonder's the vice-regal lodge, sir; in them two corners lives the two sicretirries, wishing I was them, sir. There's air here, sir, av yer plase! There's scenery here, sir! There's mountains – thim, sir! Yer coonsider it a park, sir? It is that, sir!'

Charles Dickens, from Dublin, to one of his daughters, 1858.

24 AUGUST

79 *Vesuvius erupts, burying the towns of Pompeii and Herculaneum.*

410 *Rome is captured by the Visigoths.*

1814 *The White House in Washington is burnt by British troops.*

Found heaps of letters, some of them from poets and authors, who are the pest of my life – one sending me a 'Serio-Comic Drama of Invasion, in Three Acts, including the Vision and the Battle', and referring me for his poetic credentials to three admirals and 'the late comptroller of the navy'. Another begging to know whether I was acquainted with 'any man or woman to whom money was for a time useless', who would venture £100 upon a literary speculation he had in hand.

Tom Moore, Diary, 1818.

And you are actually going to get married! you! already! And you expect me to congratulate you! or 'perhaps not'. I admire the judiciousness of that 'perhaps not'. Frankly, my dear, I wish you all happiness in the new life that is opening to you; and you are marrying under good auspices, since your father approves of the marriage. But congratulation on such occasions seems to me a tempting of Providence. The triumphal-procession-air which, in our manners and customs, is given to marriage at the outset – that singing of *Te Deum* before the battle has begun – has, ever since I could reflect, struck me as somewhat senseless and somewhat impious. If ever one is to pray – if ever one is to feel grave and anxious – if ever one is to shrink from vain show and vain babble – surely it is just on the occasion of two human beings binding themselves to one another, for better and for worse, till death part them; just on that occasion which it is customary to celebrate only with rejoicings, and congratulations, and *trousseaux*, and white ribbon! Good God!

Jane Welsh Carlyle to Miss Barnes, the daughter of her Chelsea doctor, 1859.

25 AUGUST

1875 *Captain Webb becomes the first man to swim the Channel.*

1944 *Paris is liberated by de Gaulle and the single Free French division in Normandy, whom the Americans diplomatically allow to enter the city ahead of other Allied forces.*

At two o'clock in the morning, that terrible Sheridan [the playwright] seduced Mr Creevey into Brooks's [Club] where they stayed till four when Sherry *affectionately* came home with him, and upstairs to see me. They were both so very merry, and so much pleased with each other's jokes, that, though they could not repeat them to me very distinctly, I was too much amused to scold them as they deserved.

Mrs Creevey to her daughter Miss Ord, 1806.

What it is to be ill in an emigrant train let those declare who know. I slept none till late in the morning, overcome with laudanum, of which I had luckily a little bottle. All today I have eaten nothing, and only drunk two cups of tea, for each of which, on the pretext that the one was breakfast, and the other dinner, I was charged fifty cents, and neither of them, I may add, stood by me for three full minutes. Our journey is through the ghostly deserts, sage brush and alkali, and rocks, without form or colour, a sad corner of the world. I confess I am not jolly, but mighty calm in my distresses. My illness is a subject of great mirth to some of my fellow travellers, and I smile rather sickly at their jests.

Robert Louis Stevenson to W.E. Henley, 1879. The invalid Stevenson was on his way to California to see Fanny Osbourne, the American whom eventually he married. The train was crossing south-west Wyoming, and he had been taken ill at Laramie.

26 AUGUST

55 BC *Julius Caesar's first invasion of Britain. He comes again the following year.*

1346 *British longbowmen defeat the French at the Battle of Crécy.*

1919 *19th Amendment to the US Constitution is adopted, giving women the vote.*

The reins, bit, and bridle of this wonderful beast is a small steel handle, which applies or withdraws the steam from its legs or pistons, so that a child might manage it. The coals, which are its oats, were under the bench, and there was a small glass tube affixed to the boiler, with water in it, which indicates by its fullness or emptiness when the creature wants water, which is immediately conveyed to it from its reservoirs. There is a chimney to the stove, but as they burn coke there is none of the dreadful black smoke which accompanies the progress of a steam-vessel. This snorting little animal, which I felt rather inclined to pat, was then harnessed to our carriage, and, Mr Stephenson having taken me on the bench of the engine with him, we started at about ten miles an hour . . .

We then came to a moss, or swamp, of considerable extent, on which no human foot could tread without sinking, and yet it bore the road which bore us. This had been the great stumbling-block in the minds of the committee of the House of Commons; but Mr Stephenson has succeeded in overcoming it. A foundation of hurdles, or, as he called it, basket-work, was thrown over the morass, and the interstices were filled with moss and other elastic matter. Upon this the clay and soil were laid down, and the road *does* float, for we passed over it at the rate of five and twenty miles an hour, and saw the stagnant swamp water trembling on the surface of the soil on either side of us.

Fanny Kemble goes for a trip on the Manchester-to-Liverpool Railway, 1830.

27 AUGUST

1883 *Krakatoa, a volcano in the straits between Java and Sumatra, erupts, killing 36,000 with its tsunami waves. The explosion is heard 3,000 miles away.*

1939 *First flight by the world's first jet aircraft, the German Heinkel 178.*

He was dead DRUNK when he landed . . . They drank all the wine on board the steamboat, and then applied to the whiskey punch, till he could hardly stand . . . It is a meloncholy farce from beginning to end, and they have voted him a palace! In short, palaces in the air and drunkards under the table are the order of the day.

The Countess of Glengall, quoted in the Creevey *Papers, on George IV's visit to Ireland, 1821.*

. . . I have just finished my book (very prettily indeed, I hope) and am in the first drowsy lassitude of having done so. I should be lying in the sunshine by the hour together, if there were such a thing. In its absence I prowl about in the wind and rain. Last night was the most tremendous I ever heard for a storm of both. I fear there will be sad shipwrecks in the newspapers a few days hence.

. . . The Birmingham people are arranging those readings I promised to give them. They expect to get five hundred pounds for their new Institution (a splendid idea of a Mechanics' Athenaeum) therefrom. I am going to read there three nights in the Christmas week – to two thousand working people only, on the Friday – the *Christmas Carol.* You heard the beginning of *Bleak House.* I wish (and did wish very heartily) you had been here the night before last, to hear the end.

Charles Dickens to Miss Burdett-Coutts, 1853, from Boulogne.

28 AUGUST

1879 *Cetewayo, King of the Zulus, is captured by the British but only after his warriors have inflicted a major defeat on them at Isandlwana, killing or wounding 1,300. He is reinstated in 1883 but has lost face, and so is driven out by his people.*

1994 *Sunday trading in stores is legalised in Britain.*

I should like now to promenade you round gardens – apple-tasting – pear-tasting – plum-judging – apricot-nibbling' – peach-scrunching – nectarine-sucking and melon-carving – I have also a great feeling for antiquated cherries full of sugar cracks – and a white currant tree kept for company – I admire lolling on a lawn by a water-lilied pond to eat white currants and see gold fish: and go to the fair in the evening if I'm good – There is not hope for that – one is sure to get into some mess before evening.

John Keats to Fanny Keats, 1819.

I have a dream that one day this nation will rise up and live out the true meaning of its creed: 'We hold these truths to be self-evident; that all men are created equal.'

I have a dream that one day on the red hills of Georgia the sons of former slaves and the sons of former slaveowners will be able to sit down together at the table of brotherhood.

I have a dream that one day even the state of Mississippi, a desert state sweltering with the heat of injustice and oppression, will be transformed into an oasis of freedom and justice.

I have a dream that my four little children will one day live in a nation where they will not be judged by the color of their skin but by the content of their character.

I have a dream today.

Martin Luther King, Jr speaks to 250,000 in Washington, DC on the occasion of the centenary of Abraham Lincoln's emancipation proclamation, 1963.

29 AUGUST

————◦❈◦————

1950 *The first British troops arrive in South Korea to fight as part of the United Nations force defending it from attack by Communist North Korea.*

1966 *The Beatles give their last public concert, in San Francisco.*

The mob direct all their violence against the Duke of Wellington. They tried yesterday to pull him off his horse. The police interfered and some of the mob were knocked down, some hurt in the struggle.

What an extraordinary man Brougham is! How do you think he was occupied the greatest part of Sunday morning? Playing at leap-frog with [Lord] Duncannon's children at Roehampton. They say the Queen looks cross and pale, is blooded every morning before she comes to town and scarcely returns the bows made to her as she passes.

I have almost forgotten to talk of my royal morning. I spent two hours at Cleveland House with the Duchess of Gloucester, an amiable and good soul. The Duchess of Clarence, ugly with a good *tournure* [figure] and manner; the Duchess of Kent, very pleasing indeed raving of her baby. '*C'est mon bonheur, mes délices, mon existence. C'est l'image du feu roi* [the late king].' Think of the baby. They say it is *le roi*, George in petticoats, so fat it can scarcely waddle. Augusta, good-humoured and jolly, stuffing *filets de sole* and veal cutlets, and Sophia very clever and agreeable. I had to go with each of them the whole course. 'How many children has Lady Georgiana Morpeth?' 'Eleven, ma'am.' 'God bless my soul, you don't say so, it seems but yesterday' etc.

Lady Granville to her sister Lady Morpeth, 1820. George IV and the government were intent on dissolving his marriage to Queen Caroline. The darling of the mob, her defence counsel at her trial in the House of Lords was Henry Brougham. The baby was the future Queen Victoria; Augusta and Sophia were daughters of George III.

30 AUGUST

30 BC *Cleopatra, Queen of Egypt, lover of Julius Caesar and Mark Anthony, dies.*

1982 *Yasser Arafat and the Palestine Liberation Army are forced out of Beirut in the Lebanon and take refuge in Tunisia.*

Here everything is Scotch – the curtains, the carpets, the furniture are all of different plaids, and the thistles are in such abundance that they would rejoice the heart of a donkey if they happened to look like his favourite repast, which they don't. I am told that it is *de rigueur* to clothe myself in tweed directly . . . It is very cold here, and I believe my feet were frostbitten at dinner, for there was no fire at all there, and in the drawing-room there were two little sticks which hissed at the man who attempted to light them; and the Queen, thinking, I suppose, that they meant to burn, had a large screen placed between the royal nose and the unignited wood. She seemed, I thought, particularly grateful for such small jokes as my freezing state enabled me to crack. I have a very comfortable room, however, and am now sitting on the hob writing to you . . . I must, however, be ready for kirk, where the *meenister* preaches for two hours and takes his large, rough greyhound into the pulpit with him, so no more at present.

Lord Clarendon to his wife, from Balmoral, 1856.

When he came into the room he half opened the door and then retreated and did so twice before he got courage to come inside. He was in rags, his feet, without stockings, showing through his boots, his coat torn, and no shirt. He seemed in the last stage of physical collapse . . . He explained that he was obliged to earn tenpence every day to live. This he did by waiting at the doors of theatres and calling cabs, and by selling matches in the neighbourhood of Charing Cross.

Wilfred Meynell, the editor, describes, his first meeting with the poet and opium addict Francis Thompson in 1888, to Wilfrid Scawen Blunt, 1907. Thompson's most famous poem is 'The Hound of Heaven'.

1888 *Jack the Ripper's first murder victim, a prostitute, found in Whitechapel in the East End of London.*

1997 *Death of Diana, Princess of Wales in a car crash in a Paris underpass.*

Descended. As I bounded down, noticed the moving stones under the soft moss, hurting my feet. Ascended that steep and narrow ridge. On my right that precipice and the morass at its feet. On my left the two tarns and another precipice twice as lofty as the other, but its white stones more coated and lined with moss. Am now at the top of Helvellyn . . . No words can convey any idea of this prodigious wildness. That precipice . . . its ridge, sharp as a jagged knife, level so long, and then ascending so boldly. What a frightful bulgy precipice I stand on and to my right how the crag . . . plunges down like a waterfall, reaches a level steepness, and again plunges! The moon is above Fairfield almost at the full. Now descended over a perilous peat-moss then down a hill of stones all dark, and darkling. I climbed stone after stone down a half-dry torrent and came out at the Raise Gap. And Oh! my God! how did that opposite precipice look in the moonshine – its name Stile Crags.

Coleridge describes the end of his cross-country walk from Keswick to Dove Cottage, the Wordsworths' home at Grasmere, in his Notebook, 1800. He and Wordsworth 'invented' the idea of walking for pleasure.

At eleven o'clock Coleridge came, when I was walking in the still, clear moonshine in the garden . . . We sat and chatted till half-past three, W. in his dressing-gown. Coleridge read us a part of *Christabel*.

Dorothy Wordsworth, Journal, 1800.

SEPTEMBER

1 SEPTEMBER

1853 *The first triangular postage stamp is issued, by the Cape of Good Hope.*

1939 *Germany invades Poland.*

'There [in Glenshiel]', said I, 'is a mountain like a cone.' JOHNSON. 'No, Sir, it would be called so in a book; and when a man comes to look at it, he sees it is not so. It is indeed pointed at the top; but one side of it is larger than the other.' Another mountain I called immense. JOHNSON. 'No; it is no more than a considerable protuberance . . .'

At Auchnashiel, we sat down on a green turf-seat at the end of a house; they brought us out two wooden dishes of milk, which we tasted. One of them was frothed like a syllabub. I saw a woman preparing it with such a stick as is used for chocolate, and in the same manner. We had a considerable circle about us, men, women, and children, all M'Craas, Lord Seaforth's people. Not one of them could speak English. I observed to Dr Johnson, it was much the same as being with a tribe of Indians. JOHNSON. 'Yes, Sir, but not so terrifying.' I gave all who chose it snuff and tobacco, I also gave each person a piece of wheat bread, which they had never tasted before. I then gave a penny apiece to each child. I told Dr Johnson of this: upon which he called to Joseph and our guides, for change for a shilling, and declared that he would distribute among the children. Upon this being announced in Erse, there was a great stir; not only did some children come running down from neighbouring huts, but I observed one black-haired man, who had been with us all along, had gone off, and returned, bringing a very young child. My fellow-traveller then ordered the children to be drawn up in a row, and he dealt about his copper, and made them and their parents all happy.

James Boswell, Journal of a Tour to the Hebrides, *1773*

2 SEPTEMBER

490 BC *The Greeks defeat the Persians at the Battle of Marathon and Pheidippides runs 26 miles to carry the news to Athens.*

1898 *Kitchener defeats the Sudanese dervishes under the Khalifa at the Battle of Omdurman outside Khartoum, so establishing Anglo-Egyptian control of the Upper Nile.*

The track followed the crest of a high ridge with the dales of Moldavia flowing away on either hand. We were moving through illimitable sweeps of still air. Touched with pink on their under sides by the declining sun, which also combed the tall stubble with gold, one or two thin shoals of mackerel cloud hung motionless in the enormous sky. Whale-shaped shadows expanded along the valleys below, and the spinneys were sending long loops of shade downhill. The air was so still that the smoke from Matila Ghyka's cigar hung in a riband in the wake of our cavalcade; and how clearly the bells of the flocks, which were streaming down in haloes of golden dust to the wells and the brushwood folds a few ravines away, floated to our ears. Homing peasants waved their hats in greeting, and someone out of sight was singing one of those beautiful and rather forlorn country songs they call a *doina*. A blurred line along the sky a league away marked the itinerary of the deserting storks. Those in the carriage below were snowed under by picnic things, mushroom baskets and bunches of anemones picked in the wood. It was a moment of peace and tranquillity and we rode on in silence towards the still far-off samovar and the oil lamps and heaven knew what bad news.

Patrick Leigh Fermor describes his last day of peace in 1939,
as he and his hosts in Romania return from a picnic.

3 SEPTEMBER

1658 Oliver Cromwell dies on the anniversary of the Battles of Dunbar (1650) and Worcester (1651), his two victories against the forces of Charles II.

1943 Allied troops land on mainland Europe, in southern Italy, four years to the day since the declaration of war on Germany.

The Prime Minister is to broadcast at 11.15 and we have no wireless. The housemaid has one and she comes and fixes it up in a fumbling way . . . At 11.40 we decide to stroll down to the House. I walk ahead with Leo Amery, and Anthony [Eden] and Duff [Cooper] walk behind. Hardly have we left 28 Queen Anne's Gate when a siren blows. Amery says, 'They ought not to do that after what we have heard on the wireless. People will think it is an air-raid warning.' Hardly has he said these words when another siren takes it up. 'My God!' I say, 'it *is* an air-raid warning!' . . . We reach Parliament Square. As we enter it the crowd, which had massed itself against the railings, breaks up like a flock of pigeons. They run away towards Westminster Hospital. They cut across the grass plot where the statues are . . . I give my hat up in the ordinary way and mount the stairs to the Members' Lobby. The police there are in steel helmets and tell us to go down to the air-raid refuge. I do so, and find the corridor towards the Harcourt Room blocked by all manner of people from cabinet ministers to cooks. It is very hot. People chat to each other with forced geniality. After ten minutes we are released and go on to the terrace. People assert that they heard gunfire and bombs dropping. I suggest that it was merely the carpenters nailing in the asbestos linings to the windows. The terrace is flashed with sunshine, and we watch with disapproval the slow movements of people at Lambeth trying to get a balloon to rise. It has been dampened by last night's rain.

Harold Nicolson, Diary, 1939.

4 SEPTEMBER

476 *The deposition of Romulus Augustus marks the end of the Western Roman Empire.*

1888 *George Eastman gets a patent for his roll-film camera and registers the name Kodak.*

1964 *The Forth Road Bridge is opened.*

They hurried into contradicting their own decrees as fast as they made them, pronounced property sacred and seized it everywhere, declared for universal peace, and usurped Papal and German dominions, proclaimed everybody at liberty to live where they pleased, but burnt their houses and forced them to fly, and then confiscated their estates if they did not return at the hazard of their lives. The option of perjury or starving was another benefit bestowed on all the conscientious clergy. The Bastille (where only six prisoners were found, rather a moderate number for such a capital as Paris) was destroyed, and every prison was crammed.

> *Horace Walpole to the Countess of Ossory, 1792, on the French revolutionaries.*

Lads after the stamp of the Head Filing Boy ('boy' by courtesy – he's over fifty) stand in khaki and steel helmets on duty at Richmond Bridge and along the railway lines. Yellow notices have appeared in railway carriages telling passengers to lie on the floor in an air-raid, having drawn the blinds to stop flying glass. (George Edgar, one-time soldier of the First World War, said you'd not catch him lying down on the floor of a railway carriage.) Announcement after announcement over the wireless relating to billeting, closing of schools, evacuation, addresses of public concerns like the licensing offices, where to apply for gas-masks etc. . . . one goes to the wireless to be thoroughly disheartened.

> *George Beardmore, Journal, 1939.*

5 SEPTEMBER

1800 *Britain seizes the island of Malta from the French, vital for control of the Mediterranean.*

1997 *Mother Teresa dies aged 87 in Calcutta.*

I up to the top of Barking steeple, and there saw the saddest sight of desolation that I ever saw; everywhere great fires, oil-cellars, and brimstone, and other things burning. I became afraid to stay there long, and therefore down again as fast as I could, the fire being spread as far as I could see it . . . I walked into the town, and find Fenchurch Street, Gracechurch Street, and Lombard Street all in dust. The Exchange a sad sight, nothing standing there of all the statues or pillars but Sir Thomas Gresham's picture [i.e., statue] in the corner. Into Moorfields, our feet ready to burn, walking through the town among the hot coals, and find that full of people, and poor wretches carrying their goods there, and everybody keeping his goods together by themselves; and a great blessing it is to them that it is fair weather for them to keep abroad night and day; drank there, and paid twopence for a plain penny loaf. Thence homeward, having passed through Cheapside and Newgate market, all burned . . . And took up, which I keep by me, a piece of glass of the Mercers' chapel in the street, where much more was, so melted and buckled with the heat of the fire, like parchment. I also did see a poor cat taken out of a hole in the chimney joining to the wall of the Exchange, with the hair all burned off the body, and yet alive.

Samuel Pepys, Diary, 1666.

6 SEPTEMBER

1522 *Del Cano completes the first circumnavigation of the world begun by Magellan, who had died earlier on the voyage.*

1915 *The first tank has its first trial run in England*

We (that is to say, Major Careless [Carlos] and I) went, and carried up with us some victuals for the whole day – viz., bread, cheese, small beer, and nothing else – and got up into a great oak, that had been lopped some three or four years before, and being grown out again, very bushy and thick, could not be seen through, and here we stayed all the day.

Memorandum – That while we were in this tree we see soldiers going up and down, in the thicket of the wood, searching for persons escaped, we seeing them, now and then, peeping out of the wood.

King Charles II describes hiding in an oak tree
after the Battle of Worcester, 1651.

I . . . got admittance [to Ely Cathedral], happily in total solitude: some agencies, supposed to be human, were blowing the organ, making it discourse deep solemn music; a poor little sparrow was fluttering far aloft in the topmost windows of the lantern (top of the main tower, which is almost all of glass); this sparrow, and a poor country lad, who had plucked up courage to follow on seeing me enter, were my only fellow worshippers. I declare it were a good arrangement if they would but keep the music going, in all such places, and sweep away the rest of the living lumber; and leave one alone in these enormous towering spaces, with one's own thoughts and the spirits of the Dead!

Thomas Carlyle to John Sterling, 1842.

7 SEPTEMBER

1838 *Grace Darling and her father rescue the crew of the* Forfarshire
off the Farne Islands on the Northumbrian coast.

1940 *The Luftwaffe's heavy bombing of London signals the start of
the Blitz and its abandonment of raids on airfields, strategically
much more dangerous for Britain*

I am in that state of mind which you may (once) have seen described in the
newspapers as 'bordering on distraction'; the house given up to me, the fine
weather going on (soon to break, I daresay), the painting season oozing away,
my new book waiting to be born, and

NO WORKMEN ON THE PREMISES,

along of my not hearing from you!! I have torn all my hair off, and constantly
beat my unoffending family. Wild notions have occurred to me of sending in my
own plumber to do the drains. Then I remember that you have probably written
to prepare *your* man, and restrain my audacious hand. Then Stone presents
himself, with a most exasperatingly mysterious visage, and says that a rat has
appeared in the kitchen, and it's his opinion (Stone's not the rat's) that the
drains want 'compo-ing' [sealing], for the use of which explicit language I could
fell him without remorse . . . Curtains and carpets, on a scale of awful splendour
and magnitude, are already in preparation, and still – still –

NO WORKMEN ON THE PREMISES.

*Charles Dickens to his brother-in-law, an architect, who is supervising works at
Dickens's new house, bought from the painter Frank Stone, 1851.*

I had a letter from Palmerston this morning who seems to have made up his
mind to throw over the East India Company, and asks me while *I am shaving
or walking* to think what sort of government should be established in place of
it! He has a jolly way of looking at disasters.

*Lord Clarendon to his wife, a few months after the outbreak of the Indian Mutiny,
1857. He was Foreign Secretary, Palmerston Prime Minister; the East India Company
had administered British India for the preceding two centuries.*

8 SEPTEMBER

1943 *Italy surrenders.*

1944 *The first V2 rockets land on London. They are immune to attack by planes or anti-aircraft fire and explode without warning, unlike VI doodlebugs.*

I called on Bacon at Meadyeates. He remarked how much evil communication was carried on in the gaols, where persons, for small faults comparatively, mixed with those who were incarcerated for crimes of greater magnitude. He had been sent to Shepton on a charge of poaching, although at the time he certainly was not guilty, having been found merely with a dog following at his heels in a grass field, without a gun, and on the footpath. Yet this man was sent to prison, and during his confinement associated with sheep-stealers and horse-stealers, and was made acquainted with all their tricks. I also learnt from him that one of the Camerton people, of the name of Crocum, has stolen a horse; and it is supposed he will be in danger of his life as this is not his first offence, and his father was hanged for the same malpractices.

The Revd John Skinner, Journal, 1824.

A verger took a party round [York Minster], and talked so pleasantly and gently; I did not listen to much he said, but just crept about in the holy gloom, and felt the awe of the huge solemn place, so filled with tradition and splendour, creep into my mind. That feeling is worth ten thousand cicerones telling you what everything *is*. I don't want to know; indeed, I want *not* to know; it is enough that I am deeply moved. A foolish antiquarian was with the party, asking silly questions and contradicting everything. Such a goose, and so proud of being learned! The wealth and air of *use* pleased me. Yet the spirit which built it is all gone, I think. Religion – by which I mean services and dogmas – what is it? I sometimes think it is like tobacco, chewed by hungry men to stay the famished stomach. And perhaps the real food for which we starve is death.

A. C. Benson, Diary, 1904.

9 SEPTEMBER

1513 *James IV and the flower of the Scottish nobility are killed by the English under the Earl of Surrey at the Battle of Flodden in Northumberland.*

1976 *Death of Chinese Communist leader Mao Tse-tung, who has inflicted untold misery on his people.*

The key to the business is of course the belly; difficult as it is to keep that in view in the zone of three miraculous meals a day in which we were brought up. Civilisation has become reflex with us; you might think that hunger was the name of the best sauce; but hunger to the cold solitary under a bush of a rainy night is the name of something quite different. I defend civilisation for the thing it is, for the thing it has *come* to be, the standpoint of a real old Tory. My ideal would be the Female Clan. But how can you turn these crowding dumb multitudes *back*? They don't do anything *because;* they do things, write able articles, stitch shoes, dig, from the purely simian impulse. Go and reason with monkeys!

Robert Louis Stevenson to his cousin, Bob Stevenson, 1894.

Good press on the [opening of the first] Seven Bridge – and my hat. It is almost incredible how much the spotlight is put on one's appearance by TV. Millions of people just talking about the HAT – and about the fact that I bowed instead of curtseying to the Queen. The *Sun* had a nice photo of me facing the Queen but smiling past her. I was in fact smiling at one of [Prince] Philip's cracks. When he saw my name as Minister of Transport on the commemorative plaque he said, 'That's pretty cool. It was practically finished before you came along.' 'Not a bit of it,' I replied. 'It is entirely due to me that it was finished five months ahead of schedule. Anyway I intend to be in on the act.'

Barbara Castle, Diary, 1966.

10 SEPTEMBER

1963 *The American Express credit card comes to Britain.*

1973 *The big Biba store opens in the old Derry & Toms building in High Street, Kensington, only to close two years later. Biba began as a boutique in 1964 with Thirties decadence as its supposed theme.*

The best thing I can do is to write you an account of a dinner with Lord Nelson . . . So far from appearing vain and full of himself, as one had always heard, he was perfectly unassuming and natural. Talking of popular applause and his having been mobbed and huzzaed in the city, Lady Hamilton wanted him to give an account of it, but he stopped her. 'Why,' said she, 'you like to be applauded – you cannot deny it.' 'I own it,' he answered; 'popular applause is very acceptable and grateful to me, but no man ought to be too much elated by it; it is too precarious to be depended upon, and it may be my turn to feel the tide set as strong against me as ever it did for me.' Everybody joined in saying they did not believe that could happen to him, but he seemed persuaded it might; but added: 'Whilst I live I shall do what I think right and best; the country has a right to that from me, but every man is liable to err in judgement' . . . He says nothing short of the annihilation of the enemy's fleet will do any good . . . The enemy, he says, have a hundred [ships of the line], and on being asked how many we had in all, he answered: 'Oh, I do not count our ships.'

Lady Bessborough to Lord Granville, 1805.

I know I have something else to say to you, but unfortunately I awoke this morning with collywobbles, and had to take a small dose of laudanum with the usual consequences of dry throat, intoxicated legs, partial madness and total imbecility; and for the life of me I cannot remember what it is.

Robert Louis Stevenson to Sidney Colvin, 1894.

11 SEPTEMBER

1709 *Marlborough fights the Battle of Malplaquet against the French: probably the bloodiest battle of the eighteenth century, with 40,000 killed and wounded.*

1997 *Referendum held in Scotland on devolution produces a 'Yes' vote.*

As I was framing the south tower with the cross of a nearby church in the foreground, the skyscraper collapsed . . . I thought I had all the time in the world to photograph. Only at the last moment did I realize I was about to be hit. I raced to find shelter behind the buildings on the opposite side of the street as the debris crashed down and the street was engulfed in smoke.

I knew I had to photograph the wreckage of the tower lying on the ground . . . As I was photographing, I heard what sounded like a huge waterfall in the sky above me. I looked up and saw the north tower falling straight down on me, a billowing avalanche of smoke and steel, and I understood that if I took even a moment to raise my camera to photograph it, I would not survive . . . I dashed into the hallway with the hotel elevators and then into an open lift just as the debris came crashing in . . . The only way I knew I was still alive was that I was suffocating. The ashes were so dense it was like trying to breathe through a mouthful of mud . . . A construction worker had dived into the elevator just as I did, and we held onto each other's hands as we began to crawl through the blackness. We called out to ask if there was anyone else who might need help, but no one replied. Everyone who had been in the lobby was most likely dead. I began to see small points of light in the darkness, but did not know what they might be. Then I realized they were the emergency lights of cars and that we were on the street.

Photographer James Nachtwey describes his experiences at the World Trade Center, 2001.

12 SEPTEMBER

1878 *The ancient Egyptian obelisk known as Cleopatra's Needle is erected on the Thames Embankment.*

1914 *French and British forces win the Battle of the Marne, stopping the initial German thrust into France and ushering in the stalemate of trench warfare.*

Below 14th Street is barred to those without two pieces of photo ID or proof of residence. There are further patrols at Houston and Canal. Most stores stay shut. Newspapers are impossible to find as early risers, transformed by disaster into archivists, buy up multiple copies. As reporting gives way to remorseless speculation even radios have been switched off. Neither the East nor the West Village can ever have been so bucolic. Locals cycle through the tree-lined streets. They wander around checking out their neighbourhood as if for the first time. Kids throw desultory hoops in street courts, couples spoon on benches, women walk their dogs or go for short jogs. But normal life has not really been resumed. Uniformed medics carrying clipboards are everywhere. A majority of the people out and about wear masks to stop them inhaling the sticky, acrid smoke that has started to waft uptown. Children without masks suffer allergic reactions and asthma attacks. And then there's the silence. Over the next couple of days the few subway trains that are let into Manhattan are completely quiet. In a SoHo bar friends sit round a table staring at their glasses. Those who go to dance themselves into forgetfulness at the handful of clubs that stay open shuffle home early having barely broken into a sweat. A group of girls walking late in Washington Square start laughing; 'Shuddup all that noise over there,' shouts one of the local chess-players. Even the crack dealers nearby sound solicitous – 'Wassup buddy?' One of them starts rapping about Jay-Z, only to be shoved in the chest by his pal: 'This ain't no fockin joke, man. I'm holding back tears here.'

Journalist Sukhdev Sandhu, the day after the terrorist attacks on the United States, 2001.

13 SEPTEMBER

1759 *General Wolfe captures Quebec, and so Canada, from the French but is killed during the battle.*

1993 *The Israeli Prime Minister Yitzhak Rabin and Yasser Arafat, leader of the PLO, shake hands on the White House lawn in Washington. In 1995 Rabin is assassinated in Israel by an ultra-Orthodox Jewish student in protest at the peace process.*

The room where we lay was a celebrated one. Dr Johnson's bed was the very bed in which the grandson of the unfortunate King James II [Bonnie Prince Charlie] lay on one of the nights after the failure of his rash attempt in 1745–6, while he was eluding the pursuit of the emissaries of government, which had offered thirty thousand pounds as a reward for apprehending him. To see Dr Samuel Johnson lying in that bed, in the Isle of Skye, in the house of Miss Flora Macdonald, struck me with such a group of ideas as it is not easy for words to describe, as they passed through the mind. He smiled, and said, 'I have had no ambitious thoughts in it.'

Kingsburgh conducted us in his boat across one of the lochs, as they call them, or arms of the sea, which flow in upon all the coasts of Skye . . . During our sail, Dr Johnson asked about the use of the dirk, with which he imagined the Highlanders cut their meat. He was told, they had a knife and fork besides to eat with. He asked, how did the women do? and was answered, some of them had a knife and fork too; but in general the men, when they had cut their meat, handed their knives and forks to the women, and they themselves eat with their fingers. The old tutor of Macdonald always ate fish with his fingers, alleging that a knife and fork gave it a bad taste. I took the liberty to observe to Dr Johnson, that he did so. 'Yes,' said he, 'but it is because I am short-sighted, and afraid of bones, for which reason I am not fond of eating many kinds of fish, because I must use my fingers.'

James Boswell, Journal of a Tour to the Hebrides, *1773.*

14 SEPTEMBER

1752 *The Gregorian calendar is introduced into Britain, with Parliament decreeing that the day after September 2 should be September 14, thus wiping out eleven days.*

1982 *Princess Grace of Monaco, former film star Grace Kelly, is killed in a car crash.*

The custom was, in the beginning, to bury the dead in the night only; now, both night and day will hardly be time enough to do it. For the last week, mortality did too apparently evidence that, that the dead were piled in heaps above ground for some hours together, before either time could be gained or place to bury them in. The Quakers (as we are informed) have buried in their piece of ground a thousand for some weeks together last past . . .

One week the general distempers are botches and boils; the next week as clear-skinned as may be; but death spares neither. One week, full of spots and tokens; and perhaps the succeeding, none at all. Now taken with a vomiting and looseness, and within two or three days almost a general raging madness. One while patients used to linger four or five days, at other times not forty-eight hours; and at this very time we find it more quick than ever it was. Many are sick, and few escape. Where it has had its fling, there it decreases; where it has not been long, there it increases. It reigned most heretofore in alleys, etc., now it domineers in the open streets. The poorer sort was most afflicted; now the richer bear a share.

J. Tillison to his master, Dr Sancroft, Dean of St Paul's,
about the Plague in London, 1665.

15 SEPTEMBER

In 1993 a group of scholars and scientists declare this to be the real birthday of Christ, in 8 BC.

1916 *Tanks are used for the first time, on the Somme.*

At the height of twenty yards, the balloon was a little depressed by the wind, which had a fine effect; it held me over the ground for a few seconds, and seemed to pause majestically before its departure.

On discharging a part of the ballast, it ascended to the height of two hundred yards. As a multitude lay before me of a hundred and fifty thousand people, who had not seen my ascent from the ground, I had recourse to every stratagem to let them know I was in the gallery, and they literally rent the air with their acclamations and applause, in these stratagems I devoted my flag, and worked my oars, one of which was immediately broken, and fell from me, a pigeon too escaped, which, with a dog, and cat, were the only companions of my excursions.

When the thermometer had fallen from 68° to 61° I perceived a great difference in the temperature of the air. I became very cold and found it necessary to take a few glasses of wine. I likewise ate the leg of a chicken, but my bread and other provisions had been rendered useless, by being mixed with the sand, which I carried as ballast.

When the thermometer was at fifty, the effect of the atmosphere and the combination of circumstances around, produced a calm delight, which is inexpressible, and which no situation on earth could give. The stillness, extent, and magnificence of the scene, rendered it highly awful.

Vincent Lunardi, secretary to the Neapolitan ambassador in London, makes the first balloon ascent in Britain, 1784.

16 SEPTEMBER

1859 *David Livingstone reaches the banks of Lake Nyasa.*

1992 *Black Wednesday, when Britain crashes out of the Exchange Rate Mechanism which has linked the pound to the German Mark and other currencies.*

A thickly timbered country of eight different kinds of pine, which are so covered with snow, that in passing through them we are continually covered with snow. I have been wet and as cold in every part as I ever was in my life, indeed I was at one time fearful my feet would freeze in the thin moccasins which I wore. After a short delay in the middle of the day, I took one man and proceeded on as fast as I could about six miles to a small branch passing to the right, halted and built fires for the party against their arrival which was at dusk, very cold and much fatigued. We encamped at this branch in a thickly timbered bottom which was scarcely large enough for us to lie level, men all wet, cold and hungry. Killed a second colt which we all supped heartily on and thought it fine meat.

Meriwether Lewis's and William Clark's journals of their expedition from the Missouri River to the Pacific Ocean: William Clark, 1805.

Sydney [Smith] at breakfast made me actually cry with laughing. I was obliged to start up from the table. In talking of the intelligence and concert which birds have among each other, cranes and crows, etc., showing that they must have some means of communicating their thought, he said, 'I dare say they make the same remark of us. That old fat crow there [meaning himself] what a prodigious noise he is making! I have no doubt he has some power of communicating,' etc. etc. After pursuing this idea comically for some time he added, 'But we have the advantage of them; they can't put us into pies as we do them; legs sticking up out of the crust,' etc. etc. The acting of all this makes two-thirds of the fun of it; the quickness, the buoyancy, the self-enjoying laugh.

Tom Moore, Diary, 1834.

17 SEPTEMBER

1787 *The US Constitution is signed.*

1944 *British airborne forces land at Arnhem.*

1982 *Massacres at the Sabra and Shatila Palestinian refugee camps in an area of Beirut in the hands of the Israeli army are carried out by Christian Phalangist militia.*

Madame du Barri arrived over against us below [in the chapel at Versailles], without rouge, without powder, and indeed *sans avoir fait sa toilette* . . . In the Tribune above, surrounded by prelates, was the amorous and still handsome King. One could not help smiling at the mixture of piety, pomp, and carnality. From chapel we went to the dinner of the elder Mesdames [Princesses]. We were almost stifled in the antechamber, where their dishes were heating over charcoal, and where we could not stir for the press. When the doors are opened, everybody rushes in, princes of the blood, *cordons bleus*, abbés, housemaids, and the Lord knows who and what. Yet, so used are their highnesses to this trade, that they eat as comfortably and heartily as you or I could do in our own parlours.

Horace Walpole to George Montagu, describing a visit to Versailles, 1769.
Madame du Barry was the mistress of Louis XV.

About our lives . . . It is terribly difficult to say, but I believe the universe has reason and order and meaning in it. In every part of it and so in our lives. Appearances are *dead against this* and so I can't hope to be thought reasonable in believing it. But I do somehow believe it; and more, I never doubt it. If you will read the bit in *Macbeth* beginning at 'Out, out brief candle' and ending at 'signifying nothing' – that is what I don't believe. I have heard people say morals are only shifting customs. I don't believe it. I think it's wrong to kick a pregnant woman in the stomach; but to come naked to a dinner party is not wrong. It is an eccentricity – deplorable if you like – but nothing more. Nothing will ever make me believe these two acts are breaches of good manners and have the same value.

Conrad Russell to Katharine Asquith, who was converting
to Roman Catholicism, 1924.

18 SEPTEMBER

1879 *The first Blackpool illuminations are switched on.*

1978 *The Camp David peace settlement between Egypt and Israel.*

My greenhouse is never so pleasant as when we are just upon the point of being turned out of it. The gentleness of the autumnal suns, and the calmness of this latter season, make it a much more agreeable retreat than we ever find it in summer; when, the winds being generally brisk, we cannot cool it by admitting sufficient quantity of air, without being at the same time incommoded by it. But now I sit with all the windows and the door wide open, and am regaled with the scent of every flower in a garden as full of flowers as I have known how to make it. We keep no bees, but if I lived in a hive I should hardly hear more of their music. All the bees in the neighbourhood resort to a bed of mignonette, opposite to the window, and pay me for the honey they get out of it by a hum, which, though rather monotonous, is as agreeable to my ear as the whistling of my linnets . . . The notes of all our birds and fowls please me, without one exception. I should not indeed think of keeping a goose in a cage, that I might hang him up in the parlour for the sake of his melody, but a goose upon a common, or in a farmyard, is no bad performer; and as to insects, if the black beetle, and beetles indeed of all hues, will keep out of my way, I have no objection to any of the rest; on the contrary, in whatever key they sing, from the gnat's fine treble, to the bass of the humble bee, I admire them all.

William Cowper to the Revd John Newton, 1784.

19 SEPTEMBER

1356 *The English defeat the French at the Battle of Poitiers, again thanks to the longbow.*

1819 *John Keats writes his 'Ode to Autumn' (see 21 September).*

> My prime of youth is but a frost of cares,
>   My feast of joy is but a dish of pain,
> My crop of corn is but a field of tares,
>   And all my goods is but vain hope of gain.
> The day is fled, and yet I saw no sun,
>   And now I live, and now my life is done!
>
> My spring is past, and yet it has not sprung,
>   The fruit is dead, and yet the leaves are green,
> My youth is past, and yet I am but young,
>   I saw the world, and yet I was not seen;
> My thread is cut, and yet it is not spun,
>   And now I live, and now my life is done!
>
> I sought for death, and found it in the womb,
>   I looked for life, and yet it was a shade,
> I trod the ground, and knew it was my tomb,
>   And now I die, and now I am but made,
> The glass is full, and yet my glass is run;
>   And now I live, and now my life is done!

Chideock Tichborne, a young Catholic who plotted against Queen Elizabeth, wrote this on the eve of his execution, 1586.

20 SEPTEMBER

1854 *The first battle of the Crimean War is fought, a victory for the French and British over the Russians at the river Alma. Six Victoria Crosses are later awarded.*

1870 *The unification of Italy is completed.*

Proceeded on through a country as rugged as usual. At twelve miles descended the mountain to a level pine country; proceeded on through a beautiful country for three miles to a small plain in which I found many Indian lodges. A man came out to meet me, and conducted me to a large spacious lodge which he told me (by signs) was the lodge of his great chief who had set out three days previous with all the warriors of the nation to war on a south-west direction and would return in fifteen or eighteen days. The few men that were left in the village, and great numbers of women, gathered around me with much apparent signs of fear . . . Those people gave us a small piece of buffalo meat, some dried salmon, berries and roots in different states, some round and much like an onion . . . They call themselves *Cho pun-nish* or Pierced noses. Their dialect appears very different from the Flat heads [*Tushapaws*], although originally the same people. [From Meriwether Lewis's later account:] After the long abstinence [the food] was a sumptuous treat. They returned the kindness of the people by a few small presents and then went on in company with one of the chiefs to a second village . . . and passed the night . . . The free use of food, to which he had not been accustomed, made Captain Clark very sick.

William Clark emerges west of the Rocky Mountains, 1805.

You must know our steward, the Duke of Devonshire, started the first day [of Doncaster races] with his coach and six and *twelve* outriders, and old Billy Fitzwilliam [the 4th Earl] had just the same; but the next day old Billy appeared with *two* coaches and six, and *sixteen* outriders, and has kept the thing up ever since.

Thomas Creevey to his step-daughter Miss Ord, 1827.

21 SEPTEMBER

1915 *Stonehenge is sold at auction for £6,600.*

1937 *J.R.R. Tolkien's* The Hobbit *is published.*

Yesterday . . . was a grand day for Winchester. They elected a Mayor – It was indeed high time the place should receive some sort of excitement. There was nothing going on: all asleep: not an old maid's sedan returning from a card party: and if any old woman got tipsy at Christenings they did not expose it in the streets. The first night tho' of our arrival here, there was a slight uproar took place at about 10 o' the clock. We heard distinctly a noise patting down the high Street as of a walking cane of the good old Dowager breed; and a little minute after we heard a less voice observe 'What a noise the ferril made – it must be loose' . . . The side streets here are excessively maiden-lady-like: the door steps always fresh from the flannel. The knockers have a staid serious, nay almost awful quietness about them. I never saw so quiet a collection of lions' and rams' heads. The doors most part black, with a little brass handle just above the keyhole, so that in Winchester a man may very quietly shut himself out of his own house. How beautiful the season is now – how fine the air. A temperate sharpness about it. Really, without joking, chaste weather – Dian skies. I never liked stubble fields so much as now, aye, better than the chilly green of the spring. Somehow a stubble plain looks warm – in the same way that some pictures look warm. This struck me so much in my Sunday's walk that I composed upon it ['To Autumn'].

John Keats to J.H. Reynolds, 1819.

22 SEPTEMBER

The first day of Autumn.

1735 *Sir Robert Walpole goes to live at 10 Downing Street, the first Prime Minister so to do.*

1955 *ITV programmes begin on British TV. BBC radio kills off Grace Archer as a diversion.*

Passed Interlachen – entered upon a range of scenes beyond all description – or previous conception. Passed a rock – inscription – two brothers – one murdered the other – just the place fit for it. After a variety of windings came to an enormous rock – girl with fruit – very pretty – blue eyes – good teeth – very fair – long but good features . . . bought some of her pears – and patted her upon the cheek – the expression of her face very mild – but good – and not at all coquettish. Arrived at the foot of the mountain (the Yung-frau – i.e., the Maiden). Glaciers – torrents – one of these torrents *nine hundred feet* in height of visible descent – lodge at the curate's – set out to see the valley – heard an avalanche fall – like thunder – saw glacier – enormous – storm came on – thunder – lightning – hail – all in perfection – and beautiful – I was on horseback – guide wanted to carry my cane – I was going to give it him when I recollected that it was a swordstick and I thought that the lightning might be attracted towards him – kept it myself – a good deal encumbered with it and my cloak – as it was too heavy for a whip – and the horse was stupid – and stood still every other peal. Got in – not very wet – the cloak being staunch.

Lord Byron, Alpine Journal, 1816.

23 SEPTEMBER

480 BC *The Greeks defeat the Persians at the naval battle of Salamis.*

2000 *Rower Steve Redgrave makes Olympic history by winning fifth consecutive gold medal.*

Directly across from me, three Negro boys and five girls were walking toward the side door at the south end of the school . . . They weren't hurrying. They simply strolled across perhaps fifteen yards from the sidewalk to the school steps. They glanced at the people and the police as though none of this concerned them . . . 'Oh, God, the niggers are in the school,' a man yelled . . .

They surged over and around the barricades, breaking for the police.

About a dozen policemen, in short-sleeved blue shirts, swinging billy clubs, were in front of them.

Men and women raced toward them and the policemen raised their clubs, moving this way and that as people tried to dodge around them.

A man went down, pole-axed when a policeman clubbed him.

Another, with crisp curly black hair, was quick as a rat. He dodged between two policemen and got as far as the schoolyard. There the others caught him.

With swift, professional skill, they pulled his coat half-way down his back, pinning his arms. In a flash they were hustling him back toward the barricades.

A burly, thick-bodied man wearing a construction worker's 'hard hat' charged a policeman. Suddenly, he stopped and held both hands high above his head.

I couldn't see it, but I assume the officer jammed a pistol in his ribs.

Journalist Relman Morin's Pulizer Prize-winning despatch from Little Rock, Arkansas, 1957, reporting the integration of its high school.

24 SEPTEMBER

1869 *The great Wall Street panic, in which thousands are ruined when an attempt is made to corner the market in gold.*

1938 *Don Budge wins the US Open Tennis Tournament, so becoming the first player to win all four major titles.*

We [Maynard Keynes and his Russian ballerina wife Lydia] had very brisk talk of Russia: such a hotch-potch, such a mad jumble, M. says, of good and bad, and the most extreme things that he can make no composition of it – can't yet see how it goes. Briefly, spies everywhere, no liberty of speech, greed for money eradicated, people living in common, yet some, L[ydia]'s mother for instance with servants, peasants contented because they own land, no sign of revolution, aristocrats acting showmen to their possessions, ballet respected, best show of Cezanne and Matisse in existence. Endless processions of communists in top hats, prices exorbitant, yet champagne produced, and the finest cooking in Europe, banquets beginning at 8.30 and going on till 2.30; people getting slightly drunk, say about 11, and wandering round the table . . .

But to tell the truth, I am exacerbated this morning. It is 10.25, on a fine grey still day; the starlings are in the apple trees; Leonard is in London. But why am I exacerbated? By Roger [Fry, artist and art critic]. I told him I had been ill all the summer. His reply is – silence as to that; but plentiful descriptions of his own front teeth. Egotism, egotism – it is the essential ingredient in a clever man's life I believe. It protects; it enhances; it preserves his own vital juices entire by keeping them banked in. Also I cannot help thinking that he suspects me of valetudinarianism and this enrages me; and Leonard is away and I can't have my thorn picked out by him, so must write it out. There! it is better now; and I think I hear the papers come; and will get them, my woolwork, and a glass of milk.

Virginia Woolf, Diary, 1925.

1066 *The Battle of Stamford Bridge in Yorkshire, where Harold of England defeats and kills Tostig, Earl of Northumbria, his brother, and Harold Hardrada of Norway, before having to march south to confront William of Normandy.*

1857 *The Relief of Lucknow, where a British garrison and dependants have been besieged during the Indian Mutiny.*

I did send for a cup of tee (a China drink) of which I have never had drink before.

Samuel Pepys, Diary, 1660.

Did I tell you Lady Mary Wortley Montagu is here? . . . Her dress, her avarice, and her impudence must amaze any one that never heard her name. She wears a foul mob, that does not cover her greasy black locks, that hang loose, never combed or curled; an old mazarine blue wrapper, that gapes open and discovers a canvas petticoat.

Horace Walpole to Henry Seymour Conway, from Florence, 1740.

As to Annabella [Milbanke, his future wife and Lady Melbourne's niece] she requires time and all the cardinal virtues, and in the interim I am a little verging towards one who demands neither, and saves me besides the trouble of marrying by being married already – She besides does not speak English, and to me nothing but Italian, a great point, for from certain coincidences the very sound of that language is music to me, and she has black eyes and *not* a very white skin, and reminds me of many in the Archipelago [the Aegean] I wished to forget, and makes me forget what I ought to remember, all which are against me. I only wish she did not swallow so much supper, chicken wings – sweetbreads – custards – peaches and *port* wine – a woman should never be seen eating or drinking, unless it be *lobster salad and champagne*, the only truly feminine and becoming viands.

Lord Byron to Lady Melbourne, 1812.

26 SEPTEMBER

1580 *Francis Drake arrives back in his ship the* Golden Hind, *having sailed round the world and captured much Spanish treasure en route.*

1968 *The Lord Chamberlain's censorship of British stage plays is ended.*

[The Austrians] are never lively but upon points of ceremony. There, I own, they show all their passions; and 'tis not long since two coaches, meeting in a narrow street at night, the ladies in them not being able to adjust the ceremonial of which should go back, sat there with equal gallantry till two in the morning, and were both so fully determined to die upon the spot, rather than yield in a point of that importance, that the street would never have been cleared till their deaths, if the emperor had not sent his guards to part them; and even then they refused to stir, till the expedient was found out of taking them both out in chairs exactly at the same moment; after which it was with some difficulty the *pas* was decided between the two coachmen, no less tenacious of their rank than the ladies . . . The men are not much less touched with this point of honour . . . and the pedigree is much more considered by them, than either the complexion or features of their mistresses.

Lady Mary Wortley Montagu in Vienna to Mrs Thistlethwaite, 1716.

Young Harris, who is now a mason, behaved so badly in Church I was obliged to speak to him, and on leaving the Church, I saw written upon the wall of the Church porch the same obscenity that this boy once wrote on the door of my orchard, so I am inclined to think the hardened wretch did it because I reproved him for his misbehaviour. It were better far that the lower orders knew nothing about writing if they produce such fruits as these.

The Revd John Skinner, Journal, 1830.

27 SEPTEMBER

1825 *The first proper passenger-train runs on the Stockton to Darlington railway.*

1968 *The musical show* Hair, *which incorporates nudity on stage, has its premier the day after censorship ends.*

My poor dear dearest sister in a fit of insanity has been the death of her own mother. I was at hand only time enough to snatch the knife out of her grasp. She is at present in a madhouse, from whence I fear she must be moved to an hospital. God has preserved to me my senses – I eat and drink and sleep, and have my judgment I believe very sound. My poor father was slightly wounded, and I am left to take care of him and my aunt. Mr Norris of the Bluecoat School has been very kind to us, and we have no other friend, but thank God I am very calm and composed, and able to do the best that remains to do. Write, as religious a letter as possible but no mention of what is gone and done with – with me the former things are passed away, and I have something more to do than to feel.

Mention nothing of poetry. I have destroyed every vestige of past vanities of that kind . . . I charge you don't think of coming to see me. Write. I will not see you if you come. God Almighty love you and all of us.

Charles Lamb to S.T. Coleridge, 1796. Lamb subsequently looked after his sister Mary himself so that she did not have to live out her days in an asylum.

A dreadful night of dreams – voyages on wide blue waters, interspersed with many interviews with the Prince Consort [Albert]. In one of these we were by a tea-table – we two alone. He helped himself liberally to tea, cake, etc.; then he turned to me, and said, 'You observe that I offer you no tea, Mr Benson.' I said, 'Yes, sir.' 'The reason is that I am forbidden by etiquette to do so, and would to God I could alter this!' He was overcome with emotion, but finished his tea, after which a grave man came and served me with some ceremony.

A.C. Benson, Diary, 1903. He was editing Queen Victoria's Letters.

1745 *'God Save the King' is performed for the first time at Drury Lane Theatre.*

1894 *Marks & Spencer's first Penny Bazaar opens, in Manchester.*

[In the House of Commons Neville Chamberlain] said that his conversation with Herr Hitler had convinced him that the Führer was prepared, on behalf of the Sudeten Germans, 'to risk a world war' . . . The Prime Minister had been speaking for exactly an hour. I noticed that a sheet of Foreign Office paper was being rapidly passed along the Government bench. Sir John Simon interrupted the Prime Minister and there was a momentary hush. He adjusted his pince-nez and read the document that had been handed to him. His whole face, his whole body, seemed to change. He raised his face so that the light from the ceiling fell full upon it. All the lines of anxiety and weariness seemed suddenly to have been smoothed out; he appeared ten years younger and triumphant. 'Herr Hitler', he said, 'has just agreed to postpone his mobilisation for twenty-four hours and to meet me in conference with Signor Mussolini and Signor Daladier [the French premier] at Munich.'

That, I think, was one of the most dramatic moments which I have ever witnessed. For a second, the House was hushed in absolute silence. And then the whole House burst into a roar of cheering, since they knew that this might mean peace. That was the end of the Prime Minister's speech, and when he sat down the whole House rose as a man to pay a tribute to his achievement. I remained seated. Liddall [the Conservative Member for Lincoln] behind me, hissed out, 'Stand up, you Brute!' . . .

Harold Nicolson, Diaries, 1938. The crisis was that engineered by Hitler over the rights of Sudeten Germans - those living in Czechoslovakia.

29 SEPTEMBER

1938 *Chamberlain returns, claiming 'Peace in our time', with the Munich agreement by which the Sudetenland in Czechoslovakia becomes German. No Czechoslovak has been involved, which is outrageous, neither has Russia been consulted, which is foolish.*

1960 *The Russian leader Nikita Khrushchev makes angry outbursts and bangs his desk during a speech on the Congo by Harold Macmillan at the UN in New York.*

I have employed my time (besides ditching) in finishing, correcting, amending, and transcribing my *Travels* (*Gulliver's*), in four parts complete, newly augmented and intended for the press when the world shall deserve them, or rather when a printer shall be found brave enough to venture his ears . . . The chief end I propose to myself in all my labours, is to vex the world, rather than divert it . . .

I have ever hated all nations, professions, and communities; and all my love is towards individuals . . . Upon this great foundation of misanthropy the whole building of my *Travels* is erected.

Jonathan Swift to Alexander Pope, 1725.

A land-mine floated down by parachute onto the Kodak playing-fields just over the houses opposite and rendered us homeless. It was Jean and I who had found it. Over the weekend a captured Messerschmitt had been put on show, sixpence to view, a shilling to sit in the cockpit. Jean and I had turned up first thing – were indeed the first customers because I had to go to work and the plane was only just round the corner at the top of the street. On leaving, Jean asked the gate-keeper: 'Is that tub-shaped thing with the parachute attached part of the show?' To which he replied: 'What tub-shaped thing? I don't know anything about a tub-shaped thing. I've been on fire-watch all night.' Ten minutes later the fun began. The police arrived at the double and turned the whole street out of doors, advising them to leave doors and windows wide open and then to make themselves scarce while the bomb was defused. While I went to work, Jean took the baby to some cousins in Kenton . . . Someone came and removed fuse and detonator and here we are back home again.

George Beardmore, Journal, 1940.

30 SEPTEMBER

1929 *Discovery of penicillin announced.*

1955 *Death of film star James Dean while driving his Porsche, the image of rebellious youth. He achieves cult status after his death.*

We have all our playthings; happy are they that can be contented with those they can obtain. Those hours are spent in the wisest manner that can easiest shade the ills of life, and are the least productive of ill consequences. I think my time better employed in reading the adventures of imaginary people, than the Duchess of Marlborough's, who passed the latter years of her life in paddling with her will, and contriving schemes of plaguing some and extracting praise from others, to no purpose, eternally disappointed and eternally fretting.

The active scenes are over at my age [sixty-eight]. I indulge, with all the art I can, my taste for reading. If I would confine it to valuable books, they are almost rare as valuable men. I must be content with what I can find. As I approach a second childhood I endeavour to enter into the pleasures of it. Your youngest son is, perhaps, at this very moment riding on a poker with great delight, not at all regretting that it is not a gold one, and much less wishing it an Arabian horse, which he would not know how to manage; I am reading an idle tale, not expecting wit or truth in it, and am very glad it is not metaphysics to puzzle my judgement or history to mislead my opinion. He fortifies his health by exercise, I calm my cares by oblivion. The methods may appear low to busy people, but if he improves his strength and I forget my infirmities we attain very desirable ends.

> *Lady Mary Wortley Montagu to her daughter, the Countess of Bute, 1757.*
> *Twenty-six of the Duchess of Marlborough's wills still survive.*

OCTOBER

1 OCTOBER

1908 *The Model-T motor-car is introduced by Henry Ford.*

1938 *The first issue of* Picture Post, *the pioneering photo-journalism magazine, appears in Britain.*

When the heavier men began to wrestle . . . the struggle rarely lasted more than five minutes, and into that five minutes was put all the strength and practice, skill and science, and quickness of intelligence which the two men had been gaining in wrestling ever since they were boys. It made me clench my teeth, and set into firmness and excitement every muscle and nerve in my body . . . then there was a great dinner; the whole hall was filled – two rows of tables, thousands of candles, hundreds of geese and turkeys and sirloins and partridges and veal pies, plum-puddings, pastries, jellies – soups, fishes, and millions of potatoes smoked on the board. When the rage of hunger and thirst was satisfied, all the prizes were placed before Mrs Howard. There were tankards with three, two, and one handles, barometers, clocks, opera glasses, teapots, penknives, boxes of knives and forks, watch-chains, and other things, to be given to the 'successful competitors' as they called them.

Stopford Brooke describes the sports and dinner held at Naworth Castle
in Cumbria, home of the Howards, in 1874.

Marry your children, sack your servants, forget your enemies, remember your friends, enslave your admirers, fatten yourself – and all will yet be well.

Sir Walter Raleigh to Mrs Dowdall, 1918.

2 OCTOBER

1950 *The 'Peanuts' strip cartoon by Charles M. Schulz appears for the first time.*

1968 *Britain's first sextuplets, the Thorns, are born in Birmingham. Three survive.*

My whole day has been taken up by a horrible adventure. I found a little boy almost naked, crying bitterly and nursing a baby in his arms; he told me his Mammy was dying and had nobody to help her. I asked where she was; he got up and led the way to a miserable house, so miserable that I drew back unwilling to go in. The child held my gown, and looking up piteously, said, 'Won't you come?' in such a tone, that I reproached myself for my fine Ladyship in doubting, and forced myself to go on. Indeed, dear G., I could not have imagined a human being reduced to so much wretchedness: in a miserable hole on a rug on the stones lay a creature almost naked, almost a skeleton, distorted, hideous and disgusting to the most frightful degree, so helpless that her arms, face and bosom were covered with flies, which seemed devouring her and which she had not strength to drive from her . . . The man whom I made go with me came out almost as shocked as I was, but told me a dreadful story. He knew the woman; he saw her five years ago – young, very pretty, and a decent kind of woman. She married a soldier who got drunk, beat and abandoned her, since when she gave herself up to every kind of vice; in short, her disorder is the consequence of her way of life. His expression to me was horrible, but, in short, that every part of her, inside and out, was decayed, and for this last fortnight it seems she had been completely neglected.

Lady Bessborough to Lord Granville, 1805.

3 OCTOBER

1952 *Tea rationing in Britain ends.*

1990 *East and West Germany are reunified. The capital is to be Berlin once more.*

Sunshine. Sweet concert of birds. A person in this village [Llangollen, north Wales] had lost some yarn last Wednesday. Yesterday he went to the conjurer who lives in the parish of Ruabon to discover who stole this yarn. The people of this valley attribute the violent storm which arose yesterday to the incantations the conjurer made use of to raise the Infernal Prince.

Lady Eleanor Butler, Journal, 1788.

The copious old literature, by which I can trace the gradual changes in the breeds of pigeons has been extraordinarily useful to me. I have just had pigeons and fowls *alive* from the Gambia! Rabbits and ducks I am attending to pretty carefully, but less so than pigeons. I find most remarkable differences in the skeletons of rabbits. Have you ever kept any odd breeds of rabbits, and can you give me any details? One other question. You used to keep hawks; do you at all know, after eating a bird, how soon after they throw up the pellet?

Charles Darwin to W.D. Fox, 1856. Later that month he wrote to J.D. Hooker: 'The hawks have behaved like gentlemen and have cast up pellets with lots of seeds in them; and I have just had a parcel of partridge's feet well caked with mud [to carry seeds]!!!' He signed himself, 'Your insane and perverse friend'.

4 OCTOBER

1957 *Russia launches the Sputnik satellite, the first man-made object in space.*

1976 *British Rail launches the Intercity-125 service.*

1993 *US soldiers are killed in Mogadishu, Somalia, and two Blackhawk helicopters are shot down.*

Ist Case: Mr Burgess is a common begging-letter writer – Fourpost bedstead in his room – admirable steak on the fire – handsome wife – two extraordinarily jovial children – shelves, full of glasses, crockery ware, children's toys, etc. etc. – cupboard full of provender – coals in stock – everything particularly cheerful and cosey. It was such a clear case (he was not at home himself; I think must have stepped out to fetch the beer) that I caused enquiry to be made of the Mendicity Society. They know him well, and will send me down a report of his life and career tomorrow.

2nd Case: The lady at Holloway was with her sick husband. Everything scrupulously clean – except the husband. They were in a back parlour, very briefly furnished. She has two additional pupils in her little school, and one other private pupil. They have got on up to the present time, but are again so pressed by those small creditors that certain friends of hers have determined in their small way to assist her husband with the few pounds necessary to pay the expenses of taking the benefit of the Insolvent Act. They deplored this with much apparent sincerity, saying that all the creditors, except the baker, were very little tradesmen who would suffer by the loss. They estimate their debts at £50. They were very hopeful and quiet – complained of nothing – asked for nothing – and said that on the whole their creditors had been very patient and considerate.

Charles Dickens to Miss Burdett-Coutts, whom he is
helping in her philanthropy, 1853.

5 OCTOBER

1936 *The Jarrow hunger marchers set out on their 'Crusade':
200 unemployed ship-builders walking to London from Tyneside,
where four-fifths are out of work.*

1968 *A civil rights march in Londonderry is broken up by the Royal
Ulster Constabulary.*

1969 *The first* Monty Python *programme is shown on TV.*

To the King's House [Drury Lane Theatre]: and there, going in, met with Knipp, and she took us up into the tiring-rooms: and to the women's shift, where Nell [Gwyn] was dressing herself, and was all unready, and is very pretty, prettier than I thought . . . and then below into the scene-room, and there sat down, and she gave us fruit: and here I read the cues to Knipp while she answered me, through all her part [in] *Flora's Figarys* [*Flora's Vagaries*] which was acted today. But, Lord! to see how they were both painted would make a man mad, and did make me loathe them; and what base company of men comes among them, and how lewdly they talk! and how poor the men are in clothes, and yet what a show they make on the stage by candle-light, is very observable. But to see how Nell cursed for having so few people in the pit was pretty; the other House [the Duke of York's Theatre, in Lincoln's Inn Fields] carrying away all the people at the new play, and is said nowadays to have generally most company, as being better players. By and by into the pit, and there saw the play, which is pretty good.

Samuel Pepys, Diary, 1667.

6 OCTOBER

1895 *The Henry Wood Promenade Concerts begin.*

1973 *Egyptian and Syrian forces launch a surprise attack on Israel on Yom Kippur, the Day of Atonement, the holiest day in the Jewish year. They are repulsed after heavy fighting.*

I cannot take myself seriously as an artist; the limitations are so obvious. I did take myself seriously as a workman of old, but my practice has fallen off. I am now an idler and cumberer of the ground, it may be excused to me perhaps by twenty years of industry and ill-health, which have taken the cream off the milk. As I was writing this last sentence, I heard the strident rain drawing near across the forest, and by the time I was come to the word 'cream', it burst upon my roof, and has since redoubled, and roared upon it. A very welcome change. All smells of the good wet earth, sweetly, with a kind of Highland touch; the crystal rods of the shower, as I look up, have drawn their criss-cross over everything; and a gentle and very welcome coolness comes up around me in little draughts, blessed draughts, not chilling, only equalising the temperature. Now the rain is off in this spot, but I hear it roaring still in the nigh neighbourhood – and that moment I was driven from the veranda by random raindrops, spitting at me through the Japanese blinds. These are not tears with which the page is spotted! Now the windows stream, the roof reverberates. It is good; it answers something which is in my heart; I know not what; old memories of the wet moorland belike. Well, it has blown by again, and I am in my place on the veranda once more, with an accompaniment of perpetual dripping on the veranda.

Robert Louis Stevenson to Sidney Colvin, 1894. This was the last of the Vailima Letters, *named after the estate on Samoa in the South Pacific where Stevenson had lived since 1890, and where he died in December 1894.*

7 OCTOBER

1913 *All Ford's automobile factory goes over to moving assembly-line production.*

1946 Woman's Hour *is broadcast for the first time.*

1985 *Palestinian terrorists seize the liner* Achille Lauro, *surrendering two days later after killing passenger Leon Klinghofer.*

The Bidassoa is very rapid at the place where I crossed and so very strong was the current that we were constrained to take each other by the arm, holding our swords and muskets in the air, the water being up to the armpits and knee-deep in mud. The French were stationed in the houses opposite, behind the hedges and in the ditches, keeping up a regular fire upon us as we struggled through the cold river. Many fell wounded and were drowned through the rapidity of the element. The balls splashed around us like a shower of rain. But the water was so excessively cold and strong that I was insensible to the splashing of the musketry around my chest and I struggled through mechanically, without even reflecting that I was walking to fight a few thousand devils before breakfast . . .

We dived into a wood on the slope of a hill behind every tree of which stood a Frenchman, distraction in his eye and death in his hand, popping from the ditches, between the thickets, and among the bushes. And now I first heard that hissing and plaintive whistling from balls around me. The hiss is caused by the wind but when [a ball passes] close to you a strong shrill whistle tells you of your escape. I felt no tremor or cold sensation whatever. I walked without thought or reflection . . . On the edge of the field we became exposed to an elevated battery. A heavy shot fell two yards to my left and covered me with mud and slime. The noise was so great and the splash into the earth so violent that I mechanically jumped against a tall Polack who, good-naturedly smiling, pushed me back saying, 'Don't flinch, Ensign.' Little hump-backed Bacmeister behind me also said 'Vall, Veatley, how you like dat?'

Ensign Edmund Wheatley of the King's German Legion gets his baptism of fire crossing the river that marks the boundary between Spain and France: Diary, 1813.

8 OCTOBER

1965 *The 580-foot-high Post Office Tower, now the BT Tower, is opened in London.*

1967 *The first person in Britain is breathalysed by the police.*

I believe Mr Anderson talks partially of me, as to my looks; I know nothing of the matter. It is eleven years since I have seen my figure in a glass: the last reflexion I saw there was so disagreeable, I resolved to spare myself such mortifications for the future, and shall continue that resolution to my life's end. To indulge all pleasing amusements, and avoid all images that give disgust, is, in my opinion, the best method to attain or confirm health.

Lady Mary Wortley Montagu to her daughter, the Countess of Bute, 1757.

A certain bishop in the House of Lords rose to speak, and announced that he should divide what he had to say into twelve parts, when the Duke of Wharton interrupted him, and begged he might be indulged for a few minutes as he had a story to tell which he could only introduce at that moment. A drunken fellow was passing St Paul's at night, and heard the clock slowly chiming twelve. He counted the strokes and when it had finished, looked towards the clock and said, 'Damn you! Why couldn't you give us all that at once?' There was an end to the bishop's speech.

Charles Greville, Memoirs, 1820.

9 OCTOBER

1899 *The first London motor-bus goes into service.*

1967 *Che Guevara is killed in the Bolivian jungle by counter-insurgency forces.*

Called at Gullick's, where the family were all at dinner [and where the mother had just died]. The sorrow of the children is vehement at first, but soon wears off; the poor man will feel it much more, because he will find his own comfort so much connected with his loss. But happy is it that people in the lower ranks of life are not possessed of the same sensibility as their superiors; certain am I that all things are conducted on a much more equal footing than they appear to be at first sight – if enjoyment be less, privation is in proportion.

The Revd John Skinner, Journal, 1823.

I attended a meeting of Mrs Ronnie Greville's executors . . . [Her will was] a most interesting and complex subject, involving an estate of some £2 million. Mrs Greville has left Marie Antoinette's necklace to the Queen, £20,000 to Princess Margaret Rose, and £25,000 to the Queen of Spain. Everyone in London is agog to learn the terms of Mrs G's will. She was a lady who loved the great because they were great, and apparently had a tongue dipped in gall. I remember old Lady Leslie once exclaiming, when her name was mentioned, 'Maggie Greville! I would sooner have an open sewer in my drawing-room.'

James Lees-Milne, Diary, Ancestral Voices, 1942. Mrs Greville had left her house, Polesden Lacey in Surrey, to the National Trust. She was the illegitimate child of the wealthy brewer William McEwan and the wife of a watchman at the brewery, put for convenience on the night-shift.

10 OCTOBER

1980 *Mrs Thatcher gives her 'This lady's not for turning' speech at the Conservative Conference.*

1999 *The Millennium Wheel is erected on the South Bank.*

There was a most lovely combination at the head of the vale of the yellow autumnal hills wrapped in sunshine, and overhung with partial mists, the green and yellow trees, and the distant snow-topped mountains. It was a most heavenly morning. The Cockermouth traveller came with thread, hardware, mustard, etc. She is very healthy; has travelled over the mountains these thirty years. She does not mind the storms, if she can keep her goods dry. Her husband will not travel with an ass, because it is the tramper's badge; she would have one to relieve her from the weary load.

Dorothy Wordsworth, Journal, 1800.

As to the truth of the readings, I cannot tell you what the demonstrations of personal regard and respect are. How the densest and most uncomfortably-packed crowd will be hushed in an instant when I show my face . . . How common people and gentlefolks will stop me in the streets and say: 'Mr Dickens, will you let me touch the hand that has filled my home with so many friends?' And if you saw the mothers, and fathers, and sisters, and brothers in mourning, who invariably come to 'Little Dombey', and if you studied the wonderful expression of comfort and reliance with which they hang about me, as if I had been with them, all kindness and delicacy, at their own little death-bed, you would think it one of the strangest things in the world . . . At the end of 'Dombey' yesterday afternoon, in the cold light of day, they all got up, after a short pause, gentle and simple, and thundered and waved their hats with that astonishing heartiness and fondness for me, that for the first time in all my public career they took me completely off my legs, and I saw the whole eighteen hundred of them reel on one side as if a shock from without had shaken the hall.

Charles Dickens to John Forster, 1858.

11 OCTOBER

1216 *King John loses his crown jewels when crossing the Wash.*

1899 *The Boer War begins in South Africa.*

I was interrupted and drawn to the window by the most discordant sounds I ever heard – long cries and groans; in short, the Irish Howl. It was a funeral passing, the coffin borne upon an open hearse, at one end of which sat a woman with her back to the horses hanging over the coffin, sometimes throwing herself upon it, tearing her hair, beating her breast, with every appearance of despair, and making the most dismal scream I ever heard. I was quite affected with the excessive misery she expressed, when the waiter told me she was hired to do all this, and that it was a trade like any other. I cannot bear this. But sometimes they say it really is the nearest relation of the dead person. Everybody who meets the funeral is expected (as a mark of respect to the dead) to turn and follow it a little way, so that the noise increases every step they go, and is really very extraordinary. The lakes are as beautiful as it is possible for immense mountains, rocks, woods and water to make them, and answer all that is said of them. As we rowed by a beautiful mountain glen, the boatmen began lamenting themselves, shaking their heads and saying it was fine once, but spoilt now – all *gone to England*. I could not understand till the master of the vessel explained to me that it had shared the fate of several other fine woods near, and what probably would soon render this as bare of trees as the rest of Ireland. Lord Kenmare and Mr Herbert live in England; they make the most of estates they never see: the trees are all to be cut down for timber, and the money sent to them, and this is pretty nearly the history of all the miseries in Ireland.

Lady Bessborough to Lord Granville, from Killarney, 1808.

12 OCTOBER

1948 *The first Morris Minor comes off the production line.*

1984 *An IRA bomb goes off at the Brighton hotel where the Tory leadership is staying for the party conference, killing five.*

I gave some of them red bonnets and glass beads which they hung round their necks, and many other things of small value, at which they were so delighted and so eager to please us that we could not believe it. Later they swam out to the boats to bring us parrots and balls of cotton thread and darts, and many other things, exchanging them for such objects as glass beads and hawk bells. They took anything, and gave willingly whatever they had . . . They carry no weapons, and are ignorant of them; when I showed them some swords they took them by the blade and cut themselves.

Christopher Columbus lands in the Americas, 1492.

Sir Henry talked about his bad knee, and told me he had lost a kneecap. I found myself shouting, for he is rather deaf, 'Do you find it much of a handicap having no kneecap?' After the third repetition I decided that my remark was inept. Lady Hoare is an absolute treasure, and unique. She is tall, ugly and eighty-two; dressed in a long black skirt, belled from a wasp waist and trailing over her ankles . . . She kept up a lively, not entirely coherent prattle. She said to me, 'Don't you find the food better in this war than in the last?' I replied that I was rather young during the last war, but I certainly remembered the rancid margarine we were given at my preparatory school when I was eight. 'Oh!' she said. 'You were lucky. We were reduced to eating rats.' I was a little surprised, until Sir Henry looked up and said, 'No, no, Alda. You keep getting your wars wrong. That was when you were in Paris during the Commune [1871].'

James Lees-Milne, Diary, Ancestral Voices, 1942. He was staying at Stourhead in Wiltshire with Sir Henry Hoare and his wife to discuss the transfer of the house and its outstanding eighteenth-century landscape gardens to the National Trust.

13 OCTOBER

54 *The Emperor Claudius, successful invader of Britain in 43, is poisoned, probably by his wife Agrippina.*

1992 *It is announced that 31 out of 50 deep coal pits in Britain are to be closed with the loss of 31,000 jobs.*

I went out to Charing Cross, to see Major-General Harrison hanged, drawn, and quartered; which was done there; he looking as cheerful as any man could do in that condition. He was presently cut down, and his head and heart shown to the people, at which there were great shouts of joy. It is said, that he said that he was sure to come shortly at the right hand of Christ to judge them that now had judged him; and that his wife do expect his coming again. Thus it was my chance to see the King beheaded at Whitehall,.and to see the first blood shed in revenge for the King at Charing Cross. Setting up shelves in my study.

With my father took a melancholy walk to Portholme [in Huntingdonshire], seeing the country maids milking their cows there, they being there now at grass, and to see with what mirth they come all home together in pomp with their milk, and sometimes they have musique go before them.

My Lady Castlemaine, I hear, is in as great favour as ever, and the King supped with her the very first night he come from Bath: and last night and the night before supped with her; when there being a chine of beef to roast, and the tide rising into their kitchen that it could not be roasted there, and the cook telling her of it, she answered 'Zounds! she must set the house on fire but it should be roasted!' So it was carried to Mrs Sarah's husband's [a cook] and there it was roasted.

Samuel Pepys, Diary, 1660, 1662, 1663. Major-General Thomas Harrison was a regicide, one of those who had tried Charles I. He also appears on 20 April.

14 OCTOBER

1066 *The Battle of Hastings replaces Saxon with Norman rule in England.*

1969 *The new seven-sided fifty-pence coin goes into circulation.*

Dinner proceeded, and suddenly Lambert, the butler, ushered in . . . Harold Balfour, black from head to foot. He had been standing in the smoking-room of the Carlton Club . . . drinking sherry before going in to dinner: suddenly, with a blinding flash, the ceiling had fallen, and the club collapsed on them. A direct hit. Harold swam, as he put it, through the rubble, surprised to be alive, but soon realised that his limbs were all intact; he called out to his companions to see if they were still alive, and fortunately, all answered. Somehow he got to the front door . . . to find it jammed. At that moment he saw Lord Hailsham being half led, half carried out by his son, Quintin Hogg. A few other individuals, headed by Harold, put their shoulders to the door, and it crashed into the street, and only just in time as by then a fire had started . . . Seaford House, across [Belgrave] Square, has also been struck, that huge mansion where I have been to so many balls in old days: I wonder what happened to the famous green malachite staircase? Holland House, too, has gone, and I am really sorry. It seems that it is beyond repair. I have been thinking of that last great ball there in July 1939, with the crush, the Queen, and 'the world' still aglitter.

Chips Channon, Diary, 1940. Harold Balfour was Parliamentary Under-Secretary for Air, 1938–44. The malachite staircase, installed by Lord Howard de Walden, survived the war.

15 OCTOBER

1815 *Napoleon arrives at the island of St Helena in the south Atlantic.*

1964 *Nikita Khrushchev is ousted from power in Russia.*

1969 *Massive Moratorium March across the US for peace in Vietnam, with the middle-aged and middle-class demonstrating for the first time.*

At the distance of twenty-five years I can neither forget nor express the strong emotions which agitated my mind as I first approached and entered the *eternal city*. After a sleepless night, I trod, with a lofty step, the ruins of the Forum; each memorable spot where Romulus *stood*, or Tully spoke, or Caesar fell, was at once present to my eye; and several days of intoxication were lost or enjoyed before I could descend to a cool and minute investigation . . .

It was at Rome, on the 15th of October 1764, as I sat musing amidst the ruins of the Capitol, while the barefooted friars were singing vespers in the temple of Jupiter, that the idea of writing the decline and fall of the city first started to my mind. But my original plan was circumscribed to the decay of the city rather than of the empire; and though my reading and reflections began to point towards that object, some years elapsed, and several avocations intervened, before I was seriously engaged in the execution of that laborious work.

Edward Gibbon, Autobiography. *The friars were actually singing in Santa Maria in Aracoeli, on the site of the temple of Juno.*

I caught a remarkable large spider in my wash place this morning and put him in a small glass decanter and fed him with some bread and intend keeping him.

Parson James Woodforde, Diary, 1774.

16 OCTOBER

1847 Jane Eyre *by Charlotte Brontë is published.*

1987 *A great storm hits England and hundreds of thousands of trees are blown down.*

Good God! I am just returned from the terrific burning of the Houses of Parliament. Mary and I went in a cab, and drove over the bridge. From the bridge it was sublime. We alighted, and went into a room of a public house, which was full. The feeling among the people was extraordinary – jokes and radicalism universal. If Ministers had heard the shrewd sense and intelligence of these drunken remarks! I hurried Mary away. Good God, and are that throne and tapestry gone with all their associations! The comfort is there is now a better prospect of painting a [picture for the] House of Lords.

Benjamin Robert Haydon, Memoirs, 1834. In May Haydon had suggested to Lord Grey that he might paint, 'to adorn the House of Lords, a series of subjects to illustrate the best government for mankind'. The tapestry depicted the defeat of the Spanish Armada.

Worked very hard, and delightfully. Made a sketch of one side of the House of Lords, as I propose to adorn it, with a series of subjects to illustrate the principle of the best government to regulate without cramping the liberty of man:

Anarchy	Banditti
Democracy	Banishment of Aristides
Despotism	[Nero's] Burning of Rome
Revolution	La dernière charette
Moral Right	Establishment of Jury
Limited Monarchy	King, Lords and Commons

Benjamin Robert Haydon, Memoirs, 1835. Aristides (530–468 BC) was an Athenian statesman exiled when he came into conflict with the democratic leader Themistocles. La dernière charette: the last tumbril taking victims to the guillotine in the French Revolution. This overblown scheme never got any further.

17 OCTOBER

1651 *Charles II escapes to France after the Battle of Worcester and hiding in the oak tree.*

1956 *The Queen switches on the world's first full-scale nuclear power station, at Calder Hall (Windscale) in Cumberland.*

Four quires of writing paper from Wood of Salop. Ill cut. Wrote to scold him for it . . . My Love and I spent from five 'til seven in the shrubbery and in the field endeavouring to talk and walk away our little sorrows.

Our old chimney sweeper with the little Prince of the Isles of Ebony was perceived coming down the field which occasioned a general joy throughout the whole household. Every hand was instantly employed in removing the pictures, globes, tables, china from the library preparatory to this very necessary operation.

Lady Eleanor Butler, Journal, 1785 and 1788. It is doubtful whether the chimney sweep's boy, whose job it was to climb up inside the stacks, saw himself as a 'Prince of the Isles of Ebony'.

You once – only once – gave the world assurance of a waistcoat. You wore it, sir, I think, in *Money*. It was a remarkable and precious waistcoat, wherein certain broad stripes of blue or purple disported themselves as by a combination of extraordinary circumstances, too happy to occur again. I have seen it on your manly chest in private life. I saw it, sir, I think, the other day in the cold light of morning – with feelings easier to be imagined than described. Mr Macready, sir, are you a father? If so, lend me that waistcoat for five minutes. I am bidden to a wedding (where fathers are made), and my artist cannot, I find (how should he?), imagine such a waistcoat. Let me show it to him as a sample of my tastes and wishes; and – ha, ha, ha, ha! – eclipse the bridegroom!

Charles Dickens to the actor William Charles Macready, 1845.

18 OCTOBER

1689 *The Revocation of the Edict of Nantes by Louis XIV drives the Protestant Huguenots out of France and many come to Britain, bringing their skills with them.*

1860 *British troops burn the Summer Palace of the Chinese emperors outside Peking, already looted by French troops, in retaliation for the torture of prisoners by the Chinese in the Second Opium War.*

As for another grandchild – your *grand quiver* is so full of them already, that I suppose you hardly have room for any more. I think it would be such a good plan, if after people have as many children as they like, they were allowed to lie in of any other article they fancied better; with the same pain and trouble, of course (if that is necessary), but the result to be more agreeable. A set of Walter Scott's novels, or some fine china, or in the case of poor people, fire-irons and a coal scuttle, or two pieces of Irish linen. It would certainly be more amusing and more profitable, and then there would be such anxiety to know *what* was born. Now it can be only a boy or a girl.

My purse is quite perfection, and I cannot thank you enough for it. I am only afraid it is still more attractive than the last you gave me, which so took the fancy of one of those men who sell oranges in the street, that he snatched it off the seat of the carriage in which I was sitting and ran away with it.

Emily Eden to Lady Charlotte Greville, 1834.

I am quite recovered, astonishingly recovered. It must be owned these climates and this voyage have given me more strength than I could have thought possible. And yet the sea is a terrible place, stupefying to the mind and poisonous to the temper, the sea, the motion, the lack of space, the cruel publicity, the villainous tinned foods, the sailors, the captain, the passengers – but you are amply repaid when you sight an island, and drop anchor in a new world. Much trouble has attended this trip, but I must confess more pleasure. Nor should I ever complain, as in the last few weeks, with the curing of my illness indeed, as if that were the bursting of an abscess, the cloud has risen from my spirits and to some degree from my temper.

Robert Louis Stevenson, in Tahiti, to Sidney Colvin, 1888.

19 OCTOBER

1605, 1682 *The birth and death day of the writer and doctor Sir Thomas Browne, author of* Religio Medici *and* Urn Burial.

1781 *Cornwallis capitulates at Yorktown and thus signals American victory in the war for independence.*

1987 *Black Monday, as the world's stock markets crash.*

I rushed to the potager – you know my weakness – and walked up and down between spinach and dahlias in ecstasy . . . There is the repose, a freedom, and a security in a *vie de château* that no other destiny offers one. I feel when I set out to walk as if alone in the world – nothing but trees and birds; but then comes the enormous satisfaction of always finding a man dressing a hedge, or a woman in a gingham [apron] and a black bonnet on her knees picking up weeds, the natural *gendarmerie* of the country, and the most comfortable well-organised country . . .

The idea of being at Chatsworth! with dearest Hart is transport mixed with awe and timidity.

Lady Granville to her sister, now Lady Carlisle, 1828, from Trentham, home of Lord Granville's half-brother, the Marquess of Stafford. 'Hart' was her brother, the Duke of Devonshire.

It looks almost as if Devon [the Duke of Devonshire] had rather more than his share of this world's goods, but I suppose there is a compensation somewhere; and, with thirty people dining in the housekeeper's room and eighty in the [servants'] hall, there must be a bother of house accounts and cheating, and quarrels between butlers and housekeepers that may be taken as a slight set-off. But then again his deafness helps him. It has long been clear to me that he is only deaf to what he does not like to hear; anything that amuses him he hears fast enough.

Emily Eden to Lord Clarendon, on staying at Chatsworth, 1843.

20 OCTOBER

1968 *Jackie Kennedy marries Greek shipping tycoon Aristotle Onassis.*

1972 *The Dalai Lama, leader of Tibetans in exile, comes to Britain for the first time.*

I see the winter approaching without much concern, though a passionate lover of fine weather and the pleasant scenes of summer; but the long evenings have their comforts too, and there is hardly to be found upon the earth, I suppose, so snug a creature as an Englishman by his fireside in the winter. I mean however an Englishman that lives in the country, for in London it is not very easy to avoid intrusion. I have two ladies to read to, sometimes more, but never less. At present we are circumnavigating the globe, and I find the old story with which I amused myself some years since, through the great felicity of a memory not very retentive, almost new. I am however sadly at a loss for Cook's voyage, can you send it? I shall be glad of Foster's too. These together will make the winter pass merrily, and you will much oblige me.

William Cowper to Joseph Hill, 1783. 'The old story' was A Voyage Round the World, *the account of Lord Anson's journey, published in 1748; Foster was the botanist who accompanied Captain Cook on his second voyage (1772-5).*

We have at last good weather: and the harvest is just drawing to a close in this place. It is a bright brisk morning, and the loaded waggons are rolling cheerfully past my window . . . Ah, Master Tennyson, we in England have our pleasures too. As to Alfred [Tennyson], we in England have heard nothing of him since May: except that some one saw him going to a packet which he believed was going to Rotterdam . . . When shall you and I go to an Opera again, or hear one of Beethoven's Symphonies together? You are lost to England, I calculate: and I am given over to turnips and inanity.

Edward FitzGerald to Frederick Tennyson, 1841.

21 OCTOBER

1917 *US soldiers go into action for the first time on the Western Front.*

1966 *A slag-heap at Aberfan in Wales is made unstable by heavy rain and buries a school, killing 116 children and 28 adults.*

At daylight saw the enemy's combined fleet from East to ESE; bore away; made the signal for order of sailing, and to prepare for battle; the enemy with their heads to the southward; at seven the enemy wearing in succession. May the Great God, whom I worship, grant to my country, and for the benefit of Europe in general, a great and glorious victory; and may no misconduct in anyone tarnish it; and may humanity after victory be the predominant feature in the British fleet. For myself, individually, I commit my life to Him, who made me, and may his blessing light upon my endeavours for serving my country faithfully. To him I resign myself and the just cause which is entrusted to me to defend. Amen. Amen. Amen.

Lord Nelson, Diary, before the Battle of Trafalgar, 1805.

I was on the poop and quarter-deck whilst preparations for the fight were going on, and saw Lord Nelson, Captain Blackwood, and some other captains of the frigates, in earnest conversation together, and a slip of paper in the hand of the former (which Captain Blackwood had looked at), yet I have no recollection that I ever saw it pass through other hands till it was given to Pasco, who, after referring to the telegraph signal book, took it back to his lordship, and it was then that, I believe, the substitution of the words took place. I think (though not sure), the substitution was 'expects' for the word 'confides', the latter word not being in the telegraph book, and I think the word 'England' had been previously substituted for 'Nelson' for the same reason, at the suggestion of Captain Blackwood.

Lieutenant George Brown describes the sending of Nelson's signal
'England expects that every man this day will do his duty'.

22 OCTOBER

1936 *First test of the Volkswagen ('people's car') Beetle prototype commissioned from Ferdinand Porsche by the Nazis. Not produced in quantity until after the war.*

1962 *Cuban missile crisis begins with US blockade off Cuba, which only ends with removal of Soviet missiles from the island.*

[Sir Walter] Scott mentioned the contrast in the behaviour of two criminals, whom he had himself seen: the one a woman, who had poisoned her husband in some drink, which she gave him while he was ill; the man not having the least suspicion, but leaning his head on her lap, while she still mixed more poison in the drink, as he became thirsty and asked for it. The other a man, who had made a bargain to sell a *subject* (a young child) to a surgeon; his bringing it at night in a bag; the surgeon's surprise at hearing it cry out; the man then saying, 'Oh, you wanted it dead, did you?' and stepping behind a tree and killing it. The woman (who was brought up to judgment with a child at her breast) stood with the utmost calmness to hear her sentence; while the man, on the contrary, yelled out, and showed the most disgusting cowardice.

Tom Moore, Diary, 1826.

Your mother and I dined off a tray and then we turned on H. G. Wells on the wireless and we were soon both in the Land of Nod. I wonder what the point of that sort of listening in is. We can all read Wells if we want to; he has a vulgar accent and a squeaky scrannel voice. It's a wonderful invention for blind and bedridden invalids of course. Also you can hear the result of the boat race [between Oxford and Cambridge Universities] more quickly.

Conrad Russell to Katharine Asquith, 1929.

23 OCTOBER

4004 BC *According to John Lightfoot, Vice-Chancellor of Cambridge University in 1655, this was the day on which the world began, at nine o'clock in the morning. His calculation was accepted for many decades.*

1942 *The Battle of Alamein begins*

O Lord, Thou knowest how busy I must be this day; if I forget Thee, do not Thou forget me.

The Royalist Sir Jacob Astley's prayer before Edgehill, the first major battle of the English Civil War, 1642. Sir Jacob's words right at the end of the Civil War in March 1646 are also on record. He told the Parliamentary soldiers who had just scared the raw Welsh levies under his command into surrender at Stow-on-the-Wold, 'You have done your work, boys. You may go play, unless you fall out among yourselves.'

I have just finished *Copperfield* and don't know whether to laugh or cry . . . I have an idea of wandering somewhere for a day or two – to Rochester, I think, where I was a small boy – to get all this fortnight's work out of my head, but I shall be at home soon.

Charles Dickens, from Broadstairs, to Miss Burdett-Coutts, 1850.

When my Father dashed down the *Times*, after a moment of bewildered silence and said, 'Lord Palmerston is gone,' I only said, 'Le roi est mort, vive le roi.' Still it is a great event, greater far in its consequences, I think, than men suspect. He was the last barrier against the next great stride of Democracy, and I believe he has been left so long that he might keep back the incoming of the next wave till the shore of England's national life was ready to receive it.

Stopford Brooke to his wife, 1865. The Second Reform Act,
extending the right to vote, came in 1867.

24 OCTOBER

1648 *The Treaty of Westphalia brings the Thirty Years' War to an end, lifting the threat of Hapsburg domination of Germany but leaving the country devastated.*

1795 *Poland is partitioned by Prussia, Russia and Austria. She only reappears as an independent country in 1918.*

You have heard of our taking of New Amsterdam, which lies just by New England. 'Tis a place of great importance to trade. It did belong to England heretofore, but the Dutch by degrees drove our people out and built a very good town, but we have got the better of it, and 'tis now called New York.

King Charles II to his sister Henrietta, 1664.

Around eleven o'clock the deluge broke. It came with a speed and ferocity that left men dazed. The bottom simply fell out of the market. From all over the country a torrent of selling orders poured onto the floor of the Stock Exchange and there were no buying orders to meet it . . .

The animal roar that rises from the floor of the Stock Exchange and which on active days is plainly audible in the Street outside, became louder, anguished, terrifying . . . The ticker, hopelessly swamped, fell hours behind the actual trading and became completely meaningless. Far into the night, and often all night long, the lights blazed in the windows of the tall office buildings where margin clerks and bookkeepers struggled with the desperate task of trying to clear one day's business before the next began. They fainted at their desks; the weary runners fell exhausted on the marble floors of banks and slept. But within a few months they were to have ample time to rest up. By then thousands of them had been fired.

Elliott V. Bell describes the Wall Street Crash, 1929.

25 OCTOBER

———◦◦◦———

1415 *The Battle of Agincourt on St Crispin's Day. Henry V and the English archers defeat the French.*

1961 Private Eye *published for the first time.*

I must tell you all I know of departed majesty. He went to bed well last night, rose at six this morning as usual, looked, I suppose, if all his money was in his purse, and called for his chocolate. A little after seven, he went into the water-closet; the German *valet de chambre* heard a noise, listened, heard something like a groan, ran in, and found the hero of Oudenarde and Dettingen on the floor, with a gash on his right temple, by falling against the corner of a bureau. He tried to speak, could not, and expired.

Horace Walpole tells George Montagu of the death of King George II, 1760.

On the 25th inst they attacked our position at Balaclava. Our cavalry got at them – it was a grand sight, in particular the charge of the Heavy Brigade, for they went at them more like madmen than anything that I can explain; the Greys and Inniskillings (one a Scotch and the other an Irish regiment) went at them first, and they did it manfully. They rode right through them, as if they'd been a lot of old women, it was a most exciting scene. I hear that the Light Cavalry have been cut to pieces, particularly the 11th Hussars and the 17th Lancers. The rumour in camp is that someone has been blundering, and that the Light Cavalry charge was all a mistake; the truth will come out some day.

Sergeant Gowing, of the Royal Fusiliers, writes to his
parents during the Crimean War, 1854.

26 OCTOBER

1881 *Gunfight at the OK Corral in Tombstone, Arizona.*

1965 *The Beatles each receive the MBE from the Queen.*

I have been faithful to my honest liaison with Countess Guiccioli – and I can assure you that *She* has never cost me directly or indirectly a sixpence – indeed the circumstances of herself and family render this no merit. I never offered her but one present – a broach of brilliants – and she sent it back to me with her *own hair* in it (I shall *not* say of *what part* but *that* is an Italian custom) and a note to say that she was not in the habit of receiving presents of that value – but hoped that I would not consider her sending it back as an affront – nor the value diminished by the enclosure. I have not had a whore this half-year – confining myself to the strictest adultery . . .

As to 'Don Juan' – confess – confess – you dog – and be candid – that it is the sublime of *that there* sort of writing – it may be bawdy – but is it not good English? – it may be profligate – but is it not *life*, is it not *the thing*? – Could any man have written it – who has not lived in the world? – and tooled in a post-chaise? in a hackney coach? in a gondola? against a wall? in a court carriage? In a vis à vis? – on a table? – and under it?

> *Lord Byron to Douglas Kinnaird, about his 'last attachment',*
> *Teresa Guiccioli, and his poem 'Don Juan', 1819.*

27 OCTOBER

1958 *The first* Blue Peter *children's programme is televised by the BBC.*

1986 *'Big Bang' on the London Stock Exchange when automated price quotation is introduced, heralding the transformation of the City of London.*

It was nice to see the uncertain yellow faces [of the ferrets] again, turning this way and that at the mouth of a bury. Their red eyes blink vaguely at the waiting guns. They snuffle along outside the caverns, or turn back into them with a look of resignation. They hasten slowly. It is as if their long subjugation to man, their confinement generally in rather insanitary little boxes, had made them forget about the open air. Aimlessly, forgetfully, prisoners on ticket-of-leave, no longer quick like a weasel, they cock short-sighted heads and stare at you. They turn and loom back into the hole. The head goes, the back presents itself, the tail vanishes with a little quiver.

I got more interested in them than the shooting, and generally volunteered to stay when one of them laid up. We muzzle our ferrets with string, behind the tusks and under and over the jaws: in Sussex we used to line them. We tied a bell on the collar, so that you could tell where the ferret was. When a ferret does lay up you are supposed to gut a rabbit at the mouth of the bury, and the smell brings the ferret out. Unfortunately, in my case it has never done so. A far better way is to fire a gun down the mouth of the hole. The noise inside must be prodigious, and the ferret generally pops out immediately afterwards, shaking its head and saying 'What the hell was that?'

T. H. White, England Have My Bones, *1934. A laid-up ferret is one that stays down a rabbit burrow, refusing to come back to the surface.*

28 OCTOBER

1957 *The* Today *programme goes out for the first time on BBC morning radio.*

1962 *The Cuban Missile Crisis ends.*

She is very willing to talk, and make talk, in the evening, and she plays her three rubbers of whist like any other old lady – horribly badly, but with great interest. It was so like her: George [Emily's brother, Lord Auckland] scolded her for playing some wrong card, and she said, 'Yes, I know you wanted trumps, but my system at whist is to distrust my partner. In fact, I like to thwart him because I hate the way in which he draws the good cards out of my hands.'

Emily Eden, staying with Lord Lansdowne at Bowood, to Lord Clarendon, about the formidably egotistical Whig hostess Lady Holland, 1844.

It was Abdul Hamid [the Sultan of Turkey] who first suggested to the Emperor [Wilhelm II of Germany] to get rid of Bismarck. On his first visit to Constantinople they were talking about Bismarck's great power in Europe, and the Sultan said, 'I should not like to have so powerful a servant, would your Majesty like to see how I treat mine?' William said, 'Yes.' Abdul Hamid then touched a bell, and when the attendant entered said, 'Send for Kiamil', the then Grand Vizier. Instantly horsemen were despatched at a gallop through the city seeking the Minister, who presently appeared and stood, with head bowed and folded hands, before them. The Sultan for a while took no notice, and let him stand, then casually 'You need not wait, it is of no consequence, go', and the Grand Vizier went. William took this lesson to heart, and dismissed his Chancellor hardly less brusquely.

Wilfrid Scawen Blunt, Diary, 1898.

1975 *The end of General Franco's 36-year rule in Spain is signalled by the announcement that Prince Juan Carlos will take over as provisional head of state.*

1986 *The M25, London's orbital motorway, is completed.*

As he went from Westminster Hall to the Gatehouse, he espied Sir Hugh Beeston in the throng and calling to him prayed he would see him die tomorrow. Sir Hugh to make sure work got a letter from Secretary Lake to the Sheriff to see him placed conveniently, and meeting them as they came near to the scaffold delivered his letter; but the Sheriff by mishap had left his spectacles at home and put the letter in his pocket. In the meantime, Sir Hugh being thrust by, Sir Walter bade him farewell and said, 'I know not what shift you will make, but I am sure to have a place.'

When the hangman asked him forgiveness he desired to see the axe, and feeling the edge, he said that it was a fair sharp medicine to cure him of all his diseases and miseries. When he was laid down some found fault that his face was westward, and would have him turned, whereupon rising he said it was no greater matter which way a man's head stood so his heart lay right. He had given order to the executioner that after some short meditation when he stretched forth his hands he should despatch him. After once or twice putting forth his hands, the fellow out of timorousness (or what other cause) forbearing, he was fain to bid him strike, and so at two blows he took off his head, though he stirred not a whit after the first.

> *John Chamberlain to Dudley Carleton, on the execution*
> *of Sir Walter Raleigh, 1618.*

30 OCTOBER

1961 *The USSR explodes the biggest nuclear device to date - 58 megatons, 4000 times the size of the atomic bomb dropped on Hiroshima.*

1974 *The 'Rumble in the Jungle', when Mohammed Ali fights George Foreman for the world heavyweight title in Kinshasa in the Congo.*

Shewed my companion the Louvre . . . We can never do the like in Britain. Royal magnificence can be only displayed by despotic power. In England, were the most splendid street or public building to be erected the matter must be discussed in parliament or perhaps some sturdy cobbler holds out and refuses to part with his stall and the whole plan is disconcerted. Long may such impediments exist . . .

As a literary man I cannot affect to despise public applause; as a private gentleman I have always been embarrassed and displeased with popular clamours, even when in my favour. I know very well the breath of which such shouts are composed, and am sensible those who applaud me today would be as ready to toss me tomorrow; and I would not have them think that I put such a value on their favour as would make me for an instant fear their displeasure. Now all this disclamation is sincere, and yet it sounds affected. It puts me in mind of an old woman who, when Carlisle was taken by the Highlanders in 1745, chose to be particularly apprehensive of personal violence, and shut herself up in a closet, in order that she might escape ravishment. But no one came to disturb her solitude, and she began to be sensible that poor Donald was looking out for victuals, or seeking for some small plunder, without bestowing a thought on the fair sex; by and by she popped her head out of her place of refuge with the petty question, 'Good folks, can you tell when the ravishing is going to begin?'

Sir Walter Scott, Journal, 1826.

31 OCTOBER

1971 *An IRA bomb at the top of the Post Office Tower leads to its closure to the public.*

1984 *President Indira Gandhi of India is assassinated by Sikh members of her bodyguard.*

So thick is the smoke in this cellar that I can hardly see by a candle twelve inches away, and so thick are the inmates that I can hardly write for pokes, nudges and jolts. On my left the Company Commander snores on a bench; other officers repose on wire beds behind me. At my right hand, Kellett, a delightful servant of A Company in *the old days* radiates joy and contentment from pink cheeks and baby eyes. He laughs with a signaller, to whose left ear is glued the receiver; but whose eyes rolling with gaiety show that he is listening with his right ear to a merry corporal, who appears at this distance away (some three feet) nothing [but] a gleam of white teeth and a wheeze of jokes.

Splashing my hand, an old soldier with a walrus moustache peels and drops potatoes into the pot. By him, Keyes, my cook, chops wood; another feeds the smoke with the damp wood.

It is a great life. I am more oblivious than alas! yourself, dear Mother, of the ghastly glimmering of the guns outside, and the hollow crashing of the shells.

There is no danger down here, or if any, it will be well over before you read these lines.

I hope you are as warm as I am; as serene in your room as I am here and that you think of me never in bed as resignedly as I think of you always in bed. Of this I am certain: you could not be visited by a band of friends half so fine as surround me here.

The war poet Wilfred Owen to his mother, 1918. This was his last letter before his death on 4 November, seven days before the end of the war.

NOVEMBER

1 NOVEMBER

1755 *The Lisbon earthquake. Collapsed buildings and tsunami kill more than 100,000.*

1848 *W.H. Smith opens the first railway bookstall.*

1956 *Premium Bonds are introduced.*

Tea: enter Mrs Cameron (in a funny red open-work shawl) with two of her boys. T. reappears, and Mrs C. shows a small firework toy called 'Pharaoh's Serpents', a kind of pastille, which, when lighted, twists about in a worm-like shape. Mrs C. said they were poisonous and forbade us all to touch. T. in defiance put out his hand. 'Don't touch 'em!' shrieked Mrs C. 'You shan't, Alfred!' But Alfred did. 'Wash your hands then!' But Alfred wouldn't, and rubbed his moustache instead, enjoying Mrs C's agonies. Then she said to him: 'Will you come tomorrow and be photographed?' He, very emphatically, 'No' . . .

 Tennyson now took Barnes and me to his top room. Darwinism – 'Man from ape – would that really make any difference?' . . . 'Time is nothing,' said T., 'are we not all part of Deity?' 'Pantheism?' hinted Barnes, who was not at ease in this sort of speculation. 'Well!' says T., 'I think I believe in Pantheism, of a sort.' Barnes to bed, T. and I up ladder to the roof to look at Orion. Then to my room, where more talk. He likes Barnes, he says, 'but he is not accustomed to strong views theologic.'

William Allingham, at Tennyson's home on the Isle of Wight, Diary, 1865. 'Mrs Cameron' is Julia Margaret Cameron, the pioneer photographer, and 'Barnes' the Revd William Barnes, the Dorset dialect poet.

2 NOVEMBER

1936 *The first proper television broadcast in Britain is received by 20,000 homes.*

1959 *The main section of the M1 opens.*

1960 *In the* Lady Chatterley's Lover *trial, Penguin Books are found not guilty of publishing an obscene book.*

No man ever was in love with a woman of forty, since the Deluge: a boy may be so; but that blaze of straw only lasts till he is old enough to distinguish between youth and age, which generally happens about seventeen: till that time the whole sex appears angelic to a warm constitution . . . I should think it the severest suffering to know I was a burden on the good nature of a man I loved, even if I met a mind so generous to dissemble a disgust which he could not help feeling.

Lady Mary Wortley Montagu to her daughter, the Countess of Bute, 1758.

Well, it is a hard knock on the elbow; I knew I had a life of labour before me, but I was resolved to work steadily; now they have treated me like a recusant turn-spit, and put in a red-hot cinder into the wheel alongst with [me]. But of what use is philosophy – and I have always pretended to a little of a practical character – if it cannot teach us to do or suffer? The day is glorious, yet I have little will to enjoy it, but sit here ruminating upon the difference and comparative merits of the Isle of Man and of the Abbey. Small choice betwixt them. Were a twelvemonth over, I should perhaps smile at what makes me now very serious.

Sir Walter Scott, having heard that one of his London creditors was threatening proceedings that would land him in gaol, Journal, 1827. The Isle of Man was beyond the jurisdiction of the Scottish courts, while Holyrood Abbey in Edinburgh remained an asylum for civil debtors until 1830.

3 NOVEMBER

1957 *The first living creature in space, the Russian dog Laika, 'Little Lemon', dies a few hours after blast-off.*

1964, 1976 *Two Democratic presidential election victories, for Lyndon B. Johnson and Jimmy Carter.*

1975 *North Sea oil begins to flow in commercial quantities.*

I went into Bowood Park by the Studley Gate and turned sharp to the left down a drive that brought me soon into the very heart and splendour of the beeches. As the sun shone through the roof of beech boughs overhead the very air seemed gold and scarlet and green and crimson in the deep places of the wood and the red leaves shone brilliant standing out against the splendid blue of the sky. A crowd of wood pigeons rose from the green and misty azure hollows of the plantation and flapped swiftly down the glades, the blue light glancing off their clapping wings. I went by the house down to the lakeside and crossed the water by the hatches above the cascade. From the other side of the water the lake shone as blue as the sky and beyond it rose from the water's edge the grand bank of sloping woods glowing with colours, scarlet, gold, orange and crimson and dark green. Two men were fishing on the further shore of an arm of the lake and across the water came the hoarse belling of a buck while a coot fluttered skimming along the surface of the lake with a loud cry and rippling splash.

To eye and ear it was a beautiful picture, the strange hoarse belling of the buck, the fluttering of the coot as she skimmed the water with her melancholy note, the cry of the swans across the lake; the clicking of the reels as the fishermen wound up or let out their lines, the soft murmur of the woods, the quiet rustle of the red and golden drifts of beech leaves . . .

Francis Kilvert, Diary, 1874.

4 NOVEMBER

—••••◉◎◉◎◉◉••••—

1942 *The Battle of El Alamein ends, with Rommel in retreat.*

1979 *Us Embassy in Teheran is stormed and 90 hostages taken.*

1995 *Israeli Prime Minister Yitzhak Rabin shot dead by a Jewish ultra-Orthodox student.*

Sydney is a series of bays mostly tree-bordered and really very vast and grand like Plymouth Sound going on for miles and with Trebetherick [his Cornish home] bungalows in gardens full of flowers, jacaranda trees, and tamarisks and HUGE CENTIPEDES and very loud-mouthed birds. The older houses, of which there are hundreds, are charming with rich cast-iron work and there are rows and rows of them. You expect cobbers with slouch hats and rifles to come out on to the verandahs and fire guns at kangaroos.

John Betjeman in Australia to his wife Penelope, 1961.

The capsules have been taken with some whisky. What is striking is the unreality of the situation. I feel no different . . . But suddenly the decision came that it must be done. I cannot drag on another few years in this state [he had cancer]. It's a bright sunny morning. Full of life. Such a morning as many people have died on. I am ready for it. Of course the whole thing may not work and I shall wake up. I don't really mind either way. Once the decision seems inevitable the courage needed was less than I thought. I don't quite believe anything has happened though the bottle is empty. At the moment I feel very much alive. P. W. rang and asked me to dine with him tonight. But I had already made the decision though not started the action. I cannot believe I have committed suicide since nothing has happened. No big bang or cut wrists. Sixty-five was long enough for me. It wasn't a complete failure I did some [at this point the words lapse into illegibility and stop].

Keith Vaughan, Journals, 1977.

5 NOVEMBER

1688 *William of Orange lands at Torbay and the Glorious Revolution begins. It ends with him and his wife Mary on the English throne in place of James II.*

1854 *The Battle of Inkerman in the Crimean War is fought in thick fog.*

1991 *Publisher Robert Maxwell's body found in the sea off Tenerife.*

We have been witnessing today a strong example of the spirit of contradiction. The crier has been employed all morning in forbidding bonfires, on pain of great penalties, especially on the heights, lest they should be mistaken for signals of invasion; and if nothing had been said they would probably have burnt Guy Fawkes in the market place very quietly, but, in consequence of this, every cliff round Hastings is in a blaze, and especially ours, with a faggot on the top of a long pole so like the signal for the French, that I should not wonder if the whole coast was in alarm and the people under arms from here to Dover. The pleasure of doing what is forbidden does not therefore belong exclusively to women.

Lady Bessborough to Lord Granville, 1804.

The Prime Minister makes a statement after Question Time. He is rather grim. He brings home to the House [of Commons] as never before the gravity of our shipping losses and the danger of our position in the Eastern Mediterranean . . . If Chamberlain had spoken glum words such as these the impression would have been one of despair and lack of confidence. Churchill can say them and we all feel, 'Thank God that we have a man like that!' I have never admired him more. Thereafter he slouches into the smoking-room and reads the *Evening News* intently, as if it were the only source of information available to him.

Harold Nicolson, Diary, 1940.

6 NOVEMBER

1793 *John Murray I, founder of the firm, dies.*

1956 *A cease-fire is agreed in the Suez War in Egypt, with British and French troops in control of the Canal Zone.*

1968, 1996 *Presidents Nixon and Clinton are elected, Clinton for a second term.*

It is the fashion for the greatest ladies to walk the streets, which are admirably paved; and a mask, price sixpence, with a little cloak, and the head of a domino [hood], the genteel dress to carry you everywhere. The greatest equipage is a gondola, that holds eight persons, and is the price of an English chair. And it is so much the established fashion for everybody to live their own way, that nothing is more ridiculous than censuring the actions of another. This would be terrible in London, where we have little other diversion; but for me, who never found any pleasure in malice, I bless my destiny that has conducted me to a part where people are better employed than in talking of the affairs of their acquaintance.

Lady Mary Wortley Montagu in Venice to Lady Pomfret, 1739.

I have not the heart, when an amiable lady says, 'Come to *Semiramis* in my box', to decline; but I get bolder at a distance. *Semiramis* would be to me pure misery. I love music very little – I hate acting; I have the worst opinion of *Semiramis* herself, and the whole thing (I cannot help it) seems so childish and so foolish that I cannot abide it. Moreover, it would be rather out of etiquette for a Canon of St Paul's to go to an opera; and where etiquette prevents me from doing things disagreeable to myself, I am a perfect martinet.

The Revd Sydney Smith to Lady Holland, 1842.

7 NOVEMBER

1917 *Russia's October Revolution starts, in which the Communist Bolsheviks seize power (under the old-style Russian calendar the date is October 25).*

1989 *The East German Communist government resigns as tens of thousands flee the country over the border into Czechoslovakia.*

Right reverend and worshipful brother, I recommend me unto you, desiring to hear of your welfare and prosperity, letting you weet [know] that I have received of Alweather a letter, and a noble [a coin] in gold therein. Furthermore, my creancer [tutor], Master Thomas, heartily recommended him to you, and he prayeth you to send him some money for my commons [board], for he saith ye be twenty shillings in his debt, for a month was to pay for when he had money last.

Also I beseech you to send me a hose cloth, one for the holidays of some colour, and another for the working days, how coarse so ever it be it maketh no matter; and a stomacher, and two shirts, and pair of slippers. And if it like you that I may come with Alweather by water and sport me with you at London a day or two this term time, then ye may let all this be till the time that I come. And then I will tell you when I shall be ready to come from Eton, by the grace of God, whom have you in his keeping.

William Paston III to John Paston III, 1478.

I am so old that I have shamelessly to simplify . . . I shall be glad to see you, but I *won't* – thank you, no! – come to meet with you at Claridges. One doesn't go to Claridges if one simplifies.

Henry James to André Raffalovich, 1913.

8 NOVEMBER

1920 *The first 'Rupert Bear' cartoon strip appears in the* Daily Express.

1974 *Covent Garden fruit, vegetable and flower market moves south of the Thames to Nine Elms.*

The first dish was a cabbage boiled in a great quantity of rice and hot water, the whole flavoured with cheese. I was so cold that I thought it comfortable, and so hungry that a bit of cabbage, when I found such a thing floating my way, charmed me. After that we had a dish of very little pieces of pork, fried with pigs' kidneys; after that a fowl; after that something very red and stringy, which I think was veal; and after that two tiny little new-born-baby-looking turkeys, very red and very swollen. Fruit, of course, to wind up, and garlic in one shape or another in every course. I made three jokes at supper (to the immense delight of the company), and retired early.

Charles Dickens describes dinner in an Italian inn to his wife, 1844.

Walking with William Splaine, we saw a vast multitude of starlings making an unspeakable jangle. They would settle in a row of trees; then, one tree after another, rising at a signal they looked like a cloud of specks of black snuff or powder struck up from a brush or broom or shaken from a wig; then they would sweep round in whirlwinds – you could see the nearer and further bow of the rings by the size and blackness; many would be in one phase at once, all narrow black flakes hurling round, then in another; then they would fall upon a field and so on. Splaine wanted a gun: then 'there it would rain meat', he said. I thought they must be full of enthusiasm and delight hearing their cries and stirring and cheering one another.

Gerard Manley Hopkins, Journal, 1874.
See 27 November for Coleridge on this same phenomenon.

9 NOVEMBER

1938 Kristallnacht, *the Night of Broken Glass, in Germany, when Jewish shops and synagogues are attacked by the Nazis and 91 Jews are killed.*

1960 *John F. Kennedy wins the US presidential elections.*

1989 *The Berlin Wall starts to be dismantled.*

A glorious day, in every sense of the word. Alexander's great victory [Alamein] and the invasion by the Americans of French North Africa have put the people of this country into better fettle than they have known since 1925, when, at Melbourne on the third day of the second Teat Match, Hobbs and Sutcliffe put on 283 runs for England's first wicket and sent the Stock Exchange up two points.

James Agate, Ego, 1942. The 'Torch' landings at Casablanca,
Algiers and Oran had taken place the day before.

Now that the enemy has gone, the people have pulled their copper buckets out of hiding and go to fetch water at the well as they did after the Vandals and the Goths and the Huns and the Celts had come and gone in their turn. The roads are filled with ruts and holes and the country people come along and shovel in a little earth and stones to keep them going. We have bandits roaming at night in bands and holding up lonely houses and the people who live outside the towns are setting alarm bells up that can be heard and may bring help. Our small Polish garrison, like medieval mercenaries, patrol Asolo at night. A deputation of citizens came to ask me what they were to do when the Poles, rather drunk, open doors and shout 'We want women' in bad Italian. I felt this was not my sort of job to cope with and suggested a good lock to the doors as the best answer. I enjoy living so far away and am reading histories of the Dark Ages and feel them almost contemporary.

Freya Stark from her north Italian home at Asolo to
Field Marshal Lord Wavell, Viceroy of India, 1945.

10 NOVEMBER

1960 *Penguin Books publish an unexpurgated edition of D. H. Lawrence's* Lady Chatterley's Lover *and sell 200,000 copies in a day.*

1983 *Microsoft launch the first Windows operating system.*

Knavery seems to be so much the striking feature of its [America's] inhabitants that it may not in the end be an evil that they will become aliens to this kingdom.

King George III to Lord Shelburne, 1782.

Well, we are but a mile from Ujiji [on Lake Tanganyika] now, and it is high time we should let them know a caravan is coming; so 'Commence firing' is the word passed along the length of the column, and gladly do they begin. They have loaded their muskets half full, and they roar like the broadside of a line-of-battle ship. Down go the ramrods, sending huge charges home to the breech, and volley after volley is fired The flags are fluttered; the banner of America is in front, waving joyfully . . . The guide blows his horn, and the shrill, wild clangour of it is far and near; and still the cannon muskets tell the noisy seconds . . .

We have at last entered the town. There are hundreds of people around me – I might say thousands without exaggeration, it seems to me . . . There is a group of the most respectable Arabs, and as I come nearer I see the white face of an old man among them. He has a cap with a gold band around it, his dress is a short jacket of red blanket cloth, and his pants – well, I didn't observe. I am shaking hands with him. We raise our I hats, and I say:

'Dr Livingstone, I presume?'

And he says, 'Yes.'

H. M. Stanley in the New York Herald, *1872, describes the most famous meeting of his life, in 1871.*

11 NOVEMBER

1920 *The Unknown Soldier is reburied in Westminster Abbey.*

1953 *The first edition of* Panorama *is televised.*

1992 *The Church of England votes to allow women priests.*

Twenty-five minutes ago the guns went off, announcing peace. A siren hooted on the river. They are hooting still. A few people ran to look out of windows. The rooks wheeled round, and wore for a moment the symbolic look of creatures performing some ceremony, partly of thanksgiving, partly of valediction over the grave. A very cloudy still day, the smoke toppling over heavily towards the east; and that too wearing for a moment a look of something floating, waving, drooping. So far neither bells nor flags, but the wailing of sirens and intermittent guns.

Virginia Woolf, Diary, 1918.

Following the assassination of a German diplomat in Paris, said to be by a Jew, the most appalling general pogrom broke out at 2 a.m. all over Germany [*Kristallnacht*]. Jewish shops in Berlin were looted and set on fire while the police looked on. Jews were forced to jump from second-storey windows, and to crawl on their knees for a mile or two. An old man was beaten along the street while a thirteen-year-old girl tried to protect him, screaming at the mob. The news is that Jews have been lynched, forced to resign their property, and sent to concentration camps. It's a new St Bartholomew's Day Massacre.

George Beardmore, Journal, 1938.

12 NOVEMBER

1951 *The first* Come Dancing *programme is televised.*

1984 *The withdrawal of the £1 note is announced.*

Your most kind note found me in the agonies of plotting and contriving a new book [*Martin Chuzzlewit*]; in which stage of the tremendous process I am accustomed to walk up and down the house, smiting my forehead dejectedly; and to be so horribly cross and surly, that the boldest fly at my approach at such times, even the postman knocks at the door with a mild feebleness, and my publishers always come two together, lest I should fall upon a single invader and do murder on his intrusive body.

I am afraid if I came to see you under such circumstances, you would be very glad to be rid of me in two hours at the most; but I would risk even that disgrace, in my desire to accept your kind invitation, if it were not indispensable just now, that I should be always in the way. In starting a work which is to last for twenty months there are so many little things to attend to, which require my personal superintendence, that I am obliged to be constantly on the watch; and I may add, seriously, that unless I were to shut myself up, obstinately and sullenly in my own room for a great many days without writing a word, I don't think I ever should make a beginning.

I have not answered your letter until now, because I have really been tempted and hesitating. But the lapse of every new day only gives me a stronger reason for being perseveringly uncomfortable, that out of my gloom and solitude, something comical (or meant to be) may straightway grow up.

If you should still be in your present retreat when I have got my first number written (after which, I go on with great nonchalance) we shall be more than glad to come to you for one or two days.

Charles Dickens to Miss Burdett-Coutts, 1842.

13 NOVEMBER

1914 *The brassière patented in America.*

1985 *The eruption of a volcano in northern Colombia creates a mudslide which kills 23,000.*

I got into the strangest places, among the wildest Neapolitans – kitchens, washing-places, archways, stables, vineyards – was baited by dogs, answered in profoundly unintelligible Neapolitan, from behind lonely locked doors, in cracked female voices, quaking with fear; could hear of no such Englishman or any Englishman. By and by I came upon a polenta-shop in the clouds, where an old Frenchman, with an umbrella like a faded tropical leaf (it had not rained for six weeks) was staring at nothing at all, with a snuffbox in his hand. To him I appealed concerning the Signor Larthoor. 'Sir,' said he, with the sweetest politeness, 'can you speak French?' 'Sir,' said I, 'a little.' 'Sir,' said he, 'I presume the Signor Lootheere' – you will observe that he changed the name according to the custom of his country – 'is an Englishman.' I admitted that he was the victim of circumstances and had that misfortune. 'Sir,' said he, 'one word more. *Has* he a servant with a wooden leg?' 'Great Heaven, sir,' said I, 'how do I know? I should think not, but it is possible' . . . He then took an immense pinch of snuff, wiped the dust off his umbrella, led me to an arch commanding a wonderful view of the bay of Naples, and pointed deep into the earth from which I had mounted. 'Below there, near the lamp, one finds an Englishman, with a servant with a wooden leg. It is always possible that he is the Signor Lootheere' . . . As I was going down to the lamp, I saw the strangest staircase up a dark corner, with a man in a white waist-coat (evidently hired) standing on the top of it fuming. I dashed in at a venture, found it was the place, made the most of the whole story, and was indescribably popular.

Charles Dickens describes to Georgina Hogarth his attempts
to find the house of Mr Lowther in Naples, 1853.

14 NOVEMBER

1896 *The speed limit for motor-cars raised from 4 to 14 mph in Britain.*

1922 *First regular radio programme broadcast in Britain by 2LO, precursor of the BBC.*

1940 *Coventry is bombed, perhaps worse than any other British city, with 400–500 killed.*

O Digby my dear
It is perfectly clear
    That my mind will be horribly vext,
If you happen to write
By ill luck to invite
    Me to dinner on Saturday next.

For this I should sigh at
That Mrs T. Wyatt
Already has booked me, o dear!
So I could not tend answer
To you – 'I'm your man, Sir! –
– Your loving fat friend.
    Edward Lear.'

Edward Lear to the architect Sir Matthew Digby Wyatt, 1863.

I spent the whole day, a long, rich, companionable one, with [Prince] Paul [of Yugoslavia, an old friend]. I told him of the appalling impression that the King [Edward VIII] was making, and that the House of Commons openly talked of abdication, etc. He was horrified. We discussed all the eligible princesses in Europe, and tried to agree on one whose charms we could urge on the King, but we could find none: perhaps he had better marry Wallis [Simpson] and be done with it, and brave the storm.

Chips Channon, Diary, 1936.

15 NOVEMBER

1864 *General Sherman captures and burns Atlanta, Georgia in the American Civil War.*

1899 *Winston Churchill is captured by the Boers while acting as a war correspondent.*

1968 *Colour TV broadcasting begins in Britain.*

At ten o'clock we went down to supper, and from the way Gowing and Cummings ate you would have thought they had not had a meal for a month. I told Carrie to keep something back in case Mr Perkupp [Pooter's boss] should come by mere chance. Gowing annoyed me very much by filling a large tumbler of champagne, and drinking it straight off. He repeated this action, and made me fear our half-dozen of champagne would not last out. I tried to keep a bottle back, but Lupin got hold of it, and took it to the side-table with Daisy and Frank Mutlar . . .

I turned round suddenly, and then I saw Mr Perkupp standing half-way in the door, he having arrived without our knowing it . . .

Carrie and I took him downstairs, but the table was a wreck. There was not a glass of champagne left – not even a sandwich. Mr Perkupp said he required nothing, but would like a glass of seltzer or soda water. The last syphon was empty. Carrie said: 'We have plenty of port wine left.' Mr Perkupp said with a smile: 'No, thank you. I really require nothing, but I am most pleased to see you and your husband in your own home. Goodnight, Mrs Pooter – you will excuse my very short stay, I know.' I went with him to his carriage, and he said: 'Don't trouble to come to the office till twelve tomorrow.'

George and Weedon Grossmith, The Diary of a Nobody, *1894.*

16 NOVEMBER

1959 The Sound of Music, *stage version, has its première on Broadway.*

1979 *Sir Anthony Blunt, former Surveyor of the Queen's Pictures and Director of the Courtauld Institute of Art, is revealed as the 'Fourth Man', a one-time spy for Soviet Russia alongside Guy Burgess, Donald Maclean and Kim Philby.*

Indeed, nobody but an excellent sister could be induced to write on such a gloomy, dispiriting afternoon, but I have put the table close by the fire, with one leg (belonging to the table, not to me) in the fender, to prevent it from slipping away, the armchair close behind the table, and me supported by them both, holding a pen in one hand and the poker in the other, and now, have at you.

Emily Eden to her sister Lady Buckinghamshire, 1817.

Why, you madman, I wouldn't change my present installation for any post, dignity, honour, or advantage conceivable to me. It fills the bill; I have the loveliest time. And as for wars and rumours of wars, you surely know enough of me to be aware that I like that also a thousand times better than decrepit peace in Middlesex? I do not quite like politics; I am too aristocratic, I fear, for that. God knows I don't care who I chum with; perhaps like sailors best; but to go round and sue and sneak to keep a crowd together – never. My imagination, which is not the least damped by the idea of having my head cut off in the bush, recoils aghast from the idea of a life like Gladstone's, and the shadow of the newspaper chills me to the bone.

Robert Louis Stevenson, from Samoa, to Sidney Colvin, 1891.

17 NOVEMBER

1558 *The Accession of Queen Elizabeth I.*

1869 *The Suez Canal is opened.*

My gondola is, at this present, waiting for me on the canal; but I prefer writing to you in the house, it being autumn – and rather an English autumn than otherwise. It is my intention to remain at Venice during the winter, probably, as it has always been (next to the East) the greenest island of my imagination. It has not disappointed me; though its evident decay would, perhaps, have that effect upon others. But I have been familiar with ruins too long to dislike desolation. Besides, I have fallen in love, which, next to falling into the canal (which would be of no use, as I can swim), is the best or the worst thing I could do. I have got some extremely good apartments in the house of a 'Merchant of Venice', who is a good deal occupied with business, and has a wife in her twenty-second year. Marianna (that is her name) is in her appearance altogether like an antelope.

Lord Byron to Thomas Moore, 1816. See 18 December.

I feel we should not give him [Churchill] a post at this stage. Anything he undertakes he puts his heart and soul into. If there is going to be war – and no one can say that there is not – we must keep him fresh to be our war Prime Minister.

Prime Minister Stanley Baldwin to J.C.C. Davidson, 1935.

18 NOVEMBER

1477 *William Caxton the printer publishes the first book in England,* Dictes and Sayenges of the Philosophers.

1978 *Mass suicide of 914 members of the cult People's Temple Christian Church, led by Jim Jones, in Jonestown, Guyana.*

And from the time of our being in London together, I thought you really very much in love. But you certainly are not at all – there is no concealing it. What strange creatures we are! – It seems as if your being secure of him (as you say yourself) had made you indifferent. There was a little disgust I suspect, at the races – and I do not wonder at it. His expressions there would not do for one who had rather more acuteness, penetration and taste, than love, which was your case . . .

His situation in life, family, friends, and above all his character – his uncommonly amiable mind, strict principles, just notions, good habits – *all* that *you* know so well how to value, *all* that really is of the first importance – everything of this nature pleads his cause most strongly . . .

Oh! my dear Fanny, the more I write about him, the warmer my feelings become, the more strongly I feel the sterling worth of such a young man and the desirableness of your growing in love with him again. I recommend this most thoroughly. There *are* such beings in the world perhaps, one in a thousand, as the creature you and I should think perfection, where grace and spirit are united to worth, where the manners are equal to the heart and understanding, but such a person may not come in your way, or if he does, he may not be the eldest son of a man of fortune, the brother of your particular friend, and belonging to your own county . . .

And now, my dear Fanny, having written so much on one side of the question, I shall turn round and entreat you not to commit yourself further, and not to think of accepting him unless you really do like him.

Jane Austen offers contradictory advice to her niece, Fanny Knight, 1814.

19 NOVEMBER

1863 *President Lincoln gives an address at the dedication of the cemetery on the battlefield of Gettysburg,*

1994 *The first-ever draw in Britain's National Lottery produces seven winners who get £800,000 each.*

Angels are creatures that have not so much of a body as flesh is, as froth is, as a vapour is, as a sigh is; and yet with a touch they shall moulder a rock into less atoms than the sand that it stands upon, and a millstone into smaller flour than it grinds. They are creatures *made* – yet not a minute older now than when they were first made, if they were made before all measure of time began. Nor, if they were made in the beginning of time and be now six thousand years old, have they one wrinkle of age in their face or one sob of weariness in their lungs. They are God's eldest sons. They are super-elementary meteors. They hang between the nature of God and the nature of man and are of middle condition. And (if we may without offence express it so) they are the riddles of Heaven and the perplexities of speculation.

John Donne, from a sermon preached in 1627.

I am sitting hunched up by the fire in my lodgings after a meal of tough meat and cold apple-tart. I am full of self-commiseration. It is very cold and I cannot get warm – try as I will . . . London in November from the inside of a dingy lodging-house can be very terrible indeed. This celestial isolation will drive me out of my mind. I marvel how God can stick it lonely, damp, and cold in the clouds. That is how I live too – but then I am not God.

W. N. P. Barbellion, The Journal of a Disappointed Man, *1914. He was an official at the Natural History Museum, dogged by ill-health, and died in 1919 aged 30.*

20 NOVEMBER

1992 Some important rooms at Windsor Castle are destroyed by fire.

2003 The British Consulate in Istanbul is bombed by terrorists linked to al-Qaeda. The Consul-General is killed with 31 others.

Oh, if you were to hear 'Where and oh where is my Soldier Laddie gone' played every three hours in a languid way by the chimes of Woodbridge church, wouldn't you wish to hang yourself? On Sundays we have the 'Sicilian Mariner's Hymn' – very slow indeed. I see, however, by a hand-bill in the grocer's shop that a man is going to lecture on the gorilla in a few weeks. So there is something to look forward to.

Edward FitzGerald to W. F. Pollock, 1861.

Edward Humphries married a young woman when he was 83, had a son within the year, 'Leastways his wife had,' said Mrs Hall.

The Revd Francis Kilvert, Diary, 1873.

You reduce me to mere gelatinous grovel. And the worst of it is that you know so well how. You, with a magnanimity already so marked as to be dazzling, sent me last summer a beautiful and discouraging volume which I never mastered the right combination of minutes and terms to thank you for as it deserved – and then, perfectly aware that this shameful consciousness had practically converted me to quivering pulp, you let fly the shaft [another book] that has finished me in the fashion to which I now so distressfully testify. It is really most kind and charming of you, and the incident will figure largely in all your eventual biographies: yet it is almost more than I can bear.

Henry James thanks H.G. Wells for the gift of two of his books, 1899.

21 NOVEMBER

1783 *World's first-ever balloon flight takes place in Paris, when Pilatre de Rozier goes up in a Mongolfier hot-air balloon.*

1989 *Proceedings in the House of Commons are televised for the first time.*

With Creed to a tavern, where Dean Wilkins and others: and good discourse; among the rest, of a man that is a little frantic, that hath been a kind of minister, Dr Wilkins saying that he hath read for him in his church, that is poor and a debauched man, that the College [the Royal Society] have hired for 20s. to have some of the blood of a sheep let into his body; and it is to be done on Saturday next. They purpose to let in about twelve ounces; which, they compute, is what will be let in a minute's time by a watch. On this occasion, Dr Whistler told a pretty story related by [Dr Thomas] Muffett, a good author, of Dr Caius, that built Caius College [Cambridge]; that, being very old, and living only at that time upon woman's milk, he, while he fed upon the milk of an angry, fretful woman, was so himself; and then, being advised to take it of a good-natured, patient woman, he did become so, beyond the common temper of his age. Their discourse was very fine; and if I should be put out of my office, I do take great content in the liberty I shall be at, of frequenting these gentlemen's company.

Samuel Pepys, Diary, 1667. He was in the company of
several members of the Royal Society.

22 NOVEMBER

1963 *President Kennedy is assassinated in Dallas, Texas.*

2003 *England wins the Rugby World Cup in Australia.*

I scarcely remember counting upon any happiness – I look not for it if it be not in the present hour – nothing startles me beyond the moment. The setting sun will always set me to rights – or if a sparrow come before my window I take part in its existence and pick about the gravel.

John Keats to Benjamin Bailey, 1817.

You are too much apprehensive of your complaint . . . The best way in these cases is to keep yourself as ignorant as you can – as ignorant as the world was before Galen – of the entire inner construction of the Animal Man – not to be conscious of a midriff – to hold kidneys (save of sheep and swine) to be an agreeable fiction – not to know whereabouts the gall grows – to account the circulation of the blood an idle whimsy of Harvey's – to acknowledge no mechanism not visible. For, once fix the seat of your disorder, and your fancies flux into it like bad humours . . . Above all, use exercise, take a little more spirituous liquors, learn to smoke, continue to keep a good conscience, and avoid tampering with hard terms of art – viscosity – scirrhosity, and those bugbears, by which simple patients are scared into their graves. Believe the general sense of the mercantile world, which holds that desks are not deadly. It is the mind, good B.B., and not the limbs, that taints by long sitting. Think of the patience of tailors – think how long the Chancellor sits – think of the Brooding Hen.

Charles Lamb to Bernard Barton, 1823.

23 NOVEMBER

1936 *The first issue of* Life, *the greatest of the photo-journalism magazines, is issued in the US.*

1963 *The children's science-fiction serial* Dr Who *is first broadcast on BBC TV.*

In New Street Station [Birmingham] chaos and old night were reigning, also complete ignorance of what was happening. No trains were arriving from the south and I quickly discovered that no official lived who could tell me how long a passenger from Rugby would take to go to Stafford (for this was Jean's round-about route) and come back to Birmingham. By 6 p.m. a small group of people like me had gathered in the lee of a tin-plate advertisement on the bridge crossing the lines peering out into the darkness for the first sign of an approaching train. My compassion was sufficiently roused to take a girl and young fellow, who were starving and seemed completely lost – they were waiting for the arrival of parents from Camden Town – across to the Midland Hotel and give them beef sandwiches and beer before returning to the pitchy hell of the station to meet a train that did not contain Jean. (Picture me whistling our recognition-phrase beneath the broken glass arch, trying to distinguish faces, and being accosted as 'David' or 'Tom', all the while waiting for the Bofors guns to start up and bombs to whistle down.) Then I took a WAAF to the Midland, similarly lost and starving. She was a fine strong girl who drove a lorry and trailer laden with gas tubes for barrage balloons between Runcorn and Malvern every other day.

George Beardmore, Journal, 1940. Birmingham had been bombed the two previous nights. He was there to meet his wife Jean and baby daughter, and take them to his lodgings in Bromsgrove, but as it turned out, they got there without coming through Birmingham.

24 NOVEMBER

1859 *Samuel Smiles's* Self Help *and Charles Darwin's* Origin of Species *are both published by John Murray. The 1,250 print run of the latter sells out immediately, and a new edition of 3,000 copies is put in hand.*

1963 *The first live murder on TV, of the alleged assassin of John F. Kennedy, Lee Harvey Oswald, by small-time nightclub owner Jack Ruby.*

1989 *The entire Communist Czechoslovak leadership resigns.*

A rainy morning. We all were well except that my head ached a little, and I took my breakfast in bed. I read a little of Chaucer, prepared the goose for dinner, and then we all walked out. I was obliged to return for my fur tippet and spencer [a close-fitting jacket or bodice], it was so cold . . . As we were going along we were stopped at once, at the distance perhaps of fifty yards from our favourite birch tree. It was yielding to the gusty wind with all its tender twigs, the sun shone upon it, and it glanced in the wind like a flying sunshiny shower. It was a tree in shape, with stem and branches, but it was like a spirit of water. The sun went in, and it resumed its purplish appearance, the twigs still yielding to the wind, but not so visibly to us. The other birch trees that were near it looked bright and cheerful, but it was a creature by its own self among them . . .

Peggy Ashburner talked about Thomas's having sold his land . . . she told me with what pains and industry they had made up their taxes, interest, etc. etc., how they all got up at 5 o'clock in the morning to spin and Thomas carded, and that they had paid off a hundred pounds of interest. She said she used to take such pleasure in the cattle and sheep. 'O how pleased I used to be when they fetched them down, and when I had been a bit poorly I would gang out upon a hill and look ower 't fields and see them, and it used to do me so much good you cannot think.' Molly said to me when I came in, 'Poor body! She's very ill, but one does not know how long she may last. Many a fair face may gang before her.'

> *Dorothy Wordsworth, Journal, 1801. The Ashburners were*
> *the Wordsworths' closest neighbours at Dove Cottage.*

25 NOVEMBER

1867 *Swedish chemist Alfred Nobel patents dynamite. He later founds a series of prizes with the profits.*

1952 *Agatha Christie's play* The Mousetrap *opens in London.*

When I was in spirits, I sometimes fancied that my book would be successful, but I never even built a castle in the air of such success as it has met with; I do not mean the sale, but the impression it has made on you (whom I have always looked at as chief judge) and Hooker and Huxley. The whole has infinitely exceeded my wildest hopes.

Charles Darwin to Sir Charles Lyell, the leading geologist of the day, 1859.
J. D. Hooker was the leading botanist and T. H. Huxley the leading zoologist.

Out here one's outlook on life, military life I mean, changes very rapidly – every now and then moments of excitement and almost of happiness even in the trenches, occasionally a moment almost of ecstasy when one marches in late at night after a week of dirt and bullets and finds a feather bed and a bottle of the Boy awaiting one; then horrible reactions of boredom and nausea as one's mind collapses under the pressure of prospect and retrospect and the monotony of a great desert of discomfort and danger with no visible horizon. But usually one is very equable, looking no further ahead than the next meal and feeling that really life is very much the same everywhere, war or no war.

Raymond Asquith to Lady Diana Cooper, from the Western Front, 1915. 'The Boy' was
Bollinger champagne, so called from Edward VII's habit when shooting of always
having a few bottles to hand, on ice in a wheelbarrow. When thirsty he shouted 'Boy'
to summon the youth in charge of it.

26 NOVEMBER

1942 *World première of the film* Casablanca, *New York.*

1983 *The Brinks-Mat bullion robbery at Heathrow airport, when 6,800 gold bars worth £26 million are stolen.*

Emmy, are you with child? Or have you had a husband and four children in the whooping-cough? Or have you been driven mad by Orange [Protestant] factions? If none of these evils has befallen you, you might have written me a line more. I know yours was the last letter, but think of me and all my sufferings! And above all, the standing disappointment of not seeing you, when I was literally airing the sheets and killing the fowls for you. And there I was without encumbrance, a free woman, ready to go all over the [Giant's] Causeway – and as I fear I am now beginning a child, I do not know when I shall be my own woman again . . . I hope it will not be in the power of any swindler to keep you from me next year, for I really cannot do so long without a clearance of ideas. There will be such old stores to dispose of.

Emily, I am ashamed to confess to you how I have suffered from the Orange spirit of this horrid black North. I am ashamed to tell you how wickedly irritated I was, I am getting better now. The fearful evil I feel of this party spirit is, it is so catching. It kindles all the combustibles of contradiction and retaliation within one, till, though it was *injustice* that irritated me, yet I fear I should not have dealt justly towards them. I am not sanguine, I think nothing will be done; and I wish I thought better of the [Orange] Association.

Pamela, Lady Campbell to Emily Eden, from Armagh in northern Ireland, 1828.

27 NOVEMBER

1942 *The French fleet in Toulon - 8 cruisers, 30 destroyers and 16 submarines - is scuttled to prevent it falling into the hands of the Germans as they enter Vichy France.*

1969 *Brazilian footballer Pele scores his one-thousandth professional goal. He retires in 1977 with a career total of 1,282 goals.*

I have now no other vanity but in my little housewifery, which is easily gratified in this country, where, by the help of my receipt-book, I make a very shining figure among my neighbours, by the introduction of custards, cheesecakes, and minced pies, which were entirely unknown to these parts, and are received with universal applause; and I have reason to believe will preserve my memory even to future ages, particularly by the art of butter-making, in which I have so improved them, that they now make as good as in any part of England.

Lady Mary Wortley Montagu to her daughter the Countess of Bute,
from her home in Italy, 1753.

A most interesting morning. Awoke from one of my painful coach sleeps, in the coach to London . . . The sun at length rose upon the flat plain, like a hill of fire in the distance, rose wholly, and in the water that flooded part of the flat, a deep column of light. But as the coach went on, a hill rose and intercepted the sun, and the sun in a few minutes rose over it, a complete second rising through other clouds and with a different glory. Soon after this I saw starlings in vast flights, borne along like smoke, mist, like a body unendued with voluntary power. Now it shaped itself into a circular area, inclined; now it formed a square, now a globe, now from a complete orb into an ellipse; then oblongated into a balloon with the car suspended, now a concave semicircle; still expanding, or contracting, thinning or condensing, now glimmering and shivering, now thickening, deepening, blackening!

Samuel Taylor Coleridge, Notebook, 1799. Compare this with Gerard Manley
Hopkins's comments on the flight of starlings, 8 November.

28 NOVEMBER

1520 *Ferdinand Magellan reaches the Pacific Ocean, so becoming the first European to have rounded Cape Horn.*

1990 *Mrs Thatcher leaves 10 Downing Street for the last time, having announced her resignation as Prime Minister on 22 November.*

[The Queen] kept us waiting ten minutes so we stood in the long ante-hall chatting to Sir Peter Agnew, secretary of the [Privy] Council. Dick [Crossman] is on uproariously good terms with him. Said I, 'No stools today. Dick always disgraces us by falling over them. These Winchester men have no breeding.' 'That's nothing,' said Peter Agnew. And then proceeded to tell us of the time five members of the previous Tory Government had had to be sworn in. Everything was a shambles: 'The worst swearing-in I have ever seen.' The five came streaming in and every one of them flopped on to one knee on the floor! He indicated that they should move nearer the Queen on to the stools and to his astonishment everyone moved towards the stools on his knees! 'It was an incredible sight.' When it came to kissing hands one unfortunate Privy Councillor lunged at the stool in front of the Queen, missed it and knelt there with one leg cocked in the air. He was only saved from toppling right over by clutching the Queen's hand. She looked like thunder. When it was all over, Sir Peter was summoned to see the Queen. 'Here it goes, I thought. Now I'm for it.' But it was about something else. When he apologised to her she giggled. 'Wasn't it funny!' 'I thought you looked very displeased, ma'am.' 'If I hadn't looked like that I should have burst out laughing,' was her reply.

Barbara Castle, Diary, 1967.

1975 *Bill Gates chooses Microsoft as the name for the company he is founding with Paul Allen to write the* BASIC *computer language.*

1993 *Secret meetings with the IRA begin the 'Peace Process' in Northern Ireland.*

[He and his wife are woken early in the morning by suspicious knocking sounds.] We lay both of us afraid; yet I would have risen, but my wife would not let me; besides, I could not do it without making noise; and we did both conclude that thieves were in the house, but wondered what our people did, whom we thought either killed or afraid, as we were. Thus we lay till the clock struck eight, and high day. At last I removed my gown and slippers safely to the other side of the bed over my wife, and there safely rose and put on my gown and breeches, and then, with a firebrand in my hand, safely opened the door, and saw nor heard anything. Then (with fear, I confess) went to the maid's chamber-door, and all quiet and safe. Called Jane up, and went down safely and opened my chamber, where all well. Then more freely about, and to the kitchen, where the cook-maid up and all safe. So up again, and when Jane came, and we demanded whether she heard no noise, she said, 'Yes, and was afraid,' but rose with the other maid and found nothing; but heard a noise in the great stack of chimneys that goes from Sir J. Mennes's through our house; and so we sent, and their chimneys have been swept this morning, and the noise was that, and nothing else.

Samuel Pepys, Diary, 1667.

30 NOVEMBER

1886 *The first 'floor show' is put on, at the Folies-Bergère in Paris.*

1936 *The Crystal Palace burns down at Sydenham in south London. It had re-opened there in 1854 after being moved from its original position in Hyde Park, where it had housed the Great Exhibition of 1851.*

I have sent you by the carrier eight bottles of cider in a box. Pray send me one of your socks, to make you new ones by. I believe that indisposition you felt was caused by some violent exercise: if you use to swing, let it not be violently; for exercise should be rather to refresh than tire nature. You did well to take some balsam; it is a most sovereign thing, and I purpose, if please God, to write you the virtues of it. Dear Ned, if you would have anything, send me word; or if I thought a cold pie, or such a thing, would be of any pleasure to you, I would send it you. But your father says you care not for it, and Mrs Pierson tells me, when her son was at Oxford, and she sent him such things, he prayed her that she would not. I thank you for the *Man in the Moon*. I had heard of the book, but not seen it; by as much as I have looked upon, I find it is some kind of *Don Quixote*.

Brilliana, Lady Harley to her son Edward at Oxford, 1638.

. . . the national temper not being hasty, and never inflamed by wine, drunkenness being a vice abandoned to the vulgar, and spoke of with greater detestation than murder, which is mentioned with as little concern as a drinking-bout in England, and is almost as frequent . . . As all the peasants are suffered the use of fire-arms, the slightest provocation is sufficient to shoot, and they see one of their own species lie dead before them with as little remorse as a hare or a partridge, and, when revenge spurs them on, with much more pleasure.

Lady Mary Wortley Montagu from her home in Italy to
her daughter the Countess of Bute, 1749.

DECEMBER

1 DECEMBER

Last night the male dinner party at Stornoway House consisted of Beaverbrook, Esmond Harmsworth, Perry Brownlow and Monckton, the King's Solicitor. They were all in agreement that the marriage cannot be allowed to take place, and that the only avenue of approach to the demented lovesick sovereign was Wallis Simpson herself. And they bullied Perry Brownlow into promising to see Wallis today, and warn her confidentially that the country will not accept the marriage, and that she must go away for a few weeks, and allow the talk to simmer down, and to put all thoughts of marriage out of the King's mind. Perry reluctantly but very patriotically agreed, but this morning he discovered that Wallis is at Fort Belvedere [in Windsor Great Park] and ill – so ill, with a form of nervous exhaustion, that the King refuses to leave her . . . I don't personally see how the tension can be kept up, for things are boiling over. Perhaps we can anticipate an abdication shortly. Things are moving in favour of the Yorks [the future George VI], and from a realistic point of view I must confess that this seems the best solution.

Chips Channon, Diary, 1936. Beaverbrook and Harmsworth were press barons; Lord Brownlow was a courtier close to Edward VIII.

2 DECEMBER

1805 *Russia and Austria are defeated by the French under Napoleon at the Battle of Austerlitz.*

1901 *King Camp Gillette patents the first safety razor.*

2001 *The Enron Company files for bankruptcy with a debt of $16 billion.*

A white muslin cap or hood was then drawn over his face and the Sheriff not remembering that his eyes were covered requested him to advance to the platform. The prisoner replied in his usual tone, 'You will have to guide me there.'

The breeze disturbing the arrangement of the hood, the Sheriff asked his assistant for a pin. Brown raised his hand and directed him to the collar of his coat where several old pins were quilted in. The Sheriff took the pin and completed his work.

He was accordingly led forward to the drop, the halter hooked to the beam and the officers supposing that the execution was to follow immediately took leave of him. In doing so, the Sheriff enquired if he did not want a handkerchief to throw as a signal to cut the drop. Brown replied, 'No, I don't care; I don't want you to keep me waiting unnecessarily'. . . In this position he stood for five minutes or more, while the troops that composed the escort were wheeling into the positions assigned them . . .

Colonel Smith said to the Sheriff in a low voice, 'We are ready.'

The civil officers descended from the scaffold. One who stood near me whispered earnestly, 'He trembles, his knees are shaking.'

'You are mistaken,' I replied, 'it is the scaffold that shakes under the footsteps of the officers.'

David Hunter Strother describes the execution in 1859 of John Brown, by which Brown became a martyr of the abolitionist cause in the United States.

3 DECEMBER

1931 *Alka-Seltzer goes on sale for the first time.*

1984 *A gas leak at the Union Carbide pesticide factory in Bhopal in India kills nearly 3,000. In 1989 some £470 million is paid in compensation.*

Such a pouring of hundreds into a place already full to the throat, such indescribable confusion, such a rending and tearing of dresses, and yet such a scene of good humour on the whole . . . Fifty frantic men got up in all parts of the hall and addressed me all at once. Other frantic men made speeches to the walls . . . I read with the platform crammed with people. I got them to lie down upon it, and it was like some impossible tableau or gigantic picnic; one pretty girl in full dress lying on her side all night, holding on to one of the legs of my table. It was the most extraordinary sight. And yet from the moment I began to the moment of my leaving off, they never missed a point, and they ended with a burst of cheers.

Charles Dickens to Georgina Hogarth describing one of his public readings from his books, at Edinburgh, 1861.

DEAR JOHNNIE – Well, I must say you seem to be a tremendous fellow! Before I was eight I used to write stories – or dictate them at least – and I had produced an excellent history of Moses, for which I got £1 from an uncle; but I had never gone the length of a play, so you have beaten me fairly on my own ground.

DEAR RUSSELL – When you 'grow up and write stories like me', you will be able to understand that there is scarce anything more painful than for an author to hold a pen; he has to do it so much that his heart sickens and his fingers ache at the sight or touch of it; so that you will excuse me if I do not write much.

Robert Louis Stevenson to two young boys who had written him fan letters, 1893.

4 DECEMBER

1154 *Adrian IV, the only English-born Pope, is elected.*

1679 *The philosopher Thomas Hobbes dies: 'I am about to take my last voyage, a great leap in the dark.'*

1937 *The first issue of the* Dandy *comic appears.*

The scene of action beyond Crawley, thirty-two miles from town; the combatants Randall and Turner, the former an Irishman, which was lucky, as it gave me some sort of interest in the contest. The thing altogether not so horrid as I expected. Turner's face was a good deal de-humanised, but Randall (the conqueror) had hardly a scratch. The battle lasted two hours and twenty-two minutes: a beautiful sunshine broke out at this part of the day; and had there been a proportionate mixture of women in the immense ring formed around, it would have been a very brilliant spectacle. The pigeons let off at different periods of the fight, with despatches, very picturesque.

Tom Moore, Diary, 1818. He went to this prize fight with Byron's rakish friend Scrope Davies and the boxer 'Gentleman' Jackson (see 10 April).

London is now properly divided and the King's faction grows; people process the streets singing 'God Save the King', and assemble outside Buckingham Palace, they parade all night. After the first shock the country is now reacting, and demands that their King be left in peace.

Chips Channon on the growing abdication crisis, Diary, 1936.

5 DECEMBER

1872 *The brig* Marie Celeste *is found abandoned off the Azores.*

1933 *Prohibition ends in the US.*

1958 *Britain's first stretch of motorway, the Preston bypass on the M6, opens.*

We were shown the Lavenham belfry [in Suffolk]. First, the ringing chamber, hung all round with accounts of celebrated ringings . . . Then the belfry itself, the bells balanced on large beams, with great wheels to pull them round. The man rang the B♭ bell for us. It wheeled over abruptly, and the noise clanged, swelled, grew outward on the air, trembled and then settled on the third. The evening before I had expected to see the sounds fly out at the top of the tower like black cannon-balls, but this was like a wave breaking everyway outwards, thinning, ebbing back again. Then we went up to the top of the tower to look at the view. There were to have been four pinnacles, but the architect fell off the tower.

Sylvia Townsend Warner, Diary, 1927.

The following is a list of the prices of 'luxuries'. Terrines of chicken, 16f; of rabbit, 13f; . . . a goose, 45f; one cauliflower, 3f; one cabbage, 4f; dog is 2f a pound; a cat skinned costs 5f; a rat, 1f, if fat from the drains, 1f 50c. Almost all the animals in the Jardin des Plantes have been eaten. They have averaged about 7f a pound. Kangaroo, however, has been sold for 12f the pound. Yesterday I dined with the correspondent of a London paper. He had managed to get a large piece of *moufflon*, an animal which is, I believe, only found in Corsica. I can only describe it by saying that it tasted of *moufflon*, and nothing else . . . I do not think that I shall take up my residence in Corsica, in order habitually to feed upon it.

Henry Labouchere, British MP and journalist, besieged in Paris, 1870. A moufflon *is a wild mountain sheep.*

6 DECEMBER

1921 *The Irish Free State comes into existence.*

1962 *One of the last great smogs (fogs), after the Clean Air Act of 1956, covers most of England.*

My wife and I all the afternoon at Arithmetique, and she is come to do Addition, Subtraction, and Multiplication, very well. And so I purpose not to trouble her yet with Division, but to begin with the globes to her now.

Samuel Pepys, Diary, 1663. Terrestrial and celestial globes were used to teach geography and astronomy.

This journal is a relief. When I am tired – as I generally am – out comes this, and down goes everything. But I can't read it over; and God knows what contradictions it may contain. If I am sincere with myself (but I fear one lies more to one's self than to anyone else), every page should confute, refute, and utterly abjure its predecessor . . .

Gell called – he of Troy – after I was out. Mem. – to return his visit. But my Mems. are the very landmarks of forgetfulness – something like a lighthouse, with a ship wrecked under the nose of its lantern. I never look at a Mem. without seeing that I have remembered to forget . . .

I am so far obliged to this Journal, that it preserves me from verse – at least from keeping it. I have just thrown a poem into the fire (which it has relighted to my great comfort), and have smoked out of my head the plan of another. I wish I could as easily get rid of thinking, or, at least, the confusion of thought.

Lord Byron, Journal, 1813. Sir William Gell was the author of Topography of Troy, *1804.*

7 DECEMBER

1911 *The Chinese are allowed to cut off their pigtails, a sign of subservience under the now defunct Qing dynasty.*

1941 *Surprise attack by Japanese carrier-borne aircraft on the American Pacific fleet in Pearl Harbor, Hawaii ushers both countries into the Second World War.*

I imagine I see you in your box at the coffee-house. No doubt the waiter, as ingenious and adroit as his predecessors were before him, raises the teapot to the ceiling with his right hand, while in his left the teacup descending almost to the floor, receives a limpid stream; limpid in its descent, but no sooner has it reached its destination, than frothing and foaming to the view, it becomes a roaring syllabub . . . How different is the complexion of your evenings and mine! – yours, spent amid the ceaseless hum that proceeds from the inside of fifty noisy and busy periwigs; mine, by a domestic fireside, in a retreat as silent as retirement can make it; where no noise is made but what we make for our own amusement. For instance here are two rustics, and your humble servant in company. One of the ladies has been playing on the harpsichord, while I, with the other, have been playing at battledore and shuttlecock.

William Cowper to Joseph Hill, 1782.

Awoke, and up an hour before being called; but dawdled three hours in dressing. When one subtracts from life infancy (which is vegetation), sleep, eating, and swilling – buttoning and unbuttoning – how much remains of downright existence? The summer of a dormouse.

Lord Byron, Journal, 1813.

8 DECEMBER

1980 *John Lennon shot dead outside the Dakota Building on the edge of Central Park, New York where he lives.*

1987 *Reagan and Gorbachev agree to reduce the US and USSR nuclear arsenals.*

At night I went to Covent Garden and saw *Love in a Village*, a new comic opera, for the first night. I liked it much. I saw it from the gallery, but I was first in the pit. Just before the overture began to be played, two Highland officers came in. The mob in the upper gallery roared out, 'No Scots! No Scots! Out with them!', hissed and pelted them with apples. My heart warmed to my countrymen, my Scotch blood boiled with indignation. I jumped up on the benches, roared out, 'Damn you, you rascals!', hissed and was in the greatest rage. I am very sure at that time I should have been the most distinguished of heroes. I hated the English; I wished from my soul that the Union was broke and that we might give them another battle of Bannockburn. I went close to the officers and asked them of what regiment they were of. They told me Lord John Murray's, and that they were just come from the Havana. 'And this', said they, 'is the thanks that we get – to be hissed when we come home. If it was French, what could they do worse?' 'But', said one, 'if I had a *grup o yin or twa o the tamd rascals I sud let them ken what they're about.*' The rudeness of the English vulgar is terrible. This indeed is the liberty which they have: the liberty of bullying and being abusive with their blackguard tongues. They soon gave over.

James Boswell, Journal, 1762. The British had recently captured Havana, a key Spanish fortress in the Caribbean. The Scots were particularly out of favour at this time, a reflection of the unpopularity of the new Prime Minister, Lord Bute.

9 DECEMBER

The Highland Jacobite army got nine thousand pounds at Derby, and had the books brought to them, and obliged everybody to give them what they had subscribed against them. Then they retreated a few miles, but returned again to Derby, get ten thousand pounds more, plundered the town, and burnt a house of the Countess of Exeter. They are gone again, and go back to Leake, in Staffordshire, but miserably harassed, and, it is said, have left all their cannon behind them, and twenty waggons of sick.

Horace Walpole to Sir Horace Mann, 1745.

Luckily my duties took me to the House of Commons, where a friendly policewoman told me that St Stephen's Cloister had been hit last night. I went into what was the Members' cloakroom and saw a scene of devastation; confusion, wreckage, broken glass everywhere, and the loveliest, oldest part of the vast building a shambles. Suddenly I came upon Winston Churchill wearing a fur-collared coat, and smoking a cigar; he was led by a policeman and followed by Steel, his secretary. 'It's horrible,' he remarked to me without removing his cigar; and I saw that he was much moved, for he loves Westminster; I walked with him. 'They would hit the best bit,' I said. 'Where Cromwell signed King Charles's death warrant,' he grunted. I sensed the historic significance of the scene – Winston surveying the destruction he had long predicted, of a place he loved.

Chips Channon, Diary, 1940.

10 DECEMBER

1768 *The Royal Academy is founded.*

1988 *In Armenia, an earthquake kills 50,000. The Soviet Union, on its last legs, is criticised for slowness of and failure to coordinate relief efforts.*

I always put on my thickest greatcoat to go to our church in: as fungi grow in great numbers about the communion table . . . Parson and Clerk got through the service see-saw like two men in a sawpit. In the garden I see the heads of the snowdrops and crocuses just out of the earth. Another year with its same flowers and topics to open upon us.

Edward FitzGerald to Frederick Tennyson, 1843.

The House was full, for there has not been an abdication since 1399 [that of Richard II], 537 years ago. I thought everyone subdued but surprisingly unmoved, and Lady Astor actually seemed to enjoy herself, jumping about in her frivolous way. Baldwin was greeted with cheers, and sat down on the front bench gravely. At last he went to the bar, bowed twice – 'A message from the King,' and he presented a paper to the Speaker who proceeded to read it out. At the words 'renounce the Throne' his voice broke, and there were stifled sobs in the House . . .

At last Mr Baldwin sat down, and the Speaker adjourned the House until 6 p.m. . . . It is 5.42 and the House empty, the Chamber has witnessed yet again a scene that will always live in history. As I walked to my locker and fetched this diary, Lady Astor sang out to me, 'People who have been licking Mrs Simpson's boots ought to be shot.' I was too tired to retort and pretended I did not hear.

Chips Channon, Diary, 1936. Lady Astor was American-born,
the first woman MP to take her seat (see 1 December).

11 DECEMBER

1910 *Neon lighting is demonstrated for the first time, in Paris.*

1941 *Germany and Italy declare war on the US.*

1994 *President Yeltsin orders Russian troops into Chechnya.*

'My opinion is the Regent will not attempt a divorce . . . As for the Duke of York, at his time of life and that of the Duchess, all issue, of course, is out of the question. The Duke of Clarence, I have no doubt, will marry if he can; but the terms he asks from the ministers are such as they can never comply with. Besides a settlement such as is proper for a prince who marries expressly for a succession to the throne, the Duke of Clarence demands the payment of all his debts, which are very great, and a handsome provision for each of his ten natural children [by the actress Mrs Jordan]. These are terms that no ministers can accede to. Should the Duke of Clarence not marry, the next prince in succession is myself; and although I trust I shall be at all times ready to obey any call my country may make upon me, God only knows the sacrifice it will be to make, whenever I shall think it my duty to become a married man. It is now seven-and-twenty years that Madame St Laurent and I have lived together: we are of the same age, and have been in all climates, and in all difficulties together; and you may well imagine, Mr Creevey, the pang it will occasion me to part with her.'

Thomas Creevey's notes of a conversation with the Duke of Kent, younger brother of the Prince Regent, the Duke of York and the Duke of Clarence, 1817. Princess Charlotte, the only child of the Prince Regent by his estranged wife, Caroline of Brunswick, had died early in November. Madame St Laurent was the Duke of Kent's long-standing mistress. The following year he married the Princess Victoria of Saxe-Saalfeld-Coburg, who gave birth to the future Queen Victoria in 1819; he died in 1820.

12 DECEMBER

1901 *The first transatlantic radio signal - the Morse code letter S - is transmitted by Guglielmo Morconi.*

1975 *Six-day Balcombe Street siege ends with the surrender of four IRA gunmen who had murdered Ross McWhirter, co-founder with his brother of the* Guinness Book of Records, *on 27 November.*

We had some cheetah hunting on the way [to Bhurtpore, 100 miles south of Delhi]. Antelopes abound, there are hundreds of them to be seen at a time; the cheetahs are put in carts like the common hackeries the natives use, and which the antelopes are accustomed to see, so they do not get much out of the way, and when the cart is within 400 yards, the cheetah's hood is taken off, and he makes two or three bounds and generally knocks down the antelope. If he fails after a few bounds, he gets disgusted and comes back to the cart. There were two or three good chases this morning but no antelope killed, which was rather a blessing . . . The Bhurtpore Rajah came to the durbar [audience] in the afternoon. He is the ugliest and fattest young man I ever saw. A small face that takes up the usual space of the chin, and all the rest is head.

Emily Eden, en route from Simla to Calcutta with her brother, Lord Auckland, the Governor-General of India, 1839, from Up The Country. *The Rajah owed his position to the British, who had stormed the fortified city of Bhurtpore in 1826 and reinstated him, aged six, in place of an usurping cousin.*

I beg of you also to consider my strange position. I jined a club which it was said was to defend the Union; and I had a letter from the secretary, which his name I believe was Lord Warmingpan (or words to that effect), to say I am elected, and had better pay up a certain sum of money, I forget what. Now I cannae verra weel draw a blank cheque and send to 'LORD WARMINGPAN (or words to that effect), London, England'. And, man, if it was possible, I would be dooms glad to be out o' this bit scrapie.

Robert Louis Stevenson to Charles Baxter, 1887, from America.
The real name, it turned out, was 'Lord Pollington'.

13 DECEMBER

1476 *England's oldest surviving piece of printed matter is produced by William Caxton, an indulgence in Latin absolving Henry and Katherine Langley from their sins in return for raising money for a fleet to defeat the Turks.*

1939 *The Battle of the River Plate which leads to the Germans scuttling their pocket battleship, the* Graf Spee.

My heart has been in no rest since you went. I confess I was never so full of sorrow. I fear the provision of corn and malt will not hold out, if this continue; and they say they will burn my barns; and my fear is that they will place soldiers so near me that there will be no going out. My comfort is that you are not with me, lest they should take you; but I do most dearly miss you. I wish, if it pleased God, that I were with your father. I would have written to him, but I durst not write upon paper. Dear Ned, write to me, though you write upon a piece of cloth, as this is. I pray God bless you, as I desire my own soul should be blessed. There were a thousand dragoneers came into Hereford five hours after my lord Hertford.

Brilliana, Lady Harley to her son Edward, 1642. The Civil War had begun and she was alone at the family home, Brampton Bryan Castle in Herefordshire, a largely Royalist area, while her menfolk were in London supporting the Parliamentary cause. Lord Hertford was a Royalist commander.

You may faintly imagine . . . four stage-carpenters entirely boarding on the premises, a carpenter's shop erected in the back garden, size always boiling over on all the lower fires, Stanfield [the artist, painting scenery] perpetually elevated on planks and splashing himself from head to foot, Telbin requiring impossibilities of smart gasmen, and a legion of prowling nondescripts for ever shrinking in and out. Calm amidst the wreck, you aged friend glides away on the 'Dorrit' stream, forgetting the uproar for a stretch of hours, refreshes himself with a ten or twelve miles walk, pitches headforemost into foaming rehearsals . . .

Charles Dickens to the actor William Macready about preparations for amateur dramatics at home, 1856.

14 DECEMBER

1911 *The Norwegian Roald Amundsen becomes the first to reach the South Pole.*

1995 *The war between Bosnia, Croatia and Serbia ends.*

2003 *Saddam Hussein is captured by US forces in Iraq.*

As for the girdle that my father behested [promised] me, I spake to him thereof a little before he yede [went] to London last, and he said to me that the fault was in you, that ye would not think thereupon to do make it [to have it made]; but I suppose that is not so – he said it but for a scusation [excuse]. I pray you, if ye dare take it upon you, that ye will vouchsafe to do make it against ye come home; for I had never more need thereof than I have now, for I am wax so fetis [elegant – ironic] that I may not be girt in no bar of no girdle that I have but of one.

Elizabeth Peverel [a midwife] hath lay sick fifteen or sixteen weeks of the sciatica, but she sent my mother word by Kate that she should come hither when God sent time, though she should be crod [pushed] in a barrow.

John of Damme was here, and my mother discovered me to him; and he said by his troth that he was not gladder of nothing that he heard this twelvemonth than he was thereof. I may no longer live by my craft, I am discovered of all men that see me . . .

I pray you that ye will wear the ring with the image of St Margaret that I sent you for a remembrance till ye come home. Ye have left me such a remembrance that maketh me to think upon you both day and night when I would sleep.

Margaret Paston, pregnant with her first child,
to her husband John Paston I, 1441.

15 DECEMBER

1939 *The world première of* Gone With the Wind *takes place in Atlanta, Georgia.*

1974 *Speed limits of 70, 60, and 50 mph are introduced in Britain for different types of road.*

The enemies of the people of England who would have them considered in the worst light represent them as selfish, beef-eaters, and cruel. In this view I resolved today to be a true-born Old Englishman. I went into the City to Dolly's Steak-house in Paternoster Row and swallowed my dinner by myself to fulfil the charge of selfishness; I had a large fat beefsteak to fulfil the charge beef-eating; and I went at five o'clock to the Royal Cockpit in St James's Park and saw cock-fighting for about five hours to fulfil the charge of cruelty . . .

At five I filled my pockets with gingerbread and apples (quite the method), put on my old clothes and laced hat, laid by my watch, purse, and pocket-book, and with oaken stick in my hand sallied to the pit . . . The cocks, nicely cut and dressed and armed with silver heels, are set down, and fight with amazing bitterness and resolution. Some of them were quickly despatched. One pair fought three-quarters of an hour. The uproar and noise of betting is prodigious. A great deal of money made a very quick circulation from hand to hand . . . I was shocked to see the distraction and anxiety of the betters. I was sorry for the poor cocks. I looked round to see if any of the spectators pitied them when mangled and torn in a most cruel manner, but I could not observe the smallest relenting sign in any countenance. I was therefore not ill pleased to see them endure mental torment. Thus did I complete my true English day, and came home pretty much fatigued and pretty much confounded at the strange turn of this people.

James Boswell, Journal, 1762.

16 DECEMBER

1773 *The Boston Tea Party, when chests of tea subject to British customs duty are thrown in the harbour as a protest against taxation without representation.*

1944 *The Battle of the Bulge starts in the Ardennes, Germany's last offensive in the West.*

1977 *The Piccadilly Line extension to Heathrow is opened.*

I have at this moment a raging toothache, my dearest G., and go about the house with a great bottle of tincture in my hand, whilst Newhouse [Granville's valet] is boiling pigtailed tobacco for me . . . I have no twitches, no throbbings, no sensations, but a sharp, downright violent pain in my teeth. At dinner I am obliged to avoid crusts and to sit as if I was leaning on my hand only, but really to conceal my cheek being all puffed out with port wine. I think of nothing else and look resigned at all the slops and washes, at this moment taking a sly sup (behind Lady Harrowby's back) out of Seaman's Tincture.

Lady Granville to her sister Lady Morpeth, 1811. The next day Lady Granville reported, 'A large cup of liquid tobacco, held in my mouth, nearly killed but cured me.'

I have just heard the following about Bonaparte. On a certain occasion, prior to the unfortunate campaign in Russia [1812], when everything was ready for signing a treaty of peace with the Northern Powers, Maret, by an indiscretion, decided the destiny both of France and of Napoleon . . . Maret said, 'On previous occasions, sire, it was your Majesty that gave peace; now the Powers return the gift.' At these words Napoleon turned deadly pale, and impetuously threw his pen on the table . . . With a shrug of the shoulders he walked out of the room.

Frances, Lady Shelley, Diary, 1819. Maret was Foreign Minister. Lady Granville's verdict on Frances Shelley was that she was not 'superior or clever. Indeed, indeed she is not. Do observe, pray, it is all commonplace and superficial.'

17 DECEMBER

1801 *Birth of Alderman S.J. Sadcake, who donated what subsequently became lovely, sex-maniac-haunted Sadcake Park to the borough of Stretchford in 1865.*

1904 *The sack of the newly opened refreshment room on No. 3 platform, Nerdley (Bog Lane) Station by a combined force of militant temperance workers and the dreaded No. 3 suffragette commando under the leadership of Dame Tryphosa Fawcett.*

From Peter Simple's column in the Daily Telegraph, *2004*

The Boers are making a splendid fight for their freedom, and are winning all along the line. Every honest man, English or not, ought to rejoice. Instead of this, we English are in league with the Americans, we, who were the two peoples who have posed as champions of freedom in the world, to subdue two small, weak nations, the Boers and the Philippines, fighting for their independence, and not a word of disapproval is heard amongst us.

Young Walter Gaisford, Talbot's aide de camp, was here the other day, lamenting that the Khalifa and his dervishes had all been killed, so that there would be nobody left to shoot, he complained, even in the Soudan. 'There is hope, however, that, when the Boers are polished off, we may go on to a war with Abyssinia when more sport will be to be had.' This is the way our young fellow look at war ('a high old rabbit shoot'). It is good for them and the world that they have at last met their match.

Wilfrid Scawen Blunt, Diary, 1899.

SUCCESS FOUR FLIGHTS THURSDAY MORNING ALL AGAINST TWENTY-ONE MILE WIND STARTED FROM LEVEL WITH ENGINE POWER ALONE AVERAGE SPEED THROUGH AIR THIRTY-ONE MILES LONGEST 57 SECONDS INFORM PRESS HOME CHRISTMAS

Orville Wright's telegram to his father from North Carolina, 1903.

18 DECEMBER

1833 *Sir Robert Peel's Tamworth Manifesto, establishing the principle of modern liberal Conservatism.*

1997 *A Bill giving Scotland its first Parliament since 1707 is introduced.*

I go every morning to the Armenian Convent (of *friars not nuns* – my child) to study the language – I mean the *Armenian* language – (for as you perhaps know – I am versed in the Italian which I speak with fluency rather than accuracy –) and if you ask me my reason for studying this out-of-the-way language – I can only answer that it is Oriental and difficult – and employs me – which are – as you know my Eastern and difficult way of thinking – reasons sufficient. Then I have fallen in love with a very pretty Venetian of two and twenty [Marianna Segati, see 17 November] – with great black eyes – she is married – and so am I – which is very much to the purpose – we have found and sworn an external attachment – which has already lasted a lunar month – and I am more in love than ever – and so is the lady – at least she says so – and seems so – she does not plague me (which is a wonder –) and I verily believe we are one of the happiest – unlawful couples on this side of the Alps . . . I have not heard recently from England and wonder if Murray has published the po's sent to him – and I want to know if you don't think them very fine and all that – Goosey my love – don't they make you 'put finger in eye?' – You can have no idea of my thorough wretchedness from the day of my parting from you till nearly a month ago – though I struggled against it with some strength – at present I am better – thank Heaven above – and woman beneath – and will be a very good boy.

Lord Byron to his half-sister and former lover, Augusta Leigh, from Venice, 1816. The 'po's' were the third canto of Childe Harold, *published on 18 November, and* The Prisoner of Chillon and other poems, *published on 5 December.*

19 DECEMBER

1783 *William Pitt becomes Prime Minister at the age of 24.*

1972 *The splash-down of Apollo 17 ends the US programme of manned lunar landings.*

We dined last Thursday at the Hall; I sat down to table, trembling lest the tooth, of which I told you in my last, should not only refuse its own office, but hinder all the rest. Accordingly, in less than five minutes, by a hideous dislocation of it, I found myself not only in great pain, but under an absolute prohibition not only to eat, but to speak another word. Great emergencies sometimes meet the most effectual remedies. I resolved, if it were possible, then and there to draw it. This I effected so dexterously by a sudden twitch, and afterwards so dexterously conveyed it into my pocket, that no creature present, not even Mrs Unwin, who sat facing me, was sensible either of my distress, or of the manner of my deliverance from it. I am poorer by one tooth than I was, but richer by unimpeded use of all the rest . . .

Returning from my walk today, while I was passing by some small closes at the back of the town, I heard the voices of some persons extremely merry at the top of the hill. Advancing into the large field behind our house, I there met Mr Throck[morton], wife, and brother George. Combine in your imagination as large proportions as you can of earth and water intermingled so as to constitute what is commonly called mud, and you will have but an imperfect conception of the quantity that had attached itself to her petticoats: but she had half-boots, and laughed at her own figure.

William Cowper to Lady Hesketh, 1787.

20 DECEMBER

1946 *Première of Frank Capra's film* It's a wonderful Life, *starring James Stewart.*

1979 *Five million council tenants to get the right to buy their homes at a discount of up to 50 per cent off market value, depending on how long they have lived in them.*

Two laughing chimney-sweeps on a white horse – spur, rod, sneezing fine brown soot.

Samuel Taylor Coleridge, Notebook, 1802.

I went to Edinburgh, where I had not been for ten years. I found a . . . wonderful increase of shoes and stockings, streets and houses. When I lived there, very few maids had shoes and stockings, but plodded about the house with feet as big as a family Bible, and legs as large as portmanteaus . . . My old friends were glad to see me; some had turned Methodists – some had lost their teeth – some had grown very rich – some very fat – some were dying – and, alas! alas! many were dead; but the world is a coarse enough place, so I talked away, comforted some, praised others, kissed some old ladies, and passed a very riotous week . . .

From thence to Lambton. And here I ask, what use of wealth so luxurious and delightful as to light your house with gas? What folly, to have a diamond necklace or a Correggio, and not to light your house with gas! The splendour and glory of Lambton Hall make all other houses mean. How pitiful to submit to a farthing-candle existence, when science puts such intense gratification within your reach! Dear lady, spend all your fortune on a gas-apparatus.

The Revd Sydney Smith to Lady Mary Bennet, 1820. Lambton was the home of John George Lambton, made fabulously wealthy by the coalmines beneath his land and created Earl of Durham in 1833. Creevey reported him as saying 'he considered £ 40,000 a year a moderate income - such a one as a man might jog on with': 'Jog' promptly became his nickname.

21 DECEMBER

1620 *The Pilgrim Fathers land from the* Mayflower *in Massachusetts.*

1913 *First crossword puzzle ever appears in the* New York World.

1958 *General de Gaulle is elected President of the new French Fifth Republic.*

I spent a good deal of time trying to spot Germans working on the parapet opposite and then getting one of our portable machine-guns moved along the trench and loosing off fifty rounds at them in about five seconds. We got two or three that way. It keeps the men happy and amused.

Then yesterday afternoon the Germans began firing rifle grenades into the Duck's Bill and wounded two of our men. A rifle grenade is a thing like one of those big blunt-nosed Italian fir cones on the end of a metal rod about two feet long. You put the rod into the barrel of a rifle and fire it with a blank cartridge. Ours will go about three hundred yards and the Germans' five hundred. It is a good form of sport because it is almost like shooting with a bow and arrow. You can see the missile all the time in the air. I fetched up three men who are experts in the game with a box of grenades and we gave them back volleys of these things – our plan now is always to give them back about ten times as much of any particular form of beastliness which they begin to practise on us. We made very good shooting and kicked up great columns of black muck from their trench and parapet.

The grenade explodes like a bomb only much more violently when it touches the ground. The men get very excited when one of these duels is going on and swear and sweat horribly. It is almost the only fun they get in the trenches, poor dears.

Raymond Asquith to his wife Katharine, 1915.

22 DECEMBER

1849 *Fyodor Dostoevsky, the Russian novelist, is subjected to a mock firing squad before being sent to prison in Siberia.*

1894 *Captain Alfred Dreyfus, a Jewish officer in the French army, is convicted on a trumped-up charge of spying for Russia and sentenced to imprisonment on Devil's Island.*

As we came up the White Moss, we met an old man, who I saw was a beggar by his two bags hanging over his shoulder; but, from a half laziness, half indifference, and a wanting to *try* him, if he would speak, I let him pass. He said nothing, and my heart smote me. I turned back, and said, 'You are begging?' 'Ay,' says he. I gave him a halfpenny. William, judging from his appearance, joined in. 'I suppose you were a sailor?' 'Ay,' he replied, 'I have been fifty-seven years at sea, twelve of them on board a man-of-war under Sir Hugh Palmer.' 'Why have you not a pension?' 'I have no pension, but I could have got into Greenwich hospital, but all my officers are dead.' He was seventy-five years of age, had a freshish colour in his cheeks, grey hair, a decent hat with a binding round the edge, the hat worn brown and glossy, his shoes were small thin shoes low in the quarters, pretty good. They had belonged to a gentleman. His coat was blue, frock shaped coming over his thighs, it had been joined up at the seams behind with paler blue to let it out, and there were three bell-shaped patches of darker blue behind where the buttons had been. His breeches were either of fustian or grey cloth, with strings hanging down, whole and tight; he had a checked shirt on, and a small coloured handkerchief tied round his neck . . .

When [William] came home he cleared a path to the necessary [lavatory], called me out to see it, but before we got there a whole housetopfull of snow had fallen from the roof upon the path and it echoed in the ground beneath like a dull beating upon it.

Dorothy Wordsworth, Journal, 1801.

1888 *The painter Vincent van Gogh cuts off part of his ear.*

1986 *The scientist André Sakharov, the most distinguished Russian dissident of his day, returns to Moscow after a six-year internal exile. He had been awarded the Nobel Peace Prize in 1975.*

I respond with joy to your suggestion in your beautiful letter of two days ago – that I shall enable you to find a word from me on your table on the darkest a.m. of the year [25 December]; in the first place because I am much touched by your attaching to any word of mine any power to comfort or charm; and in the second because I can well measure – by my own – your sense of a melancholy from which you must appeal. It is indeed a lugubrious feast and a miserable merriment. But it is something to spend the evil season by one's own poor hearthstone (save that yours is opulent), crouching over the embers and chuckling low over all the dreadful places where one is not! I've been literally pressed to go to two or three – one of them in Northumberland! (the cheek of some people!) and the reflection that I *might* be there and yet by heaven's mercy am not, does give a faint blush as of the rose to my otherwise deep depression . . . I have ventured into three or four [shops] – but I do it, bless you, for nine and sevenpence halfpenny, all told! No wonder you want epistolary balm if you're already in the fifties!

Henry James to W. E. Norris, 1893.

24 DECEMBER

1818 *The carol 'Silent Night' is sung for the first time, in Bavaria.*

1974 *Former Labour minister John Stonehouse, presumed drowned, is found alive in Australia, having faked his death.*

Right worshipful husband, I recommend me unto you. Please it you to weet [know] that I sent your eldest son to my Lady Morley to have knowledge what sports were used in her house in Christmas next following after the decease of my lord her husband. And she said that there were none disguisings nor harping nor luting nor singing, nor no loud disports, but playing at the tables [backgammon] and chess and cards; such disports she gave her folks leave to play, and none other.

*Margaret Paston to John Paston I, 1459. This is the
first mention of card-playing in England.*

I went yesterday to St George's Hospital to see the chloroform tried. A boy two years and a half old was cut for a stone. He was put to sleep in a minute; the stone was so large and the bladder so contracted, the operator could not get hold of it, and the operation lasted above twenty minutes, with repeated probings by different instruments; the chloroform was applied from time to time, and the child never exhibited the slightest sign of consciousness, and it was exactly the same as operating on a dead body . . . I have no words to express my admiration for this invention, which is the greatest blessing ever bestowed on mankind, and the inventor of it the greatest of benefactors, whose memory ought to be venerated by countless millions for ages yet to come.

Charles Greville, Memoirs, 1847.

25 DECEMBER

1066 *William the Conqueror is crowned in Winchester Cathedral.*

1800 *George III's German-born wife, Queen Charlotte, causes the first Christmas tree to be erected in England.*

1932 *George V makes the first Christmas broadcast by a monarch, reading a script written by Rudyard Kipling.*

This is Christmas Day 1815 with us; what it may be with you I don't know, the 12th of June next year perhaps; and if it should be the consecrated season with you, I don't see how you can keep it. You have no turkeys; you would not desecrate the festival by offering up a withered Chinese Bantam, instead of the savoury grand Norfolkian holocaust, that smokes all around my nostrils at this moment from a thousand firesides. Then what puddings have you? Where will you get holly to stick in your churches, or churches to stick your dried tea-leaves (that must be the substitute) in? What memorials you can have of the holy time, I see not. A chopped missionary or two may keep up the thin idea of Lent and the wilderness; but what standing evidence have you of the Nativity? – 'tis our rosy-checked, homestalled divines, whose faces shine to the tune of 'Unto us a child'; faces fragrant with the mince-pies of half a century, that alone can authenticate the cheerful mystery – I feel.

Charles Lamb to Thomas Manning in Canton, 1815.

I grabbed my binoculars and looking cautiously over the parapet saw the incredible sight of our soldiers exchanging cigarettes, schnapps and chocolate with the enemy. Later a Scottish soldier appeared with a football which seemed to come from nowhere and a few minutes later a real football match got under-way . . . But after an hour's play, when our commanding officer heard about it, he sent an order that we must put a stop to it. A little later we drifted back to our trenches and the fraternisation ended.

Leutnant Johannes Niemann, 133rd Royal Saxon Regiment, on Christmas Day 1914.

26 DECEMBER

1898 *Marie and Pierre Curie discover radium.*

2003 *An earthquake at Bam in Iran kills 32,000.*

2004 *The most powerful earthquake for 40 years off the north-west coast of Sumatra sets off tsunami waves which kill 200,000-300,000 people.*

On Boxing Night I was at Covent Garden. A dull pantomime was 'worked' (as we say) better than I ever saw a heavy piece worked on a first night, until suddenly and without a moment's warning, every scene on that immense stage fell over on its face, and disclosed chaos by gaslight behind! There never was such a business; about sixty people who were on the stage being extinguished in the most remarkable manner. Not a soul was hurt . . .

We have had a fire here [the offices of his magazine, *All the Year Round*, in Covent Garden], but our people put it out before the parish engine arrived, like a drivelling perambulator, with *the beadle in it*, like an imbecile baby. Popular opinion, disappointed in the fire having been put out, snowballed the beadle. God bless it! . . .

The other day there appeared before me (simultaneously with a scent of rum in the air) one aged and greasy [actor], with a pair of pumps under his arm. He said he thought if he could get down to somewhere (I think it was Newcastle), he would get 'taken on' as Pantaloon, the existing Pantaloon being 'a stick, sir – a mere muff'. I observed that I was sorry times were so bad with him. 'Mr Dickens, you know our profession, sir – no one knows it better, sir – there is no right feeling in it. I was Harlequin on your own circuit, sir, for five-and-thirty years, and was displaced by a boy, sir! – a boy!'

Charles Dickens to Mary Boyle, 1860.

27 DECEMBER

1831 *HMS* Beagle *sets out on a five-year voyage of scientific discovery with Charles Darwin on board.*

1904 *The first performance of J.M. Barrie's play* Peter Pan.

I walked quite over the fields home, by light of link, one of my watermen carrying it and I reading by the light of it, a very fine clear dry night.

Samuel Pepys, Diary, 1665.

I am told that I am in a prodigious fine way; which, being translated into plain English, means, that I have suffered more sharp pain these two days than in all the moderate fits together that I have had for these last nine years: however, Madam, I have one great blessing, there is drowsiness in all the square hollows of the red-hot bars of the gridiron on which I lie, so that I scream and fall asleep by turns like a babe that is cutting its first teeth.

Horace Walpole to the Countess of Ossory, 1784.

Smallcombe, who was married on Christmas Day, and whose wife was brought to bed the same day, sent his child to be named, as they are fearful it will die.

The Revd John Skinner, Journal, 1823.

28 DECEMBER

Childermas, the feast of the Holy Innocents, the unluckiest day of the year.

1895 *The Lumière brothers show the film* L'Arrosseur Arrossé *together with some short documentaries to a paying audience in Paris, and the film industry begins.*

1908 *The Messina earthquake in Sicily kills 80,000–100,000.*

'Now,' said Lamb, 'you old lake poet, you rascally poet, why do you call Voltaire dull?' We all defended Wordsworth, and affirmed there was a state of mind when Voltaire would be dull. 'Well,' said Lamb, 'here's Voltaire – the Messiah of the French nation, and a very proper one too' . . . Then he and Keats agreed [Newton] had destroyed all the poetry of the rainbow by reducing it to the prismatic colours. It was impossible to resist him, and we all drank 'Newton's health, and confusion to mathematics' . . .

When we retired to tea [after dinner] we found the comptroller [a perfect stranger who claimed to admire Wordsworth, and invited himself to the party] . . . After a little time the comptroller looked down, looked up and said to Wordsworth: 'Don't you think, sir, Milton was a great genius?' Keats looked at me, Wordsworth looked at the comptroller. Lamb who was dozing by the fire turned round and said: 'Pray, sir, did you say Milton was a great genius?' 'No, sir; I asked Mr Wordsworth if he were not.' 'Oh,' said Lamb, 'then you are a silly fellow.' 'Charles! My dear Charles!' said Wordsworth; but Lamb, perfectly innocent of the confusion he had created, was off again by the fire. After an awful pause the comptroller said: 'Don't you think Newton a great genius?' I could not stand it any longer. Keats put his head into my books. Ritchie squeezed in a laugh. Wordsworth seemed asking himself: 'Who is this?' Lamb got up, and taking a candle, said: 'Sir, will you allow me to look at your phrenological development?'
  Benjamin Robert Haydon's 'immortal dinner' in 1817, from his Autobiography.

29 DECEMBER

1890 *Final defeat of the Sioux Indians at the Wounded Knee massacre, where 200 are killed.*

1972 Life *magazine ceases publication, unable to compete with colour supplements and TV.*

Inspired by fury the knights called out, 'Where is Thomas Becket, traitor to the King and realm?' As he answered not they cried out the more furiously, 'Where is the Archbishop?' At this . . . he descended from the stair where he had been dragged by the monks in fear of the knights, and in a clear voice answered, 'I am here, no traitor to the King, but a priest. Why do ye seek me?' . . .

'Absolve', they cried, 'and restore to communion those whom you have excommunicated, and restore their powers to those whom you have suspended.' He answered, 'There has been no satisfaction, and I will not absolve them.' 'Then you shall die,' they cried, 'and receive what you deserve' . . . A wicked knight, fearing lest he should be rescued by the people and escape alive, leapt upon him suddenly and wounded this lamb who was sacrificed to God on the head, cutting off the top of the crown . . . and by the same blow he wounded the arm of him who tells this . . . Then he received a second blow on the head but still stood firm. At the third blow he fell on his knees and elbows . . . The third knight inflicted a terrible wound as he lay, by which the sword was broken against the pavement, and the crown which was large was separated from the head; so that the blood white with the brain and the brain red with blood, dyed the surface of the virgin mother church.

Edward Grim, a clerk in the following of Archbishop Thomas à Becket, describes his murder by four knights in Canterbury Cathedral, 1170.

30 DECEMBER

1953 *The first colour TV sets go on sale in the US, priced at $1,100 each.*

1986 *More than 200 canaries, employed to detect the presence of gas in British coal mines, are made redundant, replaced by sensor devices.*

By the invitation of Mr Herschel, I now took a walk which will sound to you rather strange; it was through his telescope and it held me upright, and without the least inconvenience; so would it have done had I been dressed in feathers and a bell hoop – such is its circumference.

Fanny Burney visits Sir Willam Herschel, the astronomer who discovered the planet Uranus, Diary, 1787.

Dearest, I wonder if you are getting any victual. There must be cocks at least, and the chickens will surely have laid their eggs. I have many an anxious thought about you; and I wonder if you sleep at nights, or if you are wandering about – on, on – smoking and killing mice. Oh, if I was there I could put my arms so close about your neck, hush you into the softest sleep you have had since I went away . . . Goodnight, my beloved. Dream of me.

Jane Welsh Carlyle, staying with her mother, to Thomas Carlyle, left at their farm in Dumfriesshire, 1828.

The trouble is, you see, that no one can live by poetry, if my verse is really poetry and I am never quite sure, and so I make my living showing off on the television and rushing about writing articles commissioned by inexorable editors.

John Betjeman to Duncan Fallowell, 1965.

31 DECEMBER

1923 *The chimes of Big Ben are broadcast by the BBC for the first time.*

1960 *The farthing coin, worth a quarter of an old penny, ceases to be legal tender.*

I have written enough for tonight: I am now going to sit down and play one of Handel's overtures as well as I can – *Semele*, perhaps, a very grand one – then, lighting my lantern, trudge through the mud to Parson Crabbe's. Before I take my pen again to finish this letter the New Year will have dawned – on some of us. 'Thou fool! this night thy soul may be required of thee!' Very well: while it is in this body I will wish my dear old F.T. a happy New Year. And now to drum out the Old with Handel. Goodnight.

Edward FitzGerald to Frederick Tennyson, 1850.

I was going to bed but Dora càme down on tiptoe in a loose wrapper with her hair falling on her shoulders, soon followed by Thersie in the same state. We sat round the fire talking of domestic matters in whispers, not to disturb my Mother who was immediately overhead sleeping the sleep of the just. At 5 minutes to midnight the bells of Chippenham Church pealed out loud and clear in the frosty air. We opened a shutter and stood round the window listening. It was a glorious moonlit night.

The Revd Francis Kilvert, Diary, 1871. Dora and Thersie were his sisters.

I have just packed off the youngest of my nephews to the little Rye annual subscription ball . . . with the sternest injunction as to his not coming back to me 'engaged' to a quadragenarian hack or a military widow – the mature women being here the most serious dancers.

Henry James to W.D. Howells, 1908.

BIOGRAPHICAL NOTES ON THE WRITERS

It was not felt necessary to include entries for kings and queens or such well-known historical figures as Nelson and Marlborough. A number of more minor figures will also not be found here, but relevant details about them are included in the notes following their extracts.

James Agate (1877–1947), outstanding drama and literary critic between the wars, both in the press and on radio. He hid his homosexuality behind his enthusiasm for hackney-carriage horses, golf, and the good things of life. His nine volumes of diary, beginning in 1932 and ending with his death, were published under the title *Ego*.

William Allingham (1824–89) came from Donegal in Ireland and worked as a customs officer there and then at Lymington in Hampshire, retiring in 1870 so that he could devote himself to his real love, literature. His poetry is not of the first rank but he was a friend of many of the literary and artistic figures of the age, and had a gift for recording his encounters and conversations with them. He was editor of *Fraser's Magazine* from 1874 to 1879 and his wife Helen Allingham is remembered for her water-colours of Surrey cottages and countryside.

Raymond Asquith (1878–1916), eldest son of the Liberal Prime Minister H.H Asquith. A scholar and wit at the centre of a brilliant circle at Balliol College, Oxford at the turn of the century, he became a barrister and married Katharine Horner in 1907. Served in the Grenadier Guards and was killed on the Somme.

Jane Austen (1788–1817), novelist who took for her subject the world she knew best: that of the gentry, living largely in the country and much taken up with the search for suitable wives and husbands. For an appreciation of her genius see the extract from Sir Walter Scott's Journal on 14 March.

Samuel Bamford (1788–1872), poet and weaver, concerned with the condition of the working class. Imprisoned after the Peterloo Massacre.

George Beardmore (1908–79), diarist, novelist and children's author, whose mother was a sister of the writer Arnold Bennett. He worked as a clerk while writing his first novels, married in 1935 and lived in North Harrow. His asthma kept him out of the armed forces, and in the early war years he worked for the BBC, before writing journalism for *Picture Post* and then acting as an Information Officer for his local council, dealing with the aftermath of bombings and doodlebugs. After the war he wrote children's books and cartoon serials for *Eagle* and *Girl*. James Lees-Milne (q.v.) found his journals 'deeply moving . . . full of humour, compassion and poignancy'.

Arthur Christopher (A.C.) Benson (1862–1925), son of an Archbishop of Canterbury and brother of the novelists E. F. and R. H. Benson. After a brilliant career as a housemaster at his old school, Eton, he was expected to become Head Master there but chose instead the life of a Cambridge don, becoming Master of Magdalene College in 1915. His volumes of musings and gentle philosophising were popular in his lifetime, but his lasting monument is his diary, begun in 1897. Though he did not keep it up for lengthy periods when he was suffering from clinical depression, it eventually ran to more than five million words.

Henrietta (Harriet), Countess of Bessborough (1761–1821), daughter of the first Earl Spencer and younger sister of Georgiana, Duchess of Devanshire. The love of her life, though she had others, was Lord Granville Leveson Gower, later Earl Granville. She had two illegitimate children by him, while among her legitimate offspring was the notorious Lady Caroline Lamb (see also Countess Granville).

John Betjeman (1906–84), poet, architectural historian and polemicist, television presenter and personality, journalist, champion of the Victorian Age, knighted 1969, Poet Laureate 1972.

Wilfrid Scawen Blunt (1840–1922), Middle Eastern traveller, poet, seducer and, together with his wife (who was Byron's granddaughter), expert on the Arabian horse. He was a vocal anti-imperialist, supporting the causes of Egyptian and Irish nationalism in particular against Britain.

James Boswell (1740–95), son of a Scottish judge, studied law before coming to London in 1762, where he met Dr Johnson. He continued his studies in Holland before setting out on a grand tour, the climax of which was a visit to Corsica; back in London he set himself up as the champion of Corsican liberty. He practised law in Edinburgh and London, married a cousin in 1769, and in 1773 toured Scotland with Dr Johnson, whose *Life* he published in 1791.

Charlotte Brontë (1816–55), brought up with her sisters Emily and Anne at Haworth Rectory in Yorkshire. She earned her living as a teacher and governess before publishing *Jane Eyre* in 1847. *Shirley* followed in 1849 and *Villete* in 1853.

Stopford Brooke (1832–1916), Irish-born preacher and man of letters. Although he attracted large congregations and was one of Queen Victoria's chaplains, he left the Church of England in 1880 and thereafter preached in Unitarian churches. He wrote many books on English literature and also lectured at University College, London.

Fanny Burney (1752–1840), daughter of the musician Dr Charles Burney. She kept a diary from the age of fifteen and published her first novel, *Evelina*, in 1778. Thereafter she was much lionised, and obtained a position in the Royal Household in 1786. In 1793 she married the French *émigré* General d'Arblay.

Lady Eleanor Butler (1739?–1829), sister of the Earl of Ormonde, eloped and set up house in North Wales with Sarah Ponsonby in 1778. The 'Ladies of Llangollen' became something of a tourist attraction in their gothicised home, a sight to break the monotony of the journey to or from Ireland via Holyhead, the ferry port in Anglesey.

Lord Byron (1788–1824) spent the years 1809 to 1811 on a grand tour, mostly in Greece. The first two cantos of his autobiographical poem *Childe Harold's Pilgrimage* appeared in 1812, and he 'awoke to find himself famous'. In 1816 his debts, the break-up of his marriage to Annabella Milbanke and his rumoured incest with his half-sister Angusta Leigh drove him abroad, never to return. After some months in Switzerland and years in Venice, he lived in Ravenna, Pisa and finally Genoa with his 'Last Attachment', Countess Teresa Guiccioli, before leaving for Greece in 1823, hoping to fight in the war for independence from the Turks.

Pamela, Lady Campbell (1796–1869), daughter of the rebel Lord Edward Fitzgerald who died in prison after the abortive Irish rising against the British in 1798 (his wife, also Pamela, seems likely to have been the daughter of Philippe Egalité, the Duc d'Orleans, and his mistress, the writer Madame de Genlis). Lady Campbell was brought up abroad by her mother, and then by her grandmother, the Duchess of Leinster. She married Major-General Sir Guy Campbell, Bt, as his second wife in 1820. Her particular Irish ancestry is perhaps her licence for the remarks she makes about the country, both North and South – and her view of the Scots.

Chichester Fortescue, Lord Carlingford (1823–98), Anglo-Irish Liberal statesman, fourth husband of the famous Liberal hostess the Countess Waldegrave and the original of Anthony Trollope's character Phineas Finn.

Jane Welsh Carlyle (1801–66), daughter of a Scottish doctor, married Thomas Carlyle in 1826. Like her husband she was – or certainly made herself – something of a martyr to ill-health and insomnia. Opinions are divided on whether she or he is the better letter-writer. On their day, both are outstanding.

Thomas Carlyle (1795–1881) came from a humble Scottish farming background, but became a giant in an age of giants, a historian and biographer who transformed his subjects with his books on the French Revolution, Cromwell and Frederick the Great. He was also a latter-day prophet and sage, denouncing the ills of the age and reaffirming what he saw as the eternal verities.

Dame Barbara Castle (1911–2002), Labour MP and holder of various ministerial posts between 1945 and 1979.

John Chamberlain (1554–1628), bachelor of private means who lived close to St Paul's in the City of London. The cathedral was an information exchange where, walking up and down the nave, you could impart and collect all the latest news and gossip. This Chamberlain relayed to the career diplomat Dudley Carleton in a series of letters between 1597 and 1626.

Sir Henry (Chips) Channon (1897–1958), born in Chicago, put 'my whole life work into my anglicisation, in ignoring my early life', much helped by his time at Christ Church, Oxford. By the 1930s he had married a Guinness, become an MP, and acquired a house in Belgrave Square.

The Earl of Clarendon (1800–70), urbane, witty and charming Whig who, after a spell as ambassador to Spain in the 1830s, was successively Lord Privy Seal, President of the Board of Trade, Lord-Lieutenant of Ireland, and then three times Foreign Secretary.

Samuel Taylor Coleridge (1772–1834), Romantic poet, philosopher, spiritual guide, polymath and opium addict.

Christopher Columbus (1451–1506) was born in Genoa, and discovered America for his patrons King Ferdinand and Queen Isabella of Spain while searching for a westerly route to the East Indies.

William Cowper (1731–1800) was educated at Westminister and then studied law. Between 1763 and 1765 he was in a private asylum during the first of his recurring bouts of insanity. He lived a retired life thereafter, writing poetry and translating Homer, mostly in Huntingdon, Olney and Weston Underwood, the last two both in Buckinghamshire.

Thomas Creevey (1768–1838), probably an illegitimate son of the Earl of Sefton. After a few years practising law he became a Whig MP and married a widow, Mrs Ord, who moved in Society. After losing his seat he went with his family to Brussels to save money. His wife died in 1818 and he came back to England; he was elected to a new seat in the House of Commons in 1820. Until 1830 he lived off the hospitality of others, moving from one Whig house party to the next, paying his way out of his stores of wit and gossip. When the Whigs eventually came back to power in 1830, he received a sinecure which allowed him to end his days in comfort.

Charles Darwin (1809–82) After attending Edinburgh and Cambridge Universities, he sailed on HMS *Beagle* in 1831 as the scientist on a surveying voyage to the southern hemisphere, returning in 1836. He may have called himself 'a hunter of beetles and pounder of stones', but his observations led him to formulate the principles of natural selection in 1844, although he did not publish them until 1859.

Charles Dickens (1812–70), novelist, conjuror, keen mounter of and performer in amateur theatricals, and a founder and editor of magazines. He attracted huge audiences when he toured the country giving readings from the more dramatic and humorous passages in his books.

John Donne (*c.* 1572–1631), metaphysical poet and divine whose early life – fighting the Spaniards on the 1596 expedition to Cadiz, writing erotic love poems, travelling on the Continent, assiduously cultivating the rich and powerful in his search for preferment – contrasts with his later years. He took orders in 1615, his wife died in 1617, and in the meantime he had begun to acquire a reputation as an outstanding preacher. In 1621 he became Dean of St Paul's.

Sir Francis Drake (*c.* 1545–96), English sea-captain who made the second voyage round the world, in the *Golden Hind*, completed in 1580. Burnt many Spanish ships in Cadiz harbour in 1587. Vice-Admiral aboard the *Revenge* during the Armada.

Emily Eden (1797–1869), one of the fourteen children of the statesman and diplomat Lord Auckland. She never married, but it was rumoured that she might have become the wife of the Prime Minister Lord Melbourne after the death of his first wife, Lady Caroline Lamb. Emily and her sister Fanny accompanied their brother, the second Lord Auckland, to India in 1836, when he was appointed Governor-General. Her letters home, published as *Up the Country*, are one of the classics of the Raj. The Edens returned to England in 1842 and Emily later published two witty and accomplished novels, *The Semi-Detached House* and *The Semi-Attached Couple*.

John Evelyn (1620–1706), diarist. He was on a grand tour during much of the Civil War. He was involved in the foundation of the Royal Society in 1660 and was particularly interested in gardening and in trees. His diary was only rediscovered in 1818.

Patrick Leigh Fermor In 1933 at the age of 18 he set out to walk from the Hook of Holland to Constantinople, arriving on New Year's Day, 1935 (see *A Time of Gifts* and *Between the Woods and the Water*). He was at the home of his love Balasha Cantacuzene in Moldavia in September 1939. As a fluent Greek-speaker he fought in Albania, Greece and Crete in 1940–41 and was later in occupied Crete for a year and a half as a member of SOE, taking part in the capture of the German commander. His other books are on the West Indies, monasticism, and Greece.

Edward FitzGerald (1809–83), translator, poet, friend of Tennyson, Thackeray and Carlyle. Though famous, above all, for his translation (or re-creation) of *The Rubáiyát of Omar Khayyám* (1859) from the Persian, he was also one of the great correspondents, in the same class as Cowper, Byron and Keats.

Thomas Gainsborough (1727–88), landscape painter and musician by inclination though a portrait painter by profession. After training in London he moved back to his home county of Suffolk before going to Bath in 1759 to find fashionable sitters. There he evolved his elegant mature style, paradoxically achieved through a technique described by his rival Reynolds as 'odd scratches and marks . . . This chaos, this uncouth and shapeless appearance, by a kind of magic, at a certain distance assumes form.'

Mahatma Gandhi (1869–1948), Indian social and political leader who, by his policy of passive resistance, did much to bring about his country's independence. Assassinated by a Hindu extremist for advocating Hindu–Muslim friendship.

Edward Gibbon (1737–94) was sent to Switzerland for five years to cure him of Catholic tendencies acquired at Oxford, and then served in the Hampshire Militia from 1759 to 1763, when he set out on his grand tour. In 1772 he began writing *The Decline and Fall of the Roman Empire*.

Harriet, Countess Granville (1785–1862), daughter of the Duke and (Georgiana) Duchess of Devonshire. In 1809 she married Lord Granville Leveson Gower, the former lover of her aunt, Lady Bessborough (q.v). The most regular recipient of her letters was her sister Georgiana, Lady Morpeth (later Countess of Carlisle), whose mother-in-law was also Lord Granville's half-sister. Between 1824 and 1841 he was ambassador at Paris, where Lady Granville shone as one of the great diplomatic hostesses.

Thomas Gray (1716–71), poet. He accompanied Horace Walpole, a friend from Eton days, on the grand tour, though they quarrelled towards the end. In 1742 he went back to Cambridge, where he spent the rest of his life, first at Peterhouse and then at Pembroke College. His *Elegy in a Country Churchyard* was published in 1751.

Charles Greville (1794–1865), through the influence of his grandfather, the Duke of Portland, became clerk to the Privy Council in 1821, an ideal vantage point from which to observe government at work. His Whig connections and ownership of racehorses also gave him a fine platform in Society.

George and Weedon Grossmith (1847–1912, 1854–1919). George created many of the famous roles in the Gilbert and Sullivan operas, while Weedon was eventually manager of Terry's Theatre. *The Diary of a Nobody* first appeared in *Punch* in 1892, with illustrations by Weedon.

Brilliana, Lady Harley (*c*. 1598–1643) was born in Brill, Holland, and married Sir Robert Harley, MP, in 1623 as his third wife. She died in 1643, shortly after enduring a seven-week siege at Brampton Bryan Castle in Herefordshire by Royalist forces.

Max Hastings (1946–), reporter, newspaper editor, military historian. Editor of the *Daily Telegraph*, 1986, and of the *Evening Standard*, 1996–2002.

Benjamin Robert Haydon (1786–1846), self-taught history painter of great pretensions but little fulfilment. As Ronald Blythe says of his Journal, 'In his compelling need to explain and justify himself as a painter he proves to the world that he is really a writer.' Chronically hard-up, he eventually committed suicide.

Patrick Henry (1736–99), American statesman, Governor of Virginia.

Mr Justice Holmes (1841–1935), son of the essayist Oliver Wendell Holmes. Fought in the American Civil War. Appointed to the Supreme Court of the United States in 1902.

Gerard Manley Hopkins (1844–89), poet and Jesuit priest. He converted to Roman Catholicism while at Balliol College, Oxford and was ordained priest in 1877. He kept his poetry and journals virtually secret for fear of condemnation by his Jesuit superiors, and they were not published until well into the twentieth century.

Henry James (1843–1916), Anglo-American novelist. He spent much of his youth in Europe and returned to England in 1869. His theme was often the impact of Europe on impressionable Americans. Among his more famous works are *The Portrait of a Lady* (1881). *The Bostonians* (1886), *The Turn of the Screw* (1898), *The Wings of the Dove* (1902), and *The Golden Bowl* (1904). Robert Louis Stevenson said, 'I think no man writes so elegant a letter, and none so kind.'

Thomas Jones (1742–1803), Welsh painter who recorded his stay in Italy between 1776 and 1783 in his Memoirs. Nowadays particularly admired for his small paintings of buildings and blank walls in Naples, which foreshadow Impressionism, and beyond.

John Keats (1795–1821), Romantic poet whose letters have long been recognised as some of the most electric written in English. He died in Rome, of consumption.

Fanny Kemble (1840–79), member of a famous theatrical family (Mrs Siddons was her aunt), she made her stage debut in 1829. She married an American in 1834 (it ended in divorce), and wrote five autobiographical volumes.

Francis Kilvert (1840–79), Church of England clergyman from a clerical family. He was curate in Clyro, Radnorshire and then at Langley Burrell in Wiltshire, before returning to Wales. He married in 1879, but died five weeks after the wedding.

Martin Luther King, Jr (1929–68), Black American evangelist and campaigner against racial segregation, awarded the Nobel Peace Prize in 1964. He was assassinated by a white escaped convict.

Charles Lamb (1775–1834), essayist and friend of the Romantic poets. Shortly after he himself suffered a period of insanity his sister Mary also went mad, and murdered their mother in 1796; she was eventually released into his care.

Edward Lear (1812–88), painter and nonsense poet famed for his water-colours of countries bordering the eastern Mediterranean, his limericks, and such verses as 'The Owl and the Pussycat', 'The Jumblies' and 'The Dong with the Luminous Nose'.

James Lees-Milne (1908–97), expert on historic buildings, biographer and diarist, who began working for the National Trust in 1936. Discharged from the army for health reasons in 1941, he eventually retired from the Trust in 1996. His diaries, which start in 1942 and new volumes of which are still being published, seem set fair to become regarded as the best kept in the twentieth century.

Jack London (1876–1916), novelist, short-story writer and socialist. A native of San Francisco, he drew on his deprived, roving early life – particularly the Klondike gold rush of 1897 – for his fiction.

Lord Macaulay (1800–59) first made his name with his essays for the *Edinburgh Review*, before entering Parliament as a staunch advocate of reform. He then spent four years on the Supreme Council in India. The five volumes of his *History of England* cover the years 1685 to 1702.

James Harris, Earl of Malmesbury (1746–1820), diplomat successively in Madrid, St Petersburg, The Hague, Berlin and Paris.

Lady Mary Wortley Montagu (1689–1762) accompanied her husband when he went to Constantinople as ambassador, and her letters written there are justly famous. She took an active part in English literary and political life before going to Italy in the 1740s, remaining there until the last year of her life.

Thomas Moore (1779–1852), a convivial Irish versifier who made his way through Whig high society on the strength of his *Irish Melodies* and his pleasant singing voice. At one stage he wanted to fight a duel with Byron, but instead became a very close friend when they met in 1811. His long oriental poem *Lalla Rookh* (1817) had a great success. Forced into exile in 1819 as a result of another's fraud, he saw Byron on the Continent and was given the manuscript of his notorious memoirs. His Life of Byron was published in 1830.

Sir Thomas More (1478–1535), author and Lord Chancellor. In 1534 he refused to take the oath of supremacy to Henry VIII as head of the Church after the split with Rome, so was imprisoned in the Tower of London and then beheaded.

Sir Harold Nicolson (1886–1962), diplomat, author, journalist and MP. Husband of Vita Sackville-West, with whom he created the garden at Sissinghurst Castle, their home in Kent. His diaries cover the 1930s to the 1950s.

Wilfred Owen (1893–1918), First World War poet.

The Pastons, important family in fifteenth-century Norfolk whose letters written between 1425 and 1495 were first published in the eighteenth century.

Samuel Pepys (1633–1702), one of the greatest British diarists. Secretary to the Admiralty from 1672.

Sir Walter Raleigh (1861–1922), the first professor of English literature at Oxford University (1904).

Robert Robinson (1733–90), pastor of the Baptist Chapel in Cambridge. Farmed in nearby Chesterton and, by 1782, owned two other farms, and did business as a corn and coal merchant. Renowned for his 'massive common sense', he also wrote hymns, and a *History of Baptism.*

John Ruskin (1819–1900), art and architectural critic, social reformer, moralist and crank. A huge influence on the opinions and outlook of his contemporaries, but much from the thirty-nine volumes of his *Collected Works* justly remains unread today. On the other hand, the best of his writing has a power and beauty second to none.

Conrad Russell (1878–1947), stockbroker and farmer, nephew of the ninth Duke of Bedford. Of the same circle as Raymond Asquith (q.v.) at Oxford, after his death Conrad proposed to his widow Katharine, but was probably rather relieved when she turned him down. However, from 1927 he was her close neighbour and tenant on a farm at Mells in Somerset. His letters to Lady Diana Cooper form a large part of the second volume of her autobiography.

Captain Robert Falcon Scott (1868–1912) led his first Antarctic expedition in 1901 and got within five hundred miles of the South Pole. His second attempt ended in tragedy, largely because of his choice of ponies over dogs to pull the sledges. He reached the Pole only to find the Norwegians had got there first, and then died with his four companions on the return journey.

Sir Walter Scott (1771–1832) first established himself as a poet but, once he saw that Byron outshone him, switched to prose fiction with *Waverley* in 1814. In 1826 his main publisher Constable went bankrupt, bringing down Ballantyne & Co., a publishing and printing firm in which Scott was a sleeping partner. Rather than go bankrupt himself, Scott undertook to pay back £120,000 of debt out of the proceeds from his existing books and ones he had yet to write. He had begun keeping his Journal in November 1825.

Sir Ernest Shackleton (1874–1922), Irish polar explorer. He was on Scott's first expedition, then led his own to within a hundred miles of the South Pole in 1909. He returned to Antarctica in 1914 in the *Endurance*, but the ship was crushed in the ice. He and his men were eventually saved in 1916, after incredible feats of perseverance and seamanship.

John Simpson (1944–) is one of the most respected foreign correspondents and BBC television reporters.

John Skinner (1772–1839), Rector of Camerton, seven miles south-west of Bath. An unhappy man, except when engaged in his antiquarian pursuits; angular, querulous, fearful, standing on his dignity, he eventually shot himself.

Sydney Smith (1771–1845), Church of England clergyman and eventually a Canon of St Paul's, essayist in the *Edinburgh Review*, wit; called by Lord Macaulay 'The Smith of Smiths'.

Sir Henry Morton Stanley (1841–1904), journalist and African explorer.

Freya Stark (1893–1993) This distinguished travel writer was brought up partly in Italy, where she served as a nurse during the First World War. Her first journey was in the Lebanon in 1927. She then lived in Baghdad and her travels while based there are described in her first book, *The Valleys of the Assassins* (1934). She made two south Arabian journeys, in 1934–5 and 1937–8. In the Second World War she set up the Brotherhood of Freedom to rally local Egyptian support for the Allies. For the rest of her life she was based in Asolo in northern Italy, writing four volumes of autobiography, and books on Turkey's classical past. She became a Dame in 1972.

Robert Louis Stevenson (1850–94), novelist, poet and essayist; born, raised and educated in Edinburgh. He travelled widely in his attempt to escape chronic ill-health, leaving Britain for the last time in 1887 for America and then the South Seas. Fame had come to him in 1883 with the publication of *Treasure Island*.

Sir Roy Strong (1936–) was a junior curator at the National Portrait Gallery when he was appointed its Director in 1967, aged thirty-one. Appointed Director of the Victoria & Albert Museum in 1974. He retired in 1987, having transformed the way museum and gallery displays and exhibitions were mounted.

David Hunter Strother (1816–88), American journalist and illustrator, under the pseudonym Porte Crayon, in *Harper's Monthly*.

John Byng, Viscount Torrington (1743–1813), after twenty years in the army retired as a lieutenant-colonel in the Foot Guards in 1776, thereafter employed in a tedious job with the Inland Revenue. As he put it, 'His early days were spent in camps / His latter days were pass'd at stamps.' Meanwhile, his wife had a long affair with the politician William Windham. Byng succeeded to his title only a few weeks before his own death.

Edward John Trelawny (1792–1881), former midshipman who was a member of the Shelley–Byron circle in Italy. He accompanied Byron to Greece in 1823 and took an active part in the war against the Turks there.

Keith Vaughan (1912–77), painter. He began as one of the Neo-Romantics whose leading figure was Graham Sutherland, and taught at Camberwell, Central and Slade Schools of Art. His figurative style moved more and more towards abstraction, though he never lost his preoccupation with the male nude in landscape.

Sir Ralph Verney (1613–96), MP, initially sympathetic to the cause of Parliament in the Civil War though his father, Sir Edmund, was killed bearing the King's standard at the battle of Edgehill in 1642. He went abroad in 1643, unhappy at Parliament's alliance with the Scots.

Horace Walpole (1717–97), third son of Sir Robert Walpole, Britain's first Prime Minister, a historian, connoisseur and, above all, indefatigable correspondent. The definitive edition of his letters fills dozens of volumes. He wrote with an eye to eventual publication, rightly expecting that his letters would be his most permanent memorial. His house, Strawberry Hill at Twickenham on the Thames, offered one of the earliest and most important displays of the new Gothick taste. He eventually inherited the earldom of Orford from his mad nephew.

Sylvia Townsend Warner (1893–1978), novelist, poet and short-story writer, particularly for the *New Yorker*, also worked for many years on the multi-volume *Tudor Church Music* project.

Edmund Wheatley (1793–1841) became an officer in the King's German Legion in 1812. Wounded at Waterloo and captured by the French, who treated him brutally until he escaped. Retired on half-pay in 1816.

T.H.White (1906–64) was a master at Stowe School when keeping the diary quoted here; his greatest achievement was his retelling of the Arthurian legend, *The Once and Future King*, of which the first volume, *The Sword in the Stone* (1939), is best known. His fantasy *Mistress Masham's Repose* (1946) draws on the eighteenth-century landscape and buildings at Stowe.

William Wilberforce (1759–1833), MP, evangelical and leader of the campaign for the abolition of slavery.

Oscar Wilde (1854–1900), Irish playwright, novelist, essayist, poet and wit sent to prison for two years in 1895 for homosexual offences.

James Woodforde (1740–1803), Church of England clergyman first in Oxford and Somerset, then for the rest of his life at Weston Longeville in Norfolk.

Virginia Woolf (1882–1941), novelist, essayist and publisher at the centre of the Bloomsbury Group. She married Leonard Woolf in 1912 and they founded the Hogarth Press in 1917.

Dorothy Wordswoth (1771–1855), devoted sister of and companion to William Wordsworth, before and after his marriage in 1802. Her journals testify to her major contribution to his poetry. Coleridge called her Wordsworth's 'exquisite sister . . . her eye watchful in minutest observation of nature'.

ARTWORK

The frontispiece and wood engravings featured for each month are by Eric Ravilious. Born in London in 1903, he studied and later taught at the Royal College of Art. A distinguished painter, lithographer and designer of textiles and pottery, he was most typically a wood engraver. His work featured in several John Murray publications, including the *Cornhill Magazine*. In 1942 he was killed on active service as a war artist for the British Admiralty, when the plane in which he was travelling disappeared near Iceland.

The engravings for the frontispiece and August first featured in prospectuses published by John Murray in 1935; the engravings for January, February, March, April, May, October, November and December were originally drawn as decorations for the *Notebook and Diary* published and printed by the Kynoch Press, 1933; the images for June and September come from illustrations and decorations for *54 Conceits* by Martin Armstrong, published by Martin Secker Limited in 1933; and the art for July comes from a label decoration for Fine Old Invalid Port for the Kemp Town Brewery, Brighton, Limited (1935).

The publisher is very grateful to Alan Powers and Anne Ullmann for their assistance in the selection.

The incidental art providing intermittent decorations was created by Reynolds Stone for John Murray's publication of the works of Freya Stark. The rules under each date heading were some of John (Jock) Murray VI's favourites.

SOURCES AND ACKNOWLEDGEMENTS

Every effort has been made to contact copyright holders; in the event of an inadvertent omission or error, the editorial department should be notified at John Murray (Publishers), 338 Euston Road, London NW1 3BH.

James Agate, *A Shorter Ego*, 3 vols, George G. Harrap & Co., 1945, 1946, 1949. Reproduced by permission of PFD on behalf of the Estate of James Agate.

Edwin (Buzz) Aldrin, from *First on the Moon: A Voyage with Neil Armstrong, Michael Collins, Edwin E. Aldrin, Jr*, ed. Gene Farmer and Dora Jane Hamblin, Michael Joseph, 1970.

William Allingham, *A Diary*, ed. Helen Allingham and D. Radford, 1907.

Anonymous, description of the meeting of Charles I and Henrietta Maria, from *Original Letters Illustrative of English History*, ed. Sir Henry Ellis, 1st series, 3 vols, 1825.

Anonymous, report of the trial and execution of Joan of Arc, from *The Trial of Joan of Arc: Being the Verbatim Report of the Proceedings from the Orleans Manuscript*, ed. and trans. W. S. Scott, 1956. Reproduced by permission of the Folio Society.

Anonymous sailor on the *Warren Hastings*, from *The Gentlest Art: A Choice of Letters by Entertaining Hands*, ed. E. V. Lucas, 1907.

Raymond Asquith, *Life and Letters*, ed. John Jolliffe, Collins, 1980. Reproduced by permission of Michael Russell (Publishing) Ltd.

Sir Jacob Astley, from C. V. Wedgwood, *The King's War 1641-1647*, 1958.

Jane Austen, *Jane Austen's Letters to her Sister Cassandra and Others*, ed. R. W. Chapman, 2 vols, 1932.

——, *The Letters of Jane Austen*, ed. R. Brimley Johnson, 1925.

Walter Bagehot, *The Collected Works of Walter Bagehot*, vols 12–13, ed. Norman St John Stevas, Economist Books, 1986. Copyright © The Economist Newspaper Ltd, London (1986). Reproduced by permission of the Economist Newspaper Ltd.

Stanley Baldwin, from Martin Gilbert, *Churchill: A Life*, Heinemann, 1991.

Samuel Bamford, *Passages in the Life of a Radical and Early Days*, ed. H. Dunckley, 1893.

George Beardmore, *Civilians at War: Journals 1938-1946*, John Murray, 1984. Reproduced by permission of John Murray (Publishers).

Admiral Lord Beatty, from *The Oxford Dictionary of Quotations*, ed. Angela Partington, revised 4th edn, 1996.

Elliot V. Bell, from George Eric Rowe Gedye and others, *We Saw It Happen: By Thirteen Correspondents of 'The New York Times'*, Simon & Schuster, 1938.

A. C. Benson, *The Diary of Arthur Christopher Benson*, ed. Percy Lubbock, 1926.

Henrietta, Countess of Bessborough, from Lord Granville Leveson Gower, *Private Correspondence, 1781-1821*, ed. Castalia, Countess Granville, 2 vols, 1916.

John Betjeman, *Betjeman Letters, Vol. II*, ed. Candida Lycett Green, Methuen Publishers, 1995. By permission of Methuen Publishing Ltd, copyright © the Estate of John Betjeman.

Louis Blériot, from Leslie William Alfred Baily, *Scrapbook, 1900 to 1914*, Frederick Muller, 1957. Reproduced by permission of The Random House Group Ltd.

Captain William Bligh, from Sir John Barrow, *The Eventful History of the Mutiny and Piratical Seizure of HMS Bounty: Its Causes and Consequences*, ed. Captain Stephen W. Roskill, The Folio Society, 1976.

Wilfrid Scawen Blunt, *My Diaries*, 2 vols, 1919, 1920.

Queen Anne Boleyn, from David Hilliam, *Monarchs, Murders and Mistresses: A Book of Royal Days*, 2000. Reproduced by permission of the Pepys Library, Magdalene College, Cambridge.

James Boswell, *Boswell in Extremes, 1776-1778*, ed. Charles McC. Weis and Frederick A. Pottle, Heinemann, 1971. Reproduced by permission of Yale University Library.

——, *Boswell: The Ominous Years, 1774-1776*, ed. Charles Ryskamp and Frederick A. Pottle, Heinemann, 1963. Reproduced by permission of Yale University Library.

——, *Boswell's London Journal, 1762-1763*, ed. Frederick A. Pottle, Heinemann, 1950. Reproduced by permission of Edinburgh University Press, www.eup.ed.ac.uk.

——, *The Life of Samuel Johnson*, 2 vols, 1791.

Harold Bride, from the *New York Times*, 19 April 1912.

Charlotte Brontë, from Elizabeth Gaskell, *The Life of Charlotte Brontë*, 1857.

Stopford Brooke, *Life and Letters of Stopford Brooke*, L. P. Jacks, 2 vols, 1917.

Lieutenant George Brown, from Edward Fraser, *The Sailors Whom Nelson Led: Their Doings Described by Themselves*, 1913.

Sir Edward Burne-Jones, *Burne-Jones Talking: His Conversations 1895-1898 Preserved by His Studio Assistant Thomas Rooke*, ed. Mary Lago, John Murray, 1982. Reproduced by permission of John Murray (Publishers).

Fanny Burney, *Diary and Letters of Madame D'Arblay (1778-1840)*, ed. Charlotte Barrett, 6 vols, 1904–5.

Lady Eleanor Butler, *A Year with the Ladies of Llangollen*, ed. Elizabeth Mavor, Viking, 1984.

Lord Byron, *Byron's Letters and Journals. The Complete and Unexpurgated Text of All the Letters Available in Manuscript and the Full Printed Version of All Others*, ed. Leslie A. Marchand, 12 vols, John Murray, 1973–82. Reproduced by permission of John Murray (Publishers).

Pamela, Lady Campbell, from *Miss Eden's Letters*, ed. Violet Dickinson, 1919.

Georgiana Capel, *The Capel Letters: Being the Correspondence of Lady Caroline Capel and Her Daughters with the Dowager Countess of Uxbridge from Brussels and Switzerland, 1814-1817*, ed. the Marquess of Anglesey, Cape, 1955. Reproduced by permission of The Random House Group Ltd.

Chichester Fortescue, Lord Carlingford, '. . . and Mr Fortescue': A Selection from the Diaries from 1851 to 1862 of Chichester Fortescue, Lord Carlingford*, ed. Osbert Wyndham Hewett, 1958.

Jane Welsh Carlyle, *Jane Welsh Carlyle: A New Selection of her Letters*, ed. Trudy Bliss, Victor Gollancz, 1949.

Thomas Carlyle, *New Letters of Thomas Carlyle*, ed. Alexander Carlyle, 2 vols, 1904.

Barbara Castle, *The Castle Diaries 1964-70*, Weidenfeld & Nicolson, 1984. Reproduced by permission of David Higham Associates Ltd.

John Chamberlain, *The Chamberlain Letters: A Selection of the Letters of John Chamberlain Concerning Life in England from 1597 to 1626*, ed. Elizabeth McClure Thomson, Putnam, 1966.

Sir Henry (Chips) Channon, *Chips: The Diaries of Sir Henry Channon*, ed. Robert Rhodes

James, 1967. Reproduced by permission of Weidenfeld & Nicholson, a division of the Orion Publishing Group.

King Charles II, from David Hilliam, *Monarchs, Murders and Mistresses: A Book of Royal Days*, 2000. Reproduced by permission of The Pepys Library, Magdalene College, Cambridge.

Winston Churchill, speech of 13 May 1940, minute of 23 April 1945. Copyright Winston S. Churchill, 1940, 1945. Reproduced by permission of Curtis Brown Ltd on behalf of the Estate of Winston S. Churchill.

George William Frederick, 4th Earl of Clarendon, *The Life and Letters of George William Frederick, Fourth Earl of Clarendon*, ed. Sir Herbert Eustace Maxwell, 2 vols, 1913.

William Clark, from *Original Journals of the Lewis and Clark Expedition, 1804-1806*, ed. Reuben Gold Thwaites, 1904–5.

Caroline Clive, *Caroline Clive*, ed. Mary Clive, Bodley Head, 1949. Reproduced by permission of David Higham Associates Ltd.

Samuel Taylor Coleridge, *Collected Letters of Samuel Taylor Coleridge*, ed. Earl Leslie Griggs, 6 vols, Clarendon Press, 1956–71. Reproduced by permission of Oxford University Press.

——, *The Notebooks of Samuel Taylor Coleridge, vol. 1: 1794-1804*, ed. Kathleen Coburn, Routledge and Kegan Paul, 1957. Reproduced by permission of Routledge.

Christopher Columbus, from *The Mammoth Book of How It Happened*, ed. Jon E. Lewis, 1998.

William Cowper, *Selected Letters*, ed. William Hadley, 1926.

J. W. Croker, *The Croker Papers*, 3 vols, 1885.

Thomas Creevey, *Creevey*, ed. John Gore, John Murray, 1948. Reproduced by permission of John Murray (Publishers).

——, *The Creevey Papers: A Selection from the Correspondence and Diaries of the Late Thomas Creevey, MP*, ed. Sir Herbert Maxwell, 1903.

Oliver Cromwell, from Samuel Rawson Gardiner, *History of the Commonwealth and Protectorate, 1649-1660*, 1894–1903.

——, *Oliver Cromwell's Letters and Speeches*, ed. Thomas Carlyle, 1845.

Charles Darwin, *Life and Letters of Charles Darwin*, ed. Francis Darwin, 3 vols, 1887.

Charles Dickens, *The Letters of Charles Dickens*, ed. Mamie Dickens and Georgina Hogarth, 1893.

——, *Letters of Charles Dickens to Baroness Burdett-Coutts*, 1931.

——, *Life of Charles Dickens*, John Forster, 2 vols, 1872–74.

John Donne, *John Donne: Complete Poetry and Selected Prose*, ed. John Hayward, 1929.

——, *No Man is an Island: A Selection from the Prose of John Donne*, ed. Rivers Scott, The Folio Society, 1997.

Sir Francis Drake, from *Principal Navigations* by Richard Hakluyt, vol. 6 of Everyman edn, 1907.

——, letter to Sir Francis Walsingham, 31 July 1588, from John Knox Laughton, *State Papers Relating to the Defeat of the Spanish Armada, Anno 1588*, vol. 1, 1895.

Emily Eden, *Miss Eden's Letters*, ed. Violet Dickinson, 1919.

——, *Up The Country*, letters from India, 1866.

Queen Elizabeth I, from David Hilliam, *Monarchs, Murders and Mistresses: A Book of Royal Days*, 2000. Reproduced by permission of The Pepys Library, Magdalene College, Cambridge.

John Evelyn, *The Diary of John Evelyn*, ed. William Bray, 1819.

Captain W. G. Evelyn, from *The Evelyns in America: Compiled from Family Papers and Other Sources, 1608-1805*, ed. G. D. Scull, 1881.

Edward FitzGerald, *FitzGerald: Selected Works*, ed. Joanna Richardson, Rupert Hart-Davis, 1962.

Colonel Richard Fitzpatrick, *The Windham Papers*, 2 vols, 1913.

Thomas Gainsborough, *The Letters of Thomas Gainsborough*, ed. Mary Woodall, Cupid Press, 1963.

Mahatma Gandhi, from *The Penguin Book of Historic Speeches*, ed. Brian MacArthur, 1995.

King George III, from Christopher Hibbert, *George III: A Personal History*, 1998.

Edward Gibbon, *The Autobiography of Edward Gibbon*, ed. Oliphant Smeaton, 1911.

Sergeant Timothy Gowing, *A Voice from the Ranks*, 1896.

Harriet, Countess Granville, *Letters of Harriet Countess Granville 1810-1845*, ed. the Hon. F. Leveson Gower, 2 vols, 1894.

——, *A Second Self: The Letters of Harriet Granville, 1810-1845*, ed. Virginia Surtees, Michael Russell, 1990. Reproduced by permission of Michael Russell (Publishing) Ltd.

Thomas Gray, *Correspondence of Thomas Gray*, ed. Paget Toynbee and Leonard Whibley, 3 vols, Clarendon Press, 1935. Reproduced by permission of Oxford University Press.

Charles Greville, *The Greville Memoirs*, ed. Roger Fulford, B. T. Batsford, 1963.

Edward Grim, from *St Thomas of Canterbury: An Account of His Life and Fame from the Contemporary Biographers and Other Chroniclers*, ed. W. H. Hutton, 1889.

George and Weedon Grossmith, *The Diary of a Nobody*, 1892.

Brilliana, Lady Harley, *The Grand Quarrel: From the Civil War Memoirs of Mrs Lucy Hutchinson; Mrs Alice Thornton; Ann, Lady Fanshawe; Margaret, Duchess of Newcastle; Anne, Lady Halkett, and the Letters of Brilliana, Lady Harley*, ed. Roger Hudson, The Folio Society, 1993.

Max Hastings, from the *Evening Standard*, 15 June 1982.

Benjamin Robert Haydon, *The Autobiography and Memoirs of Benjamin Robert Haydon, 1786-1846*, ed. Tom Taylor, 1926.

Patrick Henry, from *The World's Greatest Speeches*, ed. Lewis Copeland and Lawrence W. Lamm, Doubleday, 1942.

Mr Justice Holmes, *Yankee from Olympus: Justice Holmes and His Family*, ed. Catherine Drinker Bowen, Little, Brown & Co., 1944. Reproduced by permission of Harold Ober Associates.

Gerard Manley Hopkins, *The Notebooks and Papers of Gerard Manley Hopkins*, ed. Christopher Devlin, Arthur Humphry House and Graham Storey, 2 vols, Oxford University Press, 1959. Reproduced by permission of Oxford University Press.

Henry James, *Letters*, ed. Percy Lubbock, 2 vols, 1920.

William James, *The Letters of William James*, ed. Henry James, 2 vols, 1926.

Borijove Jevtić, from the *New York World*, 29 June 1924.

Samuel Johnson, from James Boswell, *The Life of Samuel Johnson*, vol. 1, 1791.

Thomas Jones, 'Memoirs of Thomas Jones, 1768–1769', ed. A. P. Oppé, *The Walpole Society*, vol. 32, 1951.

John Keats, *Letters of John Keats: A Selection*, ed. Robert Gittings, Oxford University Press, 1970.

Fanny Kemble, *Some Recollections of a Girlhood*, 1878.

The Revd Francis Kilvert, *Kilvert's Diary: Selections from the Diary of the Rev. Francis Kilvert*, ed. William Plomer, Jonathan Cape, 1938–40. Reproduced by permission of The Random House Group Ltd.

Sir John Kincaid, *Adventures in the Rifle Brigade, in the Peninsula, France, and the Netherlands, from 1809 to 1815*, 1830.

Martin Luther King, Jr, from *The Penguin Book of Historic Speeches*, ed. Brian MacArthur, 1995. Reproduced by permission of the Estate of Martin Luther King, Jr, c/o Writers House as agent for the proprietor, New York, NY. All material © copyright Dr Martin Luther King, Jr, all material © renewed 1991 Coretta Scott King and the Heirs to the Estate of Martin Luther King, Jr.

Mary Kingsley, *Travels in West Africa, Congo Français, Corisco and Cameroons*, 1897.

Henry Labouchere, from *Paris under Siege: A Journal of the Events of 1870-1871*, ed. Joanna Richardson, The Folio Society, 1982.

Charles Lamb, *The Letters of Charles Lamb*, ed. George Woodcock, 1950.

Walter Savage Landor, *The Second Post*, ed. E. V. Lucas, 1910.

Edward Lear, *Selected Letters*, ed. Vivien Noakes, Clarendon Press, 1988. Reproduced by permission of Oxford University Press and Watson, Little Ltd.

James Lees-Milne, *Ancestral Voices*, Chatto & Windus, 1975. Reproduced by permission of David Higham Associates Ltd.

——, *Prophesying Peace*, Chatto and Windus, 1977. Reproduced by permission of David Higham Associates Ltd.

——, *A Mingled Measure*, John Murray, 1994. Reproduced by permission of David Higham Associates Ltd.

Patrick Leigh Fermor, *Words of Mercury*, ed. Artemis Cooper, 2003. Reproduced by permission of John Murray (Publishers).

Meriwether Lewis, from *Original Journals of the Lewis and Clark Expedition, 1804-1806*, ed. Reuben Gold Thwaites, 1904–5.

Jack London, from *Collier's Weekly*, 5 May 1906.

Vincent Lunardi, *An Account of the First Aerial Voyage in England, in a Series of Letters to Chevalier Gherarde Compagni Written under the Impressions of the Various Events that Affected the Undertaking*, 1784.

Lord Macaulay, from George Otto Trevelyan, *The Life and Letters of Lord Macaulay*, 2 vols, 1876.

James Harris, 1st Earl of Malmesbury, *Diaries and Correspondence of James Harris, First Earl of Malmesbury*, vol. 3, 1844.

John Churchill, Duke of Marlborough, from Correlli Douglas Barnett, *Marlborough*, 1974.

Lady Mary Wortley Montagu, *The Letters and Works of Lady Mary Wortley Montagu*, ed. Lord Warncliffe and W. May Thomas, 2 vols, 1893.

Tom Moore, *The Memoirs, Journal and Correspondence of Thomas Moore*, ed. Lord John Russell, 8 vols, 1853–56.

Sir Thomas More, *The Works of Sir Thomas More Knyght, Sometyme Lorde Chauncellour of England, Wrytten by Him in the Englysh Tonge*, ed. William Rastell, 1557.

Relman Morin, from the *Associated Press*, 23 September 1957.

James Nachtwey, *The Eye of War*, Weidenfeld & Nicolson, 2003. By permission of James Nachtwey.

Horatio, Lord Nelson, *The Dispatches and Letters of Vice Admiral Lord Viscount Nelson*, ed. Sir Nicholas Harris Nicolas, 1844–6.

John Nichol, from Edward Fraser, *The Sailors Whom Nelson Led: Their Doings Described by Themselves*, 1913.

Harold Nicolson, *Diaries and Letters*, vols 1 and 2, ed. Nigel Nicolson, Collins, 1966–7. Reproduced by permission of the Orion Publishing Group.

——, *Peacemaking, 1919*, Constable, 1933. Reproduced by permission of Constable & Robinson Ltd.

Leutnant Johannes Neimann, from Lyn Macdonald, *1914-1918: Voices and Images of the Great War*, 1988.

Wilfred Owen, *Selected Letters*, ed. John Bell, Oxford University Press, 1985. Reproduced by permission of Oxford University Press.

The Pastons, *The Paston Letters: A Selection in Modern Spelling*, ed. Norman Davis, Oxford University Press, 1963. Reproduced by permission of Oxford University Press.

Samuel Pepys, *The Diary of Samuel Pepys*, ed. The Revd J. Smith and Richard, Lord Braybrooke, 1906.

——, *A Pepys Anthology: Passages from the Diary of Samuel Pepys*, ed. Robert and Linnet Latham, Unwin Hyman, 1987. Reproduced by permission of HarperCollins Publishers Ltd.

William Pitt, the Elder, Earl of Chatham, *Chatham Correspondence*, 4 vols, ed. W. S. Taylor and W. H. Pringle, 1838.

William Pitt, the Younger, *The War Speeches of William Pitt the Younger*, ed. R. Coupland, 1915.

Sir Walter Raleigh, *The Letters of Sir Walter Raleigh, 1879-1922*, ed. Lady Lucie Gertrude Raleigh, 2 vols, 1926.

The Revd Robert Robinson, from *The Gentlest Art: A Choice of Letters by Entertaining Hands*, ed. E. V. Lucas, 1907.

John Ruskin, *Fors Clavigera: Letters to the Workmen and Labourers of Great Britain*, January 1871–March 1878, and irregularly thereafter.

——, *Notes on Educational Series*, 1870.

Conrad Russell, *Letters of Conrad Russell, 1897-1947*, ed. Georgiana Blakiston, John Murray, 1987. Reproduced by permission of John Murray (Publishers).

Sukhdev Sandhu, from the *London Review of Books*, 4 October 2001. Reproduced by permission of the *London Review of Books*, www.lrb.co.uk

Captain Robert Falcon Scott, *Scott's Last Expedition*, ed. Leonard Huxley, 2 vols, 1913.

Sir Walter Scott, *The Journal of Sir Walter Scott, from the Original Manuscript at Abbotsford*, 1891.

Chief Seattle, from *The Penguin Book of Historic Speeches*, ed. Brian MacArthur, 1995.

Sir Ernest Shackleton, *South: The Story of Shackleton's Last Expedition, 1914-1917*, 1922.

Frances, Lady Shelley, *Diary*, ed. R. Edgcumbe, 2 vols, 1912–13.

Peter Simple (Michael Wharton). Reproduced by permission of *The Daily Telegraph*.

John Simpson, from the *Observer*, January 1991. Reproduced by permission of John Simpson.

The Revd John Skinner, *Journal of a Somerset Rector, 1822-32*, 1930.

The Revd Sydney Smith, from the *The Gentlest Art: A Choice of Letters by Entertaining Hands*, ed. E. V. Lucas, 1907.

——, from *The Second Post: A Companion to 'The Gentlest Art'*, ed. E. V. Lucas, 1910.

——, *Letters of Sydney Smith*, ed. Nowell C. Smith, Oxford University Press, 1953. Reproduced by permission of Oxford University Press.

——, *The Smith of Smiths*, Hesketh Pearson, 1934.

——, *A Memoir of the Rev. Sydney Smith*, Lady Holland and Mrs Austin, 2 vols, 1855.

Sir Henry Morton Stanley, from the *New York Herald*, 10 August 1872.

Freya Stark, *Over the Rim of the World: Selected Letters*, ed. Caroline Moorehead, 1988. Reproduced by permission of John Murray (Publishers).

Robert Louis Stevenson, *Selected Letters of Robert Louis Stevenson*, ed. Ernest Mehew, Yale University Press, 1997.

——, *The Letters of Robert Louis Stevenson*, ed. Sidney Colvin, 4 vols, 1911.

——, *The Letters of Robert Louis Stevenson, vol. 8, Jan 1893-Dec 1894*, ed. Ernest Mehew and Bradford A. Booth, Yale University Press, 1995.

Roy Strong, *The Roy Strong Diaries, 1967-1987*, Weidenfeld & Nicolson, 1997. Reproduced by permission of The Orion Publishing Group.

David Hunter Strother, from *The Mammoth Book of How It Happened*, ed. Jon E. Lewis, 1998.

Jonathan Swift, *The Gentlest Art*, ed. E. V. Lucas, 1907.

Edward Thomas, 'Adlestrop', from *The Collected Poems of Edward Thomas*, ed. R. George Thomas, 1978.

Hester Thrale, *Thraliana, vol. I*, ed. Katherine C. Balderston, Clarendon Press, 1942. Reproduced by permission of Oxford University Press.

Colonel Tibbetts, from Mark Arnold-Forster, *The World at War*, Collins, 1973.

Chideock Tichborne, from *The Poems of Sir Walter Raleigh, Collected and Authenticated, with Those of Sir Henry Wotton and Other Courtly Poets from 1540 to 1650*, ed. John Hannah, 1875.

J. Tillison, from *Original Letters Illustrative of English History*, ed. Sir Henry Ellis, 2nd series, 4 vols, 1827.

John Byng, Viscount Torrington, *The Torrington Diaries, Containing the Tours through England and Wales of the Hon. John Byng, Later Fifth Viscount Torrington, between the Years 1781 and 1794*, ed. C. Bruyn Andrews, Eyre & Spottiswoode, 1934–8. Reproduced by permission of Dr James Andrews.

Edward John Trelawny, *Recollections of the Last Days of Shelley and Byron*, 1858.

Keith Vaughan, *Journals 1939-1977*, John Murray, 1989. Reproduced by permission of John Murray (Publishers).

Sir Ralph Verney, *Verney Papers: Notes of Proceedings in the Long Parliament*, ed. John Bruce, 1845.

Queen Victoria, *Queen Victoria in Her Letters and Journals: A Selection*, ed. Christopher Hibbert, John Murray, 1984. Reproduced by permission of David Higham Associates Ltd.

Sir William Waller, from C. V. Wedgwood, *The King's War 1641-1647*, 1958.

Horace Walpole, *Selected Letters*, ed. William Hadley, 1926.

Sylvia Townsend Warner, *The Diaries of Sylvia Townsend Warner*, ed. Claire Harman, Chatto & Windus, 1994. Reproduced by permission of The Random House Group Ltd.

Edmund Wheatley, *The Wheatley Diary: A Journal and Sketch-Book Kept during the Peninsular War and the Waterloo Campaign*, ed. Christopher Hibbert, Longmans, 1964.

T. H. White, *England Have My Bones*, Collins, 1936. Reproduced by permission of David Higham Associates Ltd.

Walt Whitman, *Specimen Days in America*, 1887.

William Wilberforce, from *The Penguin Book of Historic Speeches*, ed. Brian MacArthur, 1995.

Oscar Wilde, from *The Letters of Oscar Wilde*, ed. and published by Rupert Hart-Davis, 1962.

Samuel Wilkeson, from *The Faber Book of Reportage*, ed. John Carey, 1987.

William John Wills, from Ensign Andrew Jackson, *Robert O'Hara Burke, and the Australian Exploring Expedition of 1860*, 1862.

James Woodforde, *The Diary of a Country Parson, The Reverend James Woodforde, 1758-1781*, ed. John Beresford, 5 vols, 1924–31.

Virginia Woolf, *A Moment's Liberty: The Shorter Diary of Virginia Woolf*, ed. Anne Olivier Bell, Hogarth Press, 1990. Reproduced by permission of The Random House Group Ltd.

Dorothy Wordsworth, *Journals of Dorothy Wordsworth*, ed. William Knight, 1904.

Orville Wright, telegram to Bishop Milton Wright, 17 December 1903, from *Words and Deeds in American History*, American Memory Collections, Library of Congress.

Robert Wynkfielde, from *Original Letters Illustrative of English History*, ed. Sir Henry Ellis, 1st series, 3 vols, 1825.

INDEX

Charlotte, Queen Consort of George III, 29, 391

Chartist demonstration (1848), 111, 112

Chatham, Earl of *see* Pitt, William (the Elder)

Chaucer, Geoffrey, 13, 80, 358

Che Guevara, 300

Chelsea Flower Show, 154; Royal Hospital, 79

Chernobyl, 128

Chesterfield, Philip Dormer Stanhope, fourth Earl of, 43

Childe, Dr, 62

Christian, Fletcher, 130

Churchill, Charles, 130

Churchill, Winston, 16, 144, 139; appearance, 25; Commons speeches, 147, 339; death, 26; education, 162; election defeat (1945), 244; on foreign names, 125; on Iron Curtain, 73; in London blitz, 375; Munich crisis, 296; political career, 16, 107, 351

Civil War, American, 203

Civil War, English, 184, 202, 323, 379

Clairmont, Claire, 76

Clarence, Adelaide, Duchess of, 263

Clarence, George, Duke of, 54

Clarence, William, Duke of *see* William IV

Clarendon, George William Frederick Villiers, fourth Earl of, 264, 275

Clark, William, 142, 284, 288

Claudius, Emperor, 313

Clemenceau, Georges, 196

Cleopatra, 264

Clere, Edmund, 11

Clinton, Bill, 340

Clive, Caroline, 218

Clive, Robert, 191

Cobbett, William, 223

Coca-Cola, 142

Cody, Samuel, 316

Coleridge, Samuel Taylor, 13, 128, 295; on chimney-sweeps, 386; *Christabel*, 23, 128, 265; on illness, 93; letters to, 77, 178; on starlings, 361; visit to Dove Cottage, 265

Cologne Cathedral, 248

Columbus, Christopher, 312

Comet (jet airliner), 227

Concorde, 11, 23, 70

Connecticut, 161

Constantinople, 163

Conyngham, Elizabeth, Lady, 41, 173

Conyngham, Francis Nathaniel, second Maquess, 188

Cook, James, 20, 50, 105, 111, 159, 320

Cooke, Alistair, 92

Cooke, Thomas Simpson, 43

Cooper, Duff, 271

Corday, Charlotte, 213

Cornwallis, Lord, 319

Coronation Street, 375

Covent Garden, 342

Coventry, 348

Coward, Noël, 171

Cowper, Anne Florence, Lady, 5

Cowper, William: on bees, 286; on his hare, 255; on illness, 17; on periwig, 89; on the Throckmortons, 385; on town and country life, 373; on winter, 320; on workplace, 193

Crécy, battle of, 260

Creevey, Thomas, 261, 288; on Queen Caroline, 251; on Charleroi battle, 150; on Lady Conyngham, 41; on drink and crime, 73; on Duke of Kent, 377; on Lambton, 386; on Richard Brinsley Sheridan, 212, 259; on Wellington, 163, 184, 187

Crete, 154

Cricket, 61, 83, 343

Crimean War, 114, 187, 190, 325

Croker, John Wilson, 129

Cromwell, Oliver, 122, 202, 271, 375

Crossman, Richard, 362

crossword puzzles, 387

Crusoe, Robinson, 38, 71

Crystal Palace, 364

Mogadishu, 304
Mohammed Ali, 330
Mona Lisa, 255
Monck, George *see* Albemarle
Monckton, Walter Turner, 367
Monroe, Marilyn, 239
Montagu, Lady Mary Wortley, 69, 84, 120, 153, 163, 293, 294, 298, 308, 336, 340, 361, 364
Monte Cassino, 152
moon landing, 221
Moore, General Sir John, 18
Moore, Thomas, 30, 57, 76, 80, 103,113, 157, 258, 284, 322, 370
Mordkin, Mikhail, 126
More, Thomas, 205
Morin, Relman, 291
Morpeth, Lady Georgiana *see* Carlisle, Lady Georgiana
Morris Minor, 312
Mousetrap, 359
Moxon, Edward, 33
Muffett, Thomas, 355
Müller, Hermann, 196
Murray, John, I, 340
Murray, John, II, 7, 151, 195, 239, 384
Murray, John, III, 32, 104, 107, 109, 151, 218
Mussolini, Benito, 130, 296

Nabokov, Vladimir, 252
Nachtwey, James, 279
Nadar, Paul, 146
Napoleon, Bonaparte, 75, 112, 113, 127, 132, 139, 152, 184, 192, 215, 315, 368, 382
Nasser, President, 226
National Gallery, 90
National Health Service, 205
National Lottery, 353
National Trust, 14
Nazi Party, 7, 88
Nelson, Horatio, Viscount, 11, 104, 144, 221, 278, 321
New Orleans, battle of, 10

Newton, Isaac, 394
Nichol, John, 235
Nicholas II, Tsar, 83, 216
Nicolson, Harold, 25, 196, 271, 296, 339
Niemann, Johannes, 391
Nile, battle of the, 235
Nile, White, 59
Nixon, President, 242
Nobel, Alfred, 359
Norfolk, Bernard Fitzalan Howard, sixteenth Duke of, 24
North Sea Oil, 186, 337
Norway, 202

Oates, Captain Lawrence Edward Grace, 85
Olympic Games, 108
Omdurman, battle of, 270
Oran, 203
Oudenarde, battle of, 325
Owen, Wilfred, 331
Oxford English Dictionary, 121
Oxford Union, 45

Palmerston, Henry John Temple, third Viscount, 275
Panama Canal, 237
Paris, 182, 259, 355, 371
Passchendaele, battle of, 231
Paston, Agnes, 30
Paston, Clement, 30
Paston, John, I, 11, 380, 390
Paston, John, II, 154
Paston, John, III, 50, 341
Paston, Margaret, 380, 390
Paston, William, III, 341
Patmore, Coventry, 252
Paul of Yugoslavia, Prince, 348
Pavlova, Anna, 126
Peanuts, 302
Pearl Harbor, 373
Peary, Robert, 108
Peasants' Revolt (1381) 183
Peel, Robert, 33, 384

Peking, 318
Pele, 361
Penguin Books, 230, 336, 344
Peninsular War, 116
Pepsi-Cola, 184
Pepys, Samuel, 165, 293; afraid of thieves in his house, 363; on dancing, 70; on Drury Lane Theatre, 305; on execution of Harrison, milkmaids, and Lady Castlemaine, 313; on Great Fire of London, 273; on lice, 25; on plague, 175; on reading, 45; on return of Charles II, 159; on Royal Society, 355; on Valentine's Day, 50; on walking home, 393; on wife's studies, 372; on Windsor, 62
Perceval Spencer, 143
Peter Pan, 393
Peterloo Massacre (1819), 250
Philby, Kim, 350
Philip, Prince, 277
Picture Post, 301
Pilgrim Fathers, 387
Pitt, William (the Elder), 16
Pitt, William (the Younger), 11, 25, 37, 127, 385
Poitiers, battle of, 287
Poland, Partition of, 324
Polidori, John William, 239
Pope, Alexander, 297
Popeye, 19
Post Office Tower, 308, 331
Potemkin, battleship, 182
Pounds, John, 18
Prague, 157
Premium Bonds, 335
Presley, Elvis, 205, 250
Princip, Gavrilo, 196
Private Eye, 325
Prohibition 18, 37
Pym, John, 6

Qing Dynasty, 48, 373
Quarterly Review, 69

Queen Elizabeth, HMS, 165
Queensberry, John Sholto, eighth Marquess of, 64

Rabin, Yitzhak, 281, 336
Raleigh, Walter (1552–1618), 329
Raleigh, Walter (1861–1922), 301
Reagan, President, 91, 374
Redgrave, Steve, 291
Reform Bill (1831), 69, 90
Revocation of the Edict of Nantes, 318
Richard II, King, 183, 376
Richmond, Charles Lennox, fourth Duke of, 184
Richthofen, Manfred von, 123
River Plate, battle of, 379
Robert the Bruce, 192
Robinson, Robert, 160
Robson, Flora, 76
Rocket, locomotive, 260
Rockettes, the 151
Rogers, Ginger, 151
Rolls, Charles, 212
Rome, 122, 172, 258
Roosevelt, F. D., 16
Roper, Margaret, 205
Rorke's Drift, battle of, 25
Ross, Robert, 64, 118
Rossini, Gioacchino Antonio, 3
Rowling, J. K., 208
Royal Academy, 376
Royal Society, 124
Rugby Football Union, 28
Rupert Bear, 342
Rupert, Prince, 202
Ruskin, John, 61, 123
Russell, Conrad: on Austria, 256; on change, 58; on farm life, 104, 158; on manners, 77; on morals, 285; on wartime experiences, 33, 148; on wireless, 322
Russian Revolution, 292, 341
Russo-Japanese War, 44

Walpole, Horace (*cont*.)
  on newspapers, 204; on old age, 17; on end
  of Seven Years' War, 174; on Versailles, 285
Walpole, Robert, first Earl of Orford, 99, 105,
  290
Walsingham, Francis, 231
Walton, Valentine, 202
Walworth, William, 183
War of Independence, American, 253
Warner, Pelham, 78
Warner, Sylvia Townsend, 10, 121, 371
Washington, George, 72
Waterloo, battle of, 186, 187, 188, 215, 231
Watts-Dunton, Theodore, 106
Wavell, Lord, 343
Webb, Captain, 259
Wellington, Arthur Wellesley, first Duke of,
  129, 215, 219, 263; conversations with,
  163, 187; duel, 89; Duke of Richmond's
  ball, 184; Great Exhibition opening, 142
Welles, Orson, 135
Wells, H. G., 71, 251, 354
Welsh, Helen, 33
Wharton, Philip, Duke of, 308
Wheatley, Edmund, 116, 307
Whetley, J., 154
White, T. H., 223, 327
Whitman, Walt, 72
Whitney, Eli, 188
Whittle, Frank, 149
Whymper, E., 214
Wilberforce, William, 146
Wilde, Oscar, 64, 50, 107, 118
Wilhelm II, Kaiser, 328
Wilkeson, Samuel, 203
William III, King, 76, 339
William IV, King (*earlier* Duke of Clarence),
  173, 209, 377
William the Conqueror, 391
Williams, Edward, 249
Willis, John, 38
Wills, William John, 197
Wimbledon, 209

Winchester, 289
Winchilsea, George William Finch-Hatton,
  ninth Earl of, 89
Windsor, Duchess of, 105, 367, 376
Windsor Castle, 354
Wolfe, General James, 281
Wolfenden Report, 272
Women's Institute, 55
Wood, Henry, 306
Woodforde, Revd James, 21, 117, 315
Woodstock, 249
Woolf, Virginia: on armistice (1918), 345; on
  bingling, 48; on birthday, 27, at Café
  Royal, 79; on Charleston, 245; on
  Cornwall, 98; death, 96; on depression,
  191; on failure and Marie Lloyd, 110; on
  General Strike, 139, 146; on Knole, 205;
  on Russia, 292
Woolworth's store, 58
Worcester, battle of, 271, 274
Wordsworth, Dorothy: on autumn colours,
  310; on beggar, 388; on brother, 72, 91, 95,
  131; on Coleridge's visit, 265; on illness,
  86; on John's Grove, 131; on life in winter,
  13, 358; on sheep, 131; on walking, 86,
  118, 153
Wordsworth, Mary, 13
Wordsworth, William: Coleridge's visit, 265;
  dinner at Haydon's, 394; letters to, 108,
  128; life in winter, 13, 388; meeting with
  beggar, 388; reading, 91; relationship
  with sister, 86, 131; travel, 72; and
  walking, 118, 265; writing, 95
World Trade Center (2001), 279, 280
Wounded Knee, 395
Wren, Christopher, 62
Wright, Orville, 383
Wyatt, Matthew Digby, 348
Wynkfielde, Robert, 44

Yeltsin, Boris, 253, 377
York Minster, 209, 276
Yom Kippur War, 306